Leading the Sales Force

How should a sales force be managed effectively? Like aircraft pilots, managers must analyze information and make interconnected decisions in order to accomplish their missions. This book provides an integrative vision of a sales manager's function, using the concept of a dynamic sales force management process. This process adds a new dimension to the "classical" conception of sales force management, showing how sales managers can be more effective when they develop and maintain a holistic vision. Part I of the book describes the key actors and their roles, while Part II examines the tools used to implement the dynamic sales force management process. René Darmon shows how this process relies on a clear vision of successive sales missions to be accomplished over time by all members of a sales team, as they develop strategies and tactics which contribute to fulfilling the firm's overall aims.

René Darmon is Emeritus Professor of Marketing at ESSEC Business School, France, and Affiliate Professor of Marketing at Laval University, Quebec, Canada.

Leading
the Sales Force

A Dynamic Management Process

René Y. Darmon

CAMBRIDGE UNIVERSITY PRESS

Cambridge, New York, Melbourne, Madrid, Cape Town, Singapore, São Paulo
Cambridge University Press
The Edinburgh Building, Cambridge CB2 2RU, UK

Published in the United States of America by Cambridge University Press, New York

www.cambridge.org
Information on this title: www.cambridge.org/9780521848343

First published 2007

Printed in the United Kingdom at the University Press, Cambridge

A catalogue record for this publication is available from the British Library

ISBN-13 978-0-521-84834-3 hardback
ISBN-10 0-521-84834-2 hardback

To Nicole, my loyal partner in a life-time lasting relationship.

Contents

List of figures

List of tables

Preface

Why write a new book on sales force management? Obviously, sales and marketing managers have long supervised and controlled salespeople without resorting to the concept of a dynamic sales force management process. Nevertheless, this integrated vision of the control and management of a sales force is likely to add a new dimension to the "classical" conception of sales force management. This new integrative dimension brings together the multiple and complex aspects of a sales force system. This book shows how sales managers can be more effective when they develop such an integrative vision of their mission.

The concept of dynamic management process encompasses more than the traditional managerial functions of situation analysis, planning, program implementation, and control. It includes also the definition of strategic objectives, the translation of those mission objectives into operational and tactical plans and decisions, the constant adjustments of these plans over time, as well as the necessary adaptations of the organization during the process.

The dynamic sales force management process concept relies on a clear vision of a succession of sales missions to be accomplished over time by all the members of a sales team. At each level, the various members of a sales force develop their strategies and tactics that must all contribute to fulfilling the overall missions. The proposed concept builds on the prevalent philosophy of customer relationship management (CRM), and the development of long-term customer relationships that are mutually beneficial. It also includes salespeople's knowledge management, as well as the notion of salespeople's empowerment. As a consequence, both sales managers and salespeople tend to follow very similar dynamic management processes, increasing the complexity of the overall sales force management process.

The main purpose of this book is to provide sales managers with a guide for managing their fast-evolving functions more effectively, at a time when selling takes an increasing strategic role in most organizations.

Sales forces can benefit from the integrative and dynamic vision of the proposed management process. Perhaps more than any other function in a firm, sales leaders can successfully apply this vision. Sales force management is complex, requires accounting for many facets of the problem simultaneously, and necessitates a host of decisions that are interrelated and taken over time, often with immediate and lagged effects. Under such circumstances, leading a sales force with an overall vision of the process, with the constant awareness of the mission objectives to be met, and without losing sight of all the relevant details, is probably the best route to effective sales management.

Another related but central theme of this book is that the proposed process takes place at various levels of centralization/decentralization, according to sales managers' options. This provides salespeople with a more or less extended decision space, which directly affects the design of the various management programs, as well as the communication flows that are necessary for implementing those programs, and consequently, their costs.

The book is made up of two parts. Part 1 is essentially descriptive. It provides an analysis on the various elements that constitute the dynamic sales force management process: buyers, buyer-supplier relationships, salespeople (more or less autonomous managers of their customer relations and territories), and the function of a sales manager.

Part 2 is more normative than the first one. It provides a more detailed description of a sales manager's command center, the programs through which managers exert their actions, as well as the information flows that are necessary for feeding their dashboards.

Each chapter tackles a precise sales management question and takes place into the comprehensive framework outlined in the first chapter. Consequently, after reading Chapter 1 which defines essential concepts, a reader can approach the different chapters in any order without losing an understanding of the topic covered.

Sales practitioners and sales managers of industrial or consumer product organizations should find in the following pages an integrative vision of the selling management function, and hopefully, new perspectives and thought-provoking discussions that could lead to improved practice. Salespeople will also find some thoughts about their new and fast-evolving functions and an integrative vision of these functions. This vision should be a good preparation for accessing managerial levels in their organizations. Business school students, especially at MBA and doctoral levels, will find an exposure to personal selling and sales management that is somewhat novel in comparison with most traditional textbooks on this topic. Management researchers may find in this book a few original conceptual frameworks that could lead to a number of research hypotheses and research questions that still need to be tested empirically and validated. Finally, any person with some interest in personal selling and/or management may find matter of thoughts in the following pages.

René Y. Darmon

1 Introduction to the dynamic sales force management process

Case study 1: myopic sales force management at an Industrial Mechanics Corporation

A few years ago, the Industrial Mechanics Corporation (IMC), a large firm selling and leasing mechanical equipment to building contractors for use on construction sites, implemented a new compensation plan for its sales force. The objective was to provide its salespeople with a more motivating plan than the current one which was based on salary plus commission on sales volumes. The principles of the new plan were: (1) to reduce the proportion of fixed salary in the total remuneration, (2) to slightly reduce the commission rates on sales, and (3) to compensate for the decreased remuneration level by adding an individual bonus. The salespeople could earn a substantial bonus by meeting an individual annual sales target. Sales quotas were set in such a way as to be higher than the sales volumes realized the previous year in a given territory, but at levels that were deemed both realistic and achievable.

Several months after its implementation, the new plan was considered a success. By the end of the first year, most salespeople had met or exceeded their targets. The average remuneration paid to sales staff had slightly increased. At the same time, company sales and profits had increased substantially — management attributed these positive outcomes to the new compensation structure.

Soon after, however, the situation in the sales department started deteriorating. The morale of the sales force declined, several top salespeople resigned and joined competing firms. Many others did not hide their dissatisfaction and openly declared their intention to leave, should they find the right position elsewhere. All perceived that their working conditions had deteriorated considerably, and that management always expected them to work harder for less money than they would previously have been paid in a similar job with another employer.

To compensate for this increased sales force turnover, IMC launched an aggressive recruitment campaign. The results were well below the stated objectives. It seemed that one of the major causes of the company's inability to recruit high caliber salespeople was the very tight labor market prevailing at that time. Another reason given was that the compensation package that the firm offered was lower than that they could get elsewhere.

The end result was that the firm was unable to recruit the required number of salespeople. Consequently, some sales territories were left vacant or were only covered part time by salespeople from adjacent territories. IMC's sales manager had some hired salespeople, that did not meet the required standard.

By the end of the second year, IMC's sales and profits had dropped significantly.

This case illustrates some of the complex interactions that exist within a sales force. Decisions in one area may directly or indirectly affect other aspects of the sales force, sometimes immediately, and at other times, after some time lag. The decision to change the compensation plan, which seemed to be appropriate to boost sales in the short-term, happened to have subsequent adverse effects. The new compensation plan had been "motivating," in the sense that salespeople had to work harder to meet their quotas and earn a bonus. They had been given the choice of either increasing their remuneration (slightly) by achieving a higher performance level, or accepting a pay cut. The implied increase however, was not commensurate with the additional effort they had to put in, as well as with the increased risk associated with the new plan (i.e. working harder and not meeting their quota). IMC's management failed to anticipate the negative impact the plan could have on salespeople's morale, on the sales force turnover rate, and on the firm's ability to recruit new staff – all long-term effects.

This case study suggests that IMC did not have a long-term vision for the management for its sales force. In order to account for the long-term consequences of any decision, management's vision must encompass future events over some far-reaching time horizon. This requires a *dynamic* management of the sales force. In other words, to be efficient, sales managers must *develop and keep a holistic vision of the complex sales force system they must manage, over a sufficiently far-reaching time horizon.*

To properly handle such a complex human system, sales managers must be competent and possess strong *leadership qualities*. A major characteristic of leaders is their ability to develop a far-reaching vision and to induce all the people involved in a given endeavor to share this vision. Effective sales executives manage the sales force by making decisions that contribute to their firm's short- and long-term objectives. This dynamic vision was absent from IMC.

Over the last few decades, most of the books published in Europe and North America about sales force management have considered the various management areas as if they were isolated and independent from one another. Sales force management has often been presented as a juxtaposition of various decision domains. For example, the recruitment of salespeople, the organization, supervision, motivation, compensation, and control of the sales force are treated successively. This may be an extremely efficient approach from a didactical point of view, because it focuses on one decision area at a time. It fails, however, to accurately describe what managing a sales force efficiently is all about.

Sales force management involves a very large number of decisions, some strategic, others tactical, all bearing on a complex system (Darmon 1993). As suggested by the IMC case, this complexity calls for a holistic and dynamic approach to sales force management.

The selling function is gaining in importance in most organizations. Nowadays, an increasing number of firms recognize the central role and importance of their customers in their own operations. As a result, salespeople who have traditionally been assigned the role of ensuring quality relationships with customers through face-to-face interactions, tend to play a decisive role in the success of many firms. More frequently than ever before, firms involve sales management in strategic planning. In addition to operational decisions, for which they traditionally have assumed — and will continue to assume — this responsibility, sales managers must now conciliate operational responsibilities and strategic missions for the sales force. This broadening role of personal selling in an organization gives increased importance to this concept of sales force dynamic leadership.

This chapter is devoted to an analysis of the main implications of this holistic vision of sales force management on objectives setting and control decisions. After a more detailed definition of the concepts of dynamic sales force management and control, it provides an overview of the dynamic management process that serves as a guiding framework throughout this book.

The dynamic sales force management process defined

Sales force control and dynamic management process

A dynamic management process links the strategic and operational actions that take place within the framework of a specific organizational structure. It relies on a number of systems (objectives, plans, budgets, control indicators, etc.) and practices. As a result, dynamic sales force management implies meeting pre-specified objectives under the best possible conditions, within a given time frame, and within a sales strategy defined by marketing and/or sales managers.

For an organization, controlling its operations consists of devising and implementing procedures for checking, orienting, evaluating, and compensating employees (Anderson and Oliver 1987). Consequently, the concept of dynamic management goes well beyond the simple notion of control. Although the dynamic management of a sales force includes the control function, its main purpose is to meet a firm's objectives. It is the process that sales managers follow when they define and display the appropriate means at their disposal for influencing and controlling (within limits) the actors of the selling process – these include customers, salespeople, and middle sales management. The process intends to make all the actors contribute to the firm's objectives in the most efficient way possible. In this book, this process is called the 'dynamic sales force management process' ("the process").

Understanding the process: a metaphor

The dynamic sales force management process concept that has just been defined is perfectly in line with the roles, tasks, responsibilities, and duties that must fulfill the pilot of any means of transportation, be it a car, a train, an aircraft, or a vessel. However, if similarities are substantial, some differences are also important and worth noting.

Main similarities
Piloting an A380 Airbus

Let us observe the activities of a captain at the commands of (for instance) an A380 Airbus aircraft that must take off from London's Heathrow airport to Paris Charles-de-Gaulle, some Monday at 10 o'clock in the morning.

Given the exact location of the Charles-de-Gaulle airport (the objective), the date and time of departure (some constraints), the captain of this aircraft and its crew must step on board some time before the departure time. They set up and study the flight plan (the planning stage). For that purpose, the crew members in the cockpit study navigation maps. They inquire about weather forecasts over the Channel, as well as all other facts that they deem relevant for preparing for the voyage. The crew members get information about all the environmental constraints they must take into account.

On the basis of such information, the captain and crew decide which route to follow to reach Paris on time. To do this, they must analyze and take into account a large amount of data, as well as a number of unavoidable constraints. These are imposed by the airline (e.g., certain flight procedures), the control tower (e.g., the departure time and the runway for take off), or the prevailing air traffic regulations. Given these constraints, the crew selects what appears to be the best route, speed, cruising altitude, as well as other planning details. In other words, the captain selects an efficient *strategy* for the London-Paris flight.

After departure, the crew follow the flight plan (the implementation stage). In spite of the forecasts, however, pilots sometimes face unforeseen (and typically unforeseeable) situations over which they have little or no control. Exceptionally, a major dramatic event occurs — for example, an engine fails. This requires the crew to make major decisions that will mean drastic changes to the original plan. For example, the pilot may decide to land at a closer airport or to return to the original airport.

Even in less dramatic situations, the pilot frequently faces unforeseen events. For example, the aircraft may have to deal with some turbulence. To avoid causing discomfort to passengers, the pilot may ask to change altitude. These are tactical adjustments to deal with the current situation, but they do not substantially alter the original flight plan.

In the cockpit, the pilot consults a large number of displays, and numerous measuring instruments. These inform the crew of the amount of fuel still available, the altitude, the speed of the aircraft, the outside temperature, as well as many other pieces of information that are relevant to air navigation. By keeping track of these indicators, the pilot knows if he or she will keep to the intended route or not and eventually, take corrective action.

To maneuver the aircraft, a pilot must activate certain switches and levers. These control the aircraft. They allow it to take off, to increase or decrease in altitude, to veer right or left, or to land, as desired. Because of unexpected variations in the environment, however, a pilot's actions do not always have the expected results. Gaps between objectives and actual situations are generally signaled by the aircraft's instrument panel. The pilot can make tactical adjustments to bring the aircraft back to the intended route.

Aircraft pilots must have definite and specific competencies. They will have undertaken extensive training and will have acquired a vast theoretical knowledge about general air navigation. Theoretical knowledge, however, is not sufficient. Pilots cannot be considered competent unless they have actually flown an aircraft for a substantial number of hours, under various types of conditions, and have acquired the practical experience on how to handle exceptionally difficult situations on flight simulators.

In addition to general knowledge and competencies, pilots must be given and collect all the relevant information about the various missions they must perform. Competent pilots must have the ability to look for, process, and integrate relevant information for accomplishing specific missions.

Implementing the process

Sales managers fulfill functions that are in many ways very similar to those of the A380 Airbus pilot. At the beginning of every year or every quarter, general managers or marketing managers assign (or establish) sales and marketing objectives to be met by the end of a relevant planning period. Then the sales managers start planning. They try to obtain information about economic forecasts concerning their markets and their clients' industries. In other words, they collect information about relevant environmental constraints. Then, they generally define a sales strategy: an action plan, which, according to their best estimates, should permit them to reach the yearly or quarterly objectives they have been assigned, taking into account the prevailing market and economic constraints.

A sales manager may face important unforeseen events when implementing the sales plan. For example, a competitor may possibly have launched a major innovative product that could make the firm's product obsolete. Fortunately, in the same way as engine failures are relatively rare events, this type of occurrence does not happen too often. Should it happen, however, it requires drastic action on the part of the managers who must reconsider the marketing strategy that was originally planned.

Events that occur in the environment often have less dramatic consequences. They are, however, frequent and almost impossible to anticipate. The economic conditions may be better (or worse) than anticipated. These may be effects from an aggressive promotional campaign by a competitor. New laws may be adopted which affect the selling conditions for the product, as is frequently the case in the tobacco industry. These are only a few examples out of a very large number of possible events. In such cases, sales managers react by adjusting their sales programs. They make tactical adjustments that do not put the general strategy into question. For example, they may react to more difficult economic conditions by increa sing the number of calls made to prospects by salespeople. Following a promotional campaign by a competitor, they might give their salespeople more leeway to give better discounts. They may also adjust their advertising campaign to abide by the new regulations.

Like a pilot at the controls of an aircraft, sales managers cannot properly manage their sales force if they do not have precise and relevant indicators about their operations, for example salespeople's call reports, or customer satisfaction surveys.

Sales managers too, exert some control over the sales force by adjusting the elements that are under their control, for example, the compensation plan, the objective or quota plans, the direct supervision of salespeople's activities, or training sessions. Sales managers regularly compare the performance levels of their sales force with performance forecasts to make sure that everything is on track. If this is not the case, some corrective action is called for.

Sales managers, like pilots, must have acquired the necessary knowledge and competencies to manage their sales teams. They must understand the general personal selling process, the management of a sales team, the behaviors of their customers and of their salespeople. The quality of a manager's knowledge base depends on the amount and accuracy of the relevant information it contains.

Note that major differences exist among the concepts of management's information, knowledge, and competence (see Figure 1.1). A piece of information is an element that has meaning, but which becomes useful only when interpreted and integrated with other information to become knowledge. "The sales force turnover rate has increased from 10 to 20 percent this year" was information for IMC's sales manager. When this information is interpreted so that the causes of such an increase can be understood, it becomes management knowledge. Knowledge is a set of information about a topic that an individual has interpreted and integrated to understand some phenomenon or a given situation. When the increase in turnover rate can be attributed to dissatisfaction with the new compensation structure, this becomes managerial knowledge.

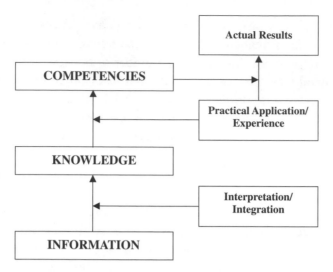

Fig. 1.1   Various levels of information integration

Competencies are a set of integrated information about a certain field of knowledge, plus a recognized and proven experience of the practical application of this knowledge. In the same way as pilots are considered as competent when they have shown they know what to do in a variety of (often difficult) situations, competent sales managers must have demonstrated their ability to manage a sales force effectively. Returning to IMC, a competent sales manager should have known exactly what to do when the sales force turnover rate had increased as a result of their dissatisfaction, and should have done it!

Sales managers must be able to look for, process, and integrate the information relative to every sales mission to make appropriate decisions and fulfill the mission. Some of a manager's knowledge and competencies apply irrespective of the firm and its sales force. Others, are firm-specific and not transferable to other selling situations.[1] Like pilots, competent sales managers must demonstrate that they can apply their knowledge in practical situations.

Some differences

Although the similarities between the functions of a pilot and that of a sales manager are substantial, there are also some major differences. From a practical point of view, a pilot controls a material entity (the aircraft),

---

[1] These are referred to as specific assets in the transaction cost analysis literature (Williamson 1975; 1983).

while a sales manager manages a team of human beings (the sales force). When pilots activate a switch, they may reasonably expect the aircraft to respond in a particular way (short of mechanical failure). When sales managers attempt to "control" a sales force, by, say, setting new norms on the number of calls to make to prospects, they cannot predict how individuals will actually react. The IMC sales manager learned this the hard way!

It may be more accurate to compare sales managers to the commander of a squadron, all displaying more or less autonomy in their actions. Even in this case, however, the metaphor can only be carried so far. Military discipline, the personal and collective danger that may result from an individual action on the part of a pilot, mean that squadron commanders have much more authority over their pilots than sales managers have over their sales force. Although sales managers can expect an average salesperson to react as anticipated, they cannot know with certainty how every salesperson, and consequently how the whole sales force, will actually react to their directives.

There is a second major difference between aircraft pilots and sales managers. To meet their objectives, sales managers, unlike pilots, can easily alter the structure of the system they control. They may, decide to increase or decrease the size of the sales force, or permanently redefine the role and assignment of every salesperson. Sales managers encompass a much larger decision domain than pilots do. This makes their function more complex.

When pilots have completed a mission, the aircraft is repaired, and put back into its original order. Sales managers must fulfill a series of missions, with the sales force in the state it was left in at the end of the preceding period. This can be a threat or an opportunity, depending on how they have accomplished their preceding missions.

In spite of these differences, however, the pilot metaphor that has been developed in the preceding paragraphs should provide a good understanding of the scope and content of the dynamic sales force management concept.

Main elements of the process

The dynamic sales force management process consists of devising procedures that induce the sales force to perform correctly to achieve the specific objectives set by management. Be it an aircraft, a vessel, or

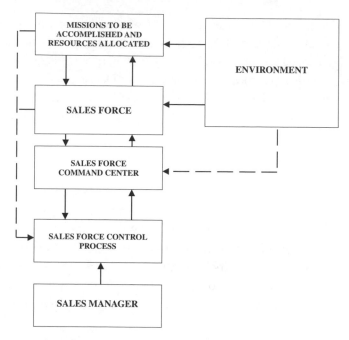

Fig. 1.2   The main elements of a dynamic sales force management process

a sales force, any system to be controlled is made up of a certain number of elements that can be conveniently grouped into five categories (Figure 1.2):

- A (sales) mission, with a number of characteristics, that must be accomplished in a given constrained context (customers and/or markets), in a typically uncertain environment, and with the resources allocated for meeting the mission (budgets, support from other functional departments, etc.);
- a system that must be managed in order to accomplish the missions in this uncertain environment (the sales force);
- a (sales force) command center;
- a dynamic (sales force) control process; and
- a leader (the sales manager) who is responsible for achieving the objectives of the missions (Darmon 1998a; Jaworski and MacInnis 1989).

Figure 1.2 describes the main links among these five sets of elements. Once the customer and market objectives of a mission are set, sales managers exercise their leadership to meet those objectives. Analyzing the information obtained from the command center, they follow managerial procedures for making and implementing adequate decisions: they utilize some resources and some tools out of the management tool kit at their disposal. The sales force reacts by taking the proper actions toward customers and markets, which results in performance outcomes. If the process has been properly followed, performance should match the mission objectives. In practice, because of more or less important disturbances in the environment, discrepancies are likely to be reported by the sales force command center. Consequently, sales managers constantly adjust their actions over time: this is a dynamic sales force management process. In the following paragraphs, the various elements of this process are discussed and described in more detail.

A selling mission

Sales and marketing missions are the central focus of sales management. They are characterized by: the type of market in which they occur, the importance and ambition of their objectives, the environment in which they are carried out, and by the resources available.

Mission objectives

Sales management processes imply that some objectives are to be met. In a sales force context, firms typically pursue several marketing objectives, that require procedures, some more complex than others. Management also generally pursue a varied type of objective — for example, short-term objectives are setting specific sales, profit, or market share goals. More and more frequently, the general sales force objectives also include long-term and more qualitative goals, such as building lasting relationships with selected customers, increasing and sustaining customer satisfaction, providing high quality services, or building customer goodwill (Anderson 1996). *By nature, marketing and sales objectives are always specified in terms of outcomes to be achieved.*

In some cases, objectives are imposed on sales managers, in others, managers select them. Sales managers have some leeway to modify, or even alter objectives according to circumstances. One should keep in mind, however, that sales managers, like other human beings, also have personal objectives which may sometimes clash with those of the firm. As a result, they may occasionally behave opportunistically.

Mission's environmental conditions

A mission is more difficult to carry out if the objectives are demanding, but also if the environmental conditions are less favorable. The "Overlord" mission, devised by the US army for invading Normandy during World

War II would have been a trivial exercise without the tremendous firepower of the enemy. Any mission must account for constraints imposed by the prevailing conditions. These are imposed not only by the general marketing policy of the firm, but also by competition, the current economic, legal, social, cultural, organizational, and technological conditions.

In addition, environmental uncertainties affect the predictions that managers make about the anticipated consequences of their actions. This is why managers try to obtain as much accurate information as possible about market conditions. This, however, can never be perfect. For example, in the IMC case, managers had not anticipated the difficulty of recruiting new highly qualified salespeople, given the prevailing labor market conditions at the time.

Mission's available resources

Few sales force missions can be carried out without the use of some material, human, and/or financial resources. They must have the right number of salespeople to meet their objectives. This is not easy, as will be seen in Chapter 7. Sales managers need a certain number of sales supervisors and other support personnel (secretaries, administrative staff, trainers, etc.) that is commensurate with the size of the sales force. In industrial selling, they often need the help of engineers and technicians. They require promotional literature on the products and services to be sold and some demonstration material — essential for facilitating salespeople's task in the field. Finally, sales managers need a sufficient budget to cover the expenses incurred by salespeople in the field (e.g., travel expenses) or for setting up tactical sales force motivation and training programs (e.g., sales contests or incentive programs). Note that all these resources can always be converted into financial terms.

A sales force to be managed

A sales force is part of a complex system that includes three types of actors: clients/prospects, salespeople, and middle sales management (Figure 1.3). Besides the general management of the sales force, every actor may be considered as a communication, information, and decision center. These centers interact with one another, and all have their own (sometimes personal) objectives and capabilities.

As already suggested, salespeople may be considered as managers of their own territories. They are responsible for building and maintaining

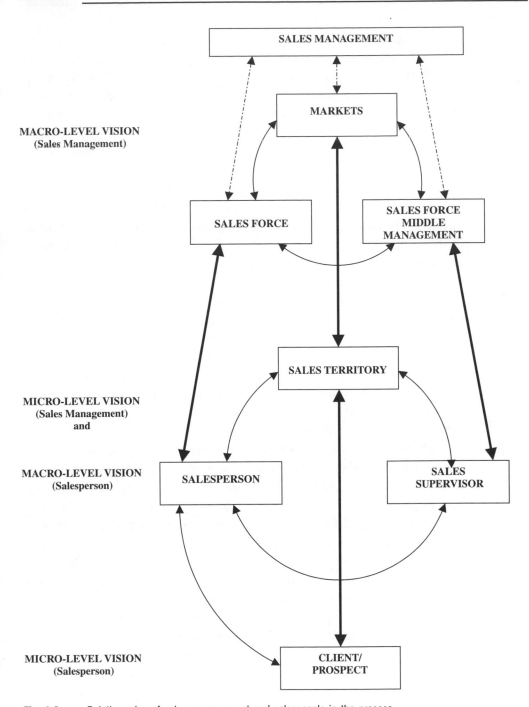

MACRO-LEVEL VISION
(Sales Management)

MICRO-LEVEL VISION
(Sales Management)
and

MACRO-LEVEL VISION
(Salesperson)

MICRO-LEVEL VISION
(Salesperson)

Fig. 1.3   Relative roles of sales management and salespeople in the process

relationships with every client and prospect in their territories. They fulfill missions that sales managers have assigned to them over a certain period of time. Management must carefully define and clearly communicate to every salesperson the extent of their *decision space*: the limits of their responsibilities and duties. Salespeople must also be given the appropriate resources to accomplish their mission. These include relevant information as well as material and financial resources. To maintain a sufficient communication level with its sales force, a firm often needs the help of intermediate sales managers. The mission of middle sales managers and the extent of their respective decision spaces, must be carefully and clearly defined. In the same way, management must provide them with the appropriate resources for completing their supervisory missions.

Figure 1.2 provides only a simplified vision of the process because all the above-mentioned entities may be split into a number of smaller units (see the dark arrows in Figure 1.3). Markets are made up of a number of sales territories. Sales territories are comprised of a number of clients and prospects. The sales force itself includes a number of salespeople. Middle sales management typically has several sales supervisors. These clusters of actors, however, display properties that may be different from those of their constitutive units. As a result, a dynamic management process takes place at different levels. At a more basic level, through their sales supervisors, sales managers try to control the client-related activities of every salesperson. At a more macro level, they make decisions that can affect the structure and organization of the whole sales force.

When managing their territories, salespeople can visualize their actions as the control of their relationships with every client or prospect. They must, however, also consider their actions as the management of the whole sales territory in order to define the best possible time and effort allocations among the various accounts and/or profit centers, or between calls to clients versus prospects, among others.

The process demands that sales managers develop not only a macro-level vision of the sales force, but also a thorough understanding of the micro-level operations that are typically carried out by middle sales management and by individual salespeople. In other words, *the selling processes that salespeople must follow to sell a firm's products or services in selected target markets must be part of a sales manager's competence and knowledge base.*

A sales force command center

A sales force command center is made up of two main parts, each one with a specific function: (1) a set of control levers that can be directly manipulated by management which constitute communication links with salespeople, and (2) a dashboard designed for management to watch the various indicators signaling, for example, whether objectives are likely to be met, or whether an individual is slipping behind target. The dashboard also includes various indicators about the state and evolution of the sales force and of the market environment.

Control levers

Because management typically pursues multiple objectives, sales force control levers are not homogeneous. They include several tools, each one playing a specific, but complementary, role. For sales managers, control levers are tools that control salespeople's decision spaces, motivation, activities, and/or competencies. Some of the control levers are devised for controlling outcomes and the behavior of others. Most frequently, hybrid control systems are often observed in practice (Oliver and Anderson 1995). For example, it is not unusual for a sales manager to closely supervise his or her staff (a behavior-based control lever) and also to use sales quota plans (a performance-based control lever). Sales managers have a certain number of control levers (also called control programs) at their disposal that they can use or not, depending upon the needs of their mission.

Nature of control levers

Sales force control levers are all the tools that sales managers can manipulate to directly or indirectly influence the activities and behaviors of salespeople. They include all managerial tools and techniques concerning training, motivation, supervision, support, and compensation. They are decisions or instructions that are directly communicated to salespeople to restrict or expand their freedom of action and their choices (i.e. their decision space) when fulfilling their duties. The decision spaces of salespeople cover numerous and varied areas. Within the constraints set by management, they may decide to display certain behaviors and activities in their sales territories. These are characterized by the relative effort intensity and by the effort allocations they imply (working hard), as well as by the quality level of those efforts (working smart) (Sujan 1986; Challagalla and Shervani 1996).

Sales managers can, for example, restrict the decision space of a salesperson by providing him or her with very precise target objectives (e.g., specifying a given sales quota). Alternatively, they can expand the decision space by giving general instructions (e.g., improve customer satisfaction level as much as possible) or by allowing some price initiative. These aspects will be discussed in detail in Chapter 5.

Selection criteria of control levers
Given that managers typically pursue multiple objectives, they also need to use a variety of control levers to meet them. Although all control levers have a specific function, they must all complement one another. Research has shown, for example, that salespeople who were compensated with a large percentage of fixed salary were also those that had a lower number of supervisors for a given sales force size and were also offered the best job opportunities and promotion in the long-run (John and Weitz 1989). Management selects the relevant control levers according to a set of criteria, the most important of which are briefly listed below.

Mission's objectives and environment   As the objectives are challenging, the means to achieve them must be multiple and elaborate. In the same way, when environmental forces are unfavorable and/or unpredictable, sales managers are likely to use a larger set of control levers.

Management style   A key idea developed in this book is that sales managers can select a more or less centralized or decentralized management style and control strategy, depending on the precision level and details of the instructions they impose on the sales force (Anderson and Oliver 1987). Consequently, management style also refers to the importance of the decision space given to salespeople when carrying out their duties (Montgomery, Silk, and Zaragoza 1971).

Under a fully centralized control system, management exerts direct control over sales activities or outcomes. It assigns very precise objectives and/or activities, and gives rewards for meeting those objectives or performing those activities (and/or the sanctions for failing to do so). Centralized controls essentially imply supervisors' authority, and tend to restrict decision space. A salesperson's decision space is essentially limited by the control decisions taken by management. For example, management may assign (i.e. impose) sales quotas for every customer/prospect and for every product line. In the most extreme cases, a salesperson's decision space is restricted to only two main possible courses of action — try to comply with management's requests, or not (and in the latter case, suffer the [likely] negative consequences).

At the other extreme, a decentralized control system is illustrated by use of the agency theory contract (Eisenhardt 1985): a firm offers a specific contract designed in such a way as to induce salespeople (who act in their own best interest), to optimize the firm's objectives at the same time. No precise objective is assigned. Only general reward/sanction or compensation programs are communicated to the sales force. For example, management may pay a commission on the gross margins of the products sold. This may induce a commission-maximizing salesperson to make effort allocations that have been shown (under restrictive conditions) to maximize a firm's profits (Farley 1964). Control is not exercised through authority. On the contrary, management implicitly gives a wide range of effort level and allocation options to choose from. Management only tries to make sure that the salespeople will pick up the option it wishes them to select.

Dashboard quality   The choice of the control levers used by management also depends on the extent to which the behaviors of the sales force are known or predictable, observable, and measurable. It also depends on the availability of adequate information about the sensitivities of sales territories to selling efforts,[2] and to the cost of collecting this type of information.

The extent and quality of the information provided by a dashboard interacts with a manager's style to specify the size of the tool kits which are actually used. Where a centralized management style is used, managers need good knowledge about territory sensitivities to selling efforts to estimate the quotas that correspond to the maximum efforts salespeople can achieve. If managers impose the use of canned sales presentations to salespeople, they need to know customer sensitivity to the various types of sales argument and features, in order to design effective sales presentations. In other words, because highly centralized management styles provide salespeople with specific targets, managers need information on how customers and salespeople react to the selected control instrument.

---

[2] Sales territory sensitivities to selling efforts are frequently called territory sales response functions in the academic sales management literature. They have been also referred to as task programmability (see Eisennhart 1985) or transformation processes (see Ouchi and McGuire 1975). Lodish *et al.* 1988 noted, however, that managers preferred the term 'sensitivities' when referring to this concept. Consequently, the latter terminology will be used throughout this book.

Sales management's dashboard

While managers make decisions about the control levers they want to use, they do not directly control the elements of their dashboard. A sales management dashboard is made up of three sets of elements: those that report and assess sales force performance, those that indicate environmental changes, and those that demonstrate any changes in the sales force.

Performance indicators

First, a dashboard allows sales managers to assess whether they are on the right track to meet their objectives (they can adjust the control levers, alter the objectives or both). A sales force dashboard allows formal comparisons between expectations (or predictions) about individual activities (behaviors), performances (outcomes) and the actual results.

The choice of which elements of this type should be in the sales force dashboard depends on the predictability (for accurate expectations), the observability (for outcome knowledge) of salespeople's activities and performance and/or on the costs of collecting sufficiently reliable information (Eisenhardt 1985; Ouchi 1979). In some cases, collecting information on calls to customers and prospects may be straightforward and inexpensive. In others, it might be more difficult and costly to monitor the quality of sales presentations and demonstrations made during calls (possibly as the result of the closer supervision that collecting this information requires).

An important question concerns the frequency with which results should be observed, analyzed, and compared to expectations. In order to obtain useful information, actual outcome levels should be compared with the proportion of the objectives that should be met at this time in order to meet the objectives for the planning period. This is why sales managers frequently use guidelines that assess whether a salesperson is achieving or missing their targets.

Environmental indicators

A second category of information that sales managers should find on the sales force dashboard describes the actual (and expected) states of various environmental indicators, for example, information about what the competition does or intends to do, economic forecasts and indices, and indications of new fashion trends. An analysis of the information collected through the dashboard should point at plausible explanations for any gaps. This new information alters the structure and content of a manager's knowledge base and competency level.

Sales force indicators

A third type of dashboard element concerns the sales force and its evolution. These indicate how the sales force and individual salespeople have actually reacted to the control levers that management has activated. For example, information about an individual's organizational commitment, job satisfaction, competency erosion, or turnover levels, provides essential data to managers about the current state of their sales force. Unfortunately, it seems that this type of element is often neglected – in the case of IMC, managers seemed to lack these vital elements. If management had been alerted that a feeling of dissatisfaction was developing in the sales force, despite the satisfactory short-term sales results, it would have tried to find the causes and implement corrective actions. Instead, the sales manager was satisfied with short-term success.

A dynamic control process

To manage a sales force dynamically, sales managers need to develop and constantly keep in mind the short- and long-term objectives of the mission. As leaders, they always should have a vision of what needs to be done, and to communicate the willingness to accomplish this mission to the whole sales force. To do this, they must devise a strategy that specifies the appropriate control levers that they intend to use, as well as the extent to which they intend to rely on them for implementing the selected strategy (Darmon 1993). This process, followed for each decision, includes three sequential stages: a planning stage; an implementation stage; and a feedback stage (Jaworski 1988). Figure 1.4, an extension of Figure 1.2, shows how the three stages of this control process affect all the other elements of the sales force management process.

Planning stage

The planning stage is described by the left hand part of Figure 1.4. To guide a sales force toward the corporate goals, a sales manager must 'plan' and contemplate which actions to undertake and consequently, which control levers to use. For that purpose, more or less formally, they estimate the sales force activities and behaviors that are necessary for meeting such objectives. For example, a sales manager might assess that the successful introduction of a given new product on the market requires some additional selling efforts from the sales force, and some additional training. This assessment can only be done on the basis of the (more or less extended and accurate)

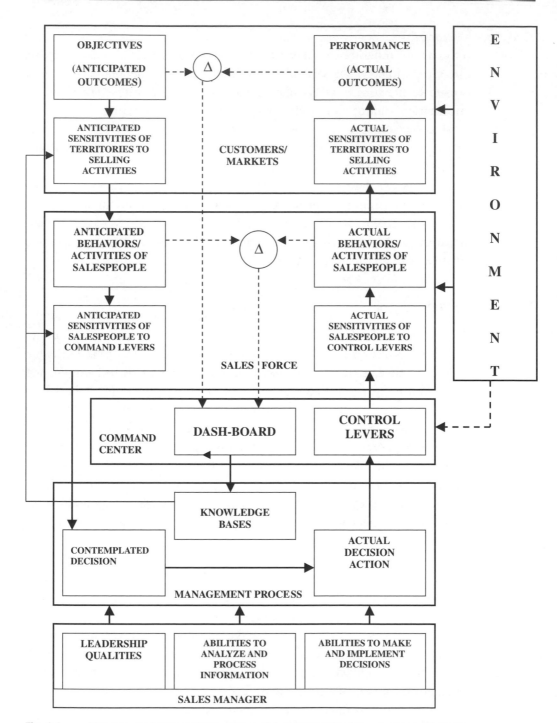

Fig. 1.4   Planning and implementation phases of a dynamic sales force management process

knowledge that management has about territory sensitivities to sales force activities. In other words, this sales manager (accurately or not) estimates that the market will react appropriately to additional selling effort and to some increase in sales force competency (given the new product introduction objectives). This can be influenced by a number of situational factors, like the economic and competitive conditions prevailing in the territory, the territory's market potential, the firm's penetration rate in the territory, and by a salesperson's abilities and competencies.

To influence salespeople's activities in the desired direction, under certain conditions, sales managers must have some (often imperfect) knowledge of the sales force sensitivities to the control levers at their disposal. For example, the sales manager may estimate that he needs ten new salespeople to deliver the required additional efforts, and that a two-day training course is sufficient to train the existing sales force to allow them to sell the new product. Although essential, this knowledge is difficult to acquire at a sufficiently accurate level. Returning to the IMC case, sales management had built the sales force compensation plan, based on certain expected sensitivities (or reactions) of the sales force to the new plan. Although the short-term sensitivities were correctly assessed, management had ignored (or underestimated) the long-term behavioral reactions of the sales force.

This planning stage constitutes the mental process that leads a manager to select appropriate control levers and to use the appropriate resources to achieve objectives. Consequently, as suggested by Figure 1.5, management's choice of specific control devices depends on the specificities of the situation, the firm, and its environment. More specifically, this choice is influenced by the predictability, observability, and measurability of the behaviors and activities of the sales force; by their performances; the availability of information about territory sensitivities to salespeople's efforts; the ability of the individual to respond to the various control devices; and by the cost of collecting such information.

Implementation phase

The implementation phase is described in the right hand part of Figure 1.4. Once the appropriate command devices are selected, managers must actually implement the contemplated actions. Planning must lead to action. This implementation phase is in reverse order, but this time, in an effective fashion (and not as a planning abstraction). Objectives will be met only as long as the plan is properly carried out. Departure from the plan is one of

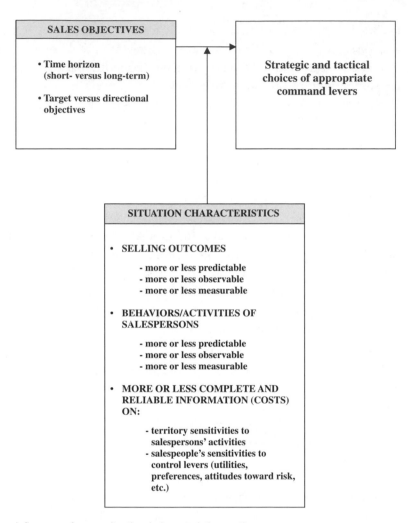

Fig. 1.5   Influences of some situational characteristics on the process

the major reasons why objectives may not be met. Using the preceding example, if only five salespeople were hired instead of ten, or if only half the salespeople in the sales force actually undertook the training program, it is unlikely that the sales force will meet its objectives. If, however, the planning process has been accurate, and the plan fully implemented, the implementation phase should result in achieving the mission objectives. If the size of sales force increases and the training program has produced sales force efforts and competencies at the required levels, *and* if these actions are sufficient to induce the sales force to sell the new product effectively, the objectives should be met.

Feedback

The feedback phase of the process is described by the middle part of Figure 1.4. Although managers take action to achieve definite results over a certain period of time, as discussed above, in practice, the results will almost always deviate (by a more or less important margin) from anticipated outcomes. Assuming the decisions have been implemented correctly, this may result from inaccurate forecasts of the prevailing conditions at the time the decisions are actually implemented. For example, in the preceding example, new product sales may fall short of the target objectives because management may have overestimated the territory sensitivities to sales effort. Possibly twenty more salespeople (instead of ten) would have been needed to meet the objectives. Alternatively, although the effort size could have been properly estimated, management may have underestimated the strength of retaliatory actions from competitors. Such causes suggest imperfect knowledge and anticipation of the actual territory sensitivities to selling effort (former case) or imperfect anticipation of (more or less predictable) occurrences in the environment. The latter tends to prevail when the environment is uncertain. It may also happen that management has made an inaccurate estimate of the sales force sensitivities to the control levers – for example if the two-day training period was too short to train the sales force properly.

For all these reasons, differences are frequently observed (Δ) between anticipated and actual outcomes, as well as between anticipated and actual sales force activities and behaviors. The quality of a dynamic management process may be assessed by the sizes of the various deltas reflecting the different dimensions of sales force performances and activities. As they get closer to zero, especially at the end of the mission period, they tend to reflect higher quality management.

By observing the gaps between actual and expected results (outcome-based controls), or the gaps between actual and expected activities (behavior-based controls), management can make tactical adjustments and use its sales force control levers accordingly. As seen above, this phase of the management process was deficient in the case of IMC.

The feedback loops are essential to the process. When managers see on the sales force dashboards that results are departing from their objectives by too great a margin, they must consider corrective action. To react properly, they need to start their decision process all over again – at least until the mission is fully accomplished.

Through observation (and interpretation of the data) from their dashboards, the knowledge bases of sales managers are constantly updated and increased, as well as their competencies. This should allow experienced managers to make better decisions.

Sales leaders

To be effective, sales managers must be competent and display appropriate behaviors. They must have developed extensive appropriate knowledge bases, a proper ability to analyze and process information, as well as making and implementing decisions. These different aspects of sales force management are essential (see Chapter 5).

More importantly, managers must possess definite leadership qualities. In the present framework of a dynamic sales management process, leadership must be a pervasive quality exercised throughout the sales organization (Ingram *et al.* 2005). Leadership is the ability to influence others to achieve common goals for the collective welfare of the firm. According to the traditional view, leadership is typically exercised by top managers. In the perspective of the sales management process described above, however, self-leadership must also be performed by salespeople themselves, because they must manage relationships with clients (Ingram *et al.* 2006) and/or with members of their selling teams (Ingram, LaForge, and Leigh 2002). This vision of extended leadership prevails throughout this book.

Conclusion

This chapter has introduced the concept of a dynamic sales force management process. This process comprises a set of elements and procedures designed to accomplish a firm's selling missions, under the conduct of a leader — the sales manager. The process is characterized by the more or less centralized management style of the leader, and is shaped by the variable availability, gathering, and cost of information flows within the system.

To effectively manage a sales force, managers have a whole series of control levers (or control devices) at their disposal. Each control lever accomplishes specific functions and must be selected with discrimination, depending on the goals to be reached, the situation at hand, and sometimes, the individuals involved. This is why the quality of sales management depends on the size and quality of the control levers as well as the completeness and accuracy of the information (and consequently the information flows) provided to sales management by what has been designated as the sales manager's dashboard.

The remainder of this book is devoted to a detailed analysis of the main aspects of this process. Part I is devoted to an analysis of the various actors of such a process and to their respective roles. It underscores the need for sales managers to have a thorough comprehension of the dynamics of the system they must manage. It is essentially descriptive, and more specifically, it covers the purchase behavior of clients and sensitivities of sales territories to selling efforts (Chapter 2). This is essential for understanding how salespeople must dynamically manage the relationships they build and maintain with their clients and prospects, as well as with their territories (Chapter 3). Chapter 4 provides an analysis of salespeople's behavior. Chapter 5 is devoted to an analysis of the means available to managers for accomplishing their mission, and especially the knowledge bases and competencies that managers must possess to efficiently fulfill them. Chapter 6 is devoted to an analysis of the selling environment, its current evolution, as well as to the probable impact of this evolution on sales force management.

The second part provides an analysis of a sales manager's command center. It is more normative than the first part. It describes (and prescribes) the various control levers that are available to management, especially, the means to assess the required sales effort levels and sales force organization (Chapter 7), target objective programs (Chapter 8), directional objective programs (Chapter 9), as well as programs designed to maintain and increase salespeople's competencies (Chapter 10). Chapter 11 provides indications and prescriptions on how to set up effective sales force dashboards. Finally, the book ends with a few concluding comments.

Part I

The actors in the process and their roles

What knowledge should sales managers have acquired in order to properly carry their missions? What qualities should they possess? These are questions that are addressed in Part I of this book. As underlined in Chapter 1, a sales force must be managed at two levels. A sales manager must attempt to influence market and customer behaviors through the sales force and salespeople. Three chapters of Part I (Chapters 2, 4, and 5) are devoted to a description and analysis of the behaviors of the three main actors of the dynamic sales management process: buyers, salespeople, and sales managers. Chapters 3 and 5 assess the roles of these actors in building and maintaining strong and lasting relationships. The rationale for this structure is provided in Figure I.1.

Chapter 2 describes the key actors of the sales management process that salespeople attempt to "influence," that is at a basic level, customers and prospects whose behaviors must be understood, predicted, and influenced, and at an aggregate level, the whole sales territory.

Chapter 3 analyzes the role salespeople play in developing relationships with clients and in managing their own sales territories. In order to establish business relationships between suppliers (through their sales representatives) and customers, a number of interactions must take place. Salespeople as well as sales managers cannot properly accomplish their missions unless they understand their customers' purchase and selling behaviors and grasp the influence and persuasion mechanisms that are activated during the selling and negotiation processes.

Chapter 4 is devoted to a description and analysis of the second type of actors of the process: at the micro-level, salespeople, and at the macro-level, the whole sales force. The dynamic management of a sales force implies making a series of decisions to lead salespeople and the sales force to perform at the highest possible level. Sales managers attempt to directly or

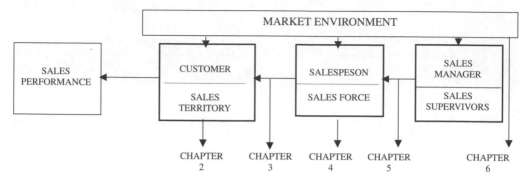

Fig. I.1   Structure of Part I

indirectly influence the behavior of salespeople and/or the selling process. As seen in Chapter 1, sales management is a difficult process because, unlike their colleagues in other functions, sales managers must influence both salespeople and customers and markets, to behave in the best long-term interests of the firm.

Chapter 5 outlines the knowledge and competencies that are required from the third type of actor of the process, sales managers. Specific knowledge and competencies are essential to effectively manage a complex system like a sales force. This chapter also discusses the main sales strategies that managers can pursue to accomplish their missions.

Chapter 6 describes market environment as well as the main evolutionary trends that are currently observed. As already noted in Chapter 1, understanding the main environmental forces and predicting their likely evolution is a prerequisite to effective dynamic management processes.

2 Buyers: key actors in the process

A salesperson's constant fear: the unexpected loss of a key account

Jim Harris, one of the most appreciated salespeople employed by the Heavy Duty Division (HDD) of an international manufacturer of automotive products had been negotiating an important contract for some time. This involved the replacement of the larger part of the truck fleet at a major transport company, a long-term client of the truck manufacturer's division. The contract involved the sale of about 200 vehicles, to be delivered over a six-month period. The deal was estimated at several billion euros. Two suppliers had made it to the last round of negotiations for this important contract, and discussions were tight. The customer's choice was going to be made on essentially economic criteria. A key decision criterion used by Tom Hilton, the procurement manager, was the transportation cost of one ton of goods per one hundred kilometers. These costs included operating and maintenance costs as well as the depreciation costs of the vehicles over their life expectancy.

Jim was about to obtain the contract. Although the offer was quoted at a price somewhat higher than most of the competing offers, the price premium could be explained by the high engineering quality of their trucks and by the strong reputation the firm enjoyed in this market. The vehicles' average life expectancy was substantially longer than those of competing trucks, and maintenance costs over a truck's expected life were considered lower for the HDD products. This gave HDD trucks a definite advantage when the cost of one ton of goods per one hundred kilometers was considered.

Jim had reached the stage of an informal agreement with the main decision makers at the transportation firm, when Tom Hilton was promoted to another position in the client's organization and was replaced by Jane Toledano. Shortly after this, Jim learned that the client had signed a contract with the other firm.

Jim immediately asked for an appointment with Jane Toledano. Given the importance of the contract, Jim asked the division sales manager to come along. During the meeting, the new procurement manager explained that when she took over, she undertook a thorough review of the data provided by the two truck manufacturers. She felt that the life expectancy of the competitor's vehicles had been somewhat underestimated by her predecessor. Obviously there was a risk that the truck life expectancy would be shorter than the competitor had claimed, but this risk seemed relatively small to her. Based on a longer life expectancy of the competitor's trucks, the competitor came up with a more advantageous transportation cost of one ton of goods per one hundred kilometers. As a result, the competitor had won the contract.

Jim Harris, his manager, and Jane Toledano separated with the definite promise from Jane that HDD would be asked to submit a proposal at their following call for offers, within a two to three-year time period.

Had Jim Harris, fully understood the behavior of his customers, he probably would have correctly assessed the threat posed by the change of a customer's key decision maker at that particular point in the negotiations. He could have called a meeting with her, and identified the behavioral characteristics and choice criteria that were important to this new individual. He could then have modified his offer accordingly.

This situation is not unusual. In the same way as sales managers control and manage their sales forces, salespeople control and manage their relationships with clients and prospects, as well as with their sales territories. Salespeople that are constantly firefighting and running from one client to another may be (although not always) a caricature of reality. They are no longer in control of the situation. This chapter is more concerned with the latter than the former kind of situation, when salespeople actually manage their activities and territories effectively to meet their objectives within usual constraints.

Because the process implies a thorough knowledge of the system to be controlled, purchasing behavior is described first. The analysis will then be extended to the management of a whole sales territory.

Relationships with buyers

Relationships between a firm (represented by a salesperson or a selling team) and a customer (often represented by a procurement manager or committee) have specific characteristics. They involve a variable number of actors. They evolve over time as the result of the (sales and purchase) behaviors of the various parties involved.

Nature and actors of buyer—supplier relationships

A business transaction can only take place when the various actors involved expect to obtain some benefits from it. At the beginning of a negotiation, it is often the case that one of the parties does not perceive clearly the benefits it could obtain from a transaction with the other. This "myopia" generally results from a lack of information. To reduce the informational gap that prevents the transaction or a long-term relationship from taking place, the two parties engage in an information exchange, generally over a specific period of time. This constitutes the selling process (or the purchase process, depending on the party's point of view).

Beyond a selling transaction that focuses on a single specific exchange, firms often attempt to adopt a long-term perspective to build customer loyalty, and consequently, to establish and maintain lasting relationships over a number of years. Such relationships imply that the two parties will not just participate in a single transaction, but in a series of transactions over an extended period of time.

Why should a client be interested in such a relationship? In many cases, firms may look for a stable relationship with certain suppliers. It is sometimes costly for a firm to build new relationships. There are substantial costs involved in looking for potential new suppliers and in collecting the information to establish new relationships. (In the HDD case above, for example, a switch of truck suppliers involves the major cost of changing spare part inventories.) In addition, a client also risks not being fully satisfied with a new supplier. As a result, it may be logical for customers to try to keep, and even build strong relationships with their current suppliers rather than constantly looking for new ones, especially when they are reasonably satisfied with them. In addition, because they work together in close relationships and have built some mutual trust, a customer may share relevant, and sometimes confidential information with suppliers.

Business-to-business relationships seldom involve one single individual in the client's organization, especially in the case of larger organizations and/or important procurements (Robinson *et al.* 1967). In such cases, the person in charge of the purchasing function plays a key role in establishing and maintaining business relationships with suppliers. In practice, the procurement function is increasingly held by professionals who have received formal training to that effect (Van Weele 2004). Research suggests that because of the rapid changes in the business environment, purchasing professionals need flexible skills, that is the ability to act entrepreneurially in managing risk, making decisions, planning, using interpersonal communication, applying influence and persuasion, being internally motivated, and being creative in solving business problems (Giunipero, Denslow, and Eltantawy 2005).

Typically, purchasing agents act on behalf of functional areas that eventually use the product, and which determine the characteristics and specifications for the product or service to be purchased. In this case, the role of purchasing agents consists of identifying potential suppliers, serving as intermediaries, and negotiating the best possible conditions on behalf of the users. Whenever a purchase involves several functional areas (e.g., the acquisition of important electronic services), several people exert an influence on the purchasing decision: the directors of the computing department, the main users, the finance managers, and the general managers (among others). In such cases, all the people involved have quite definite roles (Webster and Wind 1972).

The concept of a dynamic sales management process has a particular meaning when establishing and nurturing this type of complex relationship over time. These objectives and tasks require that salespeople plan, implement, and control their own activities. Salespeople must have acquired a thorough knowledge of how their customers are likely to think and behave, and the decisions they are likely to make.

Buyers' purchasing behavior

Just like pilots need an extended knowledge of the workings of their aircraft, a salesperson must have a thorough understanding of general customer behavior, buyers' practice in their industrial sector, and, whenever possible, of every customer with whom they have started a relationship. Some experts assert that the psychology of buying is actually more important than selling, because when a salesperson knows what prospects are thinking and how they are feeling, they have a much better chance of understanding what truly motivates them (Murphy 2004). Several models of industrial purchasing behavior have been proposed in the industrial selling literature (Ozanne and Churchill 1971; Choffray and Lilien 1978; Sheth 1973). In this chapter, only customer behavior in business-to-business (B2B) relationships is considered, because it is the most complex.

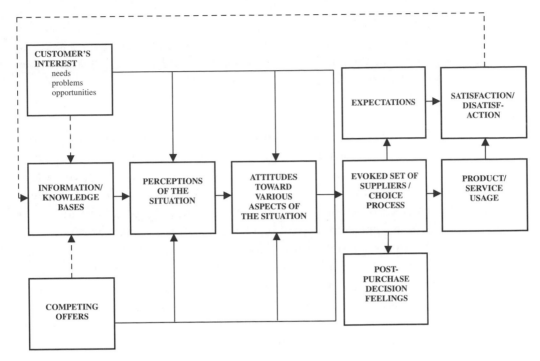

Fig. 2.1   Typical organizational purchase decision process

To establish lasting relationships between a supplier and a client, three essential conditions must be met (see the three left hand boxes in Figure 2.1). A potential client must:

- experience some felt or latent interest to even consider an offer from a supplier.
- (rightly or wrongly) perceive (or believe) that the supplier has the technical and financial capability to satisfy this interest, and the client must have developed sufficiently favorable attitudes toward this possible supplier.
- have the required resources to engage with this relationship and sees the conditions for a deal as sufficiently attractive to accept the supplier's offer.

Although these conditions are necessary for a transaction to take place, they are not sufficient. Clients are likely to assess offers from all the potential suppliers that meet the criteria above on a certain number of dimensions, and they will retain only those suppliers that are perceived as providing the highest value to them, over their own planning horizon. In addition, a transaction does not end with a purchase order. Any purchase is followed by post-decisional assessments by a buyer. Some of these are made just after the transaction has taken place. Others are made during and/or after the product or service has been used. These post-purchase feelings affect all the elements of the purchasing process as they evolve over time and as they affect the nature of the customer's experience.

Buyers' needs

In order to start a purchasing process and engage in a possible transaction, a client or a prospect must perceive or experience a latent interest. This may result from an unsatisfied need (or desire), for example, the need to feed assembly lines with raw materials or component parts for the end products they manufacture. Sometimes, a firm has recognized a problem and tries to identify the supplier that could best solve it. For example, a firm may wish to cut its administrative costs and looks for the most appropriate way to do it. In other instances, a firm may have identified an opportunity to achieve a manufacturing operation at a lower cost or has identified a better solution to an existing problem. The need can arise at a certain point in time (i.e. the purchase of a major capital asset) or it may be recurrent (i.e. the regular procurement of component parts).

For transactions to take place, buyers must have developed some incentive or motivation to make them. Motivation is an individual's willingness to spend some available, valued, but limited resources, to perform a certain activity that is expected to result in outcomes that have an even greater value to this individual. In other words, buyers must be ready to exchange some (financial, time, and/or informational) resources for other resources which are even more valued by the purchasing firm. In a given situation, the value that customers assign to various situational elements depends on their perceptions and attitudes toward those elements, especially the nature of the problem to be solved, the risks incurred, the availability of potential suppliers, and the suppliers' products, brands, and sales representatives.

Buyers' perceptions

An individual's behavior is affected by the way he or she perceives the situation at hand. It is a well known psychological phenomenon that there are often large gaps between objective and perceived situations. Typical selective attention and the need to interpret and integrate new information within a coherent mental structure, often induce individuals to unconsciously distort reality, and/or to reject part or all incongruent information. To best understand customers' behavior, objective reality is not the key factor. *What counts is how customers perceive reality.*

Self-interest

In B2B settings, purchasing agents typically have an in-depth knowledge of their firm's needs as well as of the problems faced by some of their firm's departments. Specific departments identify and express their own needs whenever such needs arise. Those needs are perceived as more or less acute depending on the quality of the solutions that have been used in the past. For example, a problem of just-in-time delivery of parts to an assembly line that has been solved satisfactorily in the past is unlikely to be perceived as a problem. In the case of the transport company described at the beginning of this chapter, the truck purchasing firm had properly perceived its problem of aging vehicles, as well as the need to replace a part of its fleet.

Generally, salespeople must inquire how customers perceive their own problems. More difficult are situations in which a firm has never found a satisfactory solution to one of its problems. This constitutes a real challenge. In such cases, it may happen that the firm does not perceive a problem any longer, because it has learned to live with it. This was the case, for example, in a wood shop that had learned to work despite the heavy saw dust that made the workshop's atmosphere almost intolerable. No satisfactory solution for cleaning the air had been found in the past, so this firm and its employees had stopped looking for a solution (Goodman 1973).

In the same way, a firm may or may not be aware of an existing opportunity. In some cases, clients themselves identify an opportunity. More frequently, however, it is up to the salesperson to identify how their offers can constitute an opportunity, and to show prospects how they could take advantage of this. In the same way, when a major innovation appears on a market, the salespersons' role consists of attracting the attention of potential customers to the opportunities that may result from using the new product.

Risk

Any industrial purchase involves some risk. This results from the incompleteness and/or inaccuracy of the information available to purchasing agents. They may trigger awareness on the part of decision makers of the negative consequences that could follow from this purchase (Henthorne, LaTour, and Natarajan 1993; Tanner and Castleberry 1993). Because of imperfect information, decision makers cannot anticipate those consequences with any reasonable degree of certainty. Purchase risks vary in nature and importance according to the decision at stake and the decision makers.

Buyers are typically subject to financial, organizational, and personal risks. A purchasing error can affect the firm's financial resources by an amount as large as the monetary value of the goods or services purchased. Product or service performances that are below expectations are organizational risks. In some cases this latter type of risk is negligible because it only has minor consequences. In other cases, the risk may be extremely high. For example, a delivery delay on one essential component part can stop production lines. Finally, poor performance of purchased products or services may result in personal risks for the purchase decision makers. Whenever purchasing mistakes have an adverse effect on an organization, purchasers may be held personally responsible and may have to suffer the consequences themselves. Consequently, personal risks are commensurate with financial and organizational risks. Researchers have recognized the importance of the two personal risks of participating and of not participating in the purchase process (with the possible consequences of such decisions) (Tanner 1996).

In addition, buyers' perceived risks vary with the importance of the purchase for the organization, with the financial resources at stake, as well as with the decision makers' informational gap. This gap is the difference between all the relevant information available to buyers at the time of purchase, on the one hand, and on the other, the relevant information level that would allow them to accurately predict the consequences of a contemplated purchase.

In the case of the transport company described above, the incurred risk was essentially linked to the actual life of the new vehicles to be purchased. Too short a life would adversely affect the transportation costs of the goods, and this cost increase could have been sufficiently high to decrease the long-term profitability of the firm, which might have threatened its survival.

Suppliers/offers

Buyers generally have a great deal of information concerning suppliers, the products and services currently on the market that are capable of satisfying their needs and solving their problems. Typically, they try to obtain information from various sources (Kennedy and Deeter-Schmelz 2001). However, this information is seldom, if ever, complete and accurate, because markets evolve constantly. The most advanced current technology will eventually be superseded by innovative new products and technologies.

As a result, firms and procurement departments constantly monitor and seek relevant market information through their own experience with current suppliers and their products, through advertising, word-of-mouth communication, interactions with other purchase agents, and of course, through the salespeople of suppliers. A firm's notoriety is commensurate with the amount and positive content of the information that customers and prospects have acquired about it. Some firms like Texas Instrument, Hewlett Packard, or IBM enjoy high notoriety levels on the market, which gives them a definite advantage for attracting prospects who have not yet dealt with them.

Obviously, information that buyers obtain from their own experience and/or from their peers is generally more credible than that received from suppliers' advertising or salespeople. As a result, information provided by salespeople is more likely to be accepted, remembered, and integrated when it is backed up with established facts (e.g., through demonstrations or objective test results).

Perceptions of salespeople

Clients perceive an efficient salesperson as a credible information source. Credibility, however, is never automatically established. It builds up over time, as they establish trust with their clients (Crosby *et al.* 1986; Swan *et al.* 1988; Hawes *et al.* 1989) and as clients develop positive perceptions of salespeople's behavior and tactics (Leigh and Summers 2002; DelVecchio *et al.* 2002).

Business relationships are frequently complex. Sometimes they involve only two individuals (the buyer and the salesperson). In this case, inter-personal relationships play a key role in the selling process. Salespeople and buyers cannot forget the fact that this is not a strictly personal relationship and that there is an even stronger relationship between the buying and the supplying firms. In other instances, as discussed above, relationships involve several people in both firms. In the above transportation company case, such an important purchase involved not only the highest management levels (the general manager and the finance and operations managers), but also the truck drivers who were the primary users of the purchased products and who had to spend a large amount of time in the new trucks.

Research suggests that interpersonal relationships may be characterized along four main dimensions (Iacobucci and Ostrom 1996):

- the power symmetry or dissymmetry of the parties involved in the relationship;

- the quality of the relationship, which may vary from very friendly and cooperative to competitive and hostile;
- the relationship intensity, and the strength of the interdependencies of the parties involved, a relationship varying possibly from aloof and superficial to very intense (and possibly friendly or hostile at the same time);
- the relationship's essentially social or professional character.

The sales force literature has investigated the hypothesis according to which interactions between purchasers and salespeople are more likely to be successful when both parties share some personal characteristics and values (Lichtenthal and Tellefsen 2001). This hypothesis is backed up by the observation that salespeople are more effective when they deal with a certain type of client. Some researchers have extended the observation by hypothesizing that salespeople had better chances to get along with purchasing agents when they shared some demographic characteristics, personality traits, common values, or attitudes (Evans 1963; Dwyer, Richard, and Shepherd 1998; Jones *et al.* 1998; McNeilly and Russ 2000). Although it is very likely that such factors facilitate business transactions (Churchill *et al.* 1975), the practice suggests that they can only partially predict the success of business relationships (Cronin 1994).

Attitudes

Buyers' attitudes are influenced by buyers' perceptions. If buyers have not developed sufficiently favorable attitudes toward a certain number of elements that characterize a purchase situation, they are unlikely to purchase from a given supplier. A positive attitude toward a supplier or a brand (for example), induces a buyer to behave positively toward this supplier or this brand. In a selling context, a customer's attitudes toward possible suppliers, their brands, and their sales representatives are especially relevant. As just seen, because any purchase involves risk, a purchaser's attitude toward risk remains one of the key factors of a purchase decision process.

Attitudes towards risk

All decision makers do not share the same risk tolerance. Some are bold and do not mind taking substantial risks. Others act cautiously and avoid risk. Typically, firms are assumed to be risk neutral, that is, they would neither seek nor avoid risk in a given situation. Observers of organizational decision making, however, know that decision makers tend to be risk averse for the same reasons that have been already mentioned: some personal risk is always involved in a purchase decision. Should the risk materialize, it could affect the status of the decision maker in his or her organization. On the contrary, making a bold decision that turns out to be a success may have positive consequences for the organization and the individual. It is unsurprising that many purchase managers avoid taking undue risks. Research suggests that for a high-risk business-to-business service, a buyer's previous experience indirectly affects his/her brand loyalty (Bennett, Hartel, and McColl-Kennedy 2005).

In the transportation company case, the main factor that induced the new procurement manager to make a decision different from her predecessor was her readiness to take a bigger risk concerning the actual life expectancy of the trucks from the competitor's company.

Suppliers and brands

Buyers generally develop variable attitudes toward suppliers and their brands. Some suppliers may enjoy quite favorable customer attitudes, others neutral, and still others, quite negative attitudes. Besides notoriety, a firm must also develop a positive image in its markets. In a B2B context, suppliers strive to build an image of a serious, dependable, and financially sound company. To build profitable and lasting relationships, it is essential for suppliers to develop positive attitudes among clients, not only toward the firm, but also toward its products and its brands. Satisfied customers are likely to keep and reinforce their positive attitudes. In the long-term, marketing relationships cannot last without a high level of customer satisfaction (Colletti and Mahoney 1991; Johnson 1991; Farber and Wycoff 1991).

Attitudes to salespeople

Relationships between buyers and salespeople are essentially human relationships. The type and intensity of the relationship that a customer develops with a sales representative has a strong impact on the success and quality of a business relationship. A customer is more likely to have developed a favorable attitude toward a salesperson (and consequently toward the firm) if the salesperson behaves professionally. Over a long period of time, purchasers come to trust a particular salesperson, so they tend to perceive a lower risk when dealing with this person's firm.

In any case, it is easier for a salesperson who enjoys a relationship of trust with buyers to influence them. Research suggests that these types of salespeople can influence clients concerning the price, quantities, and the mix of goods ordered. Manufacturers may have a stronger influence concerning the service level, inventory levels, and presentations. A customer's attitude toward a supplier's salesperson have been shown to be a key factor in the success of business relationships (Zemanek 1997).

Resources and constraints

As suggested by the lower part of the path in Figure 2.1, a firm may well need to renew part or all its fleet of automotive vehicles (necessary condition 1). It may think of (for example) Volvo or Mercedes-Benz as possible suppliers and may even have developed quite favorable attitudes toward both suppliers (necessary condition 2). Although both conditions are necessary for a purchase to take place, they are not in themselves sufficient. Even though both conditions 1 and 2 have been met, it is quite possible that neither of these firms is being seriously considered as a potential supplier. For example, it is quite possible that the price range of these two suppliers is beyond what the firm can afford, given its limited resources. Alternatively, both firms may have too scarce a network of agents throughout the country to insure the maintenance and repair of their trucks.

A third necessary condition for suppliers to be part of a customer's "evoked set of potential suppliers" is that their marketing programs do not disqualify them straightaway as a result of negative perceptions by the client (especially concerning price and distribution policies).

All those suppliers that meet those three conditions are part of a customer's evoked set, out of which the winning supplier(s) will be selected eventually.

Decisions and expectations

Through more or less formal procedures, customers have included in their evoked sets a number of potential suppliers that could *a priori* (and given the incomplete information at their disposal) have the capacity to fulfill their needs, solve their problems, or help them to take advantage of some new opportunity. Now, they must select the right supplier out of their evoked set.

Decisional conflicts

When contemplating making a major purchase, like any individual facing an important decision, customers are subject to a number of economic, psychological, and personal forces and impulses (Lewin 1935). These forces may push in essentially positive or negative directions and vary in intensity.

Positive impulses (or forces) result from desirable features of the supplier's offer, and induce purchasers to act in favor of a certain solution and/or a given supplier. In contrast, negative forces (or inhibitions) are generated by less appealing features of an offer, and tend to prevent purchasers from opting for a particular solution and/or supplier, but for an alternative course of action. In some cases, buyers may even prefer to postpone a purchase. Positive and negative impulses are materialized as positive selling arguments or as buyers' objections.

The forces or impulses implied in a given purchase decision and for a given decision maker may be represented by the right or left plates of a weighing scale, depending on whether they are positive or negative. The weights of these arguments reflect their relative importance to the decision maker. The sets of positive and negative forces and impulses involved in a decision process generate the internal conflict that any decision maker faces when making an important purchase decision.

For buyers, this conflict triggers a state of psychological tension the intensity of which is directly linked to the number and intensity of the forces involved in the process. This conflict can be solved in different ways, with different outcomes. One possible outcome (Figure 2.2a) is for the decision maker to remain in a non-purchase situation. In this case, the sum of the negative forces outweighs the sum of the positive arguments. Alternatively, a customer may fall into a purchase situation, if following some selling demonstration (for example), the sum of argument weights is larger for the positive than for the negative forces (Figure 2.2b).

This representation of an industrial purchase has the advantage of highlighting that any purchase is the outcome of an internal conflict. Purchases take place when the positive forces or impulses that induce the decision maker to sign an order override the negative ones. Note that in any selling situation, negative forces are always present. They reflect the numerous and various risks that the decision maker incurs, especially the risks of obtaining suboptimal benefits from the purchase or even of foregoing the amount of money that is involved in the transaction. As will be discussed in the following chapter, only relevant information and new evidence can change the equilibrium of the various forces at work and produce a shift to the positive direction.

Conflict resolution processes

In order to understand how buyers solve the decisional conflict described above, one should recognize that their conflict resolution process is

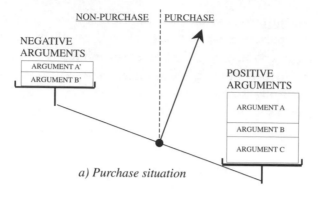

a) Purchase situation

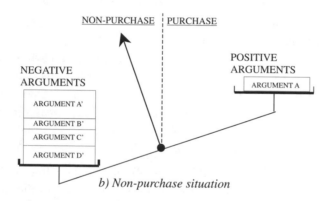

b) Non-purchase situation

Fig. 2.2   Purchase and non-purchase situations

essentially *rational* and involves a series of very precise *criteria*. In addition, every organization has its own *decision-making style*.

Purchases as rational decision processes   A firm's purchase decision is generally the outcome of a structured and rational process. When it contemplates making a certain purchase, a firm attempts to meet precise objectives. They consider a number of options that may lead them to meet those objectives (including the option to postpone the purchase). In any situation, there exist many uncertainties linked to the fact that it is practically impossible for decision makers to enjoy complete and accurate information on all possible options. Buyers typically use (formally or not) a certain number of criteria to assess the intensity of the forces at work, and consequently, for selecting what they perceive as the best solution.

Purchases based on economic choice criteria   Industrial purchasers generally take into account (but are not limited to) economic criteria. Suppliers typically evaluate suppliers and their offers according to the perceived value they can get from them. Although prices are almost always a factor, they may not be the most important decision criterion. Product and service quality, the suppliers' ability to solve customer's problems satisfactorily are at least as important as the basic price of the goods and services provided.

As already mentioned, however, beyond those objective and economic criteria that are often effectively stated by organizational purchasers, more subjective and often affective criteria are always present and may have a more or less important influence on purchase decisions. These subjective criteria are seldom recognized by purchasers, but are often used to reduce the personal risks that the decision makers perceive in the purchase decision (Wilson 1994). Note that, even though decision makers use such subjective and personal criteria, this does not subtract from the essentially rational character of their decision processes.

Characteristics of purchase decision processes   Because industrial purchases frequently involve many firms and several individuals, they follow decision processes that are more or less complex depending on the organizations involved and the importance of the negotiation (Mattson 1988; Jennings and Plank 1995). When a purchase situation involves one buyer or a limited number of decision makers, it requires simpler processes that take place over a typically short period of time. At the other extreme of the continuum, when the contemplated purchase is important and involves high risks for an organization, several decision makers are typically involved in a step-by-step decision process. When several decision makers are involved, everyone has his/her own preferences, interests and perceptual biases. This can result in conflict and opposition. In this case the final outcome depends on a number of factors such as the organization's decision-making style, the personalities and/or the tactics used by each decision maker to influence the decision toward the preferred solution (Sheth 1973).

When several individuals take part in the decision-making process, *creeping commitment* frequently occurs. Creeping commitment refers to the fact that, as the decision-making process unfolds over a certain period of time, decisions are made to keep some options open and to discard others. This narrowing-down process continues until a final choice is made from two or three possible solutions. As a result, when the purchase process has reached a certain stage, some options (and consequently some suppliers) have been set aside at an early stage of the process. Consequently, this prevents them from exerting any influence over the final choice.

In addition, purchase decision processes are dynamic. Perceptions, attitudes, and preferences change as customers obtain new information, or as new events occur and alter the situation. This is why a process is needed for constantly adapting the selling process to these changes. Research has proposed that a supplier's relationship activities develop a buyer's attentiveness toward the supplier, which, in turn, leads to profitable buyer-purchasing behaviors (Bonner and Calantone 2005). At any time, customers may decide to accelerate the process and make a final decision, depending on their analysis of the situation, the urgency of solving a problem, or their willingness to take advantage of some market opportunity. In such cases, they choose the best possible option given the information they have acquired at this time. They may also decide to postpone a purchase decision to obtain additional relevant information (and consequently, reduce the perceived risk).

Purchase decisions are always linked to customer's expectations. Based on information at hand, customers develop definite expectations concerning the benefits they must obtain from the purchased goods and services. False, inaccurate, or exaggerated information provided by salespersons may well induce a customer to select their firm as a supplier. However, this means that the customer develops expectations that cannot be fulfilled by the products or services. This is likely to result in customer disappointment and a decision to shift suppliers as quickly as possible.

Purchase decision-making styles   Research suggests that industrial purchasers develop their own decision styles and decision processes. Three decision styles have been identified:

- entrepreneurial organizations mainly delegate purchase decisions to one or two decision makers;
- planning organizations make purchase decisions by relying on experts from various functional departments;
- bureaucratic organizations have formalized purchase decision procedures.

As a result, purchasing behaviors of individuals tend to reflect the decision-making style of their own organization. Organizations that have different decision styles show definite preferences for specific selling strategies from their suppliers. Entrepreneurial organizations prefer to deal with an individual salesperson and are more sensitive to product-oriented selling strategies. Planning organizations prefer to deal with a group of experts and are more likely to appreciate a customer-oriented selling strategy. Finally, bureaucratic organizations wish to involve the supplier's various functional departments in the purchase process (Sharma and Pillai 1996).

Post-decision reaction

Once a purchase has taken place, customers have acquired more than just a product or a contract of service. They have also acquired the promise that their legitimate expectations will be met. They expect their needs to be fulfilled, their problem solved, or to have taken advantage of the opportunity they have identified. In other words, they are entitled to be satisfied with the transaction. In some cases, customers can easily and immediately verify that the promise has been kept. In most cases, however, products have long usage cycles, and several months or even years may be necessary for customers to assess whether the products and services sold to them by some supplier have actually met their expectations. For example, there is the case of important capital assets. In such cases, one must make a distinction between post-purchase and post-usage feelings. Post-purchase feelings follow immediately after the order has been signed. They refer to the uncertainty about the appropriateness of the purchase decision. Post-usage feelings are experienced after customers have had a chance to properly evaluate the extent to which the purchased goods or services have met their expectations.

Post purchase feelings

Once a major purchase has taken place, a customer's psychological tension generally does not vanish right away. It is a well-known marketing phenomenon that after major purchases, customers experience more or less important post-purchase psychological tensions (Festinger 1967). These may have two causes. First, they may result from a fear experienced by buyers that they have not made the best possible purchase decision. They may fear that they have not "optimized" their purchase as a result of their lack of information and knowledge. Second, once the decision has been made, customers have definitively given up all the advantageous conditions that could have been granted by other suppliers, and which had to be foregone to benefit from the (hopefully) more important advantages from the current supplier's deal. In other words, this psychological tension results from the fact that it was impossible for the customer to obtain an "ideal offer" from suppliers that could exactly match their needs and desires. In most purchase situations customers must accept trade-offs and make compromises. They select among offers (and suppliers) the product or service that they perceive as closest to this ideal. In the transportation company case discussed above, the client had to give up some product quality and expected product life expectancy to obtain a lower price. Obviously, none of the two competing suppliers that were kept in the transportation firm's evoked set could have offered both advantages simultaneously.

To reduce this state of psychological tension, customers may have different kinds of reaction. They may, for example, be alert to new information that could confirm that they have made the best possible choice. Researchers have found that car advertisements were more frequently read by consumers who had just bought a car of the advertised make. Customers may avoid information that tends to suggest that they have made a poor purchase decision. Alternatively, they may cancel their order.

Satisfaction/dissatisfaction

As time elapses, post-purchase feelings fade away and post-usage feelings appear. These feelings result from a comparison between a product's actual performance and the customer's expectations concerning that performance. Satisfied customers are obviously one of the prime goals for most firms. Therefore, it is important to realize that customers are not satisfied in absolute terms. Customers are more or less satisfied (or dissatisfied) depending on whether the product performance has met or surpassed (or remained above) their expectations. This has important selling implications: customers with high expectations are more difficult to satisfy and *vice versa*. In other words, raising customer expectations may not payoff in the long-term, at a time when building customer loyalty is the name of the game! Although customer satisfaction is no guarantee of customer loyalty (satisfied customers may still find competing offers even more attractive), research has shown that satisfaction has a positive effect on customer retention (Gustafson, Johnson, and Roos 2005).

Purchase strategies

It would be erroneous to think that only a supplier's salesperson selects and applies a selling strategy and deals with an essentially passive buyer. In most cases, buyers are pro-active and select their own purchase strategy. In many markets, the offer for products and services is larger than demand, and buyers hold a better relative power position. They are more likely to impose their own strategies onto the suppliers' salespeople than the other way around. This explains why the procurement function has gained so much importance in many firms over the last few years and is now often recognized as a key function in those firms.

Buyers may select a strategy of co-operation with one or more selected suppliers. Alternatively, they may call on all potential suppliers and ask them to submit offers to select the best one. Buyers may follow different strategies depending on the potential suppliers. For example, they may provide information on competing offers to some suppliers to obtain better conditions from them. With other suppliers, they may leave some doubts about competing offers to induce the supplier to grant even better conditions and make sure that they beat all competing offers and obtain the order.

As discussed above, organizations follow strategies that often reflect their decision styles. In addition, they sometimes prefer to deal with a given type of salesperson that they wish to see apply specific selling strategies.

Dynamic sales territory management processes

A salesperson is very seldom in charge of one single customer. More frequently they are assigned the responsibility for developing relationships with a certain number of accounts. In fact, a sales territory is much more than all the different accounts of which it is comprised. Not only should salespeople manage relationships with every customer and prospect in their territories, but they also need to manage their territories. In other words, they manage their time, their most scarce resource, to perform all the activities for which they are responsible, especially among their different accounts.

Definition of a sales territory

A sales territory is always defined as the set of accounts a sales manager has assigned to a given salesperson who then has the responsibility for developing, maintaining, and nurturing relationships within them. It is frequently (but not always) defined according to geographical criteria.

Frequently, one salesperson is in charge of all accounts within a geographical zone, be it a state, city, or city block.

Sales territories may sometimes include a very small number of key accounts. Sometimes, these are geographically far away from one another. Other territories may include a large number of relatively small accounts (typically concentrated in one geographic area). The way sales territories have been designed reflects the organization of the sales force, the allocations of the selling effort, and the responsibilities of individual salespeople.

Main characteristics

A sales territory is characterized by size, geographical aspects, and the characteristics of the accounts of which it is comprised. It is also characterized by a number of indicators that are used to assess current sales performances. Other indicators allow an assessment of the long-term marketing goodwill of a firm within a sales territory.

Current sales performance indicators

A number of indicators are frequently used to assess the current sales performance in a given territory. These are: a firm or industry's sales penetration, territory sales potential, the environmental characteristics of the territory, territory sensitivity to personal selling efforts, as well as the workload required for adequate coverage (Pilling, Donthu, and Henson 1999).

Territory sales penetration

Like most markets, a sales territory is cultivated by a firm and a certain number of competitors who compete in selling their products and services to the same types of account. A firm's market sales penetration (Sf) is the sales volume that this firm currently achieves in this territory over a certain period of time (generally one year). It may be expressed in units or in monetary terms. Unless the firm enjoys a monopoly, other firms compete and sell the same type of product in the territory. In other words, the sales penetration of the competition (Sc) is the total sales amount (in units or in monetary units) sold by all the competing firms in the considered market during the same period of time. Industry sales penetration is the sum of the sales penetrations of the firm and the competitors.

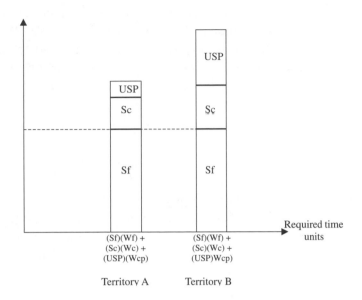

Sf   = sales to current customers
Sc   = sales to competitors' customers
USP = untapped sales potential
Wf   = time required for keeping 1€ sales to current customers
Wc   = time required for converting 1€ sales from competitors' customers
Wcp = time required for converting 1€ sales from untapped sales potential

Fig. 2.3   Comparison of two sales territories with equal sales volumes and different potential levels

These two quantities are important because their ratio, $Sf/(Sf+Sc)$ indicates a firm's market share. Market shares can be defined for any competing firm in the same way.

Territory sales potential

Unless a market is mature, none of the firms competing in a market have achieved a stage of market sales saturation. There is still some untapped potential that is up for grabs. A territory untapped sales potential (USP) for a given product is the additional product sales over some period of time that would be achieved if all the competing firms deployed quite substantial and sustained marketing efforts to promote this product. Consequently, in most cases, a firm cultivates only one part of the territory sales potential. Therefore, the total market potential of a given territory is the sum of the current industry sales and untapped market potential $(Sf+Sc+USP)$. Because a firm may consider that it can attract competitor's customers, a firm's untapped sales potential is the sum of competitors' sales penetration and the untapped market potential (Sc + USP).

It is often useful to express territory untapped market potential, a firm's, or competition's penetration in the territory as a proportion (or a percentage) of total market potential. In these cases, they are called territory untapped market potential rate, firm's, and competition's penetration rates in the territory, respectively.

Whenever a market is at maturity, there is no territory untapped market potential left (USP = 0), territory market potential is about the same as industry market penetration, and a firm's market share may be approximated by its territory sales penetration rate.

To illustrate how sales analysts can use the different concepts, Figure 2.3 provides an example of two sales territories A and B. Both territories have comparable current sales levels (Sf) and a superficial analysis may lead to a false conclusion of similar sales performances. In fact, because of different territory potentials and sales penetration rates, the sales performance in territory A is somewhat higher than in territory B.

As this figure illustrates, although equal sales levels have been achieved in both territories, Territory B, with a higher sales potential (Sc + USP) requires more of a salesperson's time for adequate coverage and could be reduced in size to yield higher sales volumes.

Sales territory environment

This refers to the conditions surrounding and affecting all the accounts of a given territory. For example, a sales territory environment may be characterized by the competition intensity in the territory, by more or less favorable local economic conditions, or by some social and/or cultural specificity affecting sales differentially. Depending on their nature and strength, such environmental characteristics can either strengthen or weaken the territory sensitivities to selling effort.

Territory sensitivity to selling efforts

Clients and prospects are more or less sensitive and reactive to sales calls from firms in various industries or even from firms from one specific industry. In the same way, this phenomenon applies at the sales territory level. The sensitivity of a territory to a salesperson's selling efforts are affected by different factors.

- They are increasing at a decreasing rate as selling efforts increase (Sinha and Zoltners 2001).

- They cannot surpass a maximum level (market potential) per period of time, no matter how high the selling effort level.
- They display carryover sales effects from efforts deployed in preceding periods.
- They display more or less important lagged effects.
- They depend on how the selling effort has been allocated over time and among the various selling activities by the salesperson in charge of the territory.

In addition, sales territory sensitivity to selling efforts is likely to depend on environmental conditions as well as on the competence level and effectiveness of the salesperson in charge of the territory (Krishnan, Netemeyer, and Boles 2002). A sales territory is more reactive to selling efforts when the salesperson in charge is experienced and competent. In the same way, the territory is more reactive when selling conditions are more favorable and the competition level is less acute. Note that the same relationships apply to individual customer sensitivities to selling effort.

Workloads

Finally, sales territories are also characterized by the workload they require from a salesperson. The workload assesses the work that a salesperson must provide to adequately cover the territory and to fully exerting his or her responsibilities toward the different territory accounts. As suggested in Figure 2.3, a salesperson's workload cannot be properly defined unless managers first define what "adequate coverage" means for them. Precise targets will have been established, either in terms of activities or sales performance. For example, a territory workload may be based on the time required to sustain one sales unit from customers (Wc), for attracting one competition's customer (Wp), and for converting a prospect entering the market (Wpc).

Coverage rate

Salespeople and sales managers must decide which customers and prospects in each category should be cultivated and how much time should be allocated to them. Assuming that all accounts in a territory deserve to be cultivated (which is generally not the case), the workload for providing an adequate coverage of the territory can be easily estimated as (Sf) (Wc) + (Sc) (Wp) + (USP) (Wcp). Frequently, a salesperson has only a limited amount of time to contact customers and prospects (W). The firm's territory coverage rate can be estimated as the proportion (or

Table 2.1. Basic sales territory concepts

	Expression	Example
Market potential of a sales territory	$Sf + Sc + USP$	1,000 units
Firm's penetration in the territory (sales)	Sf	100 units
Firm's penetration rate in the territory	$Sf / (Sf + Sc + USP)$	0.1 (or 10%)
Competition's penetration in the territory	Sc	700 units
Competition's penetration rate in the territory	$Sc / (Sf + Sc + USP)$	0.7 (or 70%)
Territory untapped market potential	USP	200 units
Territory untapped market potential rate	$USP / (Sf + Sc + USP)$	0.2 (or 20%)
Firm's untapped sales potential in the territory	$Sc + USP$	900 units
Industry sales in the territory	$Sf + Sc$	800 units
Firm's market share in the territory	$Sf / (Sf + Sc)$	0.125 (or 12.5%)
Annual workload required for sustaining one sales unit	Wc	10 hours
Annual workload required for attracting one customer away from competition	Wp	15 hours
Annual workload required for converting one prospect into a client	Wcp	12 hours
Annual number of hours available to a salesperson for customer contacts	W	1,600 hours
Optimal territory coverage	$(Sf)(Wc) + (Sc)(Wp) + (USP)(Wcp)$	13,900 hours
Firm's territory coverage rate	$W/[(Sf)(Wc) + (Sc)(Wp) + (USP)(Wcp)]$	0.115 (or 11.5%)

percentage) of the ideal coverage that can be effectively provided by a salesperson: $W/[(Sf)(Wc) + (Sc)(Wp) + (USP)(Wcp)]$.

These sales territory characteristics are useful indicators of the market position of a firm in every sales territory and are frequently used to make useful comparisons across territories. These indicators are summarized and exemplified in Table 2.1. As will be discussed in Part II of this book, they often constitute the basic indicators that sales managers want to include in their sales force control dashboards.

Goodwill indicators

In order to understand a firm's position in every sales territory, sales volume performance indicators must be supplemented by more qualitative criteria. Such indicators include, for example, the firm's notoriety level in the territory, the customers' favorable or unfavorable attitudes toward the firm, its products, and sales representatives, or their satisfaction (or dissatisfaction) levels. Some indicators are more difficult to quantify and/or to observe than others. They are, however, often the best indicators for assessing the past and predicting the future of a firm in a given sales territory. Customers' perceptions and attitudes toward a firm have been at least partially shaped by the past actions of a salesperson. Although this is no guarantee, satisfied customers are more likely to remain loyal to a supplier, which is likely to facilitate the salesperson's work in the future.

Conclusion

This chapter has provided a brief description of buyer behavior and, at a more aggregate level, of a whole sales territory's reactions to a salesperson's selling effort. Like any human behavior, buyer behavior is complex, difficult to fully understand, and to predict. Buyer behavior is likely to be influenced by a host of personal, organizational, cultural, and situational factors. As a result, a salesperson's task may be conceived as managing a set of complex and ever-changing entities.

This chapter has attempted to highlight the importance for salespeople (as well as their managers) to have a thorough understanding of buyer behavior to effectively manage their relationships with customers and sales territories. This should be an essential part of the sales department's information and knowledge bases. Customers' needs and problems, awareness of market opportunities, clients' perceptions, attitudes, decision processes, information, and satisfaction levels are essential knowledge elements that any salesperson must possess to effectively manage their sales territories.

3 Dynamic customer relationship management processes

Customer relationship management at Electronics, Inc

Jim O'Connor, the sales manager at Electronics, Inc., a leading manufacturer of electronic equipment, had devised a strict policy for developing profitable relationships with the firm's key clients. He was convinced that the future of the firm depended on its capacity to implement a customer-oriented strategy. The program consisted of an intensive and rigorous training program with two major objectives: (1) sensitize salespeople to the importance of developing strong customer relationships; and (2) teach them the methods for developing and maintaining these relationships over time.

In spite of the training program, it became evident to Jim O'Connor that after two years, the customer loyalty rate had not significantly improved. A few divisional sales managers attributed these results to the poor quality of the training program. Others pointed to the almost impossible task of keeping customers loyal when they were constantly submitted to strong pressure from competitors.

Jim O'Connor did not find these explanations convincing, so he undertook an analysis of the relationships that every salesperson had developed with his/her clients. These proved to be illuminating. First, the sales force turnover rate had averaged 25 percent per year over the last few years. As a result, sales territories had to be adjusted frequently, and customers were constantly reassigned to new salespeople. Very few customers had dealt with the same person over an eighteen-month period.

Second, the loyalty and relation development program had been effective in the sense that in many cases, salespeople had been able to establish better and stronger relationships with their clients. Unfortunately, Electronics, Inc. did not benefit from these improved relationships because in many instances, clients had become loyal, not to Electronics Inc, but to the departing salesperson, and had followed them to competing firms!

These two causes acted in tandem and jeopardized the benefits of the relationship development program. Jim made two important decisions. First, he implemented a new program which attempted to reduce the turnover rate of the sales force. At least as important as keeping customers loyal, Electronics had to develop sales force loyalty to the firm. Second a direct advertising campaign was launched toward customers to build customer loyalty not only to individual salespeople, but also to the firm itself.

As the case of Electronics, Inc. suggests, the relationship between a customer and a supplier is complex. There is a double relationship between customer and supplier as well as between the customer and the supplier's salespeople. The quality of a trust relationship between a customer and a salesperson often constitutes the basis for a good relationship with a supplier. In extreme cases, like in the above example, the customers may prefer to continue working with a salesperson with whom they have built a strong trust relationship, even when the salesperson leaves his/her employer for a competitor.

Salespeople have a duty and a responsibility to manage as best they can the relationships that they and their firm have with every client and prospect in their sales territories. They must ensure an overall well balanced management of their territories. After the brief description of buyer behavior provided in Chapter 2, this chapter is devoted to an examination of how salespeople fulfill this mission. Because salespeople manage their own sales territories, the general management process that has been outlined in Figure 1.4 also applies to them. After providing a general overview of this process, this chapter concentrates on the nature of salespersons' missions, and on the strategies and tactics they follow to manage relationships. The following chapter will emphasize salespeople's behaviors and their capability to achieve such relationship-building missions.

Dynamic customer relationship management defined

Salespeople are assigned the mission to create, maintain, nurture, and develop relationships with the accounts for which they are responsible. In addition to the objectives they must meet with every client, they are also typically assigned objectives for their whole sales territories. To successfully fulfill their mission and effectively manage a set of relationships

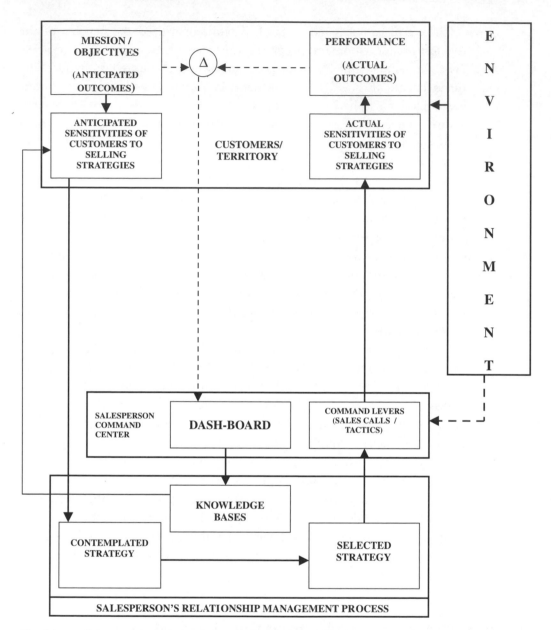

Fig. 3.1   Salesperson's dynamic relationship management process

with customers and prospects, salespeople explicitly or implicitly follow the same basic managerial process (Figure 3.1). In the same way as the dynamic sales force management process applies to sales managers, salespeople must follow a dynamic customer relationship management process.

Besides their personal competencies, salespeople have some information and knowledge about the required processes, their territory, their firm, and the market environment. Like any other manager, salespeople that are in charge of their accounts and territories, also have a command center at their disposal. They generally have large knowledge and information bases, so they collect or receive information through their own dashboards. As will be discussed in detail in the following chapter, these dashboards provide them with relevant information about customers, their own firms, or their own performance. Salespeople also receive information on the market environment, especially those forces affecting specific accounts or the whole territory. They obtain data about the economic trends affecting their customers' businesses, about competitors' actions, or about important organizational changes at one of their clients. This information originates from various sources. Part of it is observable and available only to a salesperson (such as the reaction of a client during a sales call). Another part is naturally shared with supervisors (such as sales outcomes).

Salespeople cannot content themselves with observing their environment. They must also anticipate its likely evolution. When a major account is taken over by a competitor, when a fusion or an acquisition takes place, or when a new technical innovation appears on a related market, these events should signal an opportunity or a threat to their firm's business. Consequently, salespeople must build their strategy with one eye on future events.

To meet a specific mission objective, salespeople assess and decide what actions to take. As discussed in detail in Chapter 4, they anticipate and plan their activities, even if informally. To that purpose, they need accurate information about customers' and territory's sensitivities to various possible calling strategies to select, if not the best, at least an adequate set of actions. They must take into account the resources available to accomplish their missions, as well as the market conditions that will prevail at the time of implementation, and act within these constraints.

At the implementation stage, salespeople display relationship-building activities with customers and prospects (such as sales calls and tactical actions). They allocate their time among accounts to make the most effective spatial and temporal allocations of their time and efforts among a wide range of activities. They use the control levers at their disposal.

Once a contemplated strategy is implemented and adequate tactics are used, customers and territories react in a certain way — this reveals how successful salespeople have been at carrying out their missions. Depending on which actions are taken, salespeople may observe their actual performance immediately or with a time lag. They can then assess if their planning has been sufficiently accurate and has matched their performances and their intended objectives. Frequently, salespeople may adjust their actions based on the feedback provided by customers and markets. Consequently, just like the dynamic sales force management process, the process described in Figure 3.1 must be considered as a dynamic loop and not as a simple two-way process.

Relationship-building missions

In order to fulfill their relationship-building missions, salespeople need a clear vision of the nature of these missions, a good understanding of the objectives to be met, and an accurate knowledge of the resources available to accomplish the missions.

Nature of relationship-building missions

A customer relationship management process requires different types of action. It involves initiating successful contacts with potential customers which can then evolve into a mutually profitable relationship. It also involves maintaining and enhancing strong and lasting relationships with existing customers, as well as breaking relationships that customers have already established with competing firms. Such customer-oriented activities have gained considerable importance over the last few years as many firms have adopted the Customer Relationship Management (CRM) philosophy to deal with their clients. This philosophy of relational marketing is sometimes (unduly) contrasted with that of transactional marketing. Relationship marketing often evolves as a result of successful transactions in the past. While the latter orientation emphasizes short-term selling and transactions, the former follows an approach of mutual benefits and shared value, in a long-term perspective.

Transactional selling: building customer loyalty

A business relationship with a customer implies a series of transactions and negotiations over time. A firm cannot, and probably should not, build long-term relationships with all its clients and potential customers for obvious profitability reasons. In some cases, a customer's business is insufficient to warrant the strong commitment that relationship building requires. In other cases, the type of industry in which a firm operates does not lend itself to this type of commitment from customers. This is the case, for example, when products are more or less standardized, or when they require little technical assistance from suppliers, or when suppliers essentially compete on prices and services. In such types of industry, the buyers' best interests are to let suppliers compete against one another to obtain the best possible price. They would have little to gain and much to lose by entering long-term agreements with an individual supplier. In this type of situation, a supplier's best possible approach is to try to build a trust relationship with the clients to develop some customer loyalty.

Trust relationships and customer loyalty can only be developed over time. It takes quite a few successful transactions before a business relationship evolves into customer loyalty. In other words, customer-oriented selling is a prerequisite to customer loyalty and relationship building (Schwepker 2003). In addition, customer trust and loyalty, once acquired, must be cultivated. For all these reasons, transactional selling considered in a long-term perspective, remains the most appropriate approach for most firms' customers and prospects.

Relationship selling: customer relationship management processes

In other cases, firms find it profitable to build customer relationships and to engage in long-term exclusive customer relationship management. The objective of relationship selling is to secure, build, and nurture long-term exclusive relationships with profitable customers. To achieve this goal, firms adopt a customer-focus selling approach and develop systems and procedures that they call Customer Relationship Management (CRM). As one author puts it: "CRM is a cross-functional process for achieving a continuing dialogue with customers, across all of their contact and access points, with personalized treatment of the most valuable customers, to increase customer retention ..." (Day 2001). CRM has a strategic dimension (Payne and Frow 2005). It is often technology-based (analytical dimension) and is designed to gather and process relevant customer information. In its operational dimension, it uses different selling strategies for various customer segments, and enhances the ability of firms to provide additional value to their customers (Tanner *et al.* 2005; Langerack and Verhoef 2003; see also the review by Landry, Arnold, and Arndt 2005).

Four implementation dimensions of CRM have been recognized (Hong-Kit Yim, Anderson, and Swaminathan 2004):

- focusing on key customers (Vandermerwe 2004);
- organizing around CRM (Homburg, Workman, and Jensen 2000);
- managing knowledge (Stefanou, Sarmaniotis, and Stafyla 2003); and
- incorporating CRM-based technology (Bhaskar 2004; Chen and Ching 2004).

To optimize customer relationships, firms may design integrated systems that optimize their interaction with customers, suppliers and prospects through various touch points. Touch points are possible opportunities for interacting with customers and prospects. They use call centers, salespeople, direct contact in stores or shows, company websites, and/or e-mail. CRM is a business philosophy and a process that includes customer knowledge acquisition, market planning, customer interactions, and analyses and improvement (Swift 2000).

Although the principle of CRM is simple, its implementation is fraught with difficulties (Jayachandran *et al.* 2005). There have been numerous failures, which can sometimes be attributed to the limited acceptance of the technology by end users or to poor implementation procedures (Fournier, Dolscha, and Mick 1998; Zablah, Bellenger, and Johnston 2004). More recently, however, research suggests that CRM applications increase customer satisfaction (Mithas, Krishnan, and Fornell 2005), and many firms have successfully implemented CRM systems (Rigby and Ledingham 2004). A few examples of successful CRM applications are provided in Table 3.1.

Objectives of relationship-building missions

Any relationship-building mission is generally given precise and clear objectives by higher level management. Objectives typically specify what types of result are expected. They may vary from providing only a general direction (directional objectives) to very explicit and quantified (target) objectives. Reaching the highest possible level of customer satisfaction through adequate service is an example of a directional objective. A pre-specified target level of a customer satisfaction index or a given repeat purchase level for each customer (or customer type) or for the whole sales territory is an example of a target objective. In any case, these objectives are often explicitly established for a given period of time at the end of which performances are assessed against objectives.

Table 3.1. A few examples of successful CRM implementations

In 2002, **Daiwa Securities SMBC Europe Limited** implemented an Online Customer Relationship Management Solution. Daiwa selected a CRM solution because of its cost-effectiveness, global accessibility, strong functionality, and low risk. Daiwa's investment professionals now have access to centralized real-time information that ensures a continuous relationship with clients and provides the most professional service and attention possible. Daiwa sales personnel have become more efficient in matching buyers and sellers and rapidly identifying emerging business opportunities. Within 30 days of the CRM implementation, Daiwa noted a dramatic increase in client service and customer satisfaction levels due to the capability of employees at any location to access customer data upon request. According to the company's executives, additional benefits include increased internal transparency, improved personnel management, and better coordination between capital markets and sales – all at a fraction of the cost of conventional CRM solutions.

Bell Canada has adopted a faster, more flexible CRM solution in less than two months. The objectives were to ensure customer service and support through quick implementation, data integration, ease of use, and efficient reporting capabilities. The system has been deployed to more than 200 users in less than two months. The Bell Canada staff has been quickly trained in a multilingual system. Customer service amongst seven internal groups could thus be ensured without any disruption. Flexible features created internal efficiencies and reduced total case volume. In additions, sales force customizations enabled easy data integration between systems.

Ultrak, a Honeywell subsidiary and a leading manufacturer of integrated access control and security solutions, has standardized its complete Web Services-based CRM solution as a central information center for all sales and customer information. Ultrak, which provides integrated security systems for prisons, casinos, retail, airports, government offices, banks, schools and others, has recently adopted a low-cost, quick-implementation CRM solution, eliminating the expenses and high risks often associated with CRM. Ultrak's valuable customer information was scattered throughout different departments and locations using varying systems to track and store data. This discontinuity was inefficient and awkward because there was no central place for sales and customer information to reside. Global managers found it difficult to develop reports or forecasts. In only one month, Ultrak had completely deployed salesforce.com to its offices across North America, serving the CRM needs of 100 sales, marketing, and support employees.

Nokia has customized its sales force to meet the needs of sales teams on three continents. Nokia wanted to provide its traveling sales force with anytime, anywhere accessibility CRM. The system has been set up to match the recommendations of an international CRM project team. The objectives were to produce a shorter sales cycle, more consistency across different regions and functions, a streamlined sales organization for improved collaboration and productivity, better transparency, reporting and communication across global teams, and a deeper understanding of customer buying habits. After a few months Nokia management felt that thanks to the CRM solution, the sales force had opened the lines of communication for the organization, helped shorten the sales cycle, and could respond to changes in its business model and requirements.

Source: www.salesforce.com

Resources for the customer relationship building process

Any customer relationship-building mission requires resources. Some are provided by salespeople, others by the firm itself. Salespeople provide their time and effort, which are their scarce resources. As will be discussed later, time and effort allocation are essential decision control levers for salespeople.

Other resources are given to salespeople by management to help them accomplish their mission. These resources are part of sales managers' control levers in their command centers. They will be discussed in detail in Part II of this book. They are, for example, the time allowed for customer contact and for customer relationship building. This can be controlled by management by properly specifying the size of the sales territory a salesperson must cover. Another resource is the extent of initiative and responsibility left to salespeople — this is controlled by management's specification of their decision space.

To help salespeople in their relationship-building tasks, management also provides technical help (technical personnel and literature), and marketing support (leaflets to be handed in to customers, direct supervisory support from managers, demonstration material or samples to be given away to customers and prospects). Management can also supply administrative help (such as cell phones, voice mail services, laptops with software which can help salespeople to plan their activities or hold their expense accounts, secretarial help, or travel facilities such as cars). Finally, management frequently supplies financial help in the form of expense accounts. These support devices are discussed further in Chapter 9.

Dynamic management of different types of customer relationships and situations

Short-term interactions: transactional selling

When they are given only limited decision space, salespeople must essentially rely on their ability to persuade buyers that they should enter a deal with their firm. In such cases, they are given little or no leeway for adapting the firm's offer to buyer demand. The salesperson's task is to convince buyers that the firm's offer as it stands (or with only very limited changes) will fully satisfy their needs. In such cases, salespeople have generally been taught to follow a general process (or *script*). This includes a series of typical steps

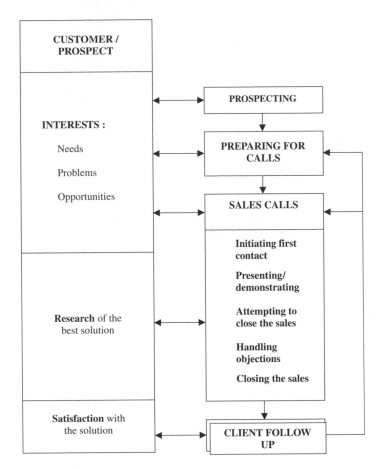

Fig. 3.2   Selling/purchasing interaction cycle

that are sometimes grouped into different categories depending on authors and training programs (Figure 3.2). Most selling methods specify a prospect identification step, followed by call preparation, actual call interactions, and customer follow up steps. The intensities of interactions and communications substantially vary at each step of the process: at the beginning of an interaction, most of the information flows from a prospect to the salesperson. The opposite tends to happen toward the end of the selling process.

Prospect identification

Identifying prospects is a difficult but essential task for a salesperson. There are a number of methods that firms generally follow to identify leads (for example, identifying firms that might need and be interested in their products or services because of the kind of business they are in). Further identification can be confirmed through "cold calls," that is, direct first contact with the prospect. Other methods for obtaining leads include referrals from current customers, a spontaneous reply from a prospect to a supplier advertisement, or increasingly, through the firm's website, direct contacts through telemarketing, call centers or e-mails. Prospect identification remains the most difficult and frustrating part of a salesperson's task as it often results in an extremely large proportion of unsuccessful contacts.

To increase the hit rate of their salespeople's prospect identification tasks, management may provide useful support. When Renault launched its Laguna model, three mailing campaigns toward different potential market segments were organized, with differing hit rate results. In the *a priori* favorable buyer segment, 5.4 percent of useful contacts were identified, against 1.7 percent for the hard core segment, and 3.2 percent for the more affluent market segments. The prospect's replies asking for product information were followed up by calls from salespeople and many of these led to definitive orders.

Besides mailing campaigns, leads can be obtained by using other methods such as call centers or through the recommendation of current clients. The Direct Bank offers gifts to clients who induce their friends and acquaintances to become clients. This sponsorship method has proven to be quite profitable for banks and other businesses to increase their customer base.

Call preparation

The purpose of this step is to prepare for a face-to-face call with clients or prospects, and to approach them in the best possible conditions. A new prospect must be approached in a professional manner and with assurance. CRM data bases provide salespeople with valuable information at this stage. The purpose is to gather as much relevant information as possible, especially about influential individuals in the decision-making process at the prospective account, and about clients' needs and sales potential for the firm. This stage is important for assessing whether there is any chance for the firm to ever become a supplier (and if yes, how) and whether the prospect has enough potential for the firm to warrant the necessary investment in a salesperson's time and effort. The outcome of this step should be to select an approach strategy. Because at this stage, salespeople are likely to have incomplete information about the prospect, the selected approach strategy must be able to adapt as new information is obtained during the call itself.

Calls to customers and prospects

At this step, intensive communication and information exchanges between a customer and a salesperson occur. Several types of activity take place in a more or less sequential fashion. All of them are important during a sales call, but their relative importance may vary according to firms and actual situations. Following an in-depth field study, Xerox Learning Systems has identified three critical salesperson behaviors for the success of a sales call: identification of customer need and opportunity, acquisition of information about customers, and proper handling of objections (Franco 1984).

Initial contact

First, initial contact takes place. Planned initial contact must account for customers' desires and constraints. Too many calls to a customer can be as bad as too few. A few years ago, AT&T realized that customers with less than ten employees wished to receive more frequent calls. Consequently, the firm set up a telemarketing program to take care of this customer category. Two years later, however, AT&T learned that customers felt they were contacted too frequently and wanted only to be contacted for valuable reasons. This story suggests that there is a "right" call frequency for every selling situation.

During initial contact, a salesperson's appearance plays quite an important role. Some trainers assert (certainly with some exaggeration) that a sales call outcome actually occurs within the first twenty seconds, with the first twenty gestures, and the first twenty words. At this point, the salesperson essentially listens to the client. Under no circumstances do they try to sell anything. They ask questions, listen rather than talk (Knowles *et al.* 1994). This is why successful salespeople are able to capture a large amount of verbal and nonverbal information from clients (Stafford 1996). Especially, salespeople identify customers' sensorial representation systems (SRS). Some customers have visual representations and wish to see the product; others have audio representations and wish to hear the product being used; still others have tactile representation and must touch the product. To that effect, salespeople are sometimes trained to use Neuro-Linguistic Programming (NLP), a (controversial) set of behavioral techniques that allow them to understand non-verbal communications (O'Connor and Seymour 1993; Spiller and Thomas 2003).

The initial contact step generally ends when the salesperson understands the customer's problem, needs, constraints, and decision criteria, and when they have some precise ideas about how they can contribute to solve the problem. In many sales training programs, salespeople are taught the SPIN sequence (Situation, Problem, Implications, and Need-payoff) (Rackham 1996). The rationale is to train salespeople to start by analyzing the situation (S) in order to find out and understand the problem (P) that the client or prospect faces. Then, the salesperson shows all the negative implications (I) that may result from the current situation if the problem is not solved satisfactorily. Only now do they start to propose a solution to the sensitized customer (Need-payoff). Sometimes firms use other sequential steps, but they all follow this general approach and rationale.

Presentation and demonstration

A presentation and demonstration stage follows the initial contact. At this stage, the salesperson may start to present and demonstrate the selling arguments that could push potential customers up the ladder of persuasive communication. Sales trainers frequently use the AIDA (Attention, Interest, Desire, and Action) scale to illustrate the concept (Strong 1925). Several other ladders have been proposed, expressing the same idea (Lavidge and Steiner 1961). A sales presentation should first attract a customer's attention (A), arouse interest (I), give the desire (D) to purchase the product or service, and result in a purchase decision and action (A).

In order to meet these objectives, the salesperson selects the most appropriate CAB (Characteristics, Advantages, and Benefits). In other words, the salesperson is trained to select the most appropriate product characteristics that are likely to appeal to the client (if possible, features that only their company provides); show the advantages provided by these characteristics, and show the benefits that buyers could obtain from such advantages. Benefits are essentially abstract and must be demonstrated through specific product (or offer) characteristics, which are more concrete. Because product characteristics can often be observed, they are more credible. Consequently, they are the best vehicle to demonstrate a firm's competitive advantages.

Attempts to close a sale

During the discussion and demonstration stage of a call, a salesperson must attempt to close the sales as soon as they have the feeling that the customer has sufficient information to make a decision. To do this, they generally ask questions that allow them to assess their progress toward a positive outcome. The answers that a client provides generally give a clear indication whether the salesperson has overcome all remaining objections. Questions such as "What do you think?" "What do you say?" or "Does that answer your concern?" should be used frequently during a sales presentation, especially once a strong argument has been voiced. They are also generally asked at the end of the presentation, after answering any objections, and in any case, before asking to sign an order and closing a sale.

Handling objections

Handling objections requires some expertise from the salesperson. Sometimes, objections are clearly voiced and can be easily rebutted. Others are hidden and are more difficult to address. Still others are almost impossible to overcome. This is the case, for example in the "too high a price" objection, the lack of customer interest, or a customer's alleged lack of time to pursue the call. An experienced salesperson knows how to overcome even such objections and avoid an abrupt end to the call (Futrell 2005).

Closing a sale

Closing a sale is the objective of any sales presentation. Salespeople are generally trained to close sales as naturally as possible. For example, a salesperson will always ask their clients which of Model A or Model B they have selected, instead of asking whether they intend to order. In other instances, they may ask: "By which date should the merchandise be delivered to your warehouse?" Sometimes, they summarize all the benefits of placing an immediate order (asking the client to explicitly agree on each point), and then bring the client to sign an order. A wide variety of closing techniques exists and these are fully discussed in the specialized literature (see e.g., Futrell 2006). They are an important part of most sales force training programs.

Customer follow-ups

A salesperson's sales relationship does not end once a client has signed an order. Salespeople must also follow up on the clients. It is a salesperson's responsibility to make sure that the product (or service) is delivered on time, and that the delivered product follows the order's precise specification. They must be sure that customers are fully satisfied that the purchased products and services have met their expectations. More generally, salespeople follow the business relationship that has just been established with a client, essentially keeping ahead of their client's evolving needs and problems. They keep the clients informed of new products or solutions that could be of interest to them. Relationships are established over time and require a dynamic management approach.

Long-term interactions: negotiation relationships

Establishing long-term relationships frequently requires elaborate negotiations during which the terms of collaboration between both parties must be agreed upon. These agreements imply that both the buyer and the supplier have sufficient leeway for making decisions and granting concessions in order to arrive at a mutually satisfying agreement. An agreement is typically reached after some compromise have been found between the initial positions of the two parties. Negotiation is an important field of study and the object of many specialized books (see e.g., Carlisle and Parker 1989; Cellich and Jain 2003). Negotiation processes typically follow a number of steps that negotiators know well.

Preparing for negotiation

Negotiations are more likely to succeed when both parties are well prepared. To prepare for negotiation, each party first decides on an initial position that should be neither too close to the target final compromise (because each party will need to make concessions before reaching a compromise agreement), nor too far away to avoid scaring the other party away right at the start of the negotiation.

The initial position must be explained and defended in front of the other party, which implies that it must be defendable. A negotiating team must also decide in advance which concessions it would be ready to accept concerning every aspect of the initial position. Short of that, it is almost impossible to react in a sensible way, if at all, to propositions from the other party during the active phase of the negotiations. It is important to set limits. These may serve as useful benchmarks in the heat of the discussion. At this stage, negotiators should gather as much information as possible about the other party. They generally strive to find out what their initial position will be, what their interests are, what aspects of the negotiation are the most important to them, and which aspects are secondary. To do this, the negotiators must display empathetic qualities. In other words, they must be able to think like the other party and to fully understand its logic (Keiser 1988).

Finally, each party should decide on a negotiation style and strategy, as well as the techniques and tactics that it will try to use during the active phase of the negotiation. Obviously, there is no guarantee that they will be able to use these, because each party will strive to impose its own style and strategies. In any case, however, it is better to decide on the general line that will be followed. The preparation stage has the advantage of ensuring that all the members of a negotiating team share the same vision and objectives, and that all of them will work in the same direction at the negotiation table. The preparation stage is also useful for defining the respective roles of the various members of the negotiating team, especially who is entitled to make concessions and/or to accept compromises.

Active negotiation phase

At the very beginning of the active phase of a negotiation, each party attempts to find out about any information it may be lacking, in order to better attune its negotiation strategies and techniques. Each party typically starts by stating and explaining its position in detail and as convincingly as possible. The other party generally listens carefully. It is a good practice for each party to summarize the position held by the other, to show that that party's position has been clearly and correctly understood.

Negotiations evolve differently, depending upon the strategies and tactics that each party attempts to follow, the characteristics of the situation, and the relative power of the two parties (Perdue and Summers 1991). A few principles, however, apply to most types of negotiation. One party must avoid making concessions that are not matched by concessions from the other. One should remain as flexible as possible and avoid getting stuck in a position that may be difficult to change. Each party must try to clearly identify all the common ground it shares with the other party, as well as all the points of disagreement. Any negotiation that is intended to build lasting relationships can only end up with a win-win solution. In other words, each party must have the feeling that it has gained or will gain something from the deal. Negotiators must bear in mind that mutual trust, shared values, and satisfaction are the major ingredients of long-term relationships.

State of current relationships

Whether it occurs now or in the future, whether it is the outcome of a negotiation or an inflexible take-it-or-leave-it transaction, a business relationship depends upon the nature of the previous relationships between both parties. In some cases, buyers and suppliers have not had previous experience of dealing with each other. In others, both parties have engaged in long-term relationships for some time and have acquired extensive knowledge of each other. A climate of mutual trust established over the years is an invaluable asset for a salesperson. It results in a drastic reduction in some dimensions of risk that a buyer may perceive in any new undertaking proposed by the supplier. Needless to say, suppliers who have succeeded in building such trust relationships with clients enjoy a strong competitive advantage.

Parties' relative power

In many negotiation situations, one party enjoys a dominant position over the other, as a result of the acquisition of different amounts and/or types of resources. Frequently, buyers hold such advantageous positions. This is the case, for example, when suppliers vie for clients in a very competitive market, or when they must rely on large scale distributors for marketing their products. Large retailers often hold dominant positions over manufacturers. In contrast, the power structure is quite different between a small retailer and a large national manufacturer. Because the dominant party typically exerts power for its own advantage, this power imbalance tends to influence the strategies and tactics that are available to both parties.

Customer relationship-building processes in various situations

Making transactions and building relationships greatly depend on the business situations in which these activities occur. Salespeople must rapidly identify the kind of situation they are facing. There are different types of buying situations, and consequently, the role of a supplier's salesperson varies accordingly — a buyer may play an active or a passive role in a transaction (Webster and Wind 1972). Although this categorization is convenient, one should not overlook that one type of situation may quickly evolve towards another — relationships evolve as a situation changes. It is up to the salespeople to adapt (Franckwick, Porter, and Crosby 2001). For example, it is not unusual for an inactive potential buyer to be alerted by a salesperson to the existence of a new market opportunity, following say, the appearance of some technological innovation. As a result, the originally passive potential buyer may become proactive, and may start searching actively among many potential suppliers for the one that can best help him take advantage of the new opportunity.

Buyers play a passive role

Buyers often play a passive role when they have no *a priori* incentive for entering a business relationship with a soliciting supplier. At the time of the first contact, they are not on the market for the kind of product and/or service provided by the salesperson's firm. Salespeople facing such situations are responsible for inducing the potential client to enter the market. Two types of situations imply some *a priori* passive buyer's attitudes: suppliers come up with a really innovative product of which they are not yet aware, and buyers are used to make routine purchases for a given type of product or service.

Innovative product or service sales

In this case, buyers are unaware that a new opportunity exists for them or that they face a problem. As seen above, a firm may have learned to cope with a problem because it has not found adequate means to solve it. For example, when a major innovative product is launched, potential buyers may not be in the market for this type of product. To induce them to enter the market, a salesperson must make them aware of the new opportunity or of their latent problem, and to arouse their interest in the new product.

In such circumstances, buyers typically lack information about the new product or innovation. There is a large information gap, and it is up to the salesperson to fill it. The salesperson's task is to make potential buyers aware of their unresolved problems or to the existence of better, more efficient, or less costly means to solve it. They must inform and educate users and the buyer's technical personnel. They must "sell" the solution to potential buyers. They must identify all the benefits that the proposed solution will bring compared with maintaining the *status quo.*

It is quite possible, at this stage, that buyers become proactive – they actively begin to look for information to see what is currently on the market to solve the problem of which they have just been made aware. Alternatively, they may start looking around to make sure that the proposed solution is the best currently available in the market.

Routine re-buys

In routine purchase situations, buyers have become used to reordering from the same suppliers. This usually happens when buyers are satisfied with their current suppliers, and when they know (or believe) that there is no opportunity available to solve their problem more effectively. For obvious efficiency reasons, they do not want to repeat the complete purchase procedure whenever they need to purchase this type of product or service. That does not mean that buyers will order exactly the same product. Orders may specify different quantities, or different product mixes, but they choose the same products and suppliers to satisfy a certain need. Routine re-buys are essentially characterized by a lack of new information gathering by buyers before signing a new order.

In this situation, the salesperson's roles differs depending on whether they represent the current supplier or are trying to attract a firm away from its current supplier. In the former case, the role is to ensure a stable and lasting relationship with the buying firm through customer satisfaction (Jap 2001). The objective is to prevent buyers from having a reason to change suppliers. The in-salesperson must keep in mind that clients are continuously solicited by competing firms. Consequently, they must constantly inform their clients of new products and innovations and must monitor the evolution of their needs and the appearance of any new problems.

A salesperson's task is even more difficult in the latter case. It implies breaking a relationship between a buyer and a competing supplier that the buyer often considers as satisfactory. In this case, the salesperson's role consists of waiting for an opportunity to arise, such as an evolution of the buyer's needs, some dissatisfaction with the current supplier, or a new product that fits the buyer's needs better than the current one. The out-salesperson must demonstrate that a better solution exists than the current supplier can offer. Like in the preceding cases, these actions can be successful only as long as the salesperson focuses on the needs and behaviors of potential buyers and can propose solutions to their actual problems.

Buyers play an active role

Buyers play an active role when they have identified a problem or a need, or when they suspect that a new opportunity exists for them. In some cases, buyers have some ideas about the type of solution that can solve their problem. Frequently, active buyers initiate contacts with potential suppliers and their representatives. In these instances, a salesperson's role consists of trying to propose a solution which is better than the competition in some key aspects of the problems to be solved. Several purchase situations fall into this category.

New customer purchases

This situation occurs when a firm must solve a problem that it faces for the first time. Buyers are confronted with a new situation and they must find solutions that they have not experienced before. They are aware of their problem, and they need to purchase a particular type of product or service. They must, however, go through a lengthy purchase process, because they must fill a more or less important information gap.

In such cases, buyers must obtain information about potential suppliers and the characteristics of the products and services offered by them. They must estimate the extent to which those products and services are likely to fulfill their needs. They must consider the selling conditions, weigh the risks incurred, evaluate the guarantees offered by each potential supplier, as well as many other relevant pieces of information. In such situations, buyers are proactive. They are actively seeking the relevant information, and they may seek expert advice and request meetings with potential suppliers. Their information sources are likely to depend upon the stage they have reached in their decision-making process.

In new purchase situations, a salesperson's role is to assess the extent and nature of the potential buyer's information gap. Salespeople must know and understand the choice criteria, and what should constitute positive and negative arguments concerning the intended purchase for the potential buyer. Then, they can give the relevant information to their customers. They should bear in mind that a lack of information means higher risks for the purchasing agent, and consequently, constitutes a strong purchase inhibitor. The best selling strategies in this case aim to reduce the buyer's perceived risks and build a relationship with whoever is influential in the firm's purchase decision process.

Modified re-buys

Buyers play also a proactive role in modified re-buy situations. In such cases, buyers wish to purchase a product or service that is slightly different from their previous purchases. This situation may arise because they are aware of some new problem or opportunity. Consequently, they are not in a first purchase situation. They may suspect that better means exist for solving their problem or their needs may have evolved. Here, buyers need to update or to increase their information base about the products or services currently available in the market. After they have completed this process, they may continue to purchase from the current supplier, or alternatively, switch to new products and suppliers (Johnson, Barksdale, and

Boles 2001). In these situations, a salesperson's role is to identify the causes of this partial information gap, and to fill it as soon as possible. They then avoid starting the selling process from scratch.

To sum up, it should be clear that buyers display different behaviors depending on the purchase situation they are facing. As a result, efficient salespeople should select selling strategies and tactics based on a thorough knowledge and understanding of general buyer behavior, as well as the specific elements that characterize the purchase behavior of each particular client. One should also stress that the quality of buyer-seller interactions also depends on how the respective characteristics of the two parties are compatible (Whittler 1994; Iacobucci and Ostrom 1996; Evans 1963; Churchill *et al.* 1975; Cronin 1994).

Strategies and tactics for building customer relationships

Strategies for building customer relationships

In order to build customer relationships, salespeople may choose from at least seven strategies, depending on the situation they face (Whittler 1994).

- A rational persuasion strategy implies using essentially logical arguments. In a B2B context, this is the most frequently used strategy.
- An inspirational appeal relies on arguments that tend to raise buyers' enthusiasm through reliance of customers' values, expectations, or ideals.
- A strategy of consultation requires listening to the customer, asking for and taking into account their opinion, advice, and suggestions.

Research suggests that these three strategies are the most frequently used and are more effective in a business context (Farrell and Schroder 1996). The four other influence strategies rely successively:

- on one's position within the organization, for example, on the use of informal legitimate power that one party may hold relative to the other;
- on the use of personal appeals to the friendship or loyalty that one party may experience toward the other;
- on coalition influence strategies, for example, the reliance on the influence that a third party may exert, in order to achieve the desired goal, and
- on exchange strategies that involve obtaining an exchange of favors in return for assistance in achieving a particular target objective.

These four last strategies may be used only occasionally and exceptionally in a business setting. Sales strategies can also be based on social influences (Harris and Spiro 1981). Influence can be exerted through:

- expert power when, for example, buyers perceive that a salesperson possesses some special knowledge that they do not possess themselves;
- legitimate power, when customers and salespeople share the same values, for example, a value for reputation;
- referent power, when a customer is willing to identify with the seller;
- reward power, whenever a salesperson provides some reward to a customer, for example, a gift; or
- impression management, a power exerted when a salesperson attempts to produce some favorable impression on a customer in order to obtain a positive reaction.

Influences of customer's purchase decisions

A salesperson's selling strategy and actions must not focus only on a customer's final decision. To obtain a favorable final decision, they must make sure that their firm remains in the customer's evoked set of potential suppliers all along the decision process. This is why a close contact with all the decision makers implied in the purchase decision is essential. Special attention is generally given to those decision makers that are in charge of analyzing the problem and its possible solutions, at the time they are influential. This follows from the creeping commitment principle discussed in the preceding chapter. In other words, especially in an industrial context, a transaction or a relationship can be initiated only when a supplier's salesperson has taken an active part all the way through the customer's decision process.

In the short-term, relationships are initiated and reinforced when salespeople help a client develop favorable perceptions and attitudes toward the various aspects of the supplying party. Whenever needed, salespeople should attempt to change a former customer's negative attitude into a positive one. In order to provoke such a change, a salesperson should provide sufficient relevant and convincing information to the potential client. In the same way, salespeople who have a good understanding of their customers' behaviors, take into account the post-purchase feelings of their clients at the follow-up stage, especially just after an order has been signed. They know also that is extremely dangerous to raise a customer's expectations above a level that cannot be met after the transaction has been completed.

In a B2B context especially, a business relationship cannot last unless a customer is fully satisfied. The reasons are obvious and numerous.

From a buyer's point of view, as already mentioned, except for quite valid reasons, a satisfied customer is unlikely to switch suppliers and destroy a relationship that has been built up over the years and incur the risks of starting a new relationship with a new supplier. From a supplier's viewpoint, especially in the case of repetitive industrial purchases, an unsatisfied customer is an irreplaceable loss. As is often the case in industrial settings, a small number of large accounts make up a firm's clientele. Consequently, it would be foolhardy for this firm not to provide such customers with satisfying deals and build up their loyalty. Moreover, unsatisfied clients are likely to propagate negative word-of-mouth communications within a small circle of important buyers. At a time when the prevalent marketing philosophy emphasizes customer-orientation, customer satisfaction must be an essential goal for any business relationship strategy.

Long-term relationship negotiation

Whenever a selling situation implies negotiations, negotiation strategies are generally carefully selected and followed. Although one accounts for some ten different negotiation strategies and hundreds of tactics, experts agree that there are only a quite limited number of broad strategic orientations for carrying out a negotiation (Cellich and Jain 2003). Thus, negotiation may be co-operative or conflictual. Co-operative negotiators show open-mindedness, and attempt to find and propose solutions that take the interests of both parties into account. In contrast, conflictual negotiators avoid compromises, and negotiations can be offensive or defensive. In offensive negotiations, a negotiator takes the initiative. In defensive negotiations, however, one negotiator avoids intervening, listens, waits, and eventually counterattacks. Negotiations can be carried out over a long or a short period of time. Negotiators can use time as a strategic tool, taking into account the specificities of the situation at hand. Negotiations can thus be dragged out over a long period of time or, strict deadlines may be imposed to arrive at a deal. In business-to-business relationships, the prevailing type of strategic orientation is co-operative negotiations that are likely to build lasting and mutually satisfying relationships.

Tactics for building customer relationships

Within a given strategy, salespeople have a wide variety of tactics to choose from. They can adopt one or several behaviors during the same round of negotiations. The choice depends on the objectives to be met, on a thorough understanding of the behaviors, strategies and tactics used by the members of the buying team, as well as on the buyers' positive and negative impulses implied by the purchase decision. Efficient salespeople know how to select the most appropriate persuasion mechanisms that have the highest probabilities of inducing a client to buy.

To arouse customers' interest and induce them to close a sale, salespeople should attempt to influence key aspects of customers' buying situations. One recalls from the preceding chapter that any buying/selling situation may be considered as an internal conflict in which a number of positive forces (or impulses or arguments) induce a buyer to purchase, and a number of negative forces, on the contrary, prevent the buyer from purchasing. Because a deal can be struck only when the number and intensities of the positive arguments override the negative ones, a salesperson's task consists of changing non-purchase situations into purchase situations. The intensity of the psychological tension experienced by a buyer is directly linked to the number and strengths of the arguments involved in a negotiation situation. As discussed below, several tactics can be used by a salesperson to change a non-purchase situation into a purchase situation. An essential part of a salesperson's role consists of reducing a potential customer's perceived risk of entering a business agreement until the client finds the risk bearable.

Identification of the driving forces involved

Before a business transaction occurs, a buyer may lean toward a solution different from the one proposed by a salesperson, because at this time, the negative arguments that tend to block a purchase are larger in number and intensity than the positive arguments. This is why effective salespeople start by identifying all the positive and negative arguments that are involved in a given selling situation, *for the decision makers involved in the purchase decision.*

As an example, consider the case of a manufacturer of automotive parts that sells electronic equipment to car manufacturers. This producer may negotiate an important contract with a major car manufacturer to supply electronic parts for the assembly lines of a popular car model. Because the parts have very precise specifications, they must be specifically manufactured by one supplier who has developed special equipment. Consequently, the car manufacturer must ensure that the parts are always delivered regularly and on time, to avoid disruption at the car plant. Any such disruptions would be extremely costly for the car manufacturer and a major responsibility of the buyer is to ensure that they are avoided. Because the buyer has no previous experience with the salesperson's firm, all the managers involved in the procurement contract decision are reluctant to sign, essentially because of the risks of possible failures in the delivery process. The financial (and personal) risks are important and difficult to assess. All the tests for evaluating the reliability, resistance, and quality of the supplier's electronic equipment have produced results that are well above the most demanding requirements of the car manufacturer. As a matter of fact, high quality is an essential prerequisite for signing the contract, because the car manufacturer has built a strong reputation in the market for the quality of this premium car model. Service, price, payment, and warranty conditions are very similar for all competing offers.

What tactic could the salesperson use to convince the buyers that they should give him the procurement contract? Salespersons could follow one (or several) of these tactics, that is, reinforce some positive arguments linked to favorable characteristics of their firm, their products and/ or services, attempt to increase the importance of some positive arguments or facilitators, or decrease the importance of some aspects of the deal that have been negatively evaluated by the contracting manufacturer.

Reinforcement of some important facilitators

A salesperson may reinforce an important client's positive argument (or facilitator), up to the point where the positive arguments outweigh the negative ones. This is described in Figure 3.3. Starting with an original non-purchase situation (Figure 3.3a), this tactic consists of changing the equilibrium toward the other side of the scale, as shown in Figure 3.3b.

In the preceding case, the salesperson could capitalize on the competitive differential advantage of his firm resulting from the much higher reliability and resistance if its equipment. He could reinforce the need for the car manufacturer to use such high quality electronic equipment in its premium cars. He could, for example, emphasize the reduced costs to the firm of providing customers with a warranty against electronic equipment failures. He could also point out that customer satisfaction would be enhanced as the result of fewer car breakdowns, or that the quality of the electronic equipment could be featured when advertising the car. For each selected argument, a salesperson could play on the CAB (Characteristic, Advantage, Benefit) sequence: the reliability of the electronic equipment (a characteristic), that should result in higher customer satisfaction (an advantage), and reduced repair costs (a benefit).

Addition of new facilitators

Another selling tactic consists of bringing a new positive argument that the buyer had not originally perceived as being important, or pointing at an important aspect of the deal that the buyer had completely overlooked. Here again the same principle applies: moving the scale towards the purchase side by making sure that the facilitating arguments have more weight than the inhibiting ones (Figure 3.3c).

In the preceding example (assuming that the fact is true and has not been already noticed by the buyer) the salesperson could show that the electronic

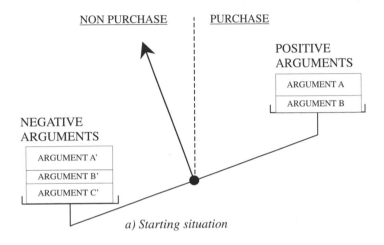

a) Starting situation

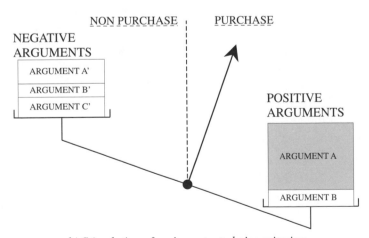

b) Stimulation of an important choice criterion

Fig. 3.3   Some possible buyer influence tactics

devices provided by his company are easier to install on the cars than the competing products, reducing the car manufacturing time, and consequently, production costs.

Suppression or importance decrease of inhibitors

A third possible tactic that can be used is to try to reduce the importance of, or possibly suppress, a major inhibiting argument that prevents a buyer

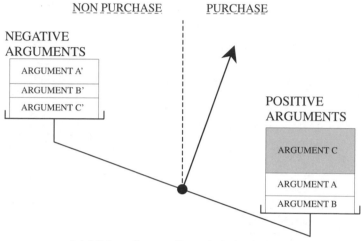

c) Addition of a new (latent) choice criterion

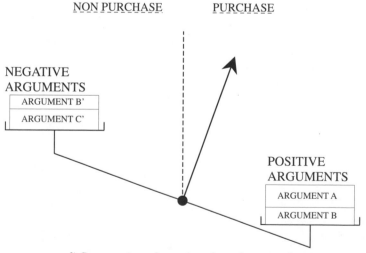

d) Suppression of a major obstacle to purchase

Fig. 3.3   *(Cont.)*

from deciding in favor of the supplier. This can be achieved by reducing the risk (rightly or wrongly) perceived by the buyer and moving the scale to the purchase position, as illustrated in Figure 3.3d.

The salesperson could also select this tactic. Understanding the situation and the behavioral dimensions of the purchase situation, he could estimate that in this case, the major inhibiting factor is the fear that the strict delivery schedule will not be met, with all the negative consequences that would imply. Assuming that he is given authority to do so, the salesperson could include a penalty clause in the contract which states that high penalties would be paid by the supplier in the case of any delivery failures that result in assembly line disruption. This would reassure the buying team and consequently, reduce the perceived risk of switching to a new supplier. By adding this penalty clause to his firm's offer, the salesperson would reduce the financial risk incurred by the prospective client in case of assembly line disruptions, as well as the purchasers' personal risk of being held responsible for the choice of a failing supplier.

Unlike the two preceding tactics that increase a buyer's psychological tension, this tactic tends to decrease it. This should be apparent when one compares the diagram of Figure 3.3d with those of Figure 3.3b and 3.3c. While the first two tactics increase the number and/or intensities of the positive and negative arguments involved in the purchase decision, the third tactic decreases them, thus reducing the conflict intensity and its associated psychological tension. As a result, the third tactic, if feasible, may be more suitable than the other two in important purchase situations with high customer implication.

Selection of sales tactics

The three tactics described above are not mutually exclusive. During an interaction with a prospect or customer, a salesperson can use several of them in turn. In the preceding example, the salesperson could demonstrate the higher reliability of his firm's equipment, then propose a delivery guarantee within set deadlines, and finally try to win the decision by pointing out the advantage of reduced production costs by using his firm's equipment. The choice and order of the selected tactics and their respective emphases depends on the salesperson's understanding of the selling situation. Using a contingency approach to personal selling (Weitz 1979), salespeople constantly adapt their talk and behavior depending on the responses and reactions of their counterparts in a negotiation. They then select the most appropriate tactics as the negotiations unfold.

Selection of negotiation tactics

Negotiation tactics are used at specific points in time and depend on the circumstances of the negotiation round. They are numerous. In acrimonious negotiations, they may run from pressure through explicit or implicit threats, to ultimatums, all or nothing statements, systematic overbidding, and stopping or suspending negotiations. Inversely, co-operative tactics are based on reciprocity, promises, mutually accepted rules, and the downplaying of difficult issues.

A salesperson may use several negotiation tactics. One is point-by-point negotiation – discussing each point in turn, as if they were independent from one another. Segmenting a negotiation consists of splitting an issue into several parts and discussing each part in turn. The idea is to start with and settle easier issues, and then move on to the more difficult points. A give-and-take negotiation tactic requires both parties to look for global solutions through mutual concessions, with advantages and cost equally shared. In enlarged negotiations, the parties may include issues that were not part of the initial negotiation. The revolving tactic consists of one party making excessively high demands on a relatively minor point which is known to be important to the other party. The negotiator then gives this up because of an important concession from the other party (Carlisle and Parker 1989).

Dynamic sales territory management processes

To fulfill their missions, salespeople must effectively manage their sales territory. This implies a proper allocation of their own resources: their time and effort, as well as those resources that are provided by management. Salespeople must decide how they should use those resources to accomplish their different tasks, according to the requirements of the selected strategies and tactics that they wish to implement, to the best of their knowledge and understanding.

Levels and quality of selling efforts

From the preceding discussions, it should be apparent that in order to accomplish their duties, salespeople must manage a large number of relationships as well as their own time. This implies a large array of activities that vary in amount (a quantitative aspect) as well as in quality (Weitz 1979). As already mentioned, salespeople must divide their time between several activities, such as selling different product lines, selling to present accounts and developing new accounts, to mention only a few. It is generally up to the individual to decide how to allocate their time.

There are at least two means for salespeople to achieve a given sales objective (Figure 3.4). Depending on the sensitivity of the territory to selling efforts (Curve A), salespeople can invest the necessary time to achieve the required sales volume. This has been called "working hard" in the literature. Alternatively, salespeople may try to "work smart" to try achieve the same result by working less, but better (Sujan 1986). This involves improving one's effort quality, and consequently, making a territory more sensitive to one's selling effort (Curve B). The same sales volume (S) can then be reached with a lesser quantity of efforts (E_B instead of E_A). Salespeople can choose one way or the other depending on the resources available to them, their ability to acquire more resources, as well as their own personal preferences.

Allocation of selling efforts

Salespeople's time management involves organizing their call schedules, their sales trips for the forthcoming days and weeks, as well as choosing the routes to be followed for calling on the different accounts. Fortunately, with the recent development of new computing and information technology and the increasing use of CRM programs, these tasks are more and more frequently being carried out for them by central office. This aspect of

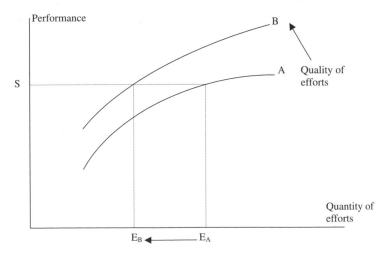

Fig. 3.4   Salesperson's effort quantity and quality

Table 3.2. Main time allocations

Time allocations among various selling activities	Space-related time allocations
Customer calls	Between clients and prospects
	Among various clients
◆ Prospecting	**Time-related time allocations**
◆ Preparing for calls	Call time spacing for every client and prospect
◆ Traveling	Selling tasks, travel, and administrative tasks
◆ Waiting	
◆ Direct customer contacts	
◆ Selling the various product lines	
Administrative tasks	
◆ Reporting to management	
◆ Preparing proposals	
◆ Collecting and processing information from head office	
Market intelligence activities	

time management is as important, as salespeople are in charge of large numbers of accounts that are scattered throughout an extended geographical area. This aspect of time management depends on the characteristics of a sales territory.

Salespeople also make a number of key time allocation decisions concerning various selling activities such as, the relative time devoted to selling the various product lines, or prospecting versus selling to current customer accounts. These time allocations are as important as the salespeople's activities are numerous and varied in nature. Consequently, they depend on the way management has defined a typical salesperson's role in the organization.

Salespeople's contact time with customers and prospects as well as the time spent preparing for those contacts are known to be the most productive parts of their day. As a result, salespeople should strive to maximize the time devoted to these tasks and keep the time spent on all other activities to a minimum. This is what most CRM programs try to achieve (Table 3.2).

Conclusion

This chapter has shown how salespeople are the managers of the various relationships with the accounts for which they are responsible. They are also the managers of their own sales territories. Like sales managers, salespeople are responsible for managing complex human entities who pursue their own interests, rather than those of the salesperson's organization. To dynamically manage their territories, salespeople must first manage a large amount of information from a huge knowledge base. They develop procedural knowledge that allows them to select appropriate strategies and tactics to accomplish their objectives and missions.

Although salespeople enjoy a certain amount of freedom in carrying out their duties, they are not independent employees. They are themselves subject to the actions of their sales managers and their intermediate sales supervisors. This aspect is discussed in Chapter 5. Consequently, to direct and manage salespeople effectively, sales managers need a thorough understanding of their behavior. This is the discussed in Chapter 4.

4 Salespeople: intermediaries in the dynamic management process

Effect of personal objectives and preferences on salespeople's behavior

Salespeople's reactions are likely to depend on their personal characteristics and preferences. This is the lesson that the management of a branch of an international corporation has learned the hard way (Darmon 1974). The International Agricultural Machine Corporation (IAM), an important producer of agricultural equipment, decided to increase its sales force motivation to improve its sales and profits. For that purpose, sales management increased the remuneration rates, partly linked to sales volume and partly to gross margins. Before it was implemented on a full scale basis, the reaction to new compensation plan had been tested by asking the opinions of a selected group of salespeople. They had been selected according to their co-operative attitudes, as perceived by their respective supervisors. Most of them were senior. As the test group recorded a unanimous favorable reaction, the new compensation plan was duly extended to the whole sales force.

The outcome of this new motivation program after a six-month period was extremely disappointing. The total sales volume was about the same as before. The compensation paid to the salespeople had substantially increased, and consequently, the total company profits had dropped.

Because of these unexpected results, the marketing manager asked an external expert to find out why the new compensation plan had failed and to propose a new solution which would effectively motivate the sales force.

The expert analyzed each individual's reactions to the new compensation plan. The results were illuminating. About one-third of the sales force reacted "positively" by working harder in order to increase their income substantially. Their attitude was that working harder was now worthwhile because increasing their sales volume paid off. This was the type of reaction that the company had anticipated, based on the advice of the test group.

The other two thirds of the sales force had reacted opportunistically (as economic theory would have predicted). This group had taken advantage of the remuneration rate increase by earning more money (and consequently increase the selling costs) but working less (and consequently decreasing sales and profits). In other words they had shared the additional welfare of the remuneration rate increase between some remuncration increase and some reduced working time and efforts (leading to a sales decrease).

At the sales force level, because some salespeople increased sales, while those of others fell, the total sales volume remained essentially unchanged. Because the whole sales force had increased their revenues (some more than others) a sharp decrease in the firm's profits followed.

This case study points to the fact that sales managers must understand their salespeople in order (1) to establish proper activity and performance norms; (2) to implement appropriate direct or indirect control procedures for monitoring salespeople's activities; and (3) to design adequate training, retraining, and support programs for the sales force. Sales managers can effectively direct and control the sales force only as long as they know and understand general and individual behavior patterns.

As one can easily surmise, every salesperson in the sales force is likely to have his/her own personality, motivation, tastes, preferences, and perceptions (Stevens and Macintosh 2003). Everyone has specific abilities and competencies. All are subject to personal, familial, and specific organizational constraints. Sales forces must be visualized as groupings of heterogeneous salespeople.

In spite of such heterogeneity, however, a number of general stable patterns apply to any salesperson. This chapter is devoted to describing such patterns, pointing out specificities whenever they are relevant. It proposes an analysis of salesperson behavior from two perspectives. First, behavioral patterns are discussed at an individual level, then at the more macro level of the whole sales force.

Objectives and motivation

Objectives

Like most human beings, salespeople are free individuals who make their own decisions. Their behavior is not always strictly aimed at fulfilling the objectives assigned by their firm – they pursue more personal objectives. Sometimes, they behave opportunistically. In other words, they sometimes take actions that, from their own perspectives, are the most satisfying to them.

The objectives that a salesperson pursues at a given point in time reflects his or her own values and preferences. For example, an individual who wants to increase his personal revenue values a bonus for performance achievement. Another individual may value personal fulfillment more than financial incentives. Both are likely to pursue different objectives, as suggested by the IAM situation, described above.

Salespeople typically try to achieve some balance between work and well-being. They try to find the best compromise between job and income security on one hand, and opportunities for promotion and advancement on the other. This makes sales force management a difficult process: sales managers must know, anticipate, and integrate the likely responses of their salespeople into their decisions as much as they can.

Far from being stable over time, individual objectives may vary over the career life cycle. For example, research carried out on insurance salespeople has shown that remuneration as well as promotion opportunities decrease in importance as they enter the latter stages in their career. Instead, they tend to give priority to characteristics such as travel frequency, the type of client to call on, or the supervision style of management (Darmon, Rigaux-Bricmont, and Balloffet 2003).

Professional objectives

Professional objectives include, for example, the kind of career salespeople intend to pursue, the promotions they expect during their career, as well as the changes they contemplate making during their professional life. Sometimes, salespeople are ambitious and consider their current position as temporary, before moving on to higher managerial levels. Alternatively, individuals who are well advanced in their career, may wish to keep their current position until they reach retirement age. People with such different work objectives are likely to display different effort levels and to behave differently.

Personal objectives

Personal and family objectives also influences behavior. Those who value their family life may avoid long and frequent traveling that would force them to be away from home. Research suggests that salespeople who are in charge of their families or who are at the beginning of their family-life cycle tend to be better performers (Churchill, Ford, and Walker 1979). In the same way, those people who are interested in sport or artistic activities may spend less time in the field than those that achieve fulfillment through their professional life.

Financial objectives

Financial objectives may also exert considerable influence over behavior. Research has shown that the financial status of a salesperson was significantly related to their performance (Churchill, Ford, and Walker 1979). This explains why financial incentives are so frequently used by sales managers as a powerful motivation device. This is also supported by empirical research. Most salespeople, if not all, have at least some financial objectives in mind. However, many of them also pursue other types of objective, as the IAM corporation case suggests. Financial objectives may be a priority or not, depending on individuals, their family situation and their needs, as well as on the stage they have reached in their family-life cycle.

Motivation

Motivation has long been a topic of considerable debate and research in social sciences, as testified by the numerous articles and books that have been devoted to the subject over the last few decades. It has led to the development of several theories, each one concentrating on one specific aspect of motivation, and each one yielding different and sometimes conflicting implications (see Table 4.1 for a non-exhaustive list). Because motivation is one of the most important aspects of sales force management, it may not be surprising that researchers and sales force practitioners have attempted to apply some of these theories to sales force situations. The research literature typically draws from one theory at a time, and overlooks other plausible motivation theories. The research stream that has stemmed from the application of expectancy theory (Vroom 1964) is a case in point (Walker, Churchill, and Ford 1977).

Salespeople's motivation to engage in certain activities relies on their anticipations and on the perceptions they have developed of various elements of the situation, as well as on their objectives and preferences. Individuals who are motivated to take a sales position are in a particular psychological state that determines the intensity of the work and effort that they decide to expend to fulfill their duties. In everyday language,

Table 4.1. Main motivation theories

Content theories of motivation

Attempt only to correlate needs and certain types of behavior, irrespective of the dynamics of motivational change.

Freud's Psychoanalytical Theory

Freud's and neo-Freudian psychoanalytical theories relate individual behavior to early childhood experience (Kassarjian and Sheffet 1981).

Maslow's Hierarchy of Need Theory (Maslow1943; 1970)

This hierarchy of need theory proposes five levels of human need: physiological needs, safety needs, need for love and affection, need for self-esteem and respect from others, and self-actualization. These five levels of need constitute a hierarchy that individuals climb sequentially from the lowest to the highest levels.

Alderfer's ERG Theory (Alderfer 1969; 1972)

Compresses Maslow's hierarchy into a three category classification: existence, relatedness, and growth needs.

Murray's Inventory of Social Needs (Costa and McCrae 1988)

Relies on the idea that needs are the basic motivating force underlying human behavior. Needs are mental forces that influence individuals to perceive and act so as to change unsatisfying situations into satisfying ones. Murray has drawn up a list of some 20 basic needs that any individual is supposed to experience to varying degrees.

Classical Economic Utility Theory

It is probably the best known motivation content theory that emphasizes value. It focuses on values individuals attach to various means that help them reach their goals. Individuals act to maximize their total utility. Utilities (or disutilities) can be considered as the benefits (or costs) associated with the outcomes of their actions.

McClelland's Theory of Learned Needs (McClelland 1962)

This theory studies the behavioral consequences of needs. Of special interest are needs for achievement (n Ach), affiliation (n Aff), and power (n Pow).

Herzberg Dual Factor Theory (Herzberg, Mausner, and Snyderman 1986)

It has been considered to be more an explanation for job satisfaction or dissatisfaction than a motivation theory (Lawler 1971, p.98). Some job factors are satisfiers (or "motivators") because they have the potential to improve job performance and contribute to job satisfaction (achievement, recognition, promotion, or responsibility). Dissatisfiers (or "hygiene" factors) are not motivators, but they tend to restrict productivity if they fall below a certain level, and contribute to job dissatisfaction (working conditions, company policies, supervision, and pay).

Process theories of motivation

Explain the processes by which motivation occurs.

Hull's Drive Theory (Hull 1952)

Motivation, or "impetus to respond" depends upon three factors: (1) a drive strength, (2) the anticipatory reactions to the amount of incentive (a forward-looking element), and (3) a habit strength which develops as a result of past stimulus-response reinforcement and experience (a past-oriented element). A drive has an energizing and directing influence on an individual's behavior.

Table 4.1 (*cont.*)

Vroom's Expectancy Theory (or expectancy-value model) (Vroom (1964)

People are motivated to perform those work activities that they find attractive and feel they can accomplish. The attractiveness of work activities depends on how well these activities lead to favorable consequences for themselves. Motivation (M) is a function of the product of the *valence* of performance outcome or performance goal (V) and the *expectancy* (E) (or subjective probability) that his/her efforts will result in the achievement of this goal. Performance acquires positive or negative valence depending on whether an employee perceives it as leading to or hindering desired job-related outcomes. This perception of the degree to which performance goal leads to the attainment of a job-related outcome is called *instrumentality* (I).

Means-End Chain Theory (Gutman 1982)

Individuals select actions that result in desired outcomes and minimize undesirable consequences. Consequences have positive or negative valences. Behavior may be considered as a means to an end following the sequence: terminal and instrumental values, psychosocial and functional consequences, and abstract and concrete goal selection.

Locke and Latham's Goal-Setting Theory (Locke and Latham's 1990)

Not only are individuals motivated to satisfy their needs, they are also motivated to strive for and reach goals. Assigned goals affect a salesperson's beliefs about their ability to perform the task (or self-efficacy) and their personal goals. These two factors, in turn, influence job performance. The underlying rationale is that goals can be motivators.

Adams's Equity Theory (Adams's 1963; 1965)

This theory has been developed for explaining workers reactions to the feelings of wage inequity in terms of work output, work quality, and attitudes toward the job. Inequity is experienced by workers when they perceive that the ratio of their outcomes (i.e. pay, fringe benefits, status, etc.) to inputs (i.e. efforts on the job, educational level, competencies, etc.) is unequal to the same ratios for "relevant others."

Porter-Lawler Motivation Model (Porter and Lawler 1968)

Integrative framework of work motivation which captures much of expectancy theory, equity theory, and performance-satisfaction research findings. Their model essentially follows an expectancy theory approach. In addition, it includes statements on how objects acquire valence, and it also takes past learning into consideration to some extent.

"motivating" salespeople is to induce them to exert more effort when carrying out one or several aspects of their duties.

According to expectancy theory, three successive relationships may explain the motivation process. In order to induce salespeople to exert some effort to accomplish the tasks for which they are responsible, three conditions must be met simultaneously:

- they believe that they can improve at least some aspects of their performance by putting in additional time and effort on this activity;
- they believe that they will obtain certain "rewards" if they do actually improve this aspect of their performance. Note that the "rewards" are not necessarily financial. They do not even need to be

under managerial control. They can come from the individual (e.g., a feeling of self-fulfillment).

• they value the expected "rewards," to engage in this activity.

When these three conditions are met, salespeople are motivated to perform an activity. If only one of these conditions is not met, the motivation program is likely to fail. The following section, discusses the perceptions of the first two relationships and their impact on motivation, as well as the typical "rewards" to which salespeople may attach some value.

Dynamics of behavior

As seen in the preceding chapter, because they have direct contact with customers, salespeople are instrumental in the success or failure of the relationships a firm wants to establish with its clients. They are often responsible for the level of satisfaction and the positive (or negative) image a client develops toward suppliers. This is true in service organizations of any personnel assuring direct interfaces with clients. In the case of an external sales force, however, the problem is compounded by the fact that salespeople are "boundary spanners". These are employees who work essentially outside of their firm, at the boundary of an organization (Singh, Goolsby, and Rhoads 1994). As a result, even under close supervision, they cannot be observed and monitored continuously. To a large extent, they are left alone when they call on clients. As a result, the quality of the relationships they develop with them depends to a large extent on the appropriateness of their behavior.

Some years ago, a performance model that has been extensively used by sales force researchers over the subsequent years was proposed (Walker, Churchill, and Ford 1977). Performance was shown to depend on five main factors: motivation, competencies, aptitudes, role perceptions, and a set of personal, organizational, and environmental factors. These last sets of factors were also hypothesized to influence the four previous ones.

The following paragraphs propose an extended description of a salesperson's behavior that integrates most aspects of this conceptualization. It attempts to reconcile many of the relevant aspects of various motivation theories listed in Table 4.1. This description emphasizes the basic dynamic characteristics of a salesperson's behaviors. It is constituted of three main parts: perception of the various relevant aspects of a sales situation, the activity planning processes, and the activity implementation phase.

Perception

Salespeople are likely to behave according to their own perceptions of the various elements that constitute their work environment (Sager, Yi, and Futrell 1998). Like buyers, they develop perceptions that sometimes depart sharply from the "objective" world — objective facts do not count as much as how salespeople *perceive* them. Management must be concerned about how salespeople perceive key aspects of their job, such as the objectives they have been assigned, their roles in the organization, their own competencies, sales territories, performances, and their situation compared with others.

Perceptions of assigned objectives

Salespeople develop perceptions of the objectives that management has assigned to them. If objectives are perceived as being too low, they may be considered as not challenging enough, which leads to a loss of motivation. If objectives are perceived as too high, they may be judged as unachievable, this may also lead to a loss of motivation. This is why it is important for management to make sure that assigned objectives are not only achievable, but are perceived as such by every person in the sales force.

Perceptions of their role

Salespeople's perception of their role depends on the activities and behaviors they think are necessary to fulfill their mission. Salespeople quickly develop such perceptions through people with whom they are in contact during their work — their "relevant others" (e.g., these could be their supervisors, clients and buyers, but also their friends and family). These work partners reveal their own expectations, constraints, and requirements to them. No doubt, those perceptions evolve as salespeople gain more experience within their work.

Research suggests that perceptions of various job characteristics (such as supervisory style, organizational communication, job significance and autonomy, job variety and completeness, and job complexity) are important antecedents of sales force motivation (Teas 1981). Three dimensions of a salesperson's role are especially relevant: role accuracy, ambiguity, and conflicts.

Role accuracy

Role accuracy covers two important aspects, one relating to the job itself, and the other to individual motivation. The former aspect of role accuracy refers to the congruence of the perceptions that salespeople and their supervisors have of the various selling job responsibilities. Some firms design very detailed job descriptions that precisely delineate a salesperson's duties and the extent of their decisional space. Others prefer to give more leeway to their salespeople to foster their initiative and provide them with some flexibility to handle unexpected situations. Obviously, in the latter case, salespeople are likely to experience many more role accuracy problems than in the former. A recent survey of sales organizations has revealed that large discrepancies exist between the perceptions that salespeople and sales managers have of the selling tasks and responsibilities in their firms. Salespeople emphasize their role in building customer loyalty and satisfaction through the provision of quality services. In contrast, managers' stated priorities were more frequently the salespeoples' roles in prospecting and selling the whole product line. For management, providing quality services was low on the list.

A second aspect of role inaccuracy occurs when salespeople develop misperceptions of the relationship between their own efforts and activities on one hand, and their performance on the other. Alternatively, the misperception may occur between their performance and the associated rewards. As they cannot know precisely how a client or their territory will respond to their actions, some role inaccuracy cannot be avoided. How important this is depends on the salespeople themselves, especially their competence levels, experience, and tenure in the position.

A salesperson may be reasonably confident that a ten percent increase in prospecting time could result in an increase of ten to twelve new accounts per month. This salesperson would perceive his/her role accurately. However, if this salesperson incorrectly estimated the number of new accounts that he/she would gain following this increased prospecting effort, or if he/she failed to properly assess the reward that would result from such an increase, he/she would have an inaccurate relational perception of the role. It would be extremely difficult, if not impossible, for a manager to motivate salespeople that (rightly or wrongly) perceive that whatever they do, they will not be able to attract new customers (if they think, for example, that the market is saturated, or that they are unable to prospect successfully).

Role ambiguity

Salespeople perceive some role ambiguity when they feel that they lack important information which prevents them from carrying out their duties properly. Alternatively, they may not understand what management expects from them in terms of duties, responsibilities, or performance. For example, individuals who have no idea of the limits of their own decision space are likely to suffer from role ambiguity.

A survey of 265 salespeople in ten hi-tech firms revealed that a large number did not know to what extent they could grant better credit conditions or use their expense accounts for entertaining a client (Ford, Walker, and Churchill 1975). Others did not know how to allocate their time among the various accounts, how to build strong customer relationships, or handle overdue accounts. Many of them had no idea what their manager's priorities or expectations were or whether they were satisfied with their performance. Finally, others did not know the limits of their authority, the firm's rules and policies, or which were the best selling methods.

Role conflicts

Salespeople experience role conflicts when they perceive that contradictory or incompatible demands are made on them. For example, in some cases, they may find it impossible to reconcile certain requests from clients with their company's policies and procedures. As boundary spanners, working at the outskirts of their organization, salespeople are bound to face such conflicts, because they typically deal with a large number of parties, each with its own demands and special requests.

In the above mentioned survey, salespeople were asked whether they were aware of conflicting requests from the various parties they had to deal with. One third of those surveyed thought that, general management and sales management had quite different expectations about how truthful and sincere salespeople should be when dealing with customers and prospects. This proportion increased to about one-half when it came to incompatible requests by general management versus those from clients (Ford, Walker, and Churchill 1975).

Some consequences of poor role perceptions

Inaccurate, ambiguous perceptions, or perceived role conflicts may have adverse psychological consequences for salespeople. Numerous studies have shown that inadequate role perceptions result in anxiety and stress (Dubinsky and Yammarino 1984), job dissatisfaction (Boles, Wood, and Johnson 2003), or lack of motivation (Dubinsky and Hartley 1986; Barktus, Peterson, and Bellanger 1989). Although salespeople tend to develop strategies for coping with stress and burnout (Nonis and Sager 2003), such faulty perceptions may also affect behavior and decrease sales productivity, favor absenteeism, and even induce salespeople to quit (Jolson, Dubinsky, and Anderson 1987; Ingram and Lee 1990). Research has also shown that customer-oriented salespeople were less likely to perceive role conflict or role ambiguity. They also tend to experience more job satisfaction and are more committed to their firms (Mengüç 1996).

Perceptions of market sensitivities to salespeople's activities

To achieve the goals set by management and/or themselves, salespeople base their decisions on their expectations about the way their territory will respond to their own selling efforts. These perceptions are called expectancies in expectancy theory. Obviously, through past experience, salespeople will have developed at least an implicit knowledge of these likely responses or sensitivities. Research has shown that, they can make reasonably accurate subjective estimates of the likely impact of an effort increase on performance in some job dimension (Lodish 1971). In some cases, however, subjective perceptions may somewhat depart from reality. As mentioned above, poor knowledge or a feeling of a lack of relevant knowledge of territory responses may lead to job ambiguity and inefficiency.

Perceptions of the performance-rewards relationship

The perceptions of the performance-reward relationships are called instrumentalities in expectancy theory. Salespeople may perceive a link between achieving a certain objective or performance level in a given dimension of their job and some positive or negative consequences. Positive consequences are either financial or non-financial rewards. Some links are explicit, for example those specified in the sales force compensation plan. Note, however, that these links are only explicit to the extent that salespeople have a clear understanding of the different features of their compensation plan. Other links may not be clearly spelt out. In some cases, the relationship is only implicit because the rewards come from within, for example a feeling of satisfaction after closing a difficult sale.

This point is well illustrated by the sales manager of a large international pharmaceutical company who was concerned about the lack of motivation in the sales force despite of a well-designed sales force incentive compensation plan. An expert was called in to investigate why the plan did not work and to propose some solutions. When the expert interviewed the sales force about their compensation plan, it became clear that most people had only a vague knowledge of its different features.

Clearly, for salespeople to be induced to change behavior in a positive way, they must comprehend how a behavioral change on their part will bring them a certain reward. They must understand the specific features of their compensation plans.

Perceptions of rewards

All salespeople do not value the same rewards equally. In expectancy theory terms, they do not attribute the same valence to various rewards. More specifically, one should make a basic distinction between extrinsic and intrinsic rewards. Extrinsic rewards are bestowed by others, for example, a supervisor or a client. They generally appeal to lower level needs and include financial rewards, such as salaries, commissions, or bonuses, as well as non-financial rewards, such as promotions, job security, or supervisors' recognition. Intrinsic rewards are bestowed by the salespersons themselves. They appeal to higher order needs, e.g., self-fulfillment or the feeling of accomplishment or success in a difficult task.

Salespeople are likely to value rewards differently, depending on the needs they have at a certain time in their lives. As a result, a given reward is unlikely to appeal equally to all salespeople or to an individual salesperson at different times in his/her life (Maslow 1970).

Perception of their own abilities

Salespeople develop a perception of how competent and efficient they are at their job (Bagozzi 1978). Research has shown that those with highest self-efficacy perceptions had also the highest expectations concerning their own performance and they logically tended to make stronger instrumentality estimates (Teas 1981).

Activity planning processes

Salespeople are more or less independent agents who decide on their own activities and behaviors. Very much like the control process discussed in Chapter 1, they make decisions based on their expectations of the plausible outcomes of their actions. They should select those courses of action that they feel will best meet their personal objectives. These actions constitute a cycle which takes place over time (Figure 4.1).

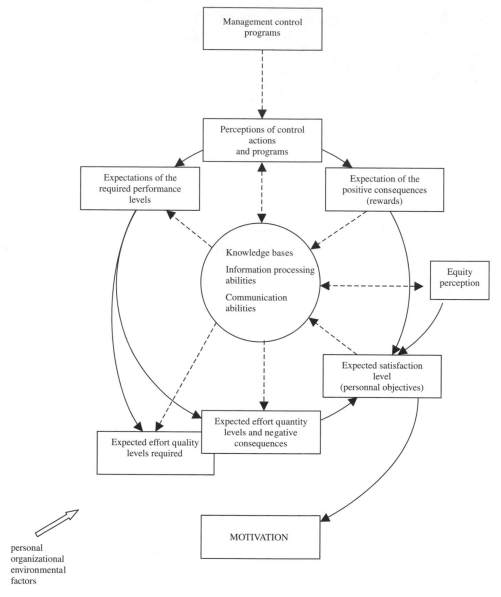

Fig. 4.1   A salesperson's expectations at the planning stage

As Figure 4.1 shows, salespeople acquire more or less perfect knowledge and develop more or less accurate perceptions of their firm's incentive programs and policies. These include not only the sales force compensation plan and the fringe benefit programs, but also other incentive programs (Hastings, Kiely, and Watkins 1988), sales contests

(Beltramini and Evans 1988), as well as the firm's stated polices and practices for promotion, and its supervisory practices. As a result, as postulated by expectancy theory, salespeople have more or less accurate perceptions of the relationship between various anticipated levels of the relevant performance dimensions on one hand, and the resulting anticipated rewards and/or sanctions on the other.

When they are working out how to achieve various levels of performance, salespeople assess the required levels of effort quality and quantity. The sales force literature emphasizes these two aspects of effort deployment as "working harder" (effort quantity) and "working smarter" (effort quality) (Sujan 1986). The adaptive selling paradigm is essentially based upon improving effort quality rather than effort quantity (Weitz, Sujan, and Sujan 1986; Park and Holloway 2003). The effort quality level that they judge to be necessary is constrained by their self-efficacy, or their own assessment of their abilities and competencies.

Given this ability constraint, salespeople assess the effort quantity that they must use to achieve a given performance level. These assessments directly depend on an individual's perception of the territory sensitivities to his/her work and efforts. In turn, such perceptions of territory sensitivities are likely to be influenced by salespeople's knowledge and forecasts of:

- the economic and competitive conditions prevailing in their territory;
- the territory market potential;
- the market penetration rate; and
- the salesperson's self-efficacy.

In addition, these instrumentalities are also directly affected by the perceived uncertainty attached to them. As predicted by economic utility theory, effort quantity has a negative valence for most salespeople. Time and effort are a salesperson's most scarce resources. Time spent on work cannot be allocated to more desirable activities. Naturally, salespeople are willing to allocate time and effort to achieve a level of performance but only as long as they perceive that the rewards that result from their work activities has an even larger positive value (or utilities).

Given a set of incentive programs, salespeople assess the various compromises between the positive and negative valence outcomes that result from different allocations of their time and effort, and select the course of action which will bring the highest positive value (or maximum utility). In practice, even if intuitively, salespeople are likely to follow a mental process which assesses the expected consequences of plausible time/effort allocations. This process continues until they find what they see as the most valuable (or utility maximizing) time/effort allocation.

Actual activities and outcomes

The mental planning process that has been outlined in the above section is followed by an implementation process described in Figure 4.2. This process goes in reverse order of the planning process.

At the implementation phase, salespeople actually behave according to their expectations and decisions. They deploy certain activities at the

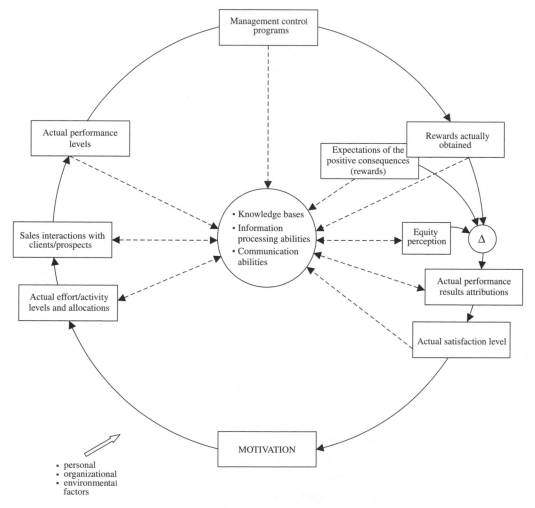

Fig. 4.2   Performance results at the implementation stage

planned quality level in the various selling tasks. Note that there are numerous reasons why their effort quantity and/or quality levels actually deployed in their territories may depart from those they had planned. For example, they may have overestimated their selling abilities, they may not have been able to sustain the planned effort level, or they may have had to attend to unexpected tasks within or outside their job.

Actual performance results from the quality and quantity of the efforts actually deployed by a salesperson. Actual performance may depart from expected performance for a number of reasons: (1) the actual effort input (in quantity and/or quality) may have departed from anticipated input; (2) the salespersons may have had a poor assessment of their territory sales sensitivities to their own efforts, that is they have made erroneous expectancy estimates; (3) salespeople may have over- or underestimated their own abilities; and/or (4) there may have been some unexpected events (i.e. a windfall sale or the bankruptcy of a major competitor) may have occurred.

Actual rewards are directly linked to actual performance. Here again, there are several reasons why actual rewards/sanctions may depart from a salesperson's expectations: (1) actual performance may have been different from expected performance for one or several of the causes outlined above; (2) salespeople may have made erroneous instrumentality estimates, possibly as a result of a poor understanding or lack of knowledge of the firm's incentive programs and policies; and/or (3) the firm has not strictly applied its official incentive programs and policies.

Effectiveness

The assessment and measurement of a salesperson's performance (or sales effectiveness) has been the object of much debate in the sales force literature (Avila, Fern, and Mann 1988; Jackson, Keith, and Schlacter 1983). The problem lies in the fact that a salesperson's performance has an important time dimension: high short-term performance may hide poor long-term performance, and vice versa. This brings us back to the differences between transactional and relational selling. Sales force performance is often measured by sales volume, market share, or generated profits. The rationale is that sales are generally the main source of revenue for a firm — sometimes its only source. Consequently, sales volume is the major source of contributions to profits and selling costs.

However, salespeople should not be given the sole responsibility for sales volumes. This is why one should make the important distinction

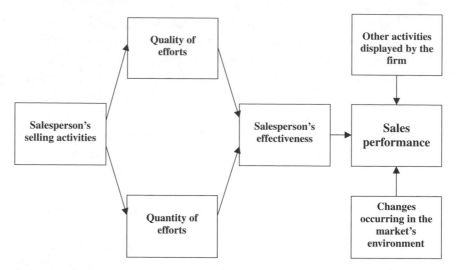

Fig. 4.3   Differences between a salesperson's effectiveness and sales performance

between a salesperson's effectiveness that actually measures a salesperson's performance (i.e. that part of sales performance that actually reflects a salesperson's effort quantity and quality) and the sales volume generated by a salesperson. Sales also result from other marketing decisions (such as product and service quality, prices, advertising, or distribution levels) as well as from environmental variables (such as competitors' actions, economic conditions, or legislation). These factors can affect sales in a positive or negative way, and salespeople should not be accountable for their impact (Figure 4.3).

In addition, a sales force does not only create revenue. It is also an important source of selling costs to a firm. As a result of its size, organization, the competence levels of its salespeople which require commensurate compensation levels, a sales force involves cost. These have a negative impact on profits. Consequently, a salesperson's performance should ideally be measured in terms of the long-term net profits that directly result from their activities. As one can easily surmise, this is a major difficulty in sales force management and control.

Multidimensional performance

A salesperson's performance should be reflected in the various dimensions of the selling job. In practice, measures such as sales volume, gross profits, sales quota achievement, and new accounts generated are frequently used.

In addition to such quantitative measures that tend to account essentially for short-term performance, more qualitative measures that include more long-term results should also be used. For example, such measures can be customer satisfaction, the quality of clients' follow-ups, or long-term relationship building.

When the objective is to build lasting relationships with key accounts, long-term customer satisfaction and/or created added value should be appropriate measures of a salesperson's performance. This suggests that no exclusive reliance on quantitative criteria can account for such qualitative aspects of a salesperson's function.

Another managerial implication is that although short-term based quantitative measures of a salesperson's performance may have some tactical value, it should not prevent managers from assessing their selling effectiveness and contribution to building lasting customer relationships. Such measures are likely to be activity- as well as outcome-based, over an appropriate period of time.

Satisfaction/dissatisfaction

The satisfaction/dissatisfaction of salespeople (SS/D) is an emotional response to an evaluation of performance outcomes (Hunt 1977). Seven dimensions to sales job satisfaction are generally recognized (Churchill *et al.* 1974):

- the job itself;
- fellow workers;
- supervision;
- company policies and support;
- pay;
- promotion and advancement opportunities; and
- customers.

They all relate either to personal job outcomes, the job itself, or the organization (Table 4.2).

Although SS/D can be assessed at a point in time, it results from a series of events, some of them having occurred long before. In the same way, performance in the short-term may be very different from performance over some period of time. Even if dissatisfied with current poor performance (or other negative but unstable events), a salesperson may be extremely satisfied with the job because the causes of poor performance (or negative events) may be perceived as exceptional and unlikely to last. Obviously, long-term SS/D builds up over a number of planning period loops.

Table 4.2. Components of a salesperson's job satisfaction/dissatisfaction

---

Satisfaction/dissatisfaction with personal job outcomes (directly related to performance)
- Fatigue and time foregone for displaying selling efforts
- Compensation
- Actual and anticipated promotions and advancement
- Recognition on the job and outside the organization
- Intrinsic rewards (feelings of personal accomplishment...)

Satisfaction/dissatisfaction with the job itself
- Difficulty of assigned sales objectives
- Customers/territory
- Difficulty of the selling tasks (uncertainties)
- Adequacy of supervision (distributive fairness)
- Perceived role conflicts and role ambiguity

Satisfaction/dissatisfaction with the organization
- Other salespeople/employees
- Support provided by the organization (product quality, advertising, call centers)
- Promotion and advancement opportunities
- Company policies and procedures (customer orientation, procedural and interactional fairness)

In addition to personal job outcomes and a salesperson's effort levels, SS/D results from the directions and sizes of the expected–actual performance/outcome gaps, the nature of the causes a salesperson attributes to the expected–actual performance/outcome gaps, and a salesperson's feelings of equity/inequity.

Directions and sizes of expected–actual outcome gaps

As mentioned above, there exist a multitude of reasons why actual performance (and actual personal outcomes) may depart from a salesperson's expectations: misperceptions of actual market responses to selling effort, unforeseen environmental events, to name only a few. Following discrepancy theory (Locke 1969; Rice *et al.* 1989) and the disconfirmation paradigm (Oliver and DeSarbo 1988; Tse and Wilton 1988), salespeople's satisfaction on each job dimension depends on the size of the gap between performance and expectations. Salespeople should develop positive or negative feelings depending on the direction and size of the discrepancy (Locke 1976). For negative disconfirmations, larger discrepancies produce higher levels of dissatisfaction (Oliver 1980).

Attributions for expected—actual outcome gaps

In addition, SS/D depends on the causes attributed to the performance—expectation gaps (Weiner 1972). According to attribution theory (Heider 1958; Kelley 1972; Mizerski *et al.* 1979), individuals try to provide explanations for events occurring in their environment. The explanations salespeople provide for their performance and departure from expectations influence job satisfaction as well as subsequent behaviors.

Attributions are characterized along two main dimensions: locus (Heider 1958) and stability (Weiner *et al.* 1972). Thus, the reason(s) a salesperson attributes to a gap between expectations and performance can be internal or external (locus) (Teas and McElroy 1986). It is internal when they believe they have been instrumental in the event outcome and external when they believe they have had no part in it. One must also make a distinction between external causes that are attributed to a firm-related factor (over which a firm has some control, e.g., the firm's advertising campaign) or to an environment-related factor (over which the firm *and* salespeople have no control, e.g., a competitor's actions). The stability dimension of attributions refers to whether a salesperson perceives these causes as stable or unstable.

Relying on research findings in consumer behavior (Folkes 1984; Folkes *et al.* 1987), Table 4.3 provides examples of situations in which salespeople may make different types of attribution. In each case, likely behavioral responses in terms of satisfaction levels and efforts are provided (Sujan 1986, pp. 41—49). One should also expect a salesperson to make different attributions depending on whether performance exceeds expectations (positive gap) or vice versa (negative gap).

These attributions affect different dimensions of the SS/D process. Internal attributions affect the personal outcome dimension of SS/D; firm-related attributions affect the organization dimension; and the environment-related attributions, the job dimension. The rationale is that salespeople interpret a positive gap as the job becoming easier, and vice versa for a negative gap.

Facing a positive gap, salespeople are more satisfied when the cause is seen as stable because they will benefit from this situation over a long period of time. This time dimension notwithstanding, salespeople are more satisfied if they can attribute the cause of the positive gap to themselves, because this should make them feel that they are in control of the situation (Silvester *et al.* 2003). When they attribute an external cause, they are less satisfied, but to a lesser extent when the cause is attributed to the firm rather than to an environmental factor. The rationale is that salespeople tend to feel that their organization will be able to take advantage of this opportunity whenever it arises in the future.

Conversely, when there is a negative gap, salespeople are as dissatisfied if the cause attributed to sub-performance is stable, because they may suffer from it for a long period of time. Their dissatisfaction level increases as the cause is successively internal, environment-related, and firm-related. The rationale is that people are more dissatisfied if they have to blame the firm, or an uncontrollable environmental factor, rather than themselves for their failing performance.

According to attribution theory, the particular cause that an individual attributes to a certain event affects his/her subsequent behavior (Jones *et al.* 1972). Whenever salespeople attribute internal and stable causes to a positive gap, their behavior is reinforced. For example, if they attribute higher than expected performance to their own abilities, their current behavior should be reinforced. If they attribute a firm-related cause, they develop higher organizational commitment because the firm is perceived as facilitating the selling task beyond expectations. This is as true as the cause is stable. When the cause is internal and unstable (e.g., a salesperson has taken advantage of a one-shot opportunity) or environment-related, no significant salesperson behavioral change will occur. Here, salespeople tend to believe that the higher than expected performance is unusual or was only a one-time occurrence.

When there is a negative gap, and the attributed cause is unstable, salespeople are unlikely to change behavior and effort levels. When it is stable, however, this attribution may affect organizational commitment, and eventually induce them to quit, if they have attributed a firm- or environment-related cause. If the attributed cause is stable and internal, it may result in a decision to change (and improve) behavior or, at the opposite, lead to a decision to quit, if they are unable or unwilling to cope with the cause of the poor performance.

Attributions are known to be linked to personality traits, especially locus of control (Teas and McElroy 1986), i.e. the extent to which individuals tend to perceive events as being internally or externally controlled (Rotter 1966). When salespeople are systematically inclined to believe they can exert control over events in their lives (internal locus of control) and make internal attributions, this affects their satisfaction level and their behavior. When they have an external locus of control, they are likely to experience different satisfaction levels and exhibit different

Table 4.3. Examples of possible causal attributions by salespeople to the gap between expected and actual sales performance

	Internal attributions	External firm-related attributions	External environment-related attributions
Unstable cause	**Attribution:** temporary salesperson's extra efforts **Possible behavioral reactions:** satisfaction, reduced effort to normal levels **Attribution:** lack of effort for family/personal reasons **Possible behavioral reactions:** moderate dissatisfaction, increased effort to normal levels	**Actual performance > Expectations** **Attribution:** successful promotional campaign of the firm **Possible behavioral reactions:** moderate satisfaction, no behavioral change **Actual performance < Expectations** **Attribution:** Poor advertising campaign of the firm **Possible behavioral reactions:** dissatisfaction, no behavioral change	**Attribution:** favorable exceptional climatic conditions **Possible behavioral reactions:** moderate satisfaction, no behavioral change **Attribution:** Successful promotional campaign of a competitor **Possible behavioral reactions:** moderate dissatisfaction, no behavioral change
Stable cause	**Attribution:** salesperson's ability to sell a product line **Possible behavioral reactions:** high satisfaction, keep increasing efforts **Attribution:** Salesperson's inability to sell a product line **Possible behavioral reactions:** High dissatisfaction, intention to quit	**Actual performance > Expectations** **Attribution:** the firm has launched a successful innovative product **Possible behavioral reactions:** moderate satisfaction, increased efforts **Actual performance < Expectations** **Attribution:** the firm sells poor uncompetitive products **Possible behavioral reactions:** high dissatisfaction, intention to quit	**Attribution:** a major competitor is out of business **Possible behavioral reactions:** satisfaction, increased efforts **Attribution:** a competitor has launched a successful innovative product **Possible behavioral reactions:** moderate dissatisfaction, sustained additional efforts

behavior (Walker *et al.* 1977). Those with a high internal locus of control should have higher expectancy estimates (Lawler 1970).

Feelings of equity/inequity

Although equity of pay has not received the attention it deserves in academic sales force compensation research (Livingtone *et al.* 1995; Ramaswami and Singh 2003), professional and textbook literature underscore the need for providing salespeople with "fair" remuneration that can ensure job satisfaction (through pay satisfaction), independently of the selected compensation plan structure (Dalrymple and Cron 1998). Reward decisions may affect the perceived equity among salespeople, and may have a knock-on effect on job satisfaction, morale and turnover.

Behavioral scientists have long recognized that individuals experience greater satisfaction when "relevant others" are perceived to be more satisfied (Linda 1979). Many research studies have found a strong link between an employee's perceived equity and job satisfaction (Berkowitz *et al.* 1987; Klein 1973; Oldham *et al.* 1986; Pritchard 1969). There is strong empirical evidence that perceived job inequity involves job dissatisfaction which may lead to poor performance, restrictions of output, and/or the intention to quit. In addition, because salespeople are likely to have numerous and close contact with co-workers, they are likely to be frequently reminded of, and confronted with, job inequity. According to equity theory, those individuals who feel inequitably treated (negative inequity) should be less productive and less satisfied than those who feel they are treated equitably. Those who feel they are treated better (positive inequity) should be more productive, but less satisfied, than equitably treated salespeople (Greenberg 1982; Lawler 1971). This conclusion has been extended to sales force contexts (Livingstone *et al.* 1995). As a corollary, job satisfaction cannot be achieved without salespeople experiencing a feeling of equity concerning various aspects of their job (Huffman and Cain (2001)).

Salespeople may experience different types of reward fairness, especially procedural and distributive fairness (Brashear *et al.* 2004; Dubinsky and Levy 1989; Roberts *et al.* 1999). Procedural inequity occurs when salespeople perceive the procedures used to distribute justice as being unfair (Lind and Tyler 1988). In such cases, inequity is likely to have a negative impact on the organization dimension of SS/D, because the organization is seen as responsible for setting inequitable procedures. Individuals may also experience distributive inequity if they perceive the actual procedure implementation as being unfair. In the latter case, the job dimension of SS/D may be affected if supervisors are responsible for applying the firm's procedures. Other authors recognize interactional fairness as another dimension of job fairness (Ramaswami and Singh 2003). This refers to the procedure that is used for communicating reward decisions (Goodwin and Ross 1992). The latter dimension, however, is not linked to the amount of reward and job outcomes.

Equity theory provides a valuable framework for analyzing salespeople's equity. It has been applied to the marketing exchange relationships between buyers and sellers (Dubinsky and Levy 1989; Geykens and Steenkamp 1997; Huppertz *et al.* 1978; Oliver and Swan 1989; Swan and Oliver 1991) and may also be applied to exchanges between a salesperson and his/her firm. According to this theory (Adams 1965; Homans 1974), a state of equity exists among different parties when their respective ratios of outputs-to-inputs (or return-to-investment) are equal (Alwin 1987). Note that perceptions rather than objective measures of inputs and outputs are relevant (Netemeyer *et al.* 1997): equity and inequity remain in the eyes of the beholder.

Another proposition of equity theory is that whenever individuals experience a feeling of inequity, they behave in such a way as to restore equity. For example, employees who feel overqualified (i.e. they perceive to be rewarded less than others, given their own inputs), have been shown to restrict their output (i.e. to perform at a lower level) to restore equity, and conversely (Adams and Jacobsen 1964).

As recognized by Geyskens and Steenkamp (1997), a major weakness of equity theory is that it is ambiguous about the "relevant others" with whom an individual compares his/her own equity ratio (Futrell and Jenkins 1978). As suggested in the literature (Ronen 1986), it is likely that salesperson equity arises at different levels (see Figure 4.4).

One basic distinction must be made between external and internal equity. External equity is concerned with the perceived fairness of one's situation relative to individuals in other organizations, either holding different types of position (equity-with-the-world) (Austin and Hatfield 1975; Brown 1986) or doing the same job (occupational equity) (Scholl *et al.* 1987). When salespeople experience occupational inequity, they may attempt to restore equity, by trying to obtain a better deal within their own firm or by leaving for another sales position with more attractive remuneration and/or work conditions. Occupational inequity may translate into high sales force turnover. Management can ensure occupational equity by providing sales

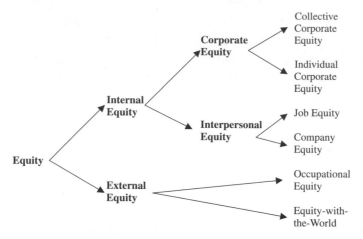

Fig. 4.4   Different types of equity at work

staff with working conditions and/or remuneration levels that are competitive for this type of work.

Internal equity (or inequity) is experienced when salespeople compare their situation with those of employees in their own organization, either in non-selling positions (company equity) (Scholl *et al.* 1987) or in sales positions (job equity). Concerning interpersonal welfare comparisons, Adams and Jacobsen (1964) have shown that perceived pay equity might have a strong impact on employee's morale and performance. Corporate equity is another type of internal equity that has not yet received much attention in the literature. Individuals often experience feelings of inequity with respect to their own firm. This is often experienced by a salesperson (individual corporate equity) following a comparison between his/her own equity ratio and the firm's perceived equity ratio. It is conceivable, that a salesperson could receive competitive (occupational equity) and equitable (job equity) remuneration, and still feel ill-treated by management, if they think the firm is not giving them a fair share of the welfare they generate. They may resent receiving only market rate wages when the firm shows higher than average industry profits. Salespeople, who always tend to feel that they are the driving force behind their firm's success, often experience a feeling of "inequity-with-the-firm". In addition, they are likely to judge whether they are being treated fairly depending on how a firm shares the welfare generated by the whole sales force with the sales force itself (collective corporate equity). In this case, the firm is the "relevant other," so corporate inequity is likely to affect the morale of the whole sales force and their feelings of trust toward the firm and organizational commitment.

Feelings of inequity are likely to affect the various dimensions of SS/D differently, depending on the nature of inequity. Among retail salespeople, internal equity was found to be more important than external equity (Dubinsky and Levy 1989), although both types of equity were found to be important (Livingstone *et al.* 1995).

Consequences of job satisfaction and feedback loops

Although the relationship between job satisfaction and organizational commitment has been largely demonstrated (Bateman and Strasser 1984; Johnston *et al.* 1990), the direction of the causal relationship has also been the object of much debate in the literature. Some authors have advocated that organizational commitment is an antecedent of job satisfaction (Bateman and Strasser 1984). The bulk of the evidence, however, suggests that organizational job satisfaction leads to organizational commitment (Bartol 1979; Bluedorn 1982a; Brown and Peterson 1993; 1994; Dailey and Kirk 1992; Johnson *et al.* 2001; Johnston *et al.* 1990; McNeilly and Russ 1992; Ramaswami and Singh 2003; Reichers 1985; Summers and Hendrix 1991). In the same way, job satisfaction has been negatively related to intention to quit and turnover (Futrell and Parasuraman 1984).

At the end of some planning period, the behavioral responses to the satisfaction/dissatisfaction formation process are likely to affect the motivation and effort levels that salespeople will display in the following planning period (Walker *et al.* 1977). In the same way, a salesperson "learns" from the anticipation-performance gaps and from the causes that have been attributed to these gaps. This affects the anticipated performance and personal outcomes for the following planning period. Then, the SS/D formation process loops endlessly.

Figure 4.5 provides an integrated view of a salesperson's behavior. It combines the two phases of planning and implementation described in Figures 4.1 and 4.2, into one single process.

Knowledge bases, skills, and competencies

The perceptions of salespeople are instrumental to their decisions and actions. They are formed through their knowledge (or lack thereof) of the relevant aspects of the situations they face. To develop accurate perceptions, salespeople need to accumulate an extensive knowledge base which has as much accurate and up to date information as possible. The size of this

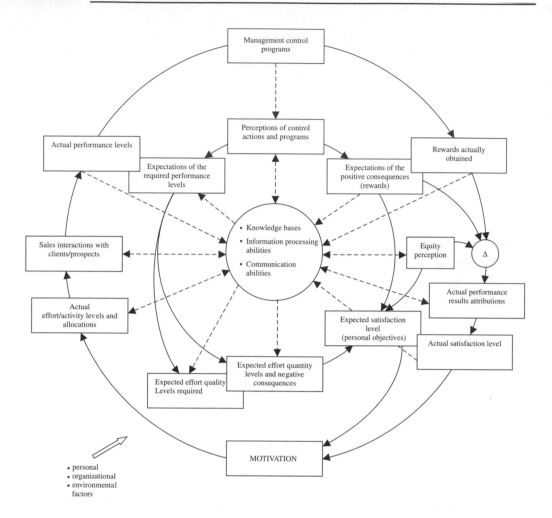

Fig. 4.5   Overview of a salesperson's behavioral process

knowledge base depends on a territory size, the number and technical level of the products and services sold, as well as on the extent of salespeople's responsibilities. When properly processed, this information constitutes a salesperson's knowledge base. Obviously, salespeople need the skills or abilities to effectively use their knowledge base and thus, increase their competence levels.

Knowledge base

In this book, a salesperson's job is essentially conceived as managing relationships with customers as well as with key people within their organization (Dubinsky *et al.* 1986). In order to carry these functions effectively, salespeople need an extensive database.

Characteristics

A salesperson's knowledge base is characterized by its size, quality, and nature. Their job is to collect, process, and dispatch information. They constantly need to blend information they have already acquired through experience with relevant information about the current situation they face during their interactions with customers and prospects (Weitz 1978). Their knowledge base must be extensive and include information that is necessary to do their job effectively. However, research suggests, that information overload can be detrimental to sales force performance (Hunter 2004).

By nature, a salespersons' knowledge base includes core, industry-specific, and firm-specific knowledge. Core knowledge is essential for holding a selling function, irrespective of the firm for which a salesperson works. Salespeople also need industry-specific knowledge. They must understand the clients' needs, the products, and the basics of the underlying technology such as electronics or real estate. Firm-specific knowledge (or specific assets, in terms of transaction cost theory), is also essential when selling for a particular firm, but this knowledge is not transferable, even to another firm within the same industry (e.g., the knowledge of a firm's specific procedures).

Another way to classify a salesperson's knowledge is whether it is elementary or aggregate. Elementary knowledge applies exclusively to one client, while aggregate knowledge applies to the whole sales territory and its environment. It is generally applicable to all the clients or market segments.

Relevant knowledge can be easily classified using the two criteria described above. Examples of information falling into each cell of this classification are provided in Table 4.4. As discussed in chapter 10, this grid can serve as a starting point for establishing a checklist and identifying essential information and knowledge to be given to salespeople, for example, through training or CRM programs.

Contents of the knowledge base

Salespeople need information and knowledge about markets, their clients and their sales territory, their firm and its products, their own selling tasks, and the selling environment.

Table 4.4. Salespeople's knowledge bases

Elementary knowledge (About every client/ prospect/product/salesperson)

Core (or general) knowledge about:

Buyer behavior
- General knowledge of buyer behavior

Selling processes
- General knowledge of the selling function
- General knowledge of selling and negotiation processes

Industry-specific knowledge about:

Buyer behavior
- Knowledge of buyer behavior specific to the firm's industrial sector

Selling processes
- General knowledge of the selling function specific to the firm's industrial sector
- General knowledge of selling and negotiation processes in the firm's industrial sector: Basic cognitive scripts

Firm-specific knowledge about:

Every customer/prospect
- Knowledge of sales potential
- Knowledge of customer's needs
- Knowledge of the history of the relationship with customer
- Knowledge of the customer's specific behaviors
- Knowledge of the customer's specific decision processes
- Knowledge of past sales results
- Knowledge of account's sensitivities to selling activities/efforts

The firm's offers
- Knowledge of the technical characteristics of the firm's products
- Knowledge of the firm's product prices
- Knowledge of each product's competitive advantages
- Knowledge of each product's relative weaknesses in comparison with competition

Other salespeople
- Knowledge of their selling objectives
- Knowledge of their territory's characteristics
- Knowledge of their sales performances
- Knowledge of their compensation level

Aggregate knowledge (About the whole sales territory/sales force/firm)

Core (or general) knowledge about:

Clients and markets
- Knowledge of environmental trends (stable economic trends)
- General declarative knowledge (types of clients, etc.)

The selling function
- General procedural knowledge of selling strategies for various types of client

Firm-specific knowledge about:

The firm's definition of the selling function
- Knowledge of a salesperson's decision space (leeway to negotiate, freedom, controls, etc.)

The firm's sales force
- Knowledge about its structure and organization
- Knowledge about the sales objectives
- Knowledge of sales force performance levels (sales, customer satisfaction, etc.)

Table 4.4 (*cont.*)

Working methods
- Knowledge of time management and work organization

Industry-specific knowledge about:

Sector's clients and markets
- Knowledge of environmental trends of the firm's industrial sector (stable economic trends)
- Declarative knowledge relative to the firm's industrial sector (client categories, etc.)
- Knowledge of the labor market in the firm's industrial sector

Selling function in the firm's industrial sector
- Procedural knowledge concerning the strategies applicable to each customer category in the firm's industrial sector

Competing firms in the industrial sector
- Knowledge concerning the various competing firms in the industrial sector (products, selling strategies, procedures, etc.)

The sales territory
- Knowledge of the sales objectives for the sales territory
- Knowledge of the territory sales potentials
- Knowledge of the territory's penetration rates and market shares
- Knowledge of the territory's competitive inroads
- Knowledge of the specific market conditions in the sales territory
- Knowledge of the territory's environment
- Knowledge of the territory's sensitivities to selling efforts
- Territory-specific declarative knowledge (firm's customer types, etc.)
- Territory-specific procedural knowledge (strategies applicable to each type of customers in the territory, etc.)

The firm
- Knowledge of the firm's selling policies and procedures (prices, delivery conditions, rebates, discounts, etc.)
- Knowledge of the firm's administrative procedures (order procedures, reporting, expense accounts, etc.)
- Knowledge of the firm's specific programs (compensation, quota, incentive plans, training, sales support programs, promotion policies, etc.)

Knowledge about markets

Salespeople need a thorough knowledge and understanding of both buyer and market behaviors, not just at a general level as described in Chapter 2, but also at a firm-specific level. Salespeople often believe that they have sufficient market knowledge. Some assert, for example, that they know their customers well when they know what they buy (Clancy and Shulman 1994). Although this is important information, it is not sufficient to understand customer needs and behaviors. Salespeople also need extensive knowledge of the trends, opportunities, and competition that characterize the markets in which they operate.

They also need to know the characteristics of their own sales territories (for each account, sales potentials, market shares, market opportunities, buying processes, etc.) Unless they have precise ideas about customer and territory sensitivities to their own efforts, they cannot properly allocate their time and selling activities.

Knowledge about the firm

Salespeople need substantial amounts of information about their own firm. Besides product knowledge (including some relevant technical aspects, and their competitive advantages), they need to know about their firm's procedures and policies. They should acquire a clear understanding of their responsibilities and rights as sales representatives, in order to avoid inadequate role perceptions. They should also have sufficient information about other salespeople in the firm, to allow them to feel part of a team, and to avoid developing unjustified feelings of inequity. Finally, they should clearly understand the structure and organization of the sales force of which they are a part, as well as its objectives and achievements.

Skills

As discussed in Chapter 1, knowledge is more than an accumulation of information. Salespeople process information to acquire knowledge and skills. More specifically, they develop procedural and declarative knowledge, working skills, and competencies.

Development of procedural and declarative knowledge

Declarative knowledge

Effective salespeople know that they must adapt their selling strategies and tactics depending on the needs, behaviors, and expectations of their customers. Their ability to recognize that different types of customers must be treated differently is called declarative knowledge. This is the opposite strategy of canned presentation where a unique selling pitch is delivered to every customer (Jolson 1975). Declarative knowledge includes all the facts related to each client category, for example, the characteristics of each type of selling situation (Weitz, Sujan, and Sujan 1986). This allows a salesperson to recognize and classify a selling situation. As seen in Chapter 3, the ability to differentiate among first purchase, modified re-buy, and routine purchase selling situations constitutes a basic declarative knowledge for a salesperson. They can often develop sub-categories of customers within each type of selling situation.

Research suggests that the top performing salespeople are best able to categorize prospects (Szymanski 1988). In addition, they tend to characterize customers using a more parsimonious number of characteristics and assign different weights to those characteristics than lower performers (Szymanski and Churchill 1990).

Cognitive scripts and procedural knowledge

For every type of selling situation they identify, salespeople have a selling script. These scripts are predetermined and stereotyped sequences of actions that are developed to deal with any given type of situation (Schank and Abelson 1977). Procedural knowledge refers to the sequence of actions associated with every selling situation (Leigh and Rethans 1984; Leigh and McGraw 1989). In other words, all the scripts that salespeople have learned constitute their procedural knowledge. This includes the general selling processes for dealing with different kinds of customers and prospects and selling know-how (such as a customer orientation). Research consistently suggests that salespeople with complex cognitive structures are more effective (Sharma, Levy, and Kumar 2001).

Development of working skills

Ability to recognize and evaluate options

In order to make strategic and tactical decisions, salespeople rationally analyze more or less formally all the possible courses of action at their disposal and anticipate the possible consequences of those actions (Porter and Inks 2000). The most efficient salespeople are those that are able to recognize and evaluate larger set of options to select the best one. In particular, salespeople evaluate possible allocations of their time and efforts, or the possible outcomes of different selling strategies with a customer. Then, they select the course of action that best fits their own personal objectives (and hopefully, those of the firm).

Vocational skills

To be efficient, salespeople need to apply effective working methods. Their objective is to make the best possible use of their most scarce resource – their time. Effective time management is part of the selling function.

Communication skills

Salespeople need to develop strong communication skills. Communication constitutes the backbone of the selling function, and good salespeople are effective communicators. Communication skills can be developed using proper techniques. Not only should salespeople be concerned with verbal skills, but they should also develop impression management skills (physical appearance, dressing, proper behaviors during sales encounters, etc.).

Competencies

Salespeople's knowledge and skills for managing relationships with customers and prospects, as well as with people in their own organization, are not sufficient. They must also be able to make decisions and take action. In order to be competent, they should also be able to demonstrate experience of effective selling, based on rational actions relying on extensive and sufficiently accurate knowledge bases.

Common sense suggests that as salespeople gain experience in their job, they acquire better knowledge of their sales territory sensitivities to selling efforts, have better understanding of the firm's policies and practices, and understand what to do in various situations encountered in the field. As a consequence, experience and tenure are positively related to expectancy and instrumentality estimates and inversely related to job ambiguity and inaccuracy.

Influence of personal and situational factors

The salesperson behavior framework described in Figure 4.6 should apply to any type of selling situation. Obviously, the variables which are shown as direct determinants of a salesperson's motivation and performance are themselves likely to vary depending on other factors. These factors can be conveniently grouped into four main categories (from micro- to macro-level factors): personal characteristics, task, organizational, and environmental factors (Teas 1981; Evans, Margheim, and Schlacter 1982).

Personal characteristics

Numerous research studies have investigated the possible relationship between a salesperson's performance and personal characteristics,

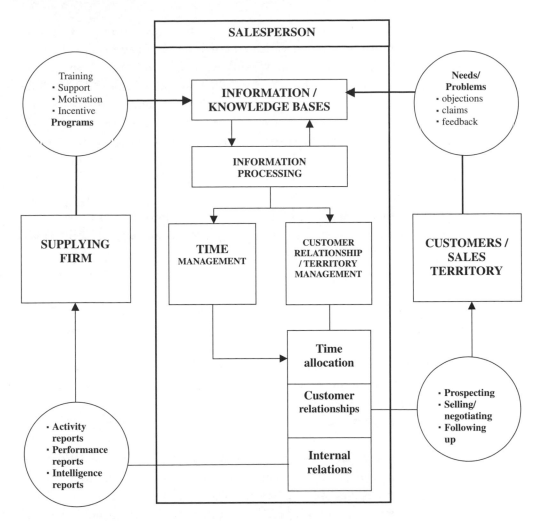

Fig. 4.6   Communication flows for customer relationship management

such as their socioeconomic profile, aptitudes, and some psychological traits.

Demographic and socioeconomic characteristics

Given the wide variety of selling positions one can find in practice (Moncrief 1986; Darmon 1998b), one challenging question is whether certain personal characteristics can be good predictors of success in personal selling. Research tends to answer no. Studies have investigated possible links of performance with age, size, weight, sex, physical appearance, and psychological characteristics of salespeople.

A research study that synthesized the findings of more than 400 previous studies has investigated whether some relationships between salespeople's performance and various personal and socio demographic variables could be generalized (Churchill, Ford, and Walker 1985). Only six such characteristics were found to be significantly, although weakly, linked to sales performance. Among them, five are related to the background and previous experience: personal and family origins, marital and social status, financial situation, and vocational and managerial aptitudes. Salespeople were more effective when they hold family responsibilities, are married with dependents, and consequently, have certain financial needs. Although those relationships are weak, the general conclusion seems to be that no one characteristic can explain sales performance.

Aptitude

There is a major difference between skills and aptitude. While skills can be acquired, an individual's aptitude (physical or mental) is innate and constitutes a natural limit to an individual's skill acquisition. One can reasonably expect a salesperson's aptitude to have a positive impact on the territory sensitivities to his or her activities. As a result, there is a minimum level of aptitude that is necessary to hold any given selling position. Research, however, suggests that there is no such a thing as a general selling aptitude.

As already suggested, selling functions involve quite diverse tasks to be performed depending on the situation. Every selling situation requires quite specific aptitudes and skills (Avila and Fern 1986). As a result, it is up to management to determine what aptitudes are necessary to hold the sales positions they design for their sales force. In other words, it is generally admitted that *salespeople are not born but they can be trained.*

Psychological traits

Mental skills, such as verbal intelligence, aptitude in mathematics, or personality traits like empathy, sociability, aggressiveness, or domination have been extensively researched. Cognitive ability is the only characteristic that was found to explain sales performance to some limited extent (Churchill *et al.* 1985).

Self-esteem is the manner in which individuals attribute and infer dispositions in themselves (Bagozzi 1980b). It seems that no systematic relationship exists between a salesperson's self-esteem and expectancy estimates (Teas 1981). *Self-efficacy*, as mentioned above, is a concept close to self-esteem. It relates to an individual's feelings of self-regard with respect to actual performance — their self-perceived ability (Bagozzi 1978). Research suggests that higher self-efficacy results in an expectation of higher performance levels and consequently in higher expectancy estimates (Teas 1981).

As seen above, salespeople may have an internal or external *locus of control*. This refers to an individual's belief that what happens to him or her is the result of their own actions. In contrast, salespeople who attribute the events to external factors such as luck, or chance, are said to have an *external locus of control*. They have been shown to be less receptive to a participative leadership style (Mitchell 1974). As can be expected, salespeople with an internal locus of control generally have higher expectancy and instrumentality estimates (Lawler 1973; Sims, Szilagyi, and McKemey 1976) and may have different perceptions of their tasks (Kimmons and Greenhaus 1976).

Given that salespeople are human beings, they are likely to display not only wide ranges of aptitude, skills, and knowledge. They are also likely to experience different values, and consequently have different *valences for rewards and sanctions*. These are themselves related to other personal characteristics such as age, job tenure, income level, and specific self-esteem, and to organizational variables like the compensation plan base, promotion opportunities, or recognition (Ingram and Bellanger 1983).

Task characteristics

Salesperson behavior is also shaped by the characteristics of their task. Such factors are sometimes easily controlled by management and are part of its control levers, for example, initiation of structure (i.e. the precision with which the task has been defined and the degree of autonomy given to a salesperson to accomplish the task), and the degree of potential job conflicts implied by the task (Hackman and Oldham 1980). Others are likely to be inherent to the sales job and cannot be easily manipulated by sales managers, such as task variety, complexity, and significance.

Task *variety* is likely to require a large range of skills and activities. Task *complexity* requires various complex tasks during sales interactions. Because of such task variety and complexity, under these circumstances, salespeople perceive more role ambiguity and have a lower understanding of their territory sensitivities to their own activities. Job challenge (implied by task variety and complexity) and variety, however, have been found to have an effect on intrinsic dimensions of instrumentality and motivation (Teas 1981; Tyagi 1982; 1985a; 1985b). *Task significance* is the extent to which performing a job has an impact on other people's lives. Job importance has been found to have an effect on intrinsic dimensions of instrumentality and motivation, but not on expectancy estimates (Tyagi 1982; 1985a; 1985b).

Organizational characteristics

A firm and its environment are likely to directly and indirectly influence sales performance. As shown in Chapter 1, management exerts direct and indirect influence on the behavior and performance of its sales force. Direct influence can be exerted through management's control levers, and this can affect salespeople's motivation, competencies, and perceptions. Performance can also be affected by organizational factors that are generally beyond sales management control, such as the firm's advertising campaigns, or the market share already achieved. The performance of the sales force is also subject to work group influences, and/or organizational commitment.

The *influence of informal work groups* on work productivity has long been recognized. The effects of such groups, which thrive within an organizational formal structure, often surpass the effects of formal goal setting and reward structures (Roethlisberger and Dickson 1946). In fact, informal groups develop norms that exert powerful influences on motivation, performance, and job satisfaction of the members of an organization. These norms may enhance or hinder organizational goals (Doyle, Pignatelli, and Florman 1985).

Salespeople who experience a high level of *organizational commitment* typically believe in, and adopt the values and goals of their firm. They are generally willing to deploy considerable levels of effort to enhance the welfare of the whole organization, and they typically intend to stay in this organization (Mowday, Steers, and Porter 1979). Research suggests that low levels of organizational commitment have negative consequences for salespeople and their firm. Inversely, highly committed salespeople are generally better performers, are more satisfied, and tend to generate lower dysfunctional turnover (Mathieu and Zajac 1990).

Environmental characteristics

The main relevant environmental factors that directly affect salespeople's behavior include economic and competitive characteristics, territory conditions (potential, supply/demand relationships, sales penetration rates, competition), and the conditions of the labor market.

Adverse *economic and competitive conditions* in a sales territory reduce (1) the actual territory sales sensitivities to a salesperson's activities, and (2) the salesperson's expected sensitivities to his/her own activities (or expectancies). The rationale for the first prediction is that it becomes more and more difficult to sell in those territories. In other words, given a certain level of effort quantity and quality, sales should decrease as the economic and competitive conditions deteriorate. As for the second prediction, it follows from the fact that salespeople are likely to be among the first to know about the prevailing economic and competitive conditions in their territories. Empirical research has found that their perceptions of increasing selling constraints are negatively related to expectancy estimates (Teas 1981).

In the same way, *sales territory characteristics* affect the two same types of territory sensitivity to selling efforts, positively when sales territory potential increases, and negatively when the sales penetration rates already achieved in a territory increases. Bearing in mind that the difference between a territory sales potential and the sales level already achieved is the territory's untapped sales potential, one could expect that larger territory's untapped sales potential correspond to: (1) higher actual sales sensitivities to a salesperson's activities, and (2) higher expectancy estimates. Such relationships have been actually found in empirical research (see, for example, Beswick and Cravens 1977).

Labor market conditions are also likely to have a strong impact on how salespeople evaluate equity. Under tight labor market conditions for the firm, they generally compare themselves with other individuals whose equity ratios are perceived to be more favorable. Consequently, they tend to be less satisfied when the labor market conditions are more favorable for the firm.

Missions and command centers

Besides their own motivation and objectives, their personal characteristics, competencies, skills, and knowledge, and their decision processes, salespeople must carry out their tasks and take the lead in establishing, maintaining, and nurturing customer relationships. Selling has been recognized as a complex mental process (Shepherd and Rentz 1990). In order to manage these relationships with customers and prospects, like other managers (including sales managers), salespeople have at their disposal a command center that also includes a dashboard and a set of control levers. A salesperson's command center is essentially based on a set of communication flows, information processing capabilities, and control levers (Darmon 1998a).

Dynamic relationship-building missions

This essentially consists of managing information and communication with customers and prospects on one hand, and with individuals at head office on the other (Figure 4.6).

Communication and information acquisition and processing are major ingredients of personal selling (Macintosh *et al.* 1992). Being part of a firm's marketing communication program, personal selling involves salespeople acquiring, processing, and disseminating marketing information effectively. A study of 568 purchasing agents found that processing, getting, and giving information best explained the difference between successful and unsuccessful salespeople (in decreasing order of importance) (Plank and Reid 1996). As a result, the personal selling function may be visualized as the management of personalized marketing relationships through effective information management.

Required information loads

Efficient relationship and time management can only result from effective information management. To manage their working time effectively, salespeople need information about their customers and prospects (in order to decide who to see, what time to call, which day of the week, etc.), routes, train and airline schedules, and so on. To allocate their time properly, they also need appropriate knowledge of customer responses to their own selling efforts, for various product lines and for different selling strategies (Lodish 1971). Obviously, the size of the information load that a salesperson in a given position should maintain depends on such factors as territory size, product technicality, or the responsibilities attached to a given sales position.

Required information processing

Generally, salespeople do more than just transmit raw information. They need to process it mentally in order to use it effectively (Williams, Spiro and Fine 1990; Weitz *et al.* 1986). They also need to process information to manage their time effectively. They must translate call timing requirements, travel times between accounts, and other relevant data into effective (if not "optimal") call schedules. They must process information they have on customers' likely responses to contact time, to make efficient allocations of their working time among customers, product lines, and other selling activities (Davis and Farley 1971; Lodish 1971). Fortunately, CRM applications now do a lot of this automatically.

Even more importantly, salespeople need to process raw information collected during sales calls to build lasting relationships with customers. They must constantly process information on customers' needs, requirements, constraints, and objections so they can select proper selling strategies, provide customers with convincing arguments, and devise adequate proposals and effective demonstrations (Leigh and McGraw 1989; Leigh and Rethans 1984; Leong, Bush, and John 1989; Sujan, Sujan, and Bettman 1988; Szymanski and Churchill 1990; Weitz, Sujan, and Sujan 1986; Macintosh *et al.* 1992). Finally, they need to process market information to which they are exposed into market intelligence by evaluating its accuracy, interpreting it, putting it in a suitable format, and transmitting it to management. This is an essential part of a salesperson's duties. Research suggests that CRM programs were less likely to be successful when sales forces were not actively involved in the process of gathering market and customer information (Pass, Evans, and Schlacter 2004).

Control levers

To do their job effectively, salespeople perform two essential mental processes: time management and relationship management (each one resulting in a number of activities). A first aspect of *time management* involves the organization of call schedules and selling trips over a certain period of time, and selecting the most appropriate routes to call on the various accounts. The sales force decision support system literature addresses the issue of finding optimal (or close to optimal) routes, work schedules, or call norms that allow the most efficient allocation of a salesperson's time among various activities (such as travels, customer contacts, and administrative duties). See, for example CALLPLAN (Lodish 1971). Time management is vital, as a salesperson is requested to make person-to-person calls to a large number of accounts scattered over an extended territory.

A second aspect of a salesperson's time management involves the decision to allocate their time among various selling and/or non-selling activities (such as selling different product lines, prospect versus customer calls, or selling versus market intelligence reporting to management). This has long been recognized in the sales management literature (see for example, Green 1987; Kerber and Campbell 1987; Weeks and Kahle 1990). Here again, the task may be so complex that it requires the use of sophisticated OR/MS techniques to be solved satisfactorily. This is the problem addressed by most sales effort (or time) allocation models (see, e.g., Davis and Farley 1971, and for a complete review, Vandenbosch and Weinberg 1993). This problem is as complex as a salesperson's selling tasks are varied. Consequently, it depends on how selling duties have been assigned to different salespeople and how their responsibilities have been defined.

Because time management results in various types of time allocation, it has a direct effect on the quantity of time (and effort) that can be devoted to relationship building. In contrast, *relationship management* is strongly linked to the quality of a salesperson's selling activities. This amounts to the distinction between working hard (effort quantity) and working smart (effort quality) (Sujan, Weitz, and Kumar 1994). Salespeople have a responsibility to maintain successful relationships with customers and prospects on the one hand, and with their home organization on the other. They typically consist of establishing new relationships with prospects, often by breaking existing relationships that prospects have already established with competing firms, and nurturing and reinforcing existing relationships with clients. Relationship selling has gained considerable importance over recent years, (Anderson 1996; Boulding *et al.* 2005). This aspect of relationship management is strongly dependent upon the type of relationships that management wants to develop with its clientele.

Salespeople must also maintain, improve, or initiate relationships with key people at head office such as their supervisors and the many people that may help them with their tasks. Secretaries, production, and technical staff, may provide help and support when dealing with clients and prospects. This second aspect of relationship management becomes more important as salespeople need more support from their home office to accomplish their tasks and with the increasing reliance on team selling (see for instance Moon and Armstrong 1994).

Sales positions vary depending on the relative importance of time management versus relationship management. At one end of the spectrum are sales positions where there is relatively little time management (e.g., in the case of a salesperson in charge of a few large accounts in one area, whose time management is limited to time allocations for better servicing his/her accounts). At the other end there are salespeople who sell a variety of product lines to accounts scattered over an extended geographical area. Here, time management is of the essence. In this case, the task is so complex that it may need the help of decision support systems (Zoltners, Sinha, and Zoltners 2001).

Dashboards

Salespeople's dashboards include all the indicators that allow them to know and assess their performance, and to compare this with their own expectations and with those of other members of the sales force. This dashboard may be structured and elaborate, or it may not. Its quality, however, influences a salesperson's ability to react adequately to managerial decisions.

Salespeople follow training programs in order to learn about customers' and prospects' needs, problems, buying processes, objectives, and constraints. Much of this training is devoted to teaching the most efficient ways to supply salespeople with this knowledge and/or on the skills for acquiring it (Chonko, Tanner, and Weeks 1993; Doyle and Roth 1992). In addition, salespeople obtain this information during their interactions with customers and prospects. They also need to secure up-to-date and accurate information from their own organization about product specification, prices, delivery times, and maintenance policies, and guarantees. As a result, they collect information from various company sources about products, inventory levels, production schedules, quotations, processes, and technical and other relevant information. Inversely, salespeople also maintain relationships with their home organization by supplying information: they transmit orders from customers and prospects; they report on their own activities and performance through call and customer reports. They are often asked to collect market information.

Customers' feedback

As they interact with customers, salespeople are in the best position to assess the effects their actions, gestures, or statements have on their clients. Depending on how they interpret those reactions, they generally respond almost immediately and adapt their selling tactics accordingly. More generally, they evaluate the quality of the relationship they are building with their customers. They can assess whether customers are satisfied with their work and with the services provided by their firm.

Management feedback

One may consider that the amount, type and quality of the information managers provide to salespeople are part of the management's control levers. These are discussed more fully in Part II of this book. However, they may also be considered to be part of a salesperson's dashboard. Salespeople receive feedback from management about various dimensions of their performance. The relevance of this information depends not only on the quantity and quality of the information provided, but also on its timeliness. In many cases, the value of some information decays over time. Consequently, salespeople must receive relevant information if this is to be of any use to them.

Environmental feedback

At a somewhat higher level, salespeople receive information about their environment, their clients, and territories. They generally use this information to predict environmental evolutions. They are likely to be exposed to relevant information on competition, changing market needs, or economic trends. This is the type of information that management wants to share with salespeoople, and that they strive to obtain, often with variable success.

Dynamics of sales force behavior

A sales force is more than a group of salespeople. It has a structure within which the tasks of every individual are defined. It is influenced by current managerial policies and practices that shape the sales force culture, typically a sub-culture within a firm. In addition, a sales force is always characterized by the turnover rate of its salespeople.

Structure and organization of the sales force

The organization of the sales force reflects the allocation of the selling responsibilities among its various individuals. There is an almost infinite number of ways to make such allocations. Geographical criteria (sales territories), the various product lines, the types of clients or product applications, customer sizes (key accounts), or any combination of these criteria in any order, are most frequently used for organizing a sales force (see Chapter 7).

Organizing a sales force also implies a specification of the type of salespeople's supervision, and consequently the controls used for managing the sales force. Tighter controls imply shorter spans of control for supervisors, and consequently, more supervisors (and/or supervision levels). This is why a sales force organization reflects the sales force control strategies followed by management.

Morale and culture

Sales force morale reflects the satisfaction levels salespeople generally experience toward their job and their firm as well as the feelings of equity or inequity they have towards other people (especially within their own sales force). Salespeople often meet during sales meetings and have ample opportunities to interact among themselves. Like in any other group, individuals who are dissatisfied may communicate their dissatisfaction to the rest of the group. Because of such interactions, a sub-culture generally develops which is specific to the sales force and different from (even if influenced by) the firm's culture.

Turnover

Sales force turnover and morale are often interrelated issues. Sales force turnover is a pervasive problem which affects more or less all sales forces. Companies that cannot retain more than fifty percent of new salespeople for more than a couple of years are not uncommon (Richardson 1999; Futrell and Parasuraman 1984). Even during economic downturns when turnover rates decrease substantially, they seldom fall below the five to seven percent levels. A sales executive poll has revealed that over fifty percent experienced average turnover rates of over 15 percent (Keenan 1993). Sales force turnover rates have been estimated at 27 percent, more than twice the national work force average (Richardson 1999). They vary widely across industries and companies (Creery 1986; Taylor 1993; Blausfuss, Murray, and Schollars 1992), reaching a high of 61 percent for car dealerships (Joetan and Kleiner 2004).

In addition, even though the costs of sales force turnover are difficult to estimate precisely (Mobley 1982; Darmon 1990b; Richardson 1999), sales managers generally agree that turnover is extremely costly. Researchers have identified and estimated the high direct costs of turnover in organizations, either in non-sales (Cawsey and Wedley 1979; Flamholtz 1974; Mirvis and Lawler 1977; Tuggle 1978) or sales contexts (Darmon 1990b; Richardson 1999). A chemical product firm has saved $10 million in direct costs since 1989 by bringing its sales turnover rate down from 15 percent to less than 7 per year (Kiesche 1997). Similar high cost estimates have been reported over the years (Weitz 1979; Williamson 1983; Learning International 1989; *Sales & Marketing Management* 1987).

Importance of turnover rates

Sales force turnover is defined as the rate at which salespeople leave the organization, due to promotion, resignation, retirement, or dismissal (Cron and DeCarlo 2006). In contrast, in the sales force research literature, it is generally limited explicitly or implicitly to people leaving voluntarily (Lucas *et al.* 1987) or its intentional counterpart, propensity to leave (Futrell and Parasuraman 1984; Jolson, Dubinsky, and Anderson 1987). It is important to consider the turnover problem in its entirety.

The sales personnel in a sales force evolves constantly. Salespeople may leave voluntarily because they have found better job opportunities in other companies. They may leave for new career opportunities, or because they have decided to change the course of their careers. This is especially the case when salespeople find the sales representative position too demanding, or when they are not overly successful at it, or when they cannot get a sense of self-actualization.

Salespeople are dismissed for many reasons, the most common of which is poor performance. A firm may also have to reduce the size of its sales force when the economic conditions do not warrant keeping so many people in the field, or when it changes the nature of its activities. Salespeople may also leave an active selling job because they are promoted to managerial positions within or outside the sales force. Promoting good sales performers to managerial levels has definite motivating consequences for the sales force. Promoting sales personnel is often a means of retaining the best sales performers and keeping a high level of morale in the sales organization. So, up to a point, this type of turnover cannot be avoided. Finally, salespeople may leave the sales force for "natural" reasons such as death, illness or retirement.

Five main factors have a direct effect on sales force turnover: the firm's environment, salespeople's characteristics, salespeople's satisfaction and motivation, salespeople's performance, and the firm's promotion and firing policies (Figure 4.7).

In addition, sales force turnover has a number of consequences that involve sometimes cost, but also, in some cases, opportunity gains. Depending on sales management's policies, sales force turnover, an essentially dynamic process, involves constant changes in the sales force and sales territory coverage. These changes may result either in decreased or sometimes in increased levels of performance and consequently, in positive or negative cost or gain variations. Contrary to commonly held beliefs, as will be seen later, sales force turnover does not systematically result in cost to a firm.

Factors that influence turnover

Most turnover research has been directed towards identifying the behavioral determinants of the decision to quit (Bluedorn 1982b; Mobley 1982; Steers and Mowday 1981). It frequently relies on the concept of employee withdrawal, which results in the decision to quit from the employee's point of view (Mobley 1977; Sager, Varadarajan, and Futrell 1988). Most research studies have tried to identify the determinants of turnover, especially environmental factors, salespeople's characteristics, the firm's policies, salespeople's motivation and satisfaction levels, and job-related factors (Busch and Bush 1978; Wells and Munchinsky 1985; Johnston *et al.* 1987; 1988; Kerber and Campbell 1987; Parasuraman and Futrell 1983; Weeks and Stark 1972).

Environmental factors

Several aspects of the sales force environment have been related to turnover. For example, turnover seems to be related to the type of product sold. During the first five years of employment, sales forces of consumer goods have the highest turnover rates, followed by service and industrial sales forces. In the same way, turnover has been found to be related to the type of selling task to be performed (Wotruba 1990) and to the sales organization.

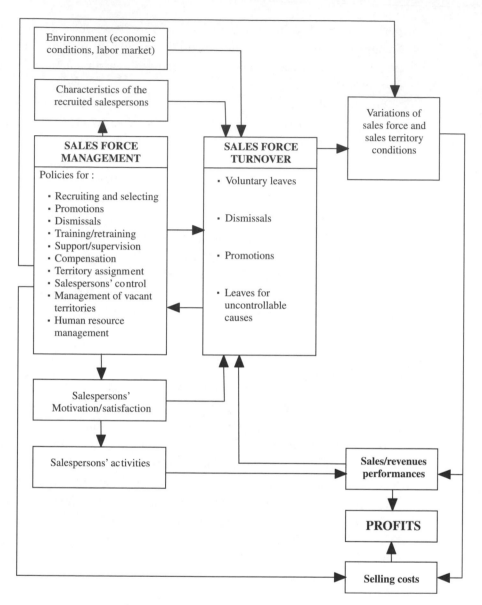

Fig. 4.7   Causes and consequences of sales force turnover

In many cases, however, it is likely that these relationships can be explained by other intervening factors such as education or training. The most influential variables influencing turnover rates are the economic climate and the labor market situation. This has been observed during the last few years. When the labor market offers the services of a limited number of people, firms have a tendency to make more attractive offers to attract individuals away from other firms. Because all the firms in a given industry tend to behave in the same way, the sales force turnover rates tend to increase. Inversely, when a large number of qualified people are on the labor market, as was the case a few years ago, the turnover rates tend to decrease.

Individual factors

As already mentioned, salespeople generally have different characteristics and bring their individual behavior and characteristics to the job. Salespeople with different profiles do not reach the same performance levels, and are not subject to the same promotion opportunities or firing threats. Experienced salespeople tend to leave the sales force for health reasons or through retirement.

Some research studies have investigated the relationships between turnover and the characteristics of salespeople (Mangione 1973). Age seems to be one of the best predictors of turnover: older salespeople have a lower propensity to quit than their younger counterparts (Munchinsky and Tuttle 1979; Munchinsky and Morrow 1980; Porter and Steers 1973; Price 1977).

The impact of job tenure is less evident. There is some support for the proposition that salespeople' propensity to quit decreases as the length of time spent within a firm increases, even though several studies could not show significant relationships. In fact, as tenure and age are likely to be correlated (salespeople with longer tenure tend to be older), it may well be that the weaker relationship that may exist between tenure and turnover is caused by the better-documented relationship between turnover and age. Although other personal characteristics have also been included in many sales force turnover and tenure studies, none has been found to be strongly linked to sales force turnover.

Organizational factors

Firms' policies   A firm's firing policies and practices have an obvious direct impact on sales force turnover. As the example of the IMC case study suggests, a firm's policies have at least three indirect impacts: (1) policies for recruiting and selecting new staff have an effect on the quality and performance of the sales force, as well as the speed at which salespeople are replaced, (2) the same policies have an impact on the sales force turnover rate through the characteristics of the newly recruited staff, and (3) the policies for promoting or firing, for providing initial training and retraining, supporting and supervising, compensating and assigning territories have also an impact on sales force turnover as they affect job satisfaction levels.

Job satisfaction   As discussed above, job satisfaction is also linked to the sales force turnover rate. Dissatisfied individuals tend to be less motivated (and consequently, to be worse performers). As a result, they often express an intention to quit, to find a more satisfying position elsewhere. Job satisfaction has several components that are affected by a firm's characteristics and decisions. For example, sales force turnover tends to be negatively related to satisfaction with pay, work, supervisors, and promotions. The most important factors for the sales staff are the firm's policies concerning promotions, dismissals, supervision, compensation, quota setting, and control procedures (Albers 1981).

Many studies have investigated the links between turnover and intrinsic and extrinsic job satisfaction (Lucas *et al.* 1987). No positive relationship has ever been found. For intrinsic job satisfaction, twenty-five out of twenty-eight studies have found a negative relationship, and only three have found to a non-significant relationship. As for extrinsic job satisfaction, the empirical evidence is less conclusive. Only eleven out of twenty-three studies have found a negative relationship, and twelve studies have reported non-significant relationships. On the other hand, research tends to support the existence of negative relationships between turnover and the various components of job satisfaction. For example, sales force turnover tends to increase when salespeople are dissatisfied with pay, work, supervisors and promotions (Newman 1974; Waters, Roach, and Waters 1976; Hom, Katerberg, and Hulin 1979; Miller, Katerberg, and Hulin 1979; Hom and Hulin 1981). The negative relationship between turnover and satisfaction with work seems to be the strongest of those relationships (Motowidlo 1983). In addition, stress (i.e. role conflict ambiguity, and overload) was found to be related to turnover (Dubinsky, Dougherty, and Wunder 1990).

Performance   Sales force turnover may well be also related to performance. Research suggests, however, that this relationship may not be simple. Some studies suggest that the turnover mainly affects very high and very low achievers. High achievers may be more likely to leave because they get promoted or are offered better opportunities elsewhere. Some studies conclude that this dysfunctional turnover is more frequent than functional turnover (Dreher 1982; Pavalko 1970). Other studies suggest that low achievers are more likely to quit: so there would be more functional than dysfunctional turnover (Keller 1984; Stumpf and Dawley 1981). The rationale is that low achievers should be more inclined to leave as they get discouraged and want to change jobs, or because they are dissatisfied with their current position (Wotruba and Tyagi 1991).

In addition, the firm itself may initiate the process by firing individuals who do not meet sufficient performance levels. Only a few studies have found no significant relationships between turnover and performance (Martin, Price, and Mueller 1981; Spencer and Steers 1981). These results suggest that there exists a curvilinear relationship between sales performance and turnover. High and low achievers should be more likely to quit the sales force (obviously, for different reasons) than average performers (McNeilly and Russ 1992).

Finally, there is an almost complete lack of research on causes of sales force turnover other than voluntary departure. For example, the characteristics of salespeople who are actually promoted to first level management and the rate at which salespeople are promoted in various kinds of organizations are questions that have yet to be researched. In the same way, very little is known about the practice of dismissal and about the reasons and the criteria used.

Conclusion

In this chapter, salespeople have been described as more or less independent agents, who strive to meet targets that have been assigned to them by their firm, but who strive also to satisfy their own personal objectives. As a result, understanding their behavior implies knowing their own objectives, perceptions, attitudes, motivation, as well as their decision-making processes.

A sales force is more than a group of individuals that hold selling functions in the same firm. Consequently, sales managers and their supervisors should always try to assess the impact of their decisions on the whole sales force. How this difficult task can be accomplished is the subject of the following chapter.

5 Sales managers: leaders of the dynamic management process

A frequent problem for large sales forces

The sales manager of an international firm selling office supply equipment followed a policy of promoting the best salespeople to managerial levels. The firm's human resource manager explained that there were several reasons for this policy. First, the prospect of being promoted was a powerful motivational device. Second, the newly promoted managers enjoyed high credibility with their salespeople because they were known to be among the best in the sales force. Third, as they were salespeople themselves, they had a thorough understanding of the job and the people they supervised.

However, when the sales manager formally assessed the performance of those people who had been promoted, it became clear that not all of them were being successful. In a significant number of cases, it became clear that the firm had exchanged one of its best salespeople for a poor regional sales manager!

Several causes could be attributed to this problem. First, the qualities that are essential for being a successful salesperson are not the same as those required for an effective leader and manager. There was no *a priori* reason why the promoted salesperson should have those required qualities. Second, promoted staff have only partial and incomplete knowledge to carry out their new duties effectively. Although they typically knew their own territory and had some knowledge of the other members of the sales force, they generally had insufficient information about the sales force, the firm, and its markets.

Following this analysis, the firm decided to alter its policy. Now, all salespeople who display the potential to be a manager are asked to follow an intensive management training program that has been specifically designed for the firm by an external training consultant. This program provides salespeople with the information and knowledge that the company and the consultant had identified as being essential for any manager. Only those who could successfully follow the program and be identified as potential leaders had a chance of being promoted.

Sales management positions are not easy to hold by any means. They involve the management and control of a number of salespeople who are more or less independent agents. These agents attempt to fulfill a mission among clients and prospects that are even more independent and less controllable. Sales managers' roles consist of shaping their sales forces and devising control programs that must develop customer loyalty (Liu and Leach 2001). The mission of sales managers consists of attempting to control entities (customers and prospects) whose actions are difficult to predict, using independent salespeople. Consequently, the position of sales manager is even more complex and difficult than that of a salesperson, as the above case suggests.

This chapter is devoted to the sales manager's leadership function. Like other managers, sales managers must have the necessary competencies to accomplishing their missions. As described in Chapter 1, the dynamic management process applies to all the management levels in a sales force (Figure 5.1). Most books on sales force management discuss the qualities and competencies that are essential for good salesmanship. Few discuss the aptitudes, qualities, and competencies that are required of sales managers. Nevertheless, management takes responsibility for the success or failure of a sales mission.

After considering the various aspects of a sales manager's competencies, this chapter considers the various resources that should be available to managers to effectively control the sales force.

Sales managers' competencies

Managerial decisions and behaviors reflect the personal characteristics of managers. Managers have personal needs and objectives. They have their own motivations, values and preferences. They develop their own perceptions and attitudes towards various aspects of a sales situation. They are risk-prone or risk-averse. In a given situation, risk-prone managers are likely to make decisions that are different from those of risk-averse managers. Research suggests that sales force executives tend to display short-term and risk-averse orientations when making such important decisions as increasing the size of the sales force (Sinha and Zoltners 2001).

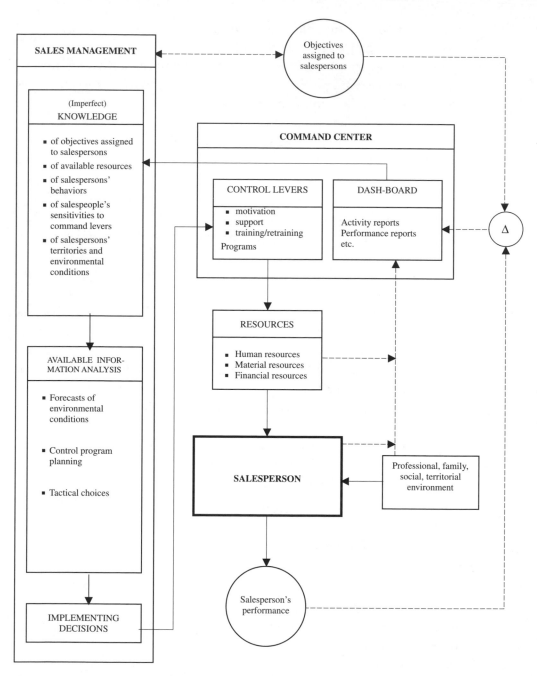

Fig. 5.1   Dynamic management of salespeople's activities

No one is born a competent sales manager, they have to be trained to be so. They must have acquired the knowledge that is necessary to fulfill their functions, and must demonstrate strong leadership qualities. They must also have demonstrated ability to analyze and process information, as well as to make and implement decisions. Managers are also competent when they have demonstrated their ability in a wide variety of selling situations.

As in the case of the office equipment company described above, these competencies do not exactly match those required from salespeople, which explains why successful salespeople do not necessarily become efficient sales managers.

Knowledge bases

Returning to the pilot metaphor of Chapter 1, just like a pilot knows how to control an aircraft, a sales manager needs the expertise to direct a sales force. In addition to this general expertise, pilots need information on the routes they could follow, and weather reports. Depending on the availability of this information (as well as its collection costs), management selects the most appropriate control devices, those that it wants to include in its dashboard as well as those that will be used as control levers.

Managers cannot effectively manage a system unless they know how it works. They must have a good idea of how a system is likely to react to various possible actions on their part. In the case of IMC, described in Chapter 1, sales managers had information about the sales force, but lacked the knowledge of how salespeople would react to a new compensation plan. In the same way, managers must be aware of current business trends, evolutions in their own industry as well as in their customers' markets (e.g., an important promotional campaign launched by a major competitor). In addition, sales managers must have precise information about their missions, and must be able to process this information and make appropriate decisions.

Characteristics of knowledge bases

Like those of salespeople, sales managers' knowledge bases are characterized by their size, quality, and nature.

Size and quality

Sales managers' competencies are limited by the amount and quality of the knowledge they have acquired and their effectiveness depends on the size and quality of their information base. Some of this knowledge is partly shared with sales staff, but a substantial part is specific to the sales management function.

Many firms spend substantial amounts of money on training their salespeople, but few of them provide their sales managers with the essential training they need for accomplishing their managerial functions effectively.

Nature of knowledge

Sales managers' have acquired core, industry-specific, and firm-specific knowledge. This knowledge concerns elementary or aggregated elements.

Core, industry-, and firm-specific knowledge   Core knowledge is essential to fulfill a sales management function. It can be applied to any sales management position, irrespective of the firm, for example, the general expertise that a sales manager has acquired for managing a team of salespeople. Industry-specific knowledge applies to all firms within a given industry (e.g., pharmaceutical product companies), and only to this industrial sector. Firm-specific knowledge can be used only for the management of the sales force of a given company. In terms of the transaction cost theory (Williamson 1975), this knowledge constitutes company-specific assets (e.g., it may be knowledge of the procedures followed by a company, its sales territories, and salespeople).

When sales managers have strong core knowledge (i.e. applicable to all sorts of situations), they can be assigned quite varied missions. Consequently, these managers have a higher value on the labor market. However, if managers have developed essentially firm-specific knowledge, they are likely to lose some mobility and value on the labor market.

Elementary and aggregate-level knowledge   A sales manager's elementary knowledge has some bearing on individual salespeople and/or specific sales territories. Sales managers have at their disposal some information on territory sensitivities to salespeople's activities and efforts. In the same way, sales managers have (and utilize) information about individual salesperson's sensitivities to managerial control levers, including preferences for rewards, aversion for efforts, sanctions, and risk, and consequently, their likely reactions to various control instruments. Aggregate knowledge bears on aggregated sets of elements, that is, on the whole market (an aggregation of sales territories) or on the whole sales force (a grouping of all salespeople).

Like salespeople in their own territories, sales managers select appropriate control levers in response to information and knowledge acquired through their dashboards (i.e. the information flows that have been organized to provide them with the necessary relevant information). As a result, the quality of their management depends to a large extent on the relevance and accuracy of the information they obtain from their dashboards.

It may be useful to classify a sales manager's information and knowledge by crossing these two characteristics (Table 5.1). The knowledge elements provided in each cell of the table should be considered as exemplars of the type of knowledge concerned, and should not be considered as exhaustive. As will be seen in Chapter 10, they may be useful for designing an adequate training program for sales managers.

Several practical implications may be drawn from Table 5.1. First, the table highlights the wide diversity of the knowledge and information that is required from sales managers. Obviously, in practice, it is impossible to enjoy complete and "perfect" knowledge, but managers must try to obtain as much relevant information as possible.

Second, compared with Table 4.1, this table highlights the relative specialization of the knowledge bases of the various persons involved in the selling process (top-level and intermediate sales managers, and salespeople). This relative specialization results from the various role definitions. Consequently, the size and content of the respective information bases remain partly under the sales manager's control. They depend on the selected sales force organizational design and on the definition of the decision spaces at the different hierarchical levels. For example, in a highly decentralized organization, in which individuals enjoy a wide responsibility for their own activities and performances, one may expect the overlapping knowledge at different hierarchical levels to be minimal. Inversely, a centralized organization requires substantial amounts of information to be conveyed to upper level command centers. This implies some overlapping knowledge and information among the various hierarchical levels.

Third, sales managers never possess every relevant piece of information. They differentially develop their knowledge bases in the different cells of Table 5.1. Psychologists call it an individual's cognitive structure. For example, when sales managers develop their aggregated information and knowledge at the expense of elementary knowledge, they are probably more inclined to manage the sales force at a macro-level rather than a micro-level (the latter being possibly delegated to lower management levels). However, when sales managers are strongly oriented toward developing elementary knowledge in their knowledge bases, they are likely to engage in micro-management, sometimes at the expense of the macro management of the

Table 5.1. Sales management's knowledge bases

Elementary knowledge (about every salesperson/sales territory/product)

Core (or general) knowledge about:

Buyer behavior
- General knowledge of buyer behavior

Selling processes
- General knowledge of the selling function
- General knowledge of selling and negotiation processes (basic cognitive scripts)

Salespeople
- General knowledge of salespeople's behavior
- Knowledge of salespeople's management and coaching

Industry-specific knowledge about:

Buyer behavior
- Knowledge of buyer behavior specific to the firm's industrial sector

Selling processes
- General knowledge of the selling function specific to the firm's industrial sector
- General knowledge of selling and negotiation processes in the firm's industrial sector: Basic cognitive scripts

Salespeople
- Knowledge of salespeople's behaviors in the firm's industrial sector

Firm-specific knowledge about:

Every salesperson
- Knowledge of their personal characteristics
- Knowledge of their backgrounds
- Knowledge of their behaviors
- Knowledge of their activities
- Knowledge of their sales and market objectives
- Knowledge of their personal objectives
- Knowledge of their responsibilities (freedom to negotiate, leeway for personal initiatives, etc.)
- Knowledge of their performance levels
- Knowledge of their remuneration levels

Every sales territory
- Knowledge of sales potentials
- Knowledge of market penetration and market shares
- Knowledge of competitive inroads
- Knowledge of specific territory conditions
- Knowledge of territory environment

Every product line
- Knowledge of technical characteristics
- Knowledge of prices
- Knowledge of competitive advantages
- Knowledge of weaknesses compared to competition

The firm
- Knowledge of firm's policies and procedures
- Knowledge of firm's specific programs (compensation plans, quota plans, motivation, support, training, etc.)

Aggregate knowledge (about the whole sales force/markets)

Core (or general) knowledge about:

Customers and markets
- Knowledge of the market environment (heavy economic trends)
- General declarative knowledge (customer types, salespeople' categories, etc.)

The sales force
- Procedural knowledge of control strategies to be followed with every type of salesperson in the firm's industrial sector

Competing firms
- Knowledge of competing firms in the firm's industrial sector (products, marketing strategies, procedures, etc.)

Table 5.1 (*cont.*)

Market sales
- General procedural knowledge of selling strategies to be followed with every type of client

The sales force
- General procedural knowledge of control strategies to be followed with every type of salesperson

Industry-specific knowledge about:

Customers and markets
- Knowledge of environmental trends in the firm's industrial sector (heavy economic trends)
- Declarative knowledge applicable to the firm's industrial sector (customer types, salespeople types, etc.)

Market sales
- Procedural knowledge of the selling strategies to be followed with every customer type in the firm's industrial sector

Firm-specific knowledge about:

The sales force
- Knowledge of its structure/organization
- Knowledge of its (aggregate) behaviors
- Knowledge of its (aggregate) activities
- Knowledge of areas of responsibility (freedom to negotiate, leeway for personal initiatives, etc.)
- Knowledge of sales force objectives
- Knowledge of sales force performances (sales, customer satisfaction levels, etc.)
- Knowledge of sales force compensation plans

The markets
- Knowledge of market sales potentials
- Knowledge of market penetration and market shares
- Knowledge of competitive inroads
- Knowledge of specific market conditions
- Knowledge of market environment
- Specific declarative knowledge (customer categories, sales force's salesperson types, etc.)
- Specific procedural knowledge (strategies to be followed with every firm's customer type, management of every salesperson type, etc.)

whole sales force. Although one could argue about what is the cause or the effect, in practice, sales managers must strive to achieve some efficient balance between the different parts of their knowledge bases.

Finally, the distinction among sales managers' core, industry-, and firm-based knowledge has more than just an academic interest. It reveals the extent of a sales manager's competencies. As managers have developed core industry-specific knowledge relative to firm-specific knowledge, they tend to be more competent. Nevertheless, they are likely to be more mobile than their colleagues with less industry-specific knowledge, because their competencies are likely to be sought by other firms, especially those in the same industrial sector.

Specific knowledge

Ideally, sales managers should possess at least the same core and industry-specific, as well as elementary and aggregated information as their salespeople. This shared information constitutes a huge knowledge base. It includes information about the characteristics of every sales territory for which a manager is responsible, about customer behavior, selling processes, the firm (its products, procedures, strategies, and policies), as well as the same declarative and procedural knowledge of the salespeople they supervise. Only the detailed information that salespeople (should) possess about individual accounts and their own territory may not be shared with management. In practice, sales managers are unlikely to have the same quality of information on sales territories as salespeople, because salespeople obtain it first hand through direct and constant contact with their customers. Consequently, in this context, there is always some information asymmetry in favor of salespeople.

In addition to the knowledge and information they share with salespeople, sales managers must possess quite specific knowledge in order to effectively manage the sales force, for example, they must know how to manage a sales team, and understand the role and purpose of the sales management function. They should have information about the market at the aggregate level and its sensitivities to selling efforts, about the behavior of their sales staff, as well as extensive declarative and procedural knowledge that is specific to sales management.

Managerial skill

Because they direct, coach, and motivate a sales team, sales managers need general managerial skills. They must have a clear and thorough understanding of the sales management function, of the duties and responsibilities it entails, as well as the limits that have been placed on their authority and initiative by upper management.

Salespeople's behavior knowledge

In order to select appropriate control programs, sales managers must understand the fundamentals of salesperson behavior in general, and especially that of the typical salesperson employed in their sales force. As much as possible, managers must know their personal characteristics, history, objectives, personality traits, strengths and weaknesses, behavior patterns, activities, and performance levels, so that they can make accurate predictions about individual reactions to various control elements. Ideally, managers should be able to predict how every salesperson in the sales force will react to increased rewards (compensation, promotions, or incentives), and be aware of the extent to which they are risk-, sanction-, and effort averse, to select the most effective control devices. At the aggregate level of the whole sales force, this knowledge is especially useful when devising sales force control programs.

Market knowledge

In addition to knowledge about each individual sales territory, managers must have extensive information about the market as a whole. They need to have data such as market potentials, sales potentials, penetration rates, market shares, the relative positions of competitors, and any specific conditions and environmental factors, such as economic trends. They must be capable of understanding the needs and problems of the market place.

Sales managers must have a good grasp of the market sensitivity to selling efforts and activities. At the elementary level, they should be able to accurately assess how every sales territory is likely to react to additional selling effort from the salesperson in charge. At the aggregate level, sales managers should also be able to assess how the whole market (or market segment) is likely to react to various levels of activity from the sales force. For example, to properly appreciate the optimal sales force size, management needs to predict how sales, costs and profits would be altered by the addition (or deletion) of various numbers of salespeople to the current sales force.

Declarative knowledge

In order to make adequate strategic and tactical decisions, sales managers must have developed their own base of extensive declarative and procedural knowledge (Weitz, Sujan, and Sujan 1986; Leigh and Rethans 1984; Leigh and McGraw 1989). Just as salespeople develop the ability to categorize customers and selling situations, sales managers develop meaningful categorizations that help them to deal with each type of situation adequately. They develop categorizations for customers, prospects and selling situations. They also categorize sales functions and salespeople.

Categorization of selling functions   In the preceding chapter, it was seen, according to the cognitive selling paradigm (Shepherd and Rentz 1990) that salespeople's performance is linked to the quality of their declarative knowledge (i.e. the quality of their selling situation classification scheme) and to the extent of their procedural knowledge (i.e., their ability to deal effectively with each category of customers) (Sujan, Sujan, and Bettman 1988). In the same way, the performance of sales managers is linked to their declarative knowledge concerning sales positions (i.e. their recognition of various types of selling functions) and of the corresponding procedural knowledge (i.e. management's practices implied by each category or type of sales function). Adequate managerial declarative and procedural knowledge is essential for specifying a sales force mission, because this implies assigning *de facto* the defined salesperson's function into given categories. Consequently, managers need to apply the proper specific procedural knowledge to every type of sales function they have created in their own sales force.

There are a wide variety of sales functions in the economy, and not surprisingly, classification of these have been regularly proposed by sales management researchers. Over one hundred methods for differentiating among sales positions have been recognized (Jolson 1977). Some typologies have been frequently reported in the sales force management literature over the past decades (McMurry 1961; Newton 1973; Moncrief 1986; Darmon 1998b).

According to the latter classification scheme, any sales function can be fully characterized along the three dimensions discussed in Chapter 4 (i.e. the relative importance of time versus relationship management, the size of the information load, and the sophistication and complexity of information processing required by this position). Note that all activities that have already been identified (Moncrief 1986; Lamont and Lundstrom 1974) are covered by these three underlying dimensions (Darmon 1998b). Obviously, only a subset of those activities generally pertains to a specific sales function. In contrast, however, any selling position displays the three underlying mental processes (dimensions) identified above, although with varying degrees of importance.

The variance displayed by sales functions on the three identified conceptual dimensions provides a useful basis for devising a classification of selling functions. For example, by characterizing each function as low or high relative to others on each dimension, every sales function falls into one of the eight-cell classification shown in Table 5.2.

The typical functions falling into each cell may be characterized successively as partnership builders, relationship builders, adaptive sellers, adaptive planners, sedentary informers, mobile informers, sedentary servicers, and mobile servicers.

As Table 5.2 suggests, this classification can encompass the whole spectrum from industrial or hi-tech sales functions to internal order-takers. This classification does not rely on job titles and/or specific industries, but on the relative importance and complexity of the mental processes

Table 5.2. A classification of sales positions with a description of a typical position falling into each category

	Relatively extensive/complex information processing		Relatively simple information processing	
	Relatively heavy information load	*Relatively light information load*	*Relatively heavy information load*	*Relatively light information load*
Relatively little time management	**Partnership builders** Sales positions implying highly technical selling of rather undiversified product lines/services to a few accounts Hi-tech industrial selling (few accounts) National Account Managers	**Adaptive sellers** Sales positions implying elaborate long-purchase-cycle selling processes (e.g., durables) to a diverse, self-selected clientele Internal advisors salespeople (furniture, appliance, automobile selling)	**Sedentary informers** Sedentary sales positions implying simple selling processes and extensive information provision on standard product line to prospective customers Telemarketing salespeople	**Sedentary servicers** Sedentary sales positions implying simple selling processes, but the provision of basic services to customers Internal order taker (sales clerks)
Relatively extensive time management	**Relationship builders** Sales positions implying highly technical selling of highly diversified product lines/services to a large number of accounts Industrial selling (large number of accounts) International negotiators	**Adaptive planners** Sales positions implying elaborate selling processes for a wide variety of long-purchase-cycle product lines to diverse (and not pre-identified) customers Door-to-door selling (encyclopedias, life-insurance, etc.)	**Mobile informers** Field sales positions implying simple selling processes, but the provision of information on a wide variety of product lines to a large number of prospective clients Medical retailers External order takers	**Mobile servicers** Field sales positions implying simple selling processes, but the provision of basic service to customers Delivery salespeople Store demonstrators Merchandisers

Note: The sales positions in each cell are only exemplars of positions falling into each category.

characteristic of a selling function. Consequently, it is conceivable that sales functions with similar titles could fall into different cells, if they imply different processes. In the same way, as a selling function evolves over time (Wotruba 1991), it is quite possible for this function to change category in the proposed classification.

Categorization of salespeople   In the same way, sales managers also learn to categorize their salespeople depending on their behavior, performance, or any other relevant criteria. This process may develop informally through experience, or be based on systematic analytical procedures. For example, some firms classify their sales staff into several groups based on their performance to try to find common characteristic that are unique to all the salespeople in that group. This information can be used, for example, at the recruitment stage, to try to hire salespeople who can be predicted to be high performers.

Categorization of selling strategies   As seen below, sales managers select selling and control strategies that may vary along several dimensions. Each type of strategy (declarative knowledge) has is associated tools and control levers (procedural knowledge). As a result, managers select their control devices from the right tool kit, that is, tools that are compatible with one another.

Procedural knowledge

Just like salespeople, sales managers develop procedural knowledge that specifies how they should behave with each type of salesperson in each type of situation, in order to achieve their goals. They, too, develop cognitive scripts, those sequences of actions that must be taken in every specific situation and which constitute their procedural knowledge. As can be surmised, managerial control procedures cannot be the same, irrespective of the cell in which the designed selling functions fall. For example, some procedural knowledge can be systematically associated with some declarative knowledge (Table 5.3).

In the same way, identifying groups of salespeople with homogeneous behaviors, characteristics, and performances within the sales force has obvious implications for recruiting, supporting, coaching, and supervising salespeople. For each group, sales managers must be able to identify those control strategies that are applicable and efficient.

Table 5.3. Sales management's procedural knowledge concerning selling functions

Procedural knowledge applicable to partnership or relationship builders, as well as to sedentary or mobile informers:

These salespeople are as efficient as:

- They keep up-to-date information bases
- They have the ability and motivation to collect and use this information
- They have strong communication skills
- They have good memories and abilities to retrieve the information they need
- They have an ethical drive to use this information appropriately

Procedural knowledge applicable to partnership or relationship builders, as well as to adaptive planners and sellers:

These salespeople are as efficient as:

- They have strong information processing abilities (high intelligence level, training, creativity, analytical skills)
- They are interested and motivated by intellectual tasks

Procedural knowledge applicable to relation builders, adaptive planners, mobile informers and servicers:

These salespeople are as efficient as:

- They have strong organizational skills
- They are mobile
- They are interested and motivated to travel and work away from their firm
- They are interested and motivated to perform a large number of different tasks as part of their function

Sales managers' abilities

In order to manage the sales force effectively, sales managers need more than knowledge. They must possess the right qualities and have developed adequate skills and abilities. More specifically, they must have developed leadership qualities and decision-making skills.

Leadership qualities

Leadership is the ability of a superior to influence the behavior of subordinates and persuade them to willingly follow a desired course of action. There are several conceptualizations of sales supervision and leadership, namely, exchanges between a leader and sales staff, transformational leadership, and behavioral self-management (Ingram *et al.* 2001). The type of leadership exercised by sales managers translates into specific control strategies, and consequently, into definite control programs.

Exchange leadership

Although it has been in existence for a number of years, the exchange conception of leadership (also called LMX), has only recently been applied to sales force management (Lagace 1991; Strutton, Pelton, and Lumpkin 1993). It relies on communication exchanges between managers and salespeople and on the interactions that management and salespeople have with one another. The idea is not for a manager to prescribe standardized behaviors, but to adapt to every situation and salespeople specificities (Shoemaker 1999). Exchange leadership allows both parties to build mutual confidence. Research in this area suggests that mutual trust and confidence between salespeople and their managers has a direct impact on the exchange relationships between the two parties (DelVecchio 1998), and creates positive perceptions and attitudes from salespeople towards their job as well as producing higher performance levels (Klein and Kim 1998). This conception of leadership is especially relevant at a time when firms emphasize the importance of building long-term relationships with customers and when mutual trust and confidence in relationships should be the rule (Beverland 2001).

Transformational leadership

Transformational leadership refers to a charismatic and inspirational type of leadership that is guided by a vision and a mission (Dubinsky *et al.* 1995). Transformational leaders intellectually stimulate others by constantly demonstrating new ways to do things or tackle problems. They are change agents. Transformational leaders give consideration and personal attention to their employees. A major characteristic of such leadership behavior is that subordinates aspire to super ordinate goals rather than focusing on narrow personal goals. This contrasts with the traditional approach of transactional leadership. This involves a contract that specifies what every employee must achieve and what they will earn once they have achieved this goal (e.g., earning a bonus for exceeding targets). In contrast with the latter leadership approach, where employees seek to achieve pre-established goals, transformational leadership induces salespeople to reach super ordinate goals (Dubinsky 1998).

Behavioral self-management

As its name implies, behavioral sales management requires planning, behaviors, activities, evaluations, rewards and sanctions that employees enforce themselves (Sauers, Hunt, and Bass 1990). This empowerment vision of leadership is especially attractive for salespeople, given the difficulty, or sometimes the impossibility, of constant individual super-vision. As a result, self-imposed discipline may be a profitable solution. It is an accepted fact that employees are more enthusiastic and committed to their work when they feel responsible for their activities. It is relatively easier to provoke lasting behavioral changes when those changes are fully accepted by salespeople than when they are imposed on them by management.

Decision-making abilities

Sales managers develop a leadership style and select control strategies. In order to make control decisions in the framework of their dynamic management process, sales managers must be able to analyze external and internal situations, to make predictions about future environmental conditions, to make strategic and tactical decisions, and to implement those decisions successfully.

Ability to analyze

To make such strategic and tactical decisions, sales managers must constantly analyze their situation. Not only should they watch the external environment (markets and customers) and their own impact on this environment (sales, market shares, etc.) in order to assess their perfor-mance, they also watch how individual salespeople and the whole sales force evolves over time. In order to understand situations and problems as they arise, they need to analyze relevant information and to process that information into knowledge.

Through current situation analysis, sales managers must also have the ability to create new knowledge that is essential for carrying a dynamic management of the sales force, and consequently, enhance their own competencies. These abilities are instrumental for predicting and anticipat-ing the outcomes of possible courses of action, in order to select the best one. They are also needed for acting and reacting effectively, whatever the circumstances. Consequently, sales managers need the ability to process large amounts of information. They must be able to synthesize information that they collect, even informally, through observing salespeople in the field or through other means. They must process this information over short periods of time, because more than ever, market successes depend on management's reaction speed.

It is recognized, however, that individuals can only process a limited amount of information at a time. This is called "bounded rationality" by economists. The maximum amount of information that individuals can process depends on their personal characteristics. Most successful sales managers tend to be able to process larger amounts of data than their less successful counterparts.

Ability to predict environmental changes

Sales managers must develop their ability to anticipate events in their environment. They must constantly scan the market to find out what is happening in as short a time as possible. The rationale of this behavior is to take advantage of any arising market opportunity, before competitors have had a chance to react. A quick reaction on their part can avoid meeting difficult situations later on. Current information about the market environment is necessary to forecast what will happen in the market place in a more or less distant future. Sales managers must draw up plans and prepare their actions based on where they anticipate the market will be at the implementation time − more an art than a science!

Most of the recent successful market innovations, such as amazon.com, Apple, Microsoft, to name but a few, have resulted from leaders that have been the first to recognize and anticipate market opportunities and future market trends. It is essential that sales managers develop the ability to identify and predict major market trends. Sales managers cannot afford to make erroneous forecasts, because sales targets are derived from them. An overly optimistic forecast by a sales manager results in targets that salespeople cannot meet. This may have a negative impact on the compensation, job satisfaction, and morale of the sales force. On the other hand, a pessimistic forecast will result in low targets that will be met easily, but will result in lower revenue and higher selling costs for the firm.

Strategic and tactical decision-making abilities

Sales managers are essentially decision makers (Lilly, Porter, and Meo 2003). They must make a large number of decisions, some of them very important, such as the design of control procedures and programs. They include, among others, decisions concerning the sales force compensation plan, motivation and incentive programs, recruitment procedures, the sales force organization and territory design decisions, as well as training and retraining. As discussed below, an important dimension of a control strategy is its level of centralization versus decentralization. Depending on the centralization-decentralization level of the process, managers provide salespeople with more or less extended decisional spaces, and give salespeople more or less detailed objectives, directives, and procedures to follow.

Besides such strategic sales force control decisions, managers must make a number of less important decisions on a daily basis. These concern the actual implementations of the above-mentioned control programs — the tactical sales force control decisions. Tactical decisions differ from strategic decisions in their shorter time scale, and their limited scope. However, they require the same planning process as strategic decisions. In any case, they never supersede strategic long-term objectives, but contribute to a long-term strategy by addressing short-term considerations.

Decision implementation abilities

Making decisions is one thing. Implementing them satisfactorily is another. This is where leadership qualities come into play. Sales leaders are able to implement their plans and make sure that they are successfully implemented by the whole sales force. Competent sales managers have not only decision-making abilities, but are also leaders who can successfully implement those decisions in the field.

The function of the sales force manager

The knowledge, skills, and abilities discussed in the preceding paragraphs constitute sales management resources. Now, we turn to the questions of how these resources are actually used by sales managers in the framework of their dynamic management process. Sales management resources are used to carry out sales missions and apply managerial decisions within the framework of a selected sales force control approach.

Sales missions

The function and responsibility of a sales manager essentially consists of carrying out sales missions successfully. Any mission assigned to a sales manager has objectives that directly follow from the firm's marketing strategy. In addition, every mission requires some resource (time, human, or financial) that generally constitute constraints to management.

Objectives

Like salespeople, sales managers must have a clear understanding of the mission that they must fulfill for their firm. Sales force missions are typically derived from a well thought-out strategy and marketing plan. A sales force is essentially a powerful tool that firms use for face-to-face communications with its markets and distribution channels. Consequently, the missions assigned to a sales force must remain within the realm of its capabilities. It must play a coherent role with the other elements of the marketing program and contribute to the general short- and long-term objectives of the firm. (Note that in practice, the relationships between the marketing and the selling functions are often strained (Rouziès *et al.* 2005).)

Being a communication tool, sales forces are generally assigned a role and a mission that is defined within the firm's marketing communication program, along with advertising, public relations, sales promotion, other direct communication (mail, e-mail advertising, and sponsorship programs). This is called Integrated Marketing Communication or IMC (Kitchen and Pelsmaker 2004; Duncan and Caywood 1996).

Depending on the selected strategy, a firm must carefully define the kind of relationship it wishes to build with customers from various segments. Following the current trend, it may decide to build strong, long-lasting, and mutually profitable relationships with selected customers or key accounts. In this case, the mission to be assigned to the salespeople in charge of such accounts is to work toward the development of relevant solutions for solving customers' problems and to build mutual trust and co-operation.

Alternatively, if the firm's communication strategy consists of ensuring that all customers and prospects are fully informed of the potential and characteristics of its products, the mission that should be given to the sales force is to act as the firm's information agents at meetings with customers and prospects. Their main tasks should be to demonstrate the product and to keep customers informed of the firm's existing and new products. Other missions could be defined as well, if the firm's marketing communication role were different.

A simple example can illustrate how a firm allocates marketing communication resources between two of its major communication tools, advertising and personal selling (Figure 5.2).

Through advertising, marketers try to stimulate market demand for their products. The stimulation of market demand pulls goods along the distribution channels and the final consumers act as a pump by keeping goods moving. This is known as a *pull strategy*. For example, Michelin,

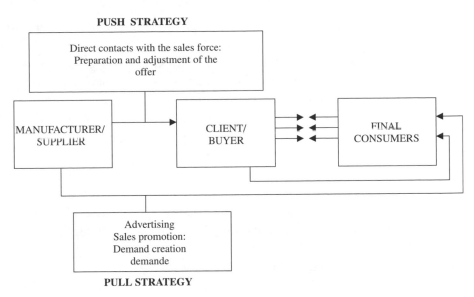

Fig. 5.2   Balance between pull and push strategies in a distribution channel

a worldwide leader and tire manufacturer, has a huge advertising budget for promoting its products to its final consumers, car owners. The objective is to develop positive attitudes, build brand awareness and notoriety among car owners to induce them to purchase, and if possible, insist on the Michelin brand when they purchase tires. In addition, the brand notoriety for Michelin's tires will eventually serve as an asset for cars that are equipped with such tires.

With personal selling, marketing managers attempt to make products flow into the distribution channel by persuading middlemen to keep inventories of their products and by ensuring that the products get their fair share of retailers' shelf space and resources. This strategy is a *push strategy*. Thus, Michelin attempts to induce car manufacturers to equip their new models with their tires. As a result, all the tire manufacturer's salespeople share the firm's objectives to push the tires in the distribution channels to deplete inventories at their firm's premises.

Push and pull strategies are complementary and must be balanced in a marketing program. Industrial firms have an incentive to deal with a given supplier when they know that the products they are going to use already have a strong positive image among final consumers. This positive image enhances the positive perceptions that the final consumer develops about these firms and their products. In the Michelin example, cars that are manufactured with Michelin tires may be perceived as more reliable and secure, provided that customers perceive Michelin as manufacturing good quality tires.

Intel and IBM are another example of firms using this type of strategy: the IBM portable ThinkPad has the label "Intel inside." Bang and Olufsen, the Danish manufacturer of high quality design audio equipment essentially relied on a push strategy when it entered the German market a few years ago. Sales started to pick up only when the firm decided to follow a more balanced strategy. This is why push and pull strategies should complement each other so that informed consumers can buy the advertised product at a point of purchase that is ready to supply it. The role and mission assigned to a sales force and its managers can only be defined within the framework of a well integrated marketing communication strategy.

Managing human resources in the sales force

As they fulfill their missions, sales managers must maintain (and even improve) the human resources in their sales force, that is, the number of salespeople and middle sales managers. They must always watch for, and try to prevent salespeople from experiencing a lack of motivation, satisfaction, or competence. Short of that, they may experience a high turnover of staff. In addition to the increased costs incurred, any decrease in the sales force may jeopardize the efforts of sales managers in their sales missions. Other resources (material and financial) are needed to achieve these goals.

Basic approaches to process implementation

One essential (lasting) decision that sales managers make before carrying their missions is to clearly and precisely define the decision space that they want to give to their sales staff, and consequently, the decision space they wish to retain for themselves. This decision defines the level of centralization/decentralization they want to implement in the sales organization, and consequently the level of direct or indirect control they will exert on the sales force. This decision determines the type of sales force control system that should be used.

Control systems

Control is one of the key problems of sales force management. It has been addressed in the descriptive professional as well as in the academic literature (Anderson and Oliver 1987; Cravens *et al.* 1993; Oliver and Anderson 1994; 1995; Stathakopoulos 1996; Challagalla and Shervani 1996; Bello and

Gilliland 1997; Darmon 1998a; Krafft 1999; Rouziès and Macquin 2002; Baldauf, Cravens, and Piercy 2001a; 2001b; 2005). In this context, a sales force control system has been defined as the set of procedures for monitoring, directing, evaluating, and compensating salespeople (Anderson and Oliver 1987). Although the research results in this area are largely inconsistent (Baldauf, Cravens, and Piercy 2005), sales force control approaches have been shown to affect performance (Agarwal 1999; Joshi and Randall 2001; Ramaswami 2002; Piercy, Cravens and Lane 2001; Cravens *et al.* 2004; Aulakh and Esra Gencturk 2000; Mengüç and Barker 2003).

Not surprisingly, a wide array of sales force control devices exist (Churchill, Ford, and Walker 1976b). From a managerial point of view, the sales force control problem may be stated as follows: what indicants of activities and/or performance should managers observe, and (based on those observations) which actions they should take in order to induce salespeople to work in the best interests of the firm? In practice, sales force dynamic management and controls are pervasive and relate to most aspects of sales operations. The training, motivation, coaching, supporting, and compensating of sales staff are part of overall sales force control (Stanton, Buskirk, and Spiro 1995, pp. 461–462). For management, controlling a sales force essentially consists of devising the most efficient methods to influence its salespeople.

The choice of specific control devices depends on the objectives of the mission assigned to sales management, as well as to the firm's and managers' control philosophy or approach. Management typically pursues several objectives that require multiple control devices with different characteristics. Each selected set of control devices and their use over time must be suited to the mission's objectives. In addition, the type of control approach that managers follow dictates the nature and quality of the information they need to exert this control.

Classifications of control approaches

Following different control theories, such as organizational theories, agency theory, or transaction cost analysis, sales force control systems have been typically characterized along different dimensions: formal versus informal, quantitative (or objective) versus qualitative (or subjective) control bases, outcome-based (or performance-based) versus behavior-based (or activity-based), and/or centralized versus decentralized controls.

Formal/informal

Formal controls are written, management-initiated mechanisms specifically aimed at influencing the activities of salespeople in the desired direction (Jaworski 1988; Jaworski and MacInnis 1989; Jaworski, Stathakopoulos, and Krishnan 1993). In contrast, informal controls are unwritten, worker-initiated mechanisms that influence behavior, such as self-control (Lawler 1976), "clan" control (Ouchi 1979), or cultural control (Wilkins and Ouchi 1983). Because sales force controls are typically management-initiated, formal controls seem to be more appropriate in this context.

Quantitative/qualitative

Quantitative controls are based on elements that can be measured easily (e.g., sales volumes or number of calls), while qualitative-based controls have more bearing on more subjectively assessed elements (such as the quality of a sales pitch). In practice, a survey of sales executives has shown that sales managers tend to rely on qualitative bases for evaluating and controlling sales forces. In addition, they use only a narrow set of quantitative bases, and evaluate salespeople over a narrow range of selling activities (Jackson, Keith, and Schlacter 1983).

Outcome- and behavior-based

Outcome-based control systems monitor final outputs (e.g., sales or profits). Such control systems are assumed to require minimal salesperson supervision, and simple performance measures and they may use, for example, a commission plan for sales force compensation. Outcome-based control has been qualified as liberal management whereby salespeople are independent entrepreneurs responsible for their own activities and performance. In other words, they imply that salespeople are given an extended decision space.

In contrast, behavior-based control systems monitor salespeople's activities (e.g., their call schedules and/or the quality of their sales presentations). Behavior-based controls monitor intermediate states in the process (such as sales activities). They require close supervision of salespeople, supervisors' interference with salespeople's activities (and consequently, a restricted decision space), and more complex and subjective evaluations of individual performances. In practice, control systems can be positioned somewhere on a continuum ranging from purely outcome-based to purely performance-based (Oliver and Anderson 1987; 1995).

Several recent studies have focused on the implications of various control philosophies for sales forces in terms of their outcome- versus behavior-based dimension. Whether it is considered through agency theory or transaction cost analysis, one can identify circumstances under which a firm should select an outcome- or an activity-based sales force control philosophy (Anderson and Oliver 1987). Thus, a series of propositions on the likely reliance on behavior- or outcome-based control systems have found some general empirical support. These studies, however, tend to reveal rather weak relationships (Oliver and Anderson 1995). To account for these weaknessess, researchers have added new control dimensions. For example, a reinforcement dimension that accounts for the rewards and sanctions built into control systems, as well as a distinction between the activity control of salespeople (i.e. daily activities) and capacity controls (i.e. control of a salesperson's competence and skills) have been added (Challagalla and Shervani 1996; 1997).

Thus, research suggests that behavior-based controls tend to be positively associated with salespeople's affective states, such as commitment to the firm, acceptance of authority, co-operation within a selling team, acceptance of evaluation systems and risk aversion, as well as with salespeople's intrinsic motivation (Oliver and Anderson 1994). A somewhat surprising result, however, is that the control system orientation might not be related to salespeople's selling strategies or performance (Cravens *et al.* 1993).

There is clear evidence, however, that most firms use hybrid forms of sales force control that includes outcome- and behavior-based elements simultaneously (Jaworski 1988; Ouchi and Maguire 1975; Oliver and Anderson 1995). Some plausible explanations as to why firms could possibly use opposite control philosophies simultaneously (e.g., for compensating salespeople with straight salaries and providing only loose supervision) have been proposed (Oliver and Anderson 1995). Although these authors recognize that firms use both types of control systems, they do not explain why in practice, one can observe the use of a wide array of outcome- and behavior-based control devices. For example, outcome-based controls run the gamut from sales quotas to commissions on sales or customer satisfaction measures. In the same way, behavior-based controls range from general call norms assigned to salespeople to canned sales presentations being imposed on them. In short, the outcome- or behavior-based control distinction provides little explanation of what induces a firm to select one (or several) specific device rather than another.

Centralized/decentralized

Although it may seem similar at first glance, the distinction between centralized and decentralized controls is somewhat different. As mentioned in Chapter 1, it focuses on the definition of salespeople's decision spaces for their various activities, and consequently, on the level of precision and details of the objectives assigned to them (those objectives being expressed either in terms of activities or performance). Under a highly centralized control system, management provides salespeople with very precise and detailed objectives (such as sales objectives for every product line and/or customer). Under a highly decentralized control system, salespeople are provided only with directional objectives (e.g., achieving as a high a customer satisfaction level or sales volume as possible).

Under a centralized control system, managers reduce the decision spaces of salespeople. It is based on the direct authority that managers exert on their salespeople. For example, when managers impose sales quotas per product line and per account, salespeople are left with the restricted choice of either trying to meet the objectives to please management, or refusing to do it and endure the negative consequences that will result.

Actually, sales control systems may range on a continuum, from fully centralized to fully decentralized systems. As discussed in Part II of this book, several factors may induce a firm to select a more centralized or decentralized control system, especially, the extent and quality of its knowledge base, as well as the quality/cost ratios of its dashboard elements.

A three-way classification of sales force controls

Although they are not completely independent from one another, the last three dimensions that characterize sales force control devices can be jointly used to classify all sales force control devices (Table 5.4). Outcome-based controls tend to be more decentralized than behavior-based controls, because in the former case, salespeople supposedly have more leeway for selecting their own activities, as long as they achieve their expected performance level. Nevertheless, the two concepts are far from being identical. As Table 5.4 shows, they imply quite different devices within the sales force control system.

Limitations of "classic" control approaches

The above-mentioned theories and conceptual frameworks for explaining sales force controls that have been described and discussed in the preceding paragraphs are somewhat complementary and each one captures some

Table 5.4. Example of sales force control devices according to the characteristics of the selected dynamic management strategy

	Outcome-based controls		Behavior-based controls	
	Quantitative (objective) elements	Qualitative (subjective) elements	Quantitative (objective) elements	Qualitative (subjective) elements
Centralized controls	• Sales quotas • Profit quotas • New business objectives Given for specific activities (e.g., for every product line, client, etc.)	• Customer satisfaction/loyalty • Long-term relationship building Objectives set for every client/prospect (or every group of clients/prospects)	• Enforced norms concerning the number of calls to clients/prospects, number of demonstrations, displays to be installed, etc, and/or on selling expenses	• Canned sales presentations imposed by management • Selling strategies imposed for certain types of clients/prospects
Decentralized controls	• Commissions on sales, profits, or market shares with the same or different rates depending on activities (e.g., product line selling)	• Evaluation/compensation/promotions based upon performance measures of: General customer satisfaction (loyalty, long-term relationship building) Directional objectives only	• Evaluation/compensation/promotions based upon - the number of calls to clients/prospects - the number of demonstrations or displays installed - the selling expenses	• Evaluation/compensation/promotions based upon - the quality of sales presentations - the quality of demonstrations - the choice of selling strategies (as perceived by management)

important aspect of sales force management. A vision that simultaneously captures all the relevant dimensions of those theories, however, is still lacking. One such attempt has integrated the choice by management of a specific control strategy to the conditions of the situation actually faced by the firm. It combines the observable character of salespeople behavior and performance as well as the sales territory sensitivities to salespeople's efforts (Stathakopoulos 1996). This proposed framework, however remains limited to the behavior- and outcome-based dimension of sales force controls.

In spite of this unique attempt at a synthesis, the above-mentioned theories have structured many sales force control research studies. They are not, however, devoid of limitations which have often been identified by the researchers themselves. These "classical" theories or conceptual frameworks are too simple to account for the complexity of the sales force dynamic management problem. As a result, mixed results and somewhat weak correlations may well be caused by some of the implicit assumptions on which most of these theories rely. Generally, these theories rely on at least three restrictive assumptions.

First, they all consider a control system as a homogeneous entity. In fact, sales force control systems are made up of several sub-systems. Although complementary, each sub-system plays a specific role in the overall control system. Sales force control problems faced by management are typically characterized by multiple objectives. It is not unusual for a firm to set sales and profit objectives for each product line to be sold in each salesperson's territory, as well as market share, market penetration, prospecting, or customer satisfaction objectives. This may explain why in practice, one can observe, for example, more complex compensation plan structures than those suggested by agency theory, or the use of more extensive sets of control devices (sometimes, from different approaches) in the same sales force.

Second, the sales force control system is often considered as a "black box." As seen previously, sales force controls are a complex influence processes. It is difficult to learn how to manage a sales force without a sound understanding of all the details of the control process. For example, few research studies have made the distinction between the *means* or *tools* by which management can exert control (or influence) over salespeople and the *measures* and *measurement devices* management uses to assess the impact of its influence.

Third, as seen above, a sales force control system is not fully characterized by its position on the single dimension, especially the outcome-based versus behavior-based dimension on which most past studies have relied. Although this is a useful distinction, it is not sufficient to fully identify a control system. In practice, one can observe a whole range of control devices either based on behaviors or on performance. This suggests that a broader conceptual framework is still needed to explain how a firm is induced to select one (or several) specific control device(s), be it based on outcome or performance measures (Baldauf, Cravens, and Piercy 2005).

The concept of a dynamic sales force management process, which is the central focus of this book, constitutes an attempt to broaden past conceptualizations, to remove some of these limitations.

Outlook of sales managers' command centers

We have seen that a sales force can be viewed as a complex network of human resources engaged in the process of establishing, maintaining, nurturing, and/or breaking existing relationships inside and outside the system. It is made up of interdependent subsystems: sales territories, human resources who display various selling activities, the outcomes of such activities deployed in sales territories, and a number of managerial decisions (Figure 5.3).

Human resources

From a human resources point of view, a sales force is made up of a number of individuals whose functions are to engage in selling activities, in direct contact with customers and prospects, and others acting as supervisors in managerial capacities. From such a perspective, a sales force is characterized along five important dimensions:

- its size (i.e. the number of active salespeople and supervisors in the sales force hierarchy)
- its organization (i.e. the various links among the members of the sales team that represent the formal lines of authority and the responsibilities assigned to every member to accomplish the firm's selling mission)
- the personal characteristics of sales force members (i.e. a set of personality traits, personal objectives, values, and aptitudes)
- the competence levels of the various team members, and

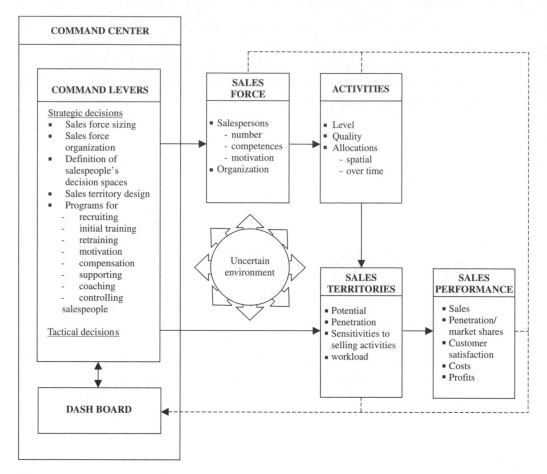

Fig. 5.3   Main command levers at the disposal of sales managers

- the motivation level of salespeople for fulfilling effectively the missions they have been assigned.

All important sales force decisions that a sales manager makes are aimed at ensuring that the sales team is the proper size and is organized effectively to accomplish the necessary selling activities, and displays the highest possible levels of competence and motivation.

The dynamic process philosophy

As discussed in Chapter 1, managing a sales force dynamically involves making a number of decisions and taking actions that affect the human resources at sales managers' disposal. This implies defining the responsibilities assigned to every member of the sales force (their sales territories) to meet the performance objectives given to the sales function. The major difficulty of such management is that sales managers cannot exert direct controls on salespeople. As we know, they are independent agents pursuing their own interests and making more or less autonomous decisions. As a result, sales managers must account for their behavior, in order to make decisions that match the firm's objectives as much as possible. These decisions are fully discussed in Part II of this book.

Main control levers

In order to accomplish their missions, sales managers have a certain number of control levers at their disposal. These are: the leeway they have to change the size of the sales force, control the decision space granted to sales staff, specify everyone's objectives and missions, and set up motivation and competence development programs for the sales force.

Size and organization controls

Determining the correct size for the sales force, and consequently deploying the adequate total selling effort over the market, are major decisions. Managers may decide to increase or decrease the size of the sales force. Obviously, these decisions must be made with utmost care, because of the time lags and costs that result from them. In addition, managers must properly allocate this selling effort over the whole market, spatially (by designing the sales territories) and qualitatively (by allocating responsibilities to the various sales force members).

Decision space controls

Sales managers can give extended or restricted decisional spaces (or responsibility extent) to salespeople, depending on the mission they assign to them and depending on their centralized or decentralized approach to sales force control. Under a restricted decisional space, salespeople have very limited leeway for adjusting the firm's offer to the needs and requirements of their customers. Offers are completely decided by management. The role of the salesperson is essentially limited to their power of persuasion for completing a sale. At the other end of the spectrum, a firm can give a salesperson an extended responsibility for negotiating, and consequently, more leeway for discussing the terms of a transaction with potential customers. Needless to say, the type of interaction and relationship development with customers are unlikely to be the same in both cases.

The level of autonomy that management gives to a salesperson is also called initiation of structure. By definition, autonomy implies a loose specification of the salesperson's role, and influences the psychological states of experienced responsibility (Tyagi 1985a; 1985b). Structure also refers to the degree to which a salesperson's role in the organization has been explicitly and precisely defined by a firm's policies and practices. A lack of structure from management leads to job inaccuracy and ambiguity. However, empowering salespeople may have a positive impact on their morale and feelings of self-accomplishment. Inversely, research suggests that when structure increases, salespeople are less likely to experience a feeling of fulfillment when a task has been successfully completed, possibly because they do not feel responsible for the success (Teas 1981).

Managers must also try to control potential job conflicts when specifying individual roles, because of their possible effect on the behavior of sales staff. Role conflict has been found to have a negative effect on intrinsic dimensions of instrumentality and motivation (Keller 1975; Tyagi 1982), although other studies have concluded the absence of a relationship (Churchill *et al.* 1976b).

Controls of objective plans

Assigning objectives to sales force members is a powerful control lever for sales management. Managers can assign sales objectives, market share objectives, profit objectives and/or customer satisfaction objectives to every salesperson or sales team. As discussed in Part II, objectives may be set precisely and on a contractual basis (e.g., sales quotas). Sometimes, objectives are only directional, in which case, salespeople are left to set their own objectives, given that higher is better for the firm (e.g., this is the case for commission plans when commissions are set at a fixed proportion of sales volume). The salespeople are then motivated to sell the largest amount possible to maximize their commission.

Motivation control programs

Motivation programs are closely linked to objective plans, because they are designed to provide salespeople with the motivation to meet their objectives. They can be financial incentive programs such as the sales force compensation plan, or sales contests that grant financial bonuses or premiums to the winners. Alternatively, they can be programs and policies that foster high morale in the sales force, such as programs that allow successful salespeople to be promoted to managerial levels, and that generally boost motivation to accomplish high quality work.

Management's supervision style can also exert some strong influence on motivation. Research has shown that when salespeople perform non-routine technical tasks, they tend to be motivated and reassured by closer supervision (House, Filley, and Kerr 1971; Evans 1970). In the same way, and although this has not always been confirmed (Teas 1981), research suggests that closer supervision leads to higher expectancy and instrumentality estimates (Churchill, Ford, and Walker 1976b).

In the same way, management can influence salespeople's behavior by providing them with proper feedback. Feedback is an important organizational factor to shape salespeople's performance. It refers to the amount of information provided by management to salespeople about their performance, as well as to the frequency with which this information is provided. Not surprisingly, as empirical research suggests (Walker, Churchill, and Ford 1977; Teas 1981), managerial feedback has different impacts on knowledge of work results (Tyagi 1985b) and on a salesperson's expectancy and instrumentality estimates, depending on whether the feedback is positive or negative. Positive feedback has been shown to increase salespeople's knowledge levels about the firm's policies as well as about their territory environmental factors.

Consideration by management is another control lever of motivation and satisfaction. This refers to managerial acts of warmth, friendship and psychological support. Management concern and awareness has been found to have an effect on intrinsic dimensions of instrumentality and motivation (Tyagi 1982). More generally, research suggests the existence of a positive relationship between consideration and a salesperson's instrumentality estimates.

In the same way, participation has a motivating impact. Participation refers to the degree to which salespeople are likely to influence their firm's decision-making process through the information/advice they provide. Research clearly shows that increasing sales personnel participation in a firm's decision-making process increases motivation through increased instrumentality and expectancy estimates (Mitchell 1973).

Competence level controls

Sales managers have also a whole set of tools at their disposal for developing salespeople's competencies. They can ensure high sales force competency levels through the recruitment of high caliber individuals with proven selling abilities or strong selling aptitudes. They can also control the sales force competency level through separation programs by dismissing those people who do not perform at the minimum acceptable performance level and who are not expected to improve substantially, even after proper training.

In addition, sales managers can design effective initial training and retraining programs to provide salespeople with the required knowledge and to enhance their skills and competencies to accomplish their selling tasks effectively. On a more routine basis, policies and practices designed for supporting, coaching, and supervising salespeople can increase knowledge bases and improve the selling skills of salespeople.

Main dashboard elements

As underlined in the first chapter, a sales manager's dashboard provides management with all the necessary information for managing and controlling sales force activities and performance over time. This information constitutes feedback from the market and the sales force and has a bearing on sales activities, as well as on short- and long-term outcomes of such activities (i.e. market performance). In addition, management's dashboard must be designed in such a way as to provide relevant information on important changes occurring in the market environment, in each territory, and in each market segment.

A sales manager's dashboard needs to be more or less elaborate, depending on the management style selected (centralized versus decentralized), as well as on the costs of collecting the required information in relation to the benefits that can be gained from it. Part II of this book, describes the various elements of a sales manager's dashboard as well as the design of the information flows that such dashboards imply.

Conclusion

This chapter has provided an overview of the role that sales managers play within the dynamic sales force management process framework. Sales managers have been shown to develop extensive knowledge bases, however, these are always incomplete and are not always fully accurate. In other words, sales managers exert their actions in an uncertain environment. In addition, sales managers are subject, like other individuals, to bounded rationality — an inability to process large amounts of relevant information simultaneously and effectively.

Sales managers are also decision makers who must make an inordinate number of decisions. Some of these decisions are important because they are *strategic decisions* and will have a long-term effect on the sales force. Others are short-term oriented, *tactical decisions* which are designed to fully implement the strategic decisions and account for casual and unanticipated every day events.

Part II of this book is devoted to a thorough description and analysis of the roles and functions of sales managers' command centers.

6 The changing environment of the dynamic management process

Successive sales organization changes at Hewlett-Packard

A few years ago, Hewlett-Packard adopted a completely new sales organization structure. The company was split into several autonomous divisions that drew their resources from headquarters, and that were entrepreneurially and autonomously managed, with complete responsibility for marketing and sales.

In addition, HP established a new CSO division (Computer Systems Organization) which was responsible for marketing a whole line of computers, ranging from individual work stations to powerful units for heavy users. By adopting more open systems, the major selling arguments shifted from equipment's performance and price to customers' added value. The new emphasis was to help customers to find the best possible solutions to their problems, even if this meant using components from a competitor.

In order to provide those services, HP salespeople needed to acquire strong expertise in their clients' problems. HP changed the geographical organization of its sales force so that it was organized by customer type (banking, insurance, industrial buyers, etc.) This was necessary so that the sales staff could understand customer problems within their sector.

However, HP soon realized that this sales force organization was not optimal. Because the salespeople always faced the same type of problems, they also tended to sell the same kind of products and so lost experience in selling the whole line of HP products, from computers to printers.

Because the clients need products from the whole HP product line, salespeople who were specialists in the various application sectors, were integrated into teams of product specialists to help them sell the whole product line. For the company's key accounts, HP created the new function of CAM (Commercial Account Manager). This 4,000-person sales force calls on large firms and acts as counselors, and is supported by product experts.

In a recent reorganization, the company has been divided into just six divisions (Brewer 1997; Louderback 1997).

More than any other industry, the data processing sector has undergone fast changes in its technological environment, as a result of the strong product development and a fierce price war. To be able to adapt to these environmental changes, HP (as well as many other firms) had to shape its selling organization according to changing market needs and expectations.

The sales force management process that has been described in the preceding chapters would not be complete without a discussion of the influence and impact of a firm's constantly evolving environment on this process. More specifically, the economic, competitive, cultural, social and technological environments impact strongly upon management processes. As already discussed, sales managers must carry out their missions, with as much knowledge as possible of the environmental forces that will affect their mission. Moreover, they need to form expectations about the environmental changes that will prevail at the time of implementation.

Clearly, this knowledge depends on the specific situations sales managers face at a given time. Common factors and evolutionary trends in the environment exist that affect all the firms, irrespective of their size, customers, and types of activity: the prevailing evolutionary trends of the selling function. Most likely, these trends will continue to prevail during the years to come.

Understanding such evolution is essential for sales managers so that they can fulfill the changing needs experienced by consumers and salespeople. Sales managers must also evolve so that they can adapt to new market expectations. This last chapter of Part I examines the factors that shape the evolution of the selling function, major evolutionary trends, as well as the problems raised by such constant change.

The environment for selling missions

Any sales mission is carried out within a specific environment. Even though sales managers have only a small chance to change this environment, they must know and understand it, because environmental forces are likely to considerably affect the effectiveness of their dynamic sales force management process. These factors are essentially economic, industry-specific, and competitive.

General economic environment

A firm's economic environment refers to the more or less favorable economic conditions that currently prevail in the market. It also refers to the prospects of evolution over a more or less extended period of time, and includes the problems and opportunities that technological and legal evolutions are likely to bring up. The economic environment affects the day-to-day operations of the sales force, as well as those of the firm as a whole. Any downturn in the economic cycle in a given market is felt by every selling unit in that market.

In contrast, the prevailing conditions of the labor market do not affect salespeople and sales managers equally. Under full employment conditions, salespeople tend to become more mobile because they are in high demand. As a result, sales forces typically experience increased dysfunctional turnover rates, and sales management operations are adversely affected. Sales managers must compensate for a higher sales force turnover rate by additional recruitment efforts in an unfavorable labor market.

Industrial sector

In addition to the general economic environment, every industry is characterized by specific economic conditions. This is of special concern to firms that operate in given industrial sectors. In addition, customers' industrial sectors may also display more or less favorable trends and experience difficult (or booming) conditions over a certain period of time. A dynamic management process must account for the conditions faced by the customers' industrial sector. Managers must constantly adjust the selling effort across more or less responsive accounts. A firm's industry may face more or less difficult economic conditions, technological or legal problems. Alternatively, it may benefit from unusual environmental opportunities. In addition, a given industrial sector may also face difficult labor market conditions, especially when salespeople are required to possess highly specialized knowledge and competencies.

Competitive environment

Markets are characterized by their competitive environment. As discussed above, knowledge about markets and competition is essential information, not only for general or sales management, but also for salespeople. As will be discussed later, all concerned parties must be aware of competitive actions to effectively manage their sales force over time. In order to do this, information channels must be set up in such a way as to provide relevant information about competitors' actions, marketing and selling strategies, pricing, distribution, and/or communication policies and practices.

Current evolution of the sales environment

Selling functions and missions evolve as a result of changes that occur in the general environment. These factors do not just affect the sales operations, they also impact on all other aspects of a firm's operations and on society as a whole. The discussion in this chapter is restricted to their impact on the selling function and its management process.

Key evolutionary factors

In Western economies, most selling functions are currently undergoing a dramatic process of evolution, and this may just be the start of even more drastic changes to come (Anderson 1996). Figure 6.1 identifies the main evolutionary trends as well as some explanatory factors from the firm's immediate environment and its more remote macro-environment.

Among the main and more striking evolutionary trends, one can identify:

- the globalization of exchanges which makes business negotiations more complex and often add a multi-cultural dimension to business transactions;
- the rapid developments that have occurred (and that will probably continue to occur) in technology-intensive sectors, such as telecommunications and electronics (including the fast-expanding use of mobiles, computers, laptops, and the internet, to name just a few);
- the uncertainty that is linked to such rapid economic and geopolitical changes that have affected most Western economies, since the mid-seventies, such as the rapid economic development of former communist

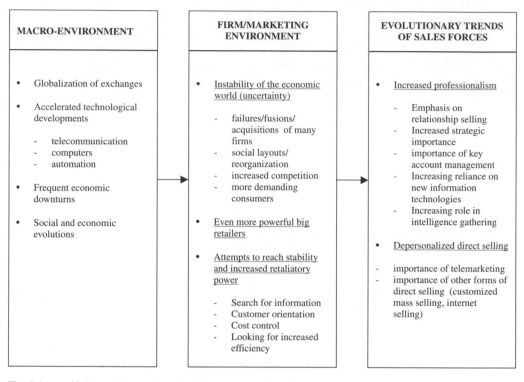

MACRO-ENVIRONMENT	FIRM/MARKETING ENVIRONMENT	EVOLUTIONARY TRENDS OF SALES FORCES

• Globalization of exchanges
 	
• Accelerated technological developments
 	
  - telecommunication
  - computers
  - automation
 	
• Frequent economic downturns
 	
• Social and economic evolutions
	• Instability of the economic world (uncertainty)
	
	  - failures/fusions/ acquisitions of many firms
	  - social layouts/ reorganization
	  - increased competition
	  - more demanding consumers
	
	• Even more powerful big retailers
	
	• Attempts to reach stability and increased retaliatory power
	
	  - Search for information
	  - Customer orientation
	  - Cost control
	  - Looking for increased efficiency
		• Increased professionalism
		
		  - Emphasis on relationship selling
		  - Increased strategic importance
		  - importance of key account management
		  - Increasing reliance on new information technologies
		  - Increasing role in intelligence gathering
		
		• Depersonalized direct selling
		
		  - importance of telemarketing
		  - importance of other forms of direct selling (customized mass selling, internet selling)

Fig. 6.1   Main evolutionary trends of the personal selling function and their causes

countries, the rise of developing economies like China, India, and Brazil, and the recurring petrol crises;

• the even greater uncertainties resulting from recent world events (including the war on terror, major earthquakes, and devastating natural disasters);

• the important social and cultural changes that have been taking place and that are still developing (e.g., the massive entry of women into the labor market). In addition, one can observe the increasing concern of the general public with environmental issues, fair trade, sustainable growth, and an increasing demand for transparency from business concerning their operations, which have been sparked by recent major corporate scandals.

All these factors operate simultaneously and provoke drastic changes in the firm's environment. This is a time of instability and uncertainty after many years of relative stability in the economic sector. They have contributed to situations in which many firms have gone bankrupt, forced into mergers, or have been absorbed by other firms. Other firms have scaled down their operations, resulting in major employee lay-offs and restructuring programs, and increased competition in mostly mature, declining, or evolving markets. As a result, consumers and buyers demand even more from their suppliers.

Increased professionalism for selling functions

As a result of these environmental evolutions, the selling function is currently divided into two opposing trends (Darmon 1998c). Selling functions bringing high added value to customer-buyer relationships tend to take a more strategic role in many firms. As a result, sales functions constantly evolve toward increased professionalism (Hawes, Rich, and Widmier 2004). In contrast, other traditional selling functions, characterized by little added value to customers, tend to disappear and to be replaced by technology-intensive functions.

The increasing importance of the dynamic CRM process

In practice, the trend towards increased professionalism is evident in the development of such widely-accepted practices as customer-oriented selling, relationship selling, or key account management. Market- and customer-orientations have the final objectives of building mutually profitable and lasting relationships with customers to ensure their long-term loyalty. This trend also results in the increasingly strategic role that many firms attribute to the selling function, and in the special attention they give to the management of key accounts (KAM). Loyal key customers ensure lasting revenue. Contrasting with these requirements, customers' expectations of their suppliers and their salespeople are endlessly increasing. The salesperson's task is much more demanding in terms of reaction speed and the extent of their knowledge bases (Jones *et al.* 2005). In addition, salespeople are often required to provide individual solutions and offers to every customer. Presently, Customer Relationship Management (CRM) capitalizes on the latest information technologies to increase sales force efficiency through better time management, more efficient information flows, and reduced sales force administrative duties (Wedell and Dempeck 1987).

Many significant examples illustrate this trend. For example, over the last few years, Rank Xerox has adopted a customer-oriented strategy. Nowadays, this company highlights the benefits that clients obtain by using its products. The Rank Xerox salespeople have been trained to systematically explain the productivity gains their customers can achieve by using Rank

Xerox products. In complex product sales, salespeople have been trained to address different parties representing the various functional departments of their customers. The sales force has increased its presence in the field (salespeople spend on average 70 percent of their time in contact with their clients). Salespeople must make a systematic analysis of their failures. They keep in close contact with customers who have bought from them, and they have developed an increased capacity to defend the listed prices.

At Accord, an international hotel group, the sales force was previously under the authority of each chain upper management. Now, personal selling is considered as a true profession, with its own training school, career plans, management and objectives.

The trend toward increased customer-orientation is helped by an increasing amount of computer software for CRM applications. A major consulting firm has reported a 30 percent increase in its CRM software package, sales of which have reached one billion euros. Sixty percent of this revenue comes from sales to large organizations.

Increased strategic roles for sales force and CRM processes

As customers are becoming the focus of many firms' concern, the strategic role of the selling function is becoming more apparent. The customer-centered approach has been followed for a number of years by the French National Railways (SNCF), after it realized that selling had become a strategic issue. The company has concluded that selling its products was an essential requirement for its future success. As a result, it has developed powerful selling aids and a computerized booking system which allows the firm to keep control of its distribution channels.

In another example, the President of Chambourcy-Nestlé, one of the leading international food product companies describes the selling function in the Switzerland-based Group as moving away from the old concept of selling as a mechanical accelerator of marketing. The top management of this company now considers that the sales and marketing functions must be put on an equal basis. Sales managers now take part in top management meetings along with their marketing colleagues. The rivalry between sales and marketing has disappeared as the prevalent strategy is now thought to be a blend of good products, effective communication policies, and efficient salespeople.

At Jaguar, the car manufacturer, the salespeople take part in the different stages of the development processes for new models. They express their opinions in terms of their knowledge of consumers' expectations and preferences. Where their suggestions are not retained, management explains why. At Peugeot, another leading car manufacturer, salespeople are increasingly involved in marketing and designing the company's loyalty building program. Salespeople are also supported by administrative personnel who have received extensive training in selling.

From an organizational standpoint, this new emphasis on the selling function requires a new definition of the respective roles of the sales and marketing departments (Rouziès *et al.* 2005). Traditionally, these have been two different departments. Logically, the selling function constitutes only one of the marketing tools, even though it is generally one of the most important (Donath 1999). The relationship between these two areas has traditionally caused problems in a lot of firms. Some have recognized the need for a strong coordination between the two functions for achieving a high performance level, and have even instituted a new functional department that is in charge of ensuring a smooth interface between the two areas. When the two functions do not have a good relationship, the interface department is torn apart!

Increased importance of key account management (KAM) and team selling

The increased professionalism of the selling function is also demonstrated by the importance that is given to key account management (KAM). The five largest clients of Procter & Gamble account for 65 percent of its sales volume. It is not surprising then, that multidisciplinary teams have been set up specifically to handle these relationships (Arnett, Macy, and Wilcox 2005). A few years ago, the P&G group pre-tested a new approach with the Wal-Mart chain stores on a worldwide basis. A multidisciplinary team was set up at the client's premises and worked on developing a strong relationship with the retail chain. As a result of the success of this new approach, P&G has progressively extended this method to its other subsidiaries. This method, which was first developed in the United States more than eight years ago has gradually been implemented in Europe by P&G, with some local adaptations, to account for each specific market.

The 3M Corporation has developed collaborative relationships with a number of international strategic accounts (such as Motorola, Hewlett Packard, IBM, and Texas Instruments). It is quite a challenge for a multinational corporation to set up and coordinate selling teams for such accounts like Nortel, Siemens, and Procter & Gamble which carry on business in more than twenty countries and require special selling conditions, technical support, prices, and differentiated products (Magrath 1997). As for IBM, salespeople who are in charge of key accounts (called *customer relationship managers*), constitute a sales force of 900, a size that should not vary substantially in the next few years. These salespeople are assigned to various industrial sectors and sell the whole IBM product and service range.

The development of KAM has resulted in the increased importance of team selling (Dixon, Gassenheimer, and Feldman Barr 2003). Team selling implies a substantial increase in the number of relationships involved in the buyer-seller interactions (within the sales team, across team members within the firm, between the selling team and the buying center members, among the selling team and other functions in the selling firm, and between the selling team and the firm's strategy) (Jones *et al.* 2005). It is worth noting, however, that team selling is not limited to KAM. At Novartis, the international pharmaceutical product group, selling has evolved towards sharing efforts and competencies. While in the past salespeople were assessed and compensated for their individual performance, they are now jointly evaluated with one or two others who work on the same customer target. The increased importance given to KAM has triggered additional research efforts in this area (Sengupta, Krapfel, and Pusateri 2000; Schultz and Evans 2002; Jones *et al.* 2005).

Increased roles for new information technologies (NIT)

The increasing bulk of administrative tasks with their ever-increasing complexity are being counterbalanced by advances in new information technologies (NIT) and computer systems. This trend also contributes to more professionalism in the sales functions (Jones, Sundaram, and Chin 2002). These days, a salesperson must be able to give up-to-date information to a client at any time during the sales and distribution processes. While in the past, computer software was essentially limited to a follow-up of the selling activities, most computer programs are now designed to personalize the customer-supplier relationships. The role of new technology in the dynamic sales management process has been already underlined, although its effect on individual's performance remains to be seen. Research suggests that initially, CRM technology enhances sales performance (Ko and Dennis 2004), but diminishing returns soon appear. After a certain point, CRM technology seems to have a disabling effect on sales performance (Ahearne, Srinivasan, and Weinstein 2004). Within certain limits, however, information systems tend to reinforce salespeople's autonomy and improve the quality of sales force control and support. Note also that advances in technology also lead to tremendous increase in customers expectation concerning response time from salespeople.

The evolution toward CRM requires sales managers and salespeople to target customers properly and to carefully prepare for sales calls. Salespeople are also required to establish efficient interactions during the contact time with customers, and management must have developed relevant performance measures, measuring instruments, and measurement processes to assess all dimensions of customer satisfaction. Thus, the need to acquire high quality and timely information has become even more vital in the last few years. In many firms, before a customer call takes place, salespeople can access the name of a client via their laptop and receive a large quantity of useful information such as the product portfolio purchased in the past, payment delays, as well as events that have taken place since the last call, such as information requests about particular products, or the number of visits to the firm's website. Consulting the potential buyer's website often provides vital information.

This evolution of the selling function has meant drastic changes to the job of salesperson. Insurance companies have been among the first to provide their sales staff with laptops. So they can accomplish a large number of tasks from their home office, for example, they can obtain information that may be needed during a sales call, or establish a proposal of an insurance policy, or send orders to the home office as soon as they are signed by a client. IBM has designed software which allows its salespeople to access any cost data that are necessary to evaluate the profitability of a transaction. Because of its high level of automation, this company has even experimented with virtual sales offices where the physical presence of salespeople is not absolutely essential (*Sales and Marketing Management* 1994).

Private Business, Inc., an American financial firm requires its 200 salespeople to use internet-based software that has been designed to provide help at every stage of the selling process. Through access to a central data bank, salespeople have all kinds of relevant customer data at their disposal. This is constantly updated. The system can be probed to find out which customers should be called next. Although many salespeople were initially skeptical of the system and resisted its introduction, they quickly realized the potential benefits they could gain from its actual implementation. Being relieved from many routine tasks, they could better devote their time to the more creative (and more challenging) aspects of their job (Dana 1999).

Even though they are sometimes difficult to implement in practice, these changes are often profitable to a firm as well as to salespeople (Erffmeyer and Johnson 2001). This trend toward sales force automation is here to last and is irreversible (Widmier, Jackson, and Brown McCabe 2002). Some firms estimate that three years after implementation of their sales force automation programs, their productivity gains have increased by over 30 percent, in addition to increasing the satisfaction levels of their clients as well as of their salesforce (Wedell and Dempeck 1987).

The importance of salespeople as market intelligence agents

Firms must constantly monitor the environment in order to react swiftly to significant changes. As a result, it may not be surprising that salespeople, who are in the unique position of collecting relevant market intelligence, are increasingly used to accomplish this important mission (LeBon and Merunka 2004). Salespeople are especially suited to communicate to management information about clients and prospects, competition, territory conditions, and customer reactions to various marketing actions. Intelligence about the competition may include such events as the launch of a new product or products being tested in their territories. Intelligence about clients may include new product applications, or major changes in a client's buying center. Intelligence about territory includes local economic trends or new market opportunities in a particular industrial sector.

One important fact deserves to be underlined: market intelligence reporting is not a selling function *per se*. It goes well beyond the selling responsibilities that are typically assigned to salespeople. This new responsibility can only reinforce their strategic role in the firm's management process. As discussed previously, sales managers should give their sales forces a major role in feeding their information flows. They should ensure that this function is well understood by their salespeople, and that it is properly organized and controlled.

The importance of ethical concerns

Over the last few years, the general public has become increasingly concerned with the ethics involved in business. In business organizations, every group of stakeholders has been observing management's practices and more than ever before, they are starting to challenge these business practices on ethical grounds. Stakeholder groups include shareholders, customers, suppliers, creditors, managers, employees, the government, and the general public (Futrell 2005). There is an increasing demand for corporations to behave ethically, that is, honestly, legally, and fairly towards all its stake-holders. Fewer people are ready to accept massive employee layoffs when a firm is making profits, like Michelin, Hewlett Packard, and other cor-porations have been doing recently. Even though outsourcing manufactur-ing operations to Third World countries might be justified from a strictly economic viewpoint, it is perceived as unacceptable by many individuals.

Personal selling, which is a firm's boundary spanning function, has always been one of the most visible parts of a business, because of its role as the interface between the firm and its customers, buyers, and/or the general public. All of these constituencies are becoming increasingly critical of some selling practices, not only any outright breach to essential ethical conducts, but even in situations that constitute subtle ethical dilemmas.

Because of this, ethical issues may arise at a sales management/salesperson level. In this context, sales managers control their relationships with salespeople. Salespeople manage relationships with sales managers and with customers.

Ethical issues in sales management

Individuals display quite different sensitivities to ethics, morale, and moral values. As leaders, sales managers are likely to have considerable influence over moral and ethical standards in their organization (Cherry and Fraedrich 2000; Chonko, Wotruba, and Loe 2002). In certain cases, sales managers may induce salespeople to behave more or less ethically toward their clients. It may be difficult for salespeople to refuse to engage in some borderline behaviors dictated by managers without risking losing their jobs. These ethical conflicts between management and staff result in low commitment to the organization and by salespeople wanting to leave (Schwepker 1999).

Putting too much pressure on salespeople to get the most out of them, engaging in unfair practices in designing or realigning sales territories or in setting quotas, and unfairly handling unexpected circumstances (such as illnesses, stress or burnout, or windfall sales) are typical examples of such ethical problems (McFarland 2003). Needless to say, strict ethical behaviors are parts of the constraints by which sales managers must abide. These are likely to become even tighter in the future, and will reinforce the professional character of the personal selling function.

Ethical issues for salespeople

There are a large number of ways in which salespeople may engage in unethical behavior that may affect their good relationships with their firm and/or managers. For example, misusing some company's assets such as a company car, shirking, cheating on expense accounts or call reports, are typical behavior that, unfortunately, is too often observed in practice.

Some of these unethical behaviors may affect customer relationships and tend to be even more damaging to an organization. Bribing or giving important gifts to a buyer are obvious extreme examples. More subtle is the question of misrepresentation. Clear cases of misrepresentation exist when salespeople promise customers benefits that they know their firm cannot deliver (note that sometimes the line between what constitutes a clear promise, an opinion, or some usual sales "puffery" is difficult to draw).

As discussed in the previous chapters, a dynamic management process is a way to control or influence behavior in the right direction. It is up to management to ensure that salespeople do not indulge in unethical behavior (Bass, Barnett, and Brown 1998). They should make it clear what constitutes acceptable and unacceptable behavior. An increasing number of companies have adopted strict and detailed codes of ethics that they enforce or provide as guidelines to the sales force. This contributes to building a strong ethical climate, and results in stronger organizational commitment and satisfaction (Weeks *et al.* 2004).

The current trend for firms, sales managers, and salespeople to include ethical considerations in their decisions and practices is becoming stronger. It is also reflected in the substantial amount of research that is taking place on sales force ethical issues (see e.g., Sivadas *et al.* 2002; Valentine and Barnett 2003; Powel Mantel 2005). As these constraints will become even more binding in the future, firms will be required to hire salespeople with high moral and ethical standards.

The decreasing importance of some selling functions

Besides the trend toward selling functions requiring additional skills and professionalism, another trend is emerging: the decreasing importance of some selling functions. In a number of direct selling situations, face-to-face contact with final consumers and buyers is becoming less important, and consequently, the high costs of personal selling can no longer be justified. They are routine selling tasks that do not require the problem-solving abilities of salespeople. This type of selling is now best handled by the new communication and automation technologies that can be used at a much lower cost. Consequently, for cost and efficiency reasons, personal selling is giving the way to telemarketing, call centers, e-marketing, computer networks — all devices that heavily rely on advanced communication technologies. Compaq estimates that a face-to-face contact with one customer costs an average of 360 euros. In contrast, a contact through the internet costs about one euro, and that through a call center somewhere between 12 and 24 euros.

One current estimate is that telephone contact with an individual client costs from 2.30 to 3.00 euros, and about 6.00 euros with a small or medium-sized firm or a professional client. The same contact with a top executive at a large corporation costs between 7.60 and 10.60 euros. Obviously such figures are definitely lower than those from face-to-face contact. While field salespeople spend from 10 to 17 percent of their time on active selling, telemarketers can spend up to 50 to 70 percent of their time on the same activities.

All kinds of direct distribution of goods and services that can be done without personal contact between sellers and buyers. These are likely to increase as new technology becomes more widespread. Note that the "depersonalization" of such relationships is often compensated for by a closer and better adjustment of the products and services to the needs and tastes of the clients. For example the manufacture of customer-tailored product through internet-collected data or the use of customer data bases that allow a detailed segmentation of markets tend to provide some "personalization" of a firm's offer. The book offers from amazon.com are a case in point.

Over the last few years, new forms of selling via the internet have appeared and tend to make certain types of selling functions obsolete. The president of a large insurance company foresees that in the next few years, more than 40 percent of sales will be done over the internet.

The French department store *Le Printemps* has developed three websites in English and in French. The first one presents the store and 200 selected products. The second site is a wedding space. The third site at the address www.boutiqueblanche.com is more original. Four salespeople (or "web-cameras") equipped with rollerskates move rapidly around the famous Boulevard Haussmann store and respond to internet requests from customers. By means of a small camera and a keyboard, these salespeople can show the products in the store and sell according to customers' requests.

Quite a few internet sites have been set up to establish relationships between firms. For example, Food Finder, a distributor of food products has an internet site which is visited by well over 20,000 interested customers every month. A firm selling media space sells over 5 percent of its services through auction bids. Cortal was one of the first banks to develop direct links with its customers by providing them with direct access to their accounts — this has now become generalized practice. Through its links with most of the world's stock exchanges, the bank allows its customers to manage their share portfolios online.

Dell, the leading manufacturer of computer products, has established a fully integrated computerized selling process. All the suppliers are linked to the manufacturer through Extranet. Thus, Dell can provide answers to the requests of any supplier. There are three sites at the customer's disposal. One is targeted at the general public. One is intended for small and medium-sized firms, and the third one for large corporations. Every customer can order directly over the internet, or use a telephone number connected to a Dell call center. This firm reports increasing current daily sales volumes from its internet sites.

And the list could go on for ever!

Under such circumstances, it may not be surprising that many firms find it more profitable to deal with part of their clientele through telemarketing or the internet. As an example, General Electric has been able to reduce its selling costs by 94 percent in one of its branches by handling its business with smaller clients through telemarketing (Anderson 1995).

An increasing number of firms rely on call centers to perform part or all of the selling functions. Pelikan Hardcopy, a firm selling printing supplies using a ten person sales force has progressively shifted to telephone selling, without any impact on its rapidly expanding customer basis. Other firms like Microsoft use a combination of call centers and a traditional field sales force. However, the fifty people employed in its call centers are sedentary technical staff who can carry out all the steps of a transaction up to its conclusion.

Evolution of salespeople's profiles

As the selling function takes on an increased role and importance in many firms and requires higher professionalism, the need to staff the selling functions and the required profile required to hold such selling positions follow parallel trends. From the firms' point of view, salespeople currently being recruited for industrial selling must be highly qualified. The recruitment of sales staff with technical backgrounds has increased by 43 percent every year over the last few years. As the selling function becomes ever more professional salespeople are required to have levels of education and ability that allow them to adapt quickly to change (Chonko *et al.* 2002; Weeks *et al.* 2004). The changes described above create heavier cognitive demands on salespeople (complex product and customer demands, ability to use computer technology, increased knowledge bases, to name but a few).

This trend results in the need to recruit better trained individuals – salespeople who can be given high levels of training, and who can adapt as their functions evolve over time. For example, at Würth's, the world leader of the binding product market, with a 1,500 individual sales force, management estimates that selling more and more technical and complex products requires salespeople who have the ability to make more specialized recommendations to solve increasingly complex customer problems. Consequently, it is vital that firms recruit well trained salespeople who can easily adapt to changing market conditions.

The socio-demographic composition of sales forces also tends to evolve. Until relatively recently, the role of a salesperson has traditionally been held by men, with some exceptions, such as retail sales jobs or cosmetic product selling which have been the preserve of female sales staffs. Most industrial sales positions were not open to women. Over the last two decades, because of the pressure from organizations that have fought for sex equality as well as the massive arrival of women on the labor market, the market has opened up for the female population, even in the industrial sector. Pernod-Ricard, one of the leading manufacturers of alcoholic beverages, with about one-third of its employees holding sales positions (500 persons at Ricard, 200 at Pernod, and 200 at Orangina), has actively recruited a substantial number of women in its sales force.

If, in some countries, women have some difficulty accessing sales positions, the situation is even worse when it comes to holding managerial roles. One could have expected, however, that in those industries where women are the main customers, female supervisors would be at least as effective as male supervisors. A female manager might be more sensitive to customers' tastes and desires in such markets than her male counterpart. Firms which have appointed female sales managers have recognized that a feminine management style is frequently smoother, less authoritarian, more open to others, and can lead to less tense negotiations.

In spite of these new developments, however, we are still far from male-female equality. In France, for example, it is estimated that women occupy no more than 16 to 20 percent of all managerial selling positions

(Shepherd and Heartfield 1991; Kelley 1991; Arnott 1995). This shows some progress from the 7 percent that was recorded in 1988, and suggests a fast progression rate. No doubt, it will still take a few years before one will be able to observe equal proportions of men and women in sales management. One sure fact, however, is that this trend is here to stay.

The evolution of sales management practices

In the preceding paragraphs, we have seen how sales managers have adapted to the new sales environment by providing salespeople with adequate objectives, organized them into selling teams, and provided them with IT and CRM techniques and tools. Many issues, on the best way to manage the new sales force remain to be solved. Up to now, research remains scarce on the best management methods to use for best conciliating short-term and long-term management objectives, especially for motivating, controlling, and compensating, not only individual salespeople, but whole sales teams (Brown *et al.* 2005).

The future of personal selling

For some years, a few authors have predicted that salespeople working in direct contact with their customers and prospects will become obsolete. Many critics have seen traditional salespeople's jobs doomed to the fate of bank tellers who have been superseded by ATMs (Sheth 1995). As underlined above, there is no doubt that the technological revolution will continue to affect selling functions and sales management.

It seems relatively safe to predict that selling functions will continue to evolve differently, depending on the creativity they require from salespeople (Darmon 1998c). Those selling functions that require only little creativity are more likely to be carried out more efficiently through the use of new technology (the internet, intranet, facsimile, mobiles, laptops, etc.). However, it is more difficult to predict how selling functions requiring elaborate customer relationship management are likely to evolve. These functions cannot rely exclusively on automation, but require strategic thinking, creativity, customized decision making, and personalized communication. The difficulty is to predict how new current and future information technologies may affect personal selling functions that imply establishing, developing and maintaining long-term buyer-seller relationships.

Most experts in the field seem to agree that face-to-face selling is not about to disappear. Research suggests that buyers and sellers generally prefer face-to-face and telephone communication media over all other media types, although all recognize that most computer-mediated communications (such as e-mails) play an important role as supporting communication devices (Rodriguez Cano, Boles, and Bean 2005). In contrast, all of them do consider that the selling function is currently undergoing major changes and that it is likely to require even more professionalism in the years to come. To try to provide some partial answers to this question, it may be appropriate to consider the key dimensions of a personal sales interaction between buyer and salesperson, and to assess how those different dimensions are likely to evolve and be affected by the new information technologies from a cost-benefit perspective.

In the preceding chapters, the selling function has been characterized along four key dimensions, namely the need for salespeople (1) to manage a more or less extensive database, (2) to submit this information to more or less extensive processing, (3) to exchange and persuasively communicate part of this information with customers and with management, and (4) to manage their time effectively. Obviously, information technologies are likely to affect all those dimensions.

Many sales forces have been equipped with laptops that can instantaneously stockpile, process, and retrieve a large number of information and intelligence data. There is no doubt that in the future, this type of equipment will become even more sophisticated, and harbor even more powerful software for sales relationship management applications. If the technological revolution considerably affects the way salespeople manage their customer relationships, one should not overlook that it also affects the way customers buy (Furey 1999). Obviously, buyers have the same technological means as selling organizations at their disposal. They, too, have increasing access to relevant information. Buyers see their information sources increase and their market surely moving toward the classical economist's dream — markets where they enjoy perfect, instant, and free market information.

Providing customers and prospects instantaneously with all the information they need may be incompatible with face-to-face selling. Geographically-distant customers and sellers must first agree on a place and time to meet physically. This may be seen as incompatible with almost instant decision making that timely and perfect information will allow. It is in this area that new information technologies could well change the practice of selling encounters. By allowing a potential customer or a client to access the information they need, when they need it, and wherever they are, new information technologies could make face-to-face contacts obsolete because of such contacts' high cost and limited efficiency superiority.

The next question that arises is: up to what point will it be possible to do without personal face-to-face contact encounters in selling? Readers may well order the latest best sellers through the internet, by clicking, for example, on amazon.com. They are provided with relevant purchase information. They receive relevant advice on other books that are likely to interest them, in an extremely efficient manner. What is earned in terms of time and savings, however, will be paid by a change (some will say by a downgrading) in lifestyle. A computerized brain can easily guess what readers might like and propose books in that category, possibly with even greater accuracy and intelligence than any bookstore employee. The warm human contact that has always prevailed between a bookstore owner and his/her loyal clients may well disappear!

Will what may now seem acceptable to most final consumers be also acceptable to customers in B-to-B? One should not overlook the importance of the personal and human factors and of physical proximity when building and entertaining lasting relationships between a firm and its customers. An e-mail exchange (without a personal contact) could well prove to be inadequate, especially over an extended period of time. "Who am I talking to?" "What does he/she look like?" "Up to what point can I trust this person?" Such questions may well remain unanswered. Trust, sympathy, or even friendship, often constitutes the basis for many lasting business relationships. Such feelings rely mainly on visual information that both parties exchange and which shape their perceptions of each other.

New technology already allows visual contact between people who are physically remote. Teleconferencing or web cameras will continue to improve in the years to come and will most likely find increased usage. Independently from the need to be present in a conference room or in front of a web cam, the question of the human factors still remains. Information that can be inferred from such simple actions as shaking hands, establishing direct eye contact, directly and deliberately (or not) observing the gestures and body language of the other party which cannot be captured by a camera may be lost, depending on its angle of vision. In the same way, lack of physical proximity prevents sharing the same environment, including smells, atmospherics, not to mention the impossibility of exchanging objects, from a simple business card to product samples.

What is the relative importance of physical proximity between the parties in a business relationship? How does this change at various stages of the relationship? What is the cost, in terms of efficiency and relationship quality, for both buyers and sellers of suppressing such physical proximity? Are such costs likely to be covered by the increased time efficiency of selling though the internet? Is the cost/benefit ratio to be the same across situations and cultures (especially in international selling contexts)? Research could shed some light on some of these basic questions, as well as on the likely future of face-to-face personal selling functions. This should be the focus of researchers over the next few years.

Conclusion

As discussed throughout Part I of this book, personal selling encompasses a wide variety of functions, sometimes even within the same firm. Personal selling involves not only salespeople and their supervisors, but also a whole range of support functions that are designed to help salespeople in their tasks. It seems that two opposite trends that currently affect the selling functions cannot be reversed or avoided. On the one hand, some selling functions require increasingly professional treatment and are becoming of considerable strategic importance for a firm. These functions require more responsibility and initiative from sales staffs. On the other hand, many selling functions evolve toward automation and increased simplification. It is likely that these will decrease in importance as their function can be carried out using modern technology.

Selling often lacks qualified people willing to work in a selling capacity. It often suffers from a poor image, even more so in countries with a Latin-origin culture than in Anglo-Saxon economies. This lack of a positive image would not be a problem, if it did not constitute an obstacle to a country's economic development and progress. How can a job with such a bad image attract the best talent? Why should talented researchers be willing to spend their time, effort, and energy to improve an activity that is despised by the general public (and also frequently, by themselves!)? As a result, many firms complain about a lack of high caliber salespeople. Despite the increased importance of the selling function and unemployment rates that are frequently in the two digit zones in several European countries, firms are still unable to fill many sales positions. A recent survey estimates that more than 120,000 sales jobs cannot be filled in France alone!

Although the selling function is rapidly becoming more professional, the image of personal selling seems to improve at a much slower pace. It is quite possible that many more years will pass before personal selling and sales management are perceived and recognized as the intellectually challenging positions that they are currently becoming.

Part II

Tools for implementing the process: the command center

In Part I of this book, we saw that controlling a sales force consists of establishing a set of procedures for supervising, coaching, motivating, evaluating, and compensating salespeople. In other words, sales force control involves all the means that induce salespeople to accomplish the firm's mission in its markets (Anderson and Oliver 1987). As also underlined, from a managerial perspective, the problem of the dynamic management of a sales force can be stated as follows: what are the indicators that sales managers should observe and what are the actions they should take as a result of such observations to induce salespeople to work towards the firm's objectives as closely as possible?

In fact, a process is exerted through all managerial actions taken in the framework of what has been called the sales manager's command center. Training, motivating, coaching, supporting, and compensating salespeople can be conceived as being parts of the sales force management and control tools. Managers have a number of means at their disposal to exert this control. They exert some control on sales effort levels, the sales force organization processes, and all kinds of programs for setting objectives, motivation and increasing competence levels. Part I was essentially descriptive. Part II is more normative. It is comprised of five chapters (Figure II.1).

The first four chapters are devoted to the various programs that constitute sales management's control levers: the programs designed for controlling the level and deployment of the selling efforts in the market (Chapter 7); the programs aimed at influencing salespeople's behaviors, first, under a more or less centralized control approach by providing salespeople with specific objectives (Chapter 8); second, under more decentralized or balanced approaches, by providing salespeople with directional objective and incentive programs (Chapter 9); and those

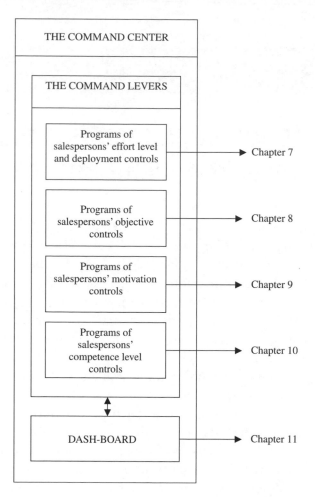

THE COMMAND CENTER

THE COMMAND LEVERS

Programs of
salespersons' effort level
and deployment controls → Chapter 7

Programs of
salespersons' objective
controls → Chapter 8

Programs of
salespersons' motivation
controls → Chapter 9

Programs of
salespersons'
competence level
controls → Chapter 10

DASH-BOARD → Chapter 11

Fig. II.1   Structure of Part II

programs that intend to maintain and increase salespeople's competencies
(Chapter 10). The firm must also have an adequate dashboard at its disposal
for exerting the right controls on individual salespeople's activities and
performances, as well as those of the whole sales force. Setting up adequate
dashboards and the necessary information flows are examined in the last
chapter (Chapter 11).

7   Controlling the overall selling effort

The dynamic management and sales force size control at Syntex Laboratories

A few years ago, Syntex Laboratories implemented a decision support system to estimate the optimal size of the sales force they should use (Lodish, Curtis, Ness, and Simpson 1988). Managers at different hierarchical levels estimated the sales market sensitivities to selling effort for various product lines and market segments. The sales force resources (reflected by mentions of a product or details) were optimally allocated to products and market segments. The objective was to allocate salespeople's time to those calls and mentions that were the most profitable to the firm. The final solution was provided as a list of the average number of mentions of each product that should be made to clients in every market segment.

The total time resources (and consequently, the required number of salespeople and the size of the sales force) were gradually increased until net profits started declining. As a result, it was possible to estimate the optimal sales force size and the optimal allocation of the resources simultaneously.

The procedure led to an increase in the size of the sales force from 433 to over 700, which was much larger than had been anticipated by management. The Syntex managers, however, had developed such confidence in the procedure that had been followed during the decision-making process, that they decided to accept those conclusions and dramatically increased their sales force.

They did not have to wait long for the results. The Syntex Laboratories showed an annual sales volume increase of about $25 million in the pharmaceutical product industry in which net profit margins are typically substantial. . .

This example shows how a firm that dynamically manages its sales force must monitor all aspects of its operations, even those that do not seem to raise problems on an *a priori* basis, as well as those that require research and analysis. One could compare the process exercised by Syntex with the complaint frequently heard from many sales managers that they have no clue as to whether their sales force is the right size.

Selecting the level of selling effort and the deployment of efforts over the market to be covered are key managerial decisions within the framework of meeting the sales manager's mission objectives. Practically, this involves deciding what the appropriate size of the sales force should be, its organization, and its deployment across sales territories. These decisions are difficult to make, often take some time to be properly implemented, and their effects are not felt for long periods of time. Through their control levers, sales managers can adjust the importance of the global selling effort, as well as its spatial and temporal allocations (Figure 7.1). In the following paragraphs, controlling the size of the sales force, its organization, and the design of its sales territory are examined in turn.

Controlling the size of the sales force

To select the sales force they need to accomplish their mission, sales managers must assess with some level of precision the "ideal" level of

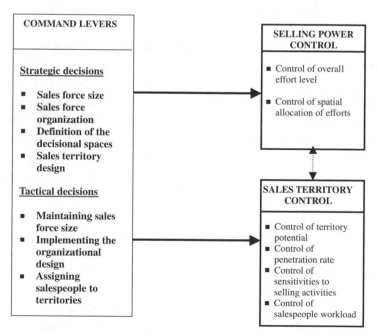

Fig. 7.1   Control effects of sales force sizing and organization

effort that is needed to cover the market and achieve the objectives of the mission that have been assigned to the sales force in the marketing plan. They must ensure that the sales force is at its ideal size.

Selecting the right size

Sales force sizing and allocation are important practical issues. The cost of personal selling is quite substantial, especially in industrial sectors. Having too many salespeople is inefficient because of unwarranted high selling costs, but, too few results in high opportunity costs. The Syntex Laboratories case study is a case in point. Any decision about the size of the sales force has a strong impact on salespeople's recruitment, the selection and training of the new hires, as well as on the number of middle sales managers available for coaching and supervising.

In spite of the profits at stake, few sales managers are confident that their sales force is the right size and is properly deployed. The main difficulty they experience is assessing what would be the additional revenues that adding one (or several) salesperson(s) to the sales force would bring, and/or by how much would the sales revenues be reduced if one (or several) salespeople were removed from the sales force. Managers frequently use their gut feeling or rely on crude decision rules to make these decisions (Fogg and Rockus 1973). Linking the sales force size to last year's sales volume or using industry guidelines (Buzzell and Farris 1976; Lilien 1979; Lilien and Weinstein 1984) are among the most frequently described methods in sales management textbooks (see, e.g., Johnston and Marshall 2006). Those methods are simple to understand and apply, but they generally lack theoretical soundness.

Alternatively, some firms use elaborate analytical procedures (see, e.g., Horsky and Nelson 1996; Zoltners and Sinha 1983). Such procedures, however, rely on elaborate analytical methods, and/or statistical techniques (Lilien, Kotler, and Moorthy 1992). As a result, they are not fully understood by analytically untrained managers. Consequently, management often lacks the confidence to use and implement the recommendations of such decision support systems. This dilemma highlights the need for decision aids that are appropriate for various types of organization (LaForge, Cravens, and Young 1986). Many small and medium-size organizations lack the resources for implementing highly sophisticated methods and often require procedures that are simple enough to be understood and accepted by managers, and at the same time, rigorous enough to provide, if not strictly optimal, at least close to optimal solutions.

Two broad types of approach to sales effort sizing and allocation have been proposed in the sales management literature. Some methods apply a workload approach. They are generally simple to implement, but they also tend to be over-simplistic. Others are based on the assessment of the market sensitivities to selling efforts. The latter methods (also called the incremental approach) are theoretically more satisfactory, but they tend to be more difficult to explain to management and to implement. Both types of approach are briefly reviewed in the following paragraphs.

Methods based on market sensitivities to selling efforts

Marketing analysts have provided some sophisticated methods for addressing the problem. They all imply estimating the market sensitivities to selling time (Parsons and Vanden Abeele 1981; Ryans and Weinberg 1987). These methods rely on the economic principle that markets are typically less and less responsive to additional selling efforts as new salespeople are added to the sales force. If one can estimate the sales revenue that one additional salesperson can yield, the rule is straightforward: keep increasing the sales force as long as an additional salesperson yields more gross profits than his/her own cost to the firm.

This is a simple principle. Its application, however, requires estimating with some precision the sales and gross margins that a sales force can generate at various size levels. Typically, this relies on analytical methods, like in the Syntex case outlined at the beginning of this chapter (see also Lodish 1975; 1976; Beswick and Cravens 1977; Zoltners and Sinha 1980).

One of the first methods of this type involved estimating the relationship between territory sales potential and sales revenues that could be expected from each territory (Semlow 1959). One should expect a direct relationship with marginally decreasing effects: in other words, if territories have a larger potential, they should yield larger sales (assuming constant effort). However, one should expect that larger potential territories yield smaller sales per unit of potential. Although Semlow's relationship specification was spurious (Weinberg and Lucas 1977), the basic principle remains, and is valid as long as the above-mentioned relationship does exist, is sufficiently strong, and can be estimated empirically with sufficient precision.

For example, the sales territory assigned to one given salesperson, with a sales potential of 10,000 units per time period could yield sales of 1,000 units per period of time. Another territory with a sales potential of 40,000 units, if assigned to the same salesperson could yield 2,000 unit sales per period. In the former case, the sales per unit of potential are equal to 0.1 units, while they are of 0.05 units in the latter case.

If the total market sales potential is estimated, for example, at 200,000 units per time period, it is relatively easy to assess the profitability of any sales force size, taking into account the sales and revenues that could be generated, as well as all the associated costs. In the example of the former territory, 20 salespeople, each one with an average territory sales potential of 10,000 units (i.e. 200,000/20) would be required to cover the whole market. Each salesperson would sell an average of 10,000 units, for total sales equal to 20,000 units. In contrast, in the latter case, only 5 salespeople would be needed, each one having a territory with an average sales potential of 40,000 units. In this case, the firm could expect sales to total 10,000 units per period. The remaining computations are straightforward and given in Figure 7.2. As a result, it is possible to estimate the size of the sales force needed to produce the highest profits.

Somewhat similar approaches have been documented in the analytical marketing literature (Lucas, Weinberg, and Clowes 1975; Horsky and Nelson 1996; Misra, Pinker, and Shumsky 2004; Zoltners, Sinha, and Zoltners 2001). Extensive reviews of such models have been proposed (see, e.g., Vandenbosh and Weinberg 1993).

All these methods assume that market sensitivities can be assessed with sufficient accuracy. Because of the data requirements as well as the difficulties of assessing customer or market sensitivities to selling effort through econometric techniques, most of these methods rely on managerial estimates (Beswick and Cravens 1977; Lodish 1975; 1976; Rangaswamy, Sinha, and Zoltners 1990; Zoltners and Sinha 1980). In fact, relationships between selling efforts and sales are not easy for management to estimate judgmentally. They require careful consideration, management experience and training, and expert analyses. Like in the Syntex example, judgmental estimates involve a lot of management time and effort. As a result, some firms prefer to use methods that are simpler to apply and implement, even if they are at the expense of scientific rigor.

Methods based on workload (or breakdown methods)

This method (Talley 1961), is described in many sales management textbooks (see, e.g., Johnston and Marshall 2006; Zoltners, Sinha, and Zoltners 2001). It is simple, even simplistic. It involves an assessment of the total sales force workload to cover the whole market. By dividing this total

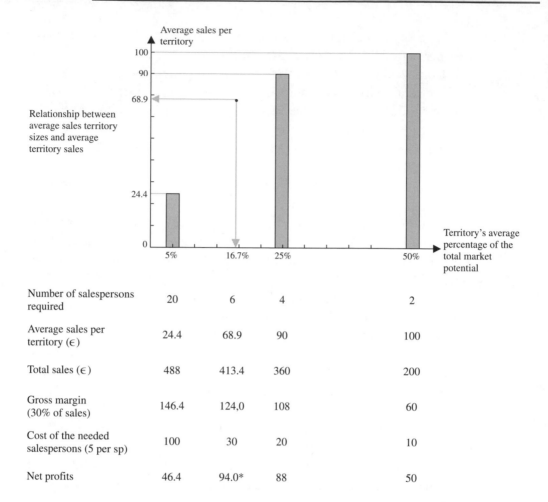

*The 6-salesperson solution maximizes net profits.

	5%	16.7%	25%	50%
Number of salespersons required	20	6	4	2
Average sales per territory (€)	24.4	68.9	90	100
Total sales (€)	488	413.4	360	200
Gross margin (30% of sales)	146.4	124,0	108	60
Cost of the needed salespersons (5 per sp)	100	30	20	10
Net profits	46.4	94.0*	88	50

Fig. 7.2   Examples of sales force size determination according to the market sensitivities to salespeople's efforts method

workload by the average workload that a salesperson can normally handle, one can roughly estimate the appropriate size of the sales force for adequate market coverage. The method implies five steps:

1. All prospect and customer accounts are classified into a relatively small number of segments that are homogeneous in terms of the selling efforts they require.
2. For each segment, appropriate call frequency and length for a typical client are estimated.

3. The total annual workload required from the whole sales force for total market coverage is derived from these estimates.
4. The annual workload that a salesperson can provide, as well as the proportion of the time he/she must spend in face-to-face contact with clients are then estimated.
5. Dividing the total workload that is necessary to cover the whole market by an average salesperson "contact time" workload provides a rough estimate of the sales force necessary to cover the market adequately.

An example using actual data is provided in Table 7.1.

The main advantage of this method is that it is easy to apply. However, it has three major drawbacks. First, it is difficult to find adequate estimates for the second stage of the procedure. These estimates require some knowledge of a typical client's sensitivities to various call policies in each segment, to decide which one is "optimal." Second, the method ignores the call time allocation problem — it makes no difference between the length of time required for making a large number of short calls to an account versus the same time spent making fewer, but longer, calls. Third, the method fails to

Table 7.1. Example of the workload approach to sales force sizing
N = 7,040 accounts and potential accounts

Step 1. *Classification of all the accounts*			Step 2. *Estimation of the contact time*		Step 3. *Computation of the total required time*
Account categories	Number of accounts in each category (1)		Number of calls/ year (2)	Typical call length (3)	Required time per year (hours) (4) = (1) x (2) x (3)
1. Key accounts	335		22.3	2.5	18,676
2. Medium-sized accounts	1,492		5.8	2.2	19,038
3. Small accounts	5,213		1.4	1.8	13,137
Total	**7,040**				**50,851**

Step 4
Annual working time available to a salesperson: 45 weeks x 35 hours = 1,575 hours
Percentage of working time spent in direct contact with clients: 44%
Contact time with clients per year and per salesperson: 1,575 x 0.44 = 693 hours.

Step 5
Number of salespeople required to cover the whole market: 50,851/693 = 73.38, i.e., 73 or 74 salespeople.

account for the revenue, cost and profit aspects of the problem, which should be of prime concern in a decision about sizing a sales force.

A method which reconciles both approaches

The two approaches that have been described in the preceding paragraphs represent the two opposite visions of control that have been discussed in Part I of this book, namely the centralized and decentralized control philosophies of management. As described in Table 7.2, while the workload (or breakdown) approach requires a centralized control (by management of salespeople's behavior through imposed call norms), the potential (or incremental) approaches to sales force sizing make decentralized controls by management of salesperson's outcomes possible.

Recently, an approach to sales force sizing has been proposed that combines the simplicity of the workload approach on which it relies, and the rigor of the market sensitivity approach (Darmon 2005). It takes into account the most desirable characteristics of market sensitivities which have

Table 7.2. Comparison between the workload and the potential methods of sales force sizing in terms of their underlying control approaches

Workload (or breakdown) methods	Potential (or incremental) methods
Salespeople are assumed to work during all (or a known fraction of) the time available	No specific assumption about selling time (salespeople work as long as is profitable (subject to the total time constraints))
Salespeople are assumed to share the firm's objective (maximizing profits), i.e., objectives must be imposed by management (call norms)	No assumption needed in terms of salespeople's objectives (no call norms required)
Allocation of accounts to territories is constrained only by a salesperson's total workload	Allocation of accounts to territories is constrained by providing salespeople with equal potential territories
Salespeople do not need information on sales response functions. They just need to follow call norms imposed by management	Salespeople need information on sales response functions to make optimal allocation of their time among accounts
Management should have information on sales response functions to set call norms	Management needs information on sales response functions to set up the territories properly
Centralized control by management of salespeople behavior required	**Decentralized controls by management of salespeople outcomes possible**

been shown to have strong impacts on sales force sizes, such as carryover effects (Sinha and Zoltners 2001). In addition, it accounts for the effects of one of the most relevant time allocations in this context, that is the allocation of a salesperson's time between the number and the length of calls (Sinha and Zoltners 2001). This five-step procedure is outlined in Table 7.3.

Because no method is free from limitations, and because of the (frequently neglected) impact of the sales force size decisions on a firm's profitability, it is always good managerial practice to use several approaches simultaneously and compare the results.

Table 7.3. Outline of the proposed optimal sales force sizing procedure

Step 1

With the help of knowledgeable managers, segment the customer base into a set of homo-
    geneous segments (in terms of size and/or responses to selling efforts). For each segment,
    estimate from call reports:
- the average number of calls actually made during a calling period
- the typical length of such calls, in hours
- the average sales volume expected during a calling period, in dollars
- the gross margin rate on those accounts, in decimal form
- the traveling cost to an account and cost of a time unit of contact time for each segment,
    in dollars
- the average number of customer contact hours available to a salesperson during a call
    period

Step 2

For each segment, secure five judgmental estimates from management:
- the maximum call frequency
- the maximum call length, in hours
- the minimum call length, in hours
- the sales level expected from a typical segment account, under a no call policy, in dollars
- the expected sales level under a maximum call policy, in dollars

Step 3

For each segment, estimate four parameters from the above data and validate them with extra
    managerial judgments.
Estimate the optimal call policies (C^*, t^*), by means of simple formulae that can be found in
    Darmon (2005). The product C^*t^* is the time required for servicing a client in a given
    segment.

Step 4

Follow the same procedures as in Steps 4 and 5 of the workload approach.

Maintenance of the sales force size

Determining the optimal sales force size is one thing. Keeping this sales force at its staffing target level is another. This is why it is impossible to manage a sales force dynamically for accomplishing its sales mission without a tight control over the sales force turnover rate. Sales force turnover is an important underlying factor to most sales force decisions. Recruiting activities are directly dependent on sales force turnover; sources of salespeople are characterized by different turnover rates; training and supporting salespeople's activities has a definite impact on salespeople's propensity to leave the sales force; compensation plans and quota procedures indirectly affect salespeople's motivation, and consequently, their willingness to stay with the company in the short or long term.

Controlling the sales force turnover rate implies a good knowledge of the causes of sales personnel attrition as well as estimates of the costs and benefits involved in the various aspects of sales force turnover. Given such knowledge, management can select the most appropriate tools for controlling salespeople's turnover.

Analysis of turnover costs and benefits

Although most sales managers cannot estimate them precisely (Mobley 1982), turnover costs are suspected to be extremely high. Researchers have identified and estimated the direct costs of turnover in organizations, although frequently in other contexts than sales forces (see, e.g., Cawsey and Wedley 1979; Flamholtz 1974; Mirvis and Lawler 1977; Tuggle 1978). Turnover, however, is often the cause of high opportunity costs. These are often hidden, only emerge in the long term, and are very difficult to estimate in practice (for estimation methods, see Darmon 1990b; Richardson 1999).

Sales force turnover generates a series of activities and decisions on the part of sales managers. When salespeople leave, they must be replaced. Consequently, turnover results in recruiting and selecting activities, training, supporting, supervising, compensating, quota setting, and controlling new salespeople using different methods from those used for those who have left. All these activities result in costs (and sometimes benefits) that affect the firm's financial results (Figure 7.3).

Figure 7.3 shows all the different costs that a firm incurs when a salesperson leaves the sales force, and consequently, leaves a territory vacant

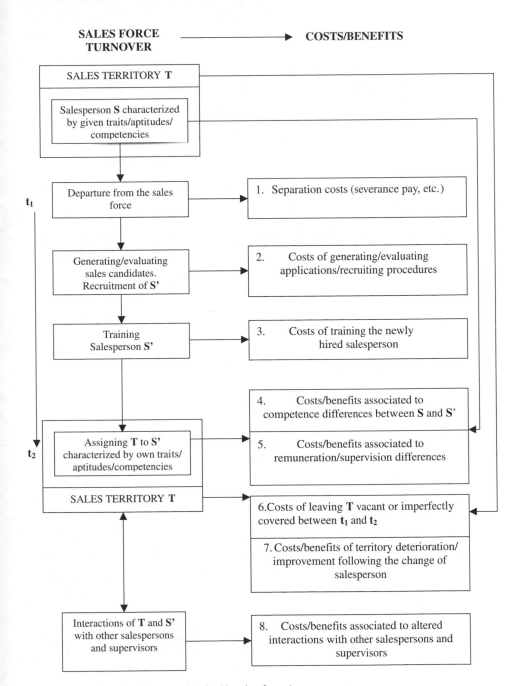

Fig. 7.3   Costs/benefits associated with sales force turnover

(at time t_0), and until a new salesperson can take over the same territory (at time t_1). These costs include:

1. Opportunity costs of decreased sales resulting from a loss of motivation and commitment to the job, as soon as a salesperson has taken the decision to quit (and possibly, even before).
2. Separation costs. These include severance pay and any other allowances a salesperson may be entitled to receive.
3. Opportunity costs of decreased sales between the time a salesperson has resigned and actual departure, assuming a salesperson is allowed to stay during the legal notification period.
4. Recruiting and selection costs. These are the costs of replacing the salesperson, unless the firm wishes to reduce the size of its sales force.
5. Training costs. These are the costs of training new salespeople before they can take charge of their territories. They also include the time managers and other salespeople spend in the field with the newly-hired salesperson for training purposes.
6. Costs of excess personnel during the time the departing and the newly hired salespeople overlap (two individuals on the payroll for one single sales territory).
7. Differential skill costs (or benefits). The new salesperson may have different skills and competencies from the old salesperson, which may result in more or less lasting differential sales (and, consequently, profits). The two individuals may also have different expected career paths and outlooks.
8. Opportunity cost of lost sales during the adaptation period for the new salesperson.
9. Differential operating costs (or benefits). If the departing and incoming salespeople require higher (or lower) remuneration levels, especially in terms of salary and other fixed components of the compensation package, or need more (or less) supervision by managers, the result may be increased (or decreased) costs.
10. Vacant territory costs caused by a decreased level of service in the vacant territory and/or the time managers must spend in the vacant territory before a replacement is found and trained. In practice, these costs are difficult to estimate because they include such long-term effects as loss of goodwill, impaired relationships with customers, and competitive inroads. Note that these costs are incurred only when managers fail to predict and make provision for the departure of the salesperson.

Sales managers can accurately predict retirements and/or promotions, but predicting voluntary departures is more difficult.

11. Vacant territory costs caused by sales decreases in adjacent territories, when these salespeople have to cover a vacant territory.

12. Sales territory quality differential costs (or benefits). Sometimes, salespeople take with them a certain number of clients who wish to remain loyal to them rather than the firm. In such cases, turnover results in some lasting downgrading of the sales territory, with the associated opportunity costs. Alternatively, the new salesperson may bring new customers from their previous business relationships, and, consequently, upgrade the territory quality. This may lead to increased profits for the firm.

13. Social and/or organizational costs (or benefits). Sales force turnover may also have a number of consequences that are even more difficult to quantify. They include disruption of social and communication structures, productivity loss (during replacement, search, and retraining), decreased satisfaction among those salespeople that stay, and negative public relations from those who have left. From the point of view of the individual who stays, other consequences include the disruption of social and communication patterns, the loss of valued co-workers, decreased satisfaction, increased workload while a replacement is found for, and decreased cohesion and lower commitment (Mobley 1982). Many of these negative consequences can turn into opportunities if the departing salesperson is a low sales producer, and/or is not especially appreciated by management and colleagues.

Outcomes of turnover analysis

Following such a cost analysis, it is possible to assess whether the turnover from different types of salesperson results in more cost than benefits (direct and opportunity costs/gains). Sales force attrition is heterogeneous and not uniformly costly to a company (Lucas *et al.* 1987). Sales force turnover is not necessarily all bad. There are cases where sales force turnover results in more benefit than cost, for example, where a poor sales producer is replaced by a high caliber salesperson. It is not always recognized that sales force turnover is heterogeneous and that the associated costs are far from being uniform. At least one part of sales force turnover may not always be a bad thing. As underlined in Chapter 3, one should make a clear distinction between *functional* and *dysfunctional* turnover (Dalton *et al.* 1982; Johnston and Futrell 1989).

Functional turnover is beneficial to a company because it affects salespeople whose performance level is below company's standard. These salespeople have not (yet) been fired because managers believe they will eventually improve or because they are former high performers whom managers tolerate as long as their performance remains at "reasonable" levels. Turnover among this type of salesperson may be beneficial: "A flushing-out of 'dead wood' is good" (Williamson 1983, p. 26).

In contrast, dysfunctional turnover affects salespeople the company definitely would like to retain because their performance is at least satisfactory. None would argue against reducing dysfunctional turnover. Functional turnover, however, raises completely different managerial issues. Why were such people hired in the first place? Why did they turn out to produce such low sales? A firm could reduce functional turnover by improving, for example, the quality of the recruiting procedures or its sales force training program.

Control of the turnover rate

As a result of typically high sales force turnover rates (often in the 20 to 30 percent range, and sometimes higher), most firms consider turnover as a serious problem and make it a priority to keep the highest performing salespeople within their sales force.

However, sales force turnover is often considered by sales managers to be a problem with no solution in sight, at least in the short term. A survey by Learning International (1987) of 500 salespeople and sales managers in the United States and Canada showed some interesting discrepancies between managers' opinions and facts. More than half the respondents thought that turnover rates were the same as five years before and would remain constant in the future. In fact, turnover had tripled in those five years, from 7.6 to 27 percent (Coleman 1989). A majority of salespeople had been with their companies for five years or less, and about 20 percent had over ten years of tenure with their present employer.

Even when sales managers report some willingness to seriously address the turnover problem, few seem to have definite policies or well established programs to do it. There are, however, a number of possible actions that can be taken to reduce this costly turnover rate in the short or long term

(Darmon 1990b). Contrasting the actions actually taken by managers and those that should be taken to rationally and systematically address the problem may be revealing. In any case, to keep the sales force at its desired size, a firm must recruit salespeople at a rate that is commensurate with the size of the sales force and with its turnover rate.

Although managers cannot equally control all the causes of turnover, there is no sound reason for limiting turnover to voluntary departure, as is often the case. Of course, they can make provisions for retirement, but they have little or no control on this part of turnover that generally affects the older members of the sales force. Firings and promotions are also, at least to an extent, under managerial control and require specific policies and decisions.

Control of promotion turnover

Salespeople may leave an active selling job because they are promoted to managerial duties within or outside the sales force. Promoting good sales performers to managerial levels has definite motivating consequences for the sales force. As a result, this part of turnover cannot be completely avoided. The extent to which managers follow this practice is a policy decision that has an impact on turnover and costs and one on which managers can exert some — even if limited — control.

A study carried among Fortune 500 companies sheds some light on how salespeople are promoted to first level management (Guest and Meric 1989). It was found that the Fortune 500 human resource managers were in general agreement with previous research findings about the type of personality traits that are crucial prerequisites to effective sales management: motivation, human relation skills, higher than average energy, ambition, persuasiveness, human interaction, behavior flexibility, perception of threshold social cues, intellectual abilities, personal impact, and tolerance of uncertainty.

What is surprising is that only a small fraction of those firms (16 percent) use psychological tests administered by professional psychologists to measure those traits. This suggests that executives in charge of these appointments have great faith in their own ability to detect these qualities in prospective candidates. Turnover rates among first level managers (excluding turnover for promotion) was relatively high (39 percent of the firms reported turnover rates over 10 percent).

This is why, before deciding to promote a salesperson, a manager should explicitly weigh the anticipated benefits to the whole organization from the promotion against the costs it will cause to the sales force. Although such benefits (which include the positive signals that promotion sends to other people in the organization, lower selection costs for managers, or possibly lower turnover rates among managers) are difficult to quantify, managers may be able to judge whether or not they are likely to override the estimated costs.

Control of voluntary dysfunctional turnover

Sales managers always try to retain their top salespeople who are tempted to leave because they receive better offers from other companies. The demand for successful salespeople has always been high, and companies try to poach top sales staff from rival companies. Despite the high cost estimates reported above, few organizations seem to have developed systematic procedures and policies to keep this type of turnover under control (Futrell and Parasuraman 1984). The following factors, among others, tend to prevent this.

First, there is a lack of relevant data about sales force attrition (Williamson 1983). Few organizations can readily answer such questions as: what are the characteristics of salespeople who decide to quit? What are the actual causes of sales force attrition? Turnover data are seldom collected and analyzed systematically. Sales managers often consider that sales force turnover is a curse that cannot be avoided, and that they have to live with it. Some observers, however, have noticed that the same managers often attribute a decrease in turnover rate to managerial actions (such as better recruiting or better support).

Second, managers tend to turn their attention to more visible and straightforward aspects of sales force management. There is a general tendency for managers to concentrate on direct (and visible) costs at the expense of opportunity (and hidden) costs. As turnover involves essentially opportunity costs, this may not be surprising.

Third, there is a general lack of recognition that sales force attrition cannot be addressed properly if it is treated as an isolated phenomenon. When attempting to reduce turnover, managers cannot ignore other related aspects of sales force management such as the validity and reliability of the recruiting process, the training program's quality and length, and remuneration levels. For that purpose, they often lack a systemic framework to manage dynamically and simultaneously all these interrelated aspects of sales force management leading to turnover control. Turnover management is part of a dynamic management process.

Control of functional turnover

Functional turnover can be handled through additional and special training, coaching, and/or support for low sales producers to bring them up to an acceptable performance level. In hopeless cases, however, sales managers have no option but to dismiss these low performers. In the latter case, the manager must determine the boundary between "acceptable" and "unacceptable" performance. To make a rational decision about this control lever, a manager must know the performance level below which it is less costly to fire a salesperson (taking into account all the associated costs including the relevant opportunity costs) than to keep them. This is difficult to assess precisely without a formal analytical procedure (Darmon 1990b).

Practical levers for turnover control   Sales force turnover is a heterogeneous phenomenon the causes of which are generally multiple and inter-related. As a result, it is impossible to manage sales force turnover effectively and rationally without understanding its mechanisms as well as the costs (and benefits) that may result. Based on the results of the survey mentioned earlier, Learning International has developed some guidelines to help sales managers to reduce high turnover:

1. Be aware of the turnover problem, and understand its causes. Exit interviews and attitude surveys should be used on a more systematic basis.
2. Pay attention to the total cost of turnover, especially hidden and opportunity costs that are not easy to quantify.
3. Adopt an open-door style of management, to encourage salespeople to speak their mind and point out sources of dissatisfaction.
4. Be sensitive to all work-related issues, not just to compensation (which tends to be overemphasized by management). Supervision, support, and training are important issues related to turnover.
5. Conduct periodic audits to identify possible sources of job dissatisfaction, and to frequently ask salespeople about their perceptions of their work.
6. Set recruiting standards carefully.
7. Re-evaluate training strategies, and make sure that salespeople are properly trained before they go out into the field (Coleman 1989).

However, there are always situations where turnover cannot be reduced, especially in the short term. The problem that a firm faces here is different. The firm must devise policies that best decrease (or minimize) turnover costs. Certain recruiting and training policies can be devised to that effect (Darmon 2004a).

Research into sales force turnover has shown that all salespeople are not equally likely to leave the sales force. By establishing relationships between salespeople's characteristics and turnover, these studies at least suggest some possible bases for turnover segmentation. For example, if turnover can be shown to be related to age, age can be used as a meaningful basis to segment the sales force. Different age groups may require different managerial actions and programs to reduce turnover. These should be based on factors that cause turnover in the specific segment and that are under managerial control.

Control of the sales force organization

Selecting the size of the sales force and deciding how to organize it are not independent issues. The selected organizational structure, and consequently, the allocation of the selling tasks within a sales force, requires adequate human resources. Research suggests that resource allocation has an even greater impact on profitability than proper sales force sizing (Sinha and Zoltners 2001). The way a sales force is organized has a strong impact on its activities and performance. When Peugeot, the car manufacturer, decided to bring the firm closer to its clients, it reorganized its sales organization and eliminated several management levels. This reduced the number of people at Peugeot headquarters with whom the firm's network agents had to deal.

Several options are opened to management when organizing a sales force. First, there is a choice between an internal versus outsourced sales force. There are an almost infinite number of ways the selling tasks can be assigned to the various sales force members. Of special concern is the way key accounts are managed. Managers need to specify the decisional space that they wish to give to every member of the sales organization, and consequently, to specify the role and mission objectives that they want to assign to every sales force member.

Choice of internal or outsourced sales forces

One of the basic decisions that management must make is whether to sell its products or services through an internally controlled sales force or through more or less independent agents (outsourced sales force, exclusive or non-exclusive agents, etc.). These two major options reflect successively a centralized control of the selling function, or a fully decentralized approach. As a result, this decision is linked to the approach selected for a dynamic management process, a fundamental characteristic of a sales organization's management. According to transaction cost analysis (Williamson 1975; 1981), when a salesperson's performance is difficult to assess, there is an increased probability that a firm will use a directly controlled sales force rather than a commission-motivated organization.

A firm should always outsource some of its activities to benefit from the best conditions they can get from competing suppliers. In this case, controls are exerted through market mechanisms (Williamson 1979). This type of control is less costly to a firm than bureaucratic controls required to systematically control an in-house sales force. In some cases, however, markets can lose efficiency, and suppliers may behave opportunistically, that is, they may acquire specific assets, competencies, and know-how that can only be used by the contracting customer. To sell a firm's products, agents may need to acquire specific technical knowledge about certain customer applications. If acquiring this knowledge is time consuming and costly, a firm may incur considerable costs if it wishes to replace its agents (because of research and training costs). As a result, these agents may take advantage of the situation and become less flexible or reduce the quality of the services they are expected to provide. In such cases, the firm may have an interest in keeping full control over such activities through vertical integration. Transaction cost analysis has been found to at least partially explain firms' behaviors (Anderson 1985; John and Weitz 1989). Many other predictions of this theory, however, have not found empirical support (Anderson 1985, p. 250).

Outsourcing a sales force can take different forms. It can mean an external organization to set up a sales force on the behalf of a firm that has no sales organization at its disposal. It may also mean using the sales force of another organization that sells other types of products or services to the same clientele, and that accomplishes all the tasks and functions that are typically carried out by an internal sales force. Sometimes, firms disband their direct sales force and commit fully to an indirect or outsourced sales strategy. In this case, a sales manager either works directly for the outsourcing firm, or hires an agency to recruit and manage the indirect sales force. A firm may also choose to retain all or part of its direct sales force and outsource other selling functions (Giannini 2005).

An increasing number of firms, especially small and medium-sized organizations, find it profitable to outsource their selling function.

There has been a sharp increase in the number of firms that have done this and it encompasses most markets (Anderson and Trinkle 2005). The following arguments are often advanced when making such a decision (Giannini 2005):

- Outsourcing firms only pay for performance, because contracted re-sellers are not compensated if they do not sell. Typically, they either receive a commission on sales, or they are sold the goods at a discount price.
- Whether contracted re-sellers are called representatives, agents, distributors, wholesalers, or partners, they are professionals that already know how to sell.
- They already specialize in selling similar products to target customers.
- They enjoy high credibility in the market place because, as established re-sellers, they have been calling on customers for years and have developed long-standing customer relationships.
- They have other products to sell, so they frequently find opportunities to sell the outsourcing firm's products as well.
- Contracted re-sellers and outsourcing firms share the same basic interests, and the contracted re-sellers are likely to provide candid and timely feedback from the field.
- The outsourcing firm's sales function is often enhanced through the outsourcing process.

To assess if a function is efficiently fulfilled internally (through vertical integration), or externally (through independent agents under decentralized contracts) a firm is likely to select the solution that minimizes direct and opportunity costs of its transactions. The firm accounts for the fact that it enjoys only limited and imperfect information, and that it can anticipate the opportunistic behaviors of some parties that can take advantage of the situation (Anderson 1985).

Research suggests that when salespeople's performances are difficult to assess, or when transactions require special skills, or when tasks that are not directly related to selling are important, a firm tends to exert a direct control on its sales force activities, and tends to use internal fully-controlled sales forces rather than agents who are compensated by commission (Anderson 1985). More than ever, cost control has become vital for most firms. It is not surprising that a control strategy through market mechanisms has become increasingly popular.

The trend toward an increasing number of firms outsourcing their sales function may, however, contrast with the importance that many firms give to the development of high quality relationships with customers. For example, one may question whether it is wise to delegate the selling function to salespeople who have not been selected and trained by the outsourcing firms.

These firms usually give several specific situational reasons to explain their decision to outsource. For some firms, it is an opportunity to cover a new market segment or use a new distribution channel. For others, it is a means to test a new product or introduce a foreign brand into the national market. In such instances, outsourcing sales activities allows a firm to test the probability of success of a new product before investing in building a new sales force. Sometimes, firms find it more profitable to concentrate selling efforts in key market segments through an internal sales force, and leave less profitable and less strategic segments to an outsourced organization. For example, the Printing Solution Division at Hewlett-Packard has a sales force which calls on wholesalers, key accounts, and important resellers. The company has contracted an external organization to call on medium-sized and small accounts and to detect the best market opportunities. American Express follows a similar strategy. It uses additional external sales forces to increasing the number of small retailers that accept the American Express credit card with all the required flexibility for operating in the most promising regions at the most appropriate time. Other companies justify outsourcing strategy as their activities are highly seasonal and do not justify a year-round sales force. Whatever the reasons they give, however, all these firms have as their objective minimizing costs, insuring maximum reactivity and flexibility while ensuring high market coverage.

Deployment of selling efforts over the market

Selecting the optimal allocations of the selling tasks to be accomplished by a sales force is another very complex problem that requires elaborate analytical optimization techniques. Obviously, these decisions are strongly related to the design of the sales territory, as these materialize an allocation of the selling responsibilities among the sales force. Research has shown that 55 percent of sales territories in a typical company are either too large (and, consequently, impossible to cover properly) or too small (salespeople spend too much time to cultivate unprofitable customers) (Zoltners and Lorimer 2000).

To solve this problem, one should account for the sensitivities of every client to the selling efforts of every salesperson when they exert various tasks (such as selling every product line and all the various tasks involved in developing and maintaining good customer relationships). An adequate solution must also account for the associated costs incurred, to identify the allocation that brings the highest benefits for each euro invested. The selected allocation must also be coherent. For example, it may not be appropriate to assign different salespeople to a client which purchases different product lines from the firm. Consequently, the selection method must account for a huge number of constraints and interactions, and makes this decision process extremely difficult. Finally, the allocation must take into account the human constraints imposed by the need to keep the motivation of the sales staff high (Smith, Jones, and Blair 2000).

As a result, the members of a sales force can be specialized according to a series of criteria such as geography, markets (and customers), product lines, and/or selling functions (Table 7.4). In practice, when a sales force must accomplish numerous, varied, and complex tasks, more allocation criteria are needed to define the tasks that are assigned to each salesperson. Note that the order according to which those criteria are applied is extremely important because different orders lead to very different allocations. For example, allocating the sales resources geographically and then by product line leads to an organization that is very different from an allocation by product line followed by a geographical criterion. In the former case, two salespeople selling different product lines cover the same geographical territory. In the latter case, two different sales forces specializing in selling different product lines do not need to have the same geographical definition of their respective territories.

As Table 7.4 shows, each type of organization has its own advantages and drawbacks, and each one tends to best apply to different market situations.

Control of key account servicing

How to organize to ensure the adequate management of key accounts is another important managerial decision. For example, should the responsibility for such accounts be assigned to a specialized sales force, or should it be shared among the whole sales force? A key account could generate a significant current or potential sales volume and that requires a coordinated approach.

Because clients are becoming scarce, it is not unusual for a single client to account for more than 20 percent of a supplier's business. As discussed in

Table 7.4. Main criteria for defining a sales force organization

Organizational structure	Advantages	Drawbacks	Appropriate selling situations
Geography	No duplication of customer or market coverage Fewer hierarchical levels Less costly	Limited specialization Difficulty of managerial controls upon effort allocations among product line and customers	Coverage of an extended geographical area for selling non complex and relatively homogeneous products and/or answering to relatively homogeneous customer needs
Markets	Salespeople have a good understanding of the specific needs of their clients Enhanced managerial ability to control sales-people's effort alloca-tions across markets	Geographical duplication of territories Higher costs	The firm sells products to clients with heterogeneous needs which require from salespeople a thorough knowledge of customers' needs and problems
Products	Salespeople can get expert knowledge of the products sold Increased managerial ability to control salespeople's effort allocations across products	Geographical duplication of territories Duplication of markets and clients	The firm sells complex product lines that are different from one another, that are typi-cally not sold to the same clients and to the same markets
Functions	Efficient performance of the various selling activities Increased managerial ability to control salespeople's effort allocations across different activities	Geographical duplication of territories Duplication of markets and clients	The selling process for the firm's products requires different functions and require quite different skills from salespeople (e.g., telemarketing, key account management, etc.)

Chapter 2, the current tendency is for buyers to purchase from a limited number of suppliers and to expect a lot of services from them. These clients require especially competent salespeople with particular management skills in order to re-establish some power equilibrium. A firm that selects this type of organization must also adopt an adequate sales force structure: to whom should such salesperson report? what is the extent of their responsibilities and decisional space? how should they be recruited, trained, and what should be their typical career path?

A study has shown that 43 percent of the firms surveyed judged that they were not quick enough to restructure their resources to build adequate dynamic management programs for serving key accounts. Barely half of them considered that their key account management programs yielded satisfactory results (Crane 2000).

For small and medium-sized firms, it is often difficult to specialize in key account management. Key accounts are frequently scattered over markets, so it is sometimes difficult for a key account manager to keep in frequent contact with all of them. This was the case of an important alarm manufacturer who, after setting up a specialized key account sales force, has been forced to assign key account responsibilities to regular salespeople.

For large firms, specialization by market rather than geography for key account management is generally more appropriate, because such clients now tend to think globally and express specific needs according to the market. This is why a branch of Alcatel (Vacuum Technology) has switched from a geographical specialization (United States, Asia, Europe, rest of the world) to a matrix organization with objectives for each zone and key account salesperson. A similar matrix organization has been adopted by Schneider Electric.

It seems that there is no universal solution for organizing the key account management function. Two factors, however, are determinant − the need for service of the key accounts, on the one hand, and the costs that are incurred by a particular organization on the other.

Control of supervision

Sales managers may decide to supervise their staff using different levels of closeness. Some select a decentralized approach because they believe in salesperson empowerment. They think that salespeople should enjoy a large autonomy and they wish to encourage individual initiative. Here, managers exert only a light control − less costly to the firm. Other managers prefer to exert centralized supervision to control salespeople's activities more tightly (and consequently, reduce their decisional space). Their objective is to take any necessary corrective action as early as possible.

Obviously, as it requires more supervision, this approach implies smaller spans of control for supervisors, and consequently, it tends to be more costly to a firm.

Whatever the approach selected, an adequate supervision and supervisory style can induce a high motivation level among salespeople by helping them to achieve the highest possible performance level. To that effect, supervisors can help every salesperson to make the most efficient time allocations, by trying to increase contact time with customers at the expense of less productive tasks. A number of decision aids have been developed to make such optimal decisions (see, e.g., Lodish 1971). In addition, salespeople often expect their managers to provide help, advice, and support, especially when they face particularly difficult situations in the field. In any case, adequate sales force dynamic management and control implies giving positive and constructive guidance to salespeople to foster a good and co-operative organizational climate.

Control of decision spaces

Sales managers can implement their control style through the control of every sales force member's decisional space. A salesperson's decisional space has at least three levels. The first set of decisions that salespeople make include the quantity and quality of efforts and resources they wish to deploy in their territories. It also includes the spatial allocation of their resources (among clients, selling the different product lines, etc.) as well as the temporal allocations (i.e. how such efforts are deployed over time). This part of salesperson's decision space depends on the closeness of their supervision. For example, when a sales manager assigns very precise sales quotas for a given product to each salesperson, the salespeople have a relatively restricted decision space. They can decide to try to meet this sales quota or not. Alternatively, if the sales manager does not assign quotas, salespeople have more leeway to set up (within limits) their own sales objectives.

The level of initiative that is left to salespeople during their interactions with clients constitutes a second dimension of their decisional space. In the case of sales negotiations, salespeople are typically given a much larger decisional space than in transactional selling. Salespeople, or more likely sales teams, can make decisions on a number of aspects of the negotiation, and can even make concessions on price, payment and/or delivery conditions (within limits). In the case of non-negotiated transactions, salespeople typically enjoy a more restricted decision space, as they cannot alter the general conditions imposed by their managers.

At a third level, salespeople may be entrusted with a more or less extended decision space depending on the initiative they have been given to select the most appropriate selling strategies, depending on the situation at hand. In many cases, salespeople enjoy complete freedom for making this type of decision. In some extreme cases which tend to disappear, though, salespeople must strictly follow a canned presentation in which nothing (if ever possible) has been left to chance (Jolson 1975). Here again, as a result of more or less close supervision and controls, salespeople may enjoy a more or less extended decisional space.

Under decentralized control, management leaves a vast decisional space to salespeople. Inversely, a very restricted decisional space reflects a more centralized control and supervision. To sum up, the definition of sales-people's decisional space, as well as the corresponding intensity of managerial controls and supervision, reflect the firm's management philosophy. It is often a part of its organizational culture.

Control of job perception

When the role and mission of a sales force are well defined, when the organization of the sales force is determined, it is relatively easy to draw a detailed and precise job description for a salesperson. Such job descriptions should precisely list all the tasks that salespeople must carry out and for which they are responsible. A detailed and precise job description must exhaustively list all the tasks for which a salesperson is accountable. Under a centralized approach, it may provide some indication of the relative importance of those responsibilities, and give salespeople some idea about the proportion of the time they must devote to fulfilling every duty. For that purpose, it is essential for management to have even an approximate idea of the relative productivities of the time that a salesperson spends on carrying out different tasks. Following economic principles, an optimal allocation of a salesperson's time implies that once all the time is allocated, an additional time unit brings exactly the same marginal profits, irrespective of the activity to which it is allocated. Although difficult to strictly apply in practice, this principle may be used by sales managers as a guideline for making better allocation decisions. Using a more decentralized approach, a salesperson's job description tends to be shorter and less detailed. However, it should clearly specify the limits of salespeople's decision spaces.

From a managerial point of view, one cannot overemphasize the benefits of actually setting up such detailed and precise job descriptions. In fact, a good job description constitutes a sound basis on which most, if not all, sales force management decisions rely. How can one make good decisions about sales force size, without a clear idea of what tasks every type of salesperson is responsible for? The job description is one starting point of the approach to sales force sizing. It would be very difficult to establish recruitment criteria for new salespeople, and set up the content and length of their initial training program without a clear description of what they will have to do once they have been recruited. How could management devise adequate motivation, support, evaluation, and supervision programs without a mutual understanding of what salespeople are responsible for? Consequently, all the managerial control decisions concerning salespeople and the sales force are much easier to make if the decisions rely on a precise and detailed job description. For a sound and rational dynamic management and control of a sales force, no sales manager can do without it.

A detailed and precise job description, known and understood by all the parties, can also prevent salespeople from developing inaccurate or ambiguous perceptions of their roles, or eliminate perceived role conflicts. Such perceptions have been shown to frequently cause a loss of motivation, stress, and low morale among salespeople. It should also be underlined that detailed sales job descriptions must be written, irrespective of the extent of the decision space granted to salespeople, and consequently, of the level of sale force centralization and control. Even when considerable leeway is given to salespeople in some areas, they must be aware of the limits of what they can or cannot do in a work situation.

Control of sales territories

Sales territory design cannot be treated independently from sales force organization. The specification of every sales territory depends on the way the salespeople's responsibilities have been defined, as well as on the criteria that have been applied to specify those responsibilities. For example, responsibilities may have been specified according to geographical criteria, product lines, types of clients and/or product application, customer sizes, or any combination of those criteria. Splitting the sales functions among salespeople according to such criteria is no easy task. The general objective is to split the total task equally. In practice, one of the major difficulties encountered by sales managers is that equal workload territories may exhibit considerable variance on other dimensions that may jeopardize the harmonious solution one is looking for.

For example, a territory in urban zone and a rural territory may have equal workloads for the respective salespeople in charge of those territories. In the former case visiting the various clients may require little traveling time. Covering the rural territory may take much longer and might represent a larger fraction of the salesperson's working time — consequently, this salesperson has a much shorter time for customer contacts. No need to specify that it will be easier and faster to penetrate the former territory than the latter.

This is why when designing a sales territory, it is important to take into account such factors as sales potential, current sales penetration rates, as well as the traveling time required for adequate coverage. Given the complexity of the problem, as well as the huge amount of information needed to solve it, firms sometimes use special software programs. One such program builds up territories by assembling smaller geographical units (or standard geographical units). At the same time, the program must abide by some workload and potential constraints. The objective is often to make territories that equalize activities or sales targets, such as the number of calls or the total workload for every salesperson. The combination of smaller geographical units is done in such a way as to build compact territories (to minimize travel costs) using only contiguous units. Technically, the program minimizes the sum of the moments of inertia defined in this case as the product of the importance of a geographical unit in terms of the selected criterion by the square distance to the center of the designed territory (Hess and Samuels 1971).

In order to assign sales territories to the different salespeople in the sales force, management also faces a number of constraints. These constraints include those imposed by the original territory configuration such as, for example, where the salespeople live, the importance of the individual relationship that every salesperson has already built with clients and which, short of mandatory reasons, should not be destroyed. In some other cases, salespeople may have special abilities for working in certain areas. The general principle that managers should strive to apply (within the above mentioned constraints) is to assign the best sales producers to the best territories, as much as possible.

Conclusion

This chapter has considered the major control levers of dynamic sales force management. These control levers are those that shape the sales force and provide the general direction in which the sales organization should move over the months ahead. Consequently, they are control levers that sales managers are likely to use with extreme care because of their long-lasting effects on a sales force and its members. As discussed above, these command levels are decisions concerning the size of the sales force and effort to be deployed over the firm's markets, as well as the means to keep the target sales force at its staffing level over time. These decisions attempt to control the sales force turnover rate, or at least to minimize its costs. Another set of command levels is constituted by all the decisions concerning the organization of the sales force and its actual deployment over the market by means of the design of sales territories. The control and sales force management through its organization implies the specification of the type of supervision and how close this supervision should be. Consequently, it implies the choice of the centralization/decentralization level that a firm wishes to exert over its sales force in general and over its salespeople in particular. It also implies the specification of detailed, precise, and formal job descriptions, as well as the clear definition of salespeople's decisional spaces.

In the following chapters, more current and "everyday" type of control levers will be examined. These are more operational control levers that are used in a more routine fashion to motivate, support, and supervise salespeople, and to raise their competence levels.

8 Tools for controlling centralized processes: specific objective programs

Two control philosophies

The president of a well-known consulting firm does not believe in quantitative objectives for salespeople. He claims that instead of focusing on quantitative objectives by asking a salesperson to meet a given sales volume target, it is better to provide qualitative objectives, such as prospecting a target segment of customers. According to this company president, sales managers should not limit themselves to assigning individual objectives because, although individual objectives induce salespeople to remain committed, only collective action makes the difference.

The president of another major corporation holds quite a different view and asserts that qualitative objectives do not work with salespeople. According to him, only two objectives matter: sales volumes and gross margins. He was reported to say in an executive meeting: "One should stop talking nonsense with those qualitative objectives, number of calls, and so on that lead to evaluate salespeople according to subjective criteria. In addition, selling is an individual sport. Consequently, except for the year end party when the total objective is met, I cannot see what can be done in common."

How can such dramatically opposed points of view be reconciled? Which of these two executives speaks the truth?

In fact, there is some truth in both arguments. They are only limited by the fact that each executive gives his own vision of the sales force dynamic management process. However, these are far from being incompatible. Each one can apply to specific selling situations, especially when it is compatible with the specific organizational culture and management styles that prevail within each firm.

Over the years, some firms have implemented centralized management and control styles. At one major producer of mattresses and related products, objectives are set by top level management according to a provisional budget, and salespeople have no input whatsoever. This does not raise any issue in their sales force. Many other firms, for example Kuoni, one of the leading tour operators, follow this centralized objective-setting procedure.

In many other firms, however, salespeople set their own objectives, and probably have as much success. These firms use a more decentralized and participative management style.

It was seen in Chapter 5 that sales managers can use either a centralized or decentralized approach for controlling and managing salespeople's activities, and to do this they have a certain number of control levers at their disposal. Because neither of these two types of management style is necessarily better than the other, both approaches are examined, together with their respective managerial tools for implementing them in an organization. This chapter focuses on the control levers that are generally used when implementing more centralized controls. These allow various levels of centralization. Chapter 9 looks at more decentralized control levers for sales force control.

The problem of controlling salespeople's activity cannot be considered independently from the types of objectives assigned to a sales force, the processes followed for setting those objectives, as well as of the way these objectives are communicated to the sales force. It also cannot be separated from the issue of defining salespeople's decision spaces. Centralized decisions at higher hierarchical levels of an organization can only be achieved at the expense of the leeway left to salespeople to make their own decisions.

The tools of centralized control can apply to salespeople's activities and/or performance. In both cases, they imply setting very precise target objectives called quotas, and they are linked to (often financial) rewards when they are met or to (typically non-financial) sanctions when they are not.

Direct control of activities

Figure 8.1a describes a centralized approach for controlling sales activities. Salespeople are assigned very precise activity levels (such as the number of calls they must make, or the number of prospects they should approach every week). By performing these activities in their territories, salespeople are supposed to obtain the desired performance results (sales, or converted

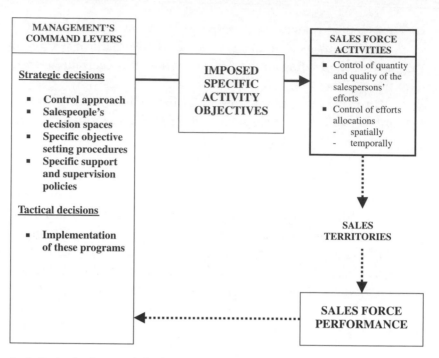

Fig. 8.1a   Centralized sales force control using specific activity objectives

prospects). To check that they have actually carried their assignments, management must establish close supervision and controls.

This may pursue two very different objectives On the one hand, supervision may permit sales managers to exert a direct control over salespeople and to evaluate them. On the other hand, it may aim at increasing their competence levels. This second managerial objective may be exerted within the framework of a centralized or decentralized policy, and is discussed in greater detail in Chapter 10.

When the supervision of salespeople aims to control their activities and/or evaluate them, it attempts to control the quantity of the efforts deployed by a salesperson as well as the effort allocation among those activities. In this case, a supervisor's role is defined as controlling whether every salesperson makes a given number of calls every day, or making sure that salespeople strictly abide by the rules set by management concerning the time allotted to each activity. The major objective is for management to control all the selling activities.

Centralized control systems often give frequent and precise feedback to salespeople. This implies that management closely watches and monitors how salespeople are progressing toward their objectives. Salespeople may interpret such managerial feedback and their own situation in different ways (Deci and Ryans 1985). Following attribution theory, salespeople may attribute various causes to managerial feedback and to the outcomes of their own actions. The causes that are attributed depend on the nature of the rewards and/or sanctions associated with the managerial feedback. For example, salespeople may attribute either an informative intention or a control intention from their supervisors following some feedback. In the former case, this may result in the salespeople feeling that they have the situation under control, which increases their self-confidence and intrinsic motivation. The latter type of feedback may have completely the opposite effect. Control strategies using management feedback underline the essential role of feedback in any control system, and on the possible conclusions that salespeople can draw from it. They cannot, however, account for the whole range of controls that are required to manage such a complex system as a sales force.

This centralized control strategy is not without cost. Closer supervision requires more time from managers, and consequently, more supervisors, each one with a smaller span of control. It is one of the major drawbacks of such a policy. Close supervision has also the disadvantage of considerably reducing salespeople's decision spaces. They may then lose interest in their job, feel less committed to their firm, as they may feel that they cannot fulfill their own personal aspirations. Centralized activity controls should only be used with the utmost care and caution.

In contrast, as discussed in Chapter 10, close supervision which has as its major objectives providing training and increasing competence levels remains an essential tool for sales force management.

Indirect control of activities

Figure 8.1b outlines the indirect control of a salesperson's activities through pre-specified performance objectives (e.g., a given sales volume or the number of converted prospects over a one-month period). In this case, salespeople are given a performance level, but are given some leeway to decide which activities to perform, as long as the performance objective is met. In other words, management exerts only an indirect control because they know that salespeople will need to exert enough efforts to meet their objective. To induce salespeople to accept the imposed objectives,

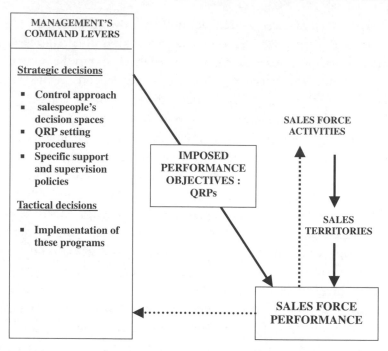

Fig. 8.1b   Centralized sales force control through specific performance objectives

rewards (sanctions) must be linked to the objective achievement (non-achievement).

Quota plans that involve financial rewards imply one or several objectives assigned to salespeople. These objectives are generally expressed as performance measures, such as sales, market shares or gross margins (Anderson 1985; Cravens *et al.* 1993; Oliver and Anderson 1994; 1995). Rewards typically take the form of a financial bonus, which is earned once quotas have been achieved. Rewards can also be in the form of gift certificates that can be redeemed at a number of stores, or travel checks that are expressed in points or euro values in retail catalogues.

For practical purposes, in this chapter, quota-reward plans (QRPs) are considered independently from compensation plans, even though the two are not completely unrelated. Several reasons support this viewpoint (Mantrala *et al.* 1994): In practice, QRPs are generally distinct from the main sales force compensation scheme and are often viewed as a supplement to a salary plan. The fixed salary usually outweighs incentive pay (e.g., by a ratio of 85 to 15 in the pharmaceutical industry). Both plans do not have the same time horizon. Compensation plans often keep the same structure over several years. This is not the case for quota-bonus plans, which last from a few weeks to a few months.

As a result, any decisions concerning the main part of the remuneration and the QRP are generally made by different decision makers within a firm. Because of its cost and financial implications, the sales force compensation plan involves not only sales managers but also the marketing, finance, and human resource manager of a firm. QRP decisions are generally taken at a more operational level. Compensation and quota-bonus decisions are usually not taken at the same time (Steinbrinck 1970).

Control objectives of a QRP

The rationale for setting QRPs is simple and well known. Quotas are set to provide salespeople with objectives that are challenging and are worth their while to achieve. To enhance performance, management gives them a reward when they reach a pre-specified performance level (the quota) which is higher than the level they would have achieved otherwise (Futrell *et al.* 1976; Locke *et al.* 1981; Winer 1973; Wotruba 1989). Conversely, failure to meet quotas may trigger a sanction. The reward usually takes the form of a financial bonus (Good and Stone 1991b), but other types of reward may also be used. Sanctions may range from no reward being given to poor evaluation by management. Note that some recent research suggests that sales force quotas can negatively affect customer orientation (Schwepker and Good 2004). This may result from the effects of quotas on sales managers' responses to salespeople's selling behaviors.

In addition to motivation, quotas may also be used to channel salespeople's efforts according to management's priorities, and/or to provide benchmarks against which actual sales performance can be assessed and controlled.

Statement of the QRP design problem

QRP design may be conceptualized as an optimization-under-constraint problem. These problems involve optimizing an objective subject to some constraints, given the available information which is captured by the different problem parameters. The QRP setting problem matches this format perfectly (Davis and Farley 1971; Mantrala *et al.* 1994): given some information on territories and salespeople (known parameters), management tries to maximize sales, profits, or market shares (the objective), by selecting the best possible QRP structure and procedures (decision variables), while ensuring that the solution is feasible by checking its effect on the likely responses from salespeople (the constraints).

QRP design procedure

There are two main aspects to setting sales-quotas (Figure 8.2). First, sales managers must establish the quota-setting procedure itself. This tends to be rather stable over time. It is generally applied in a given sales force over several quota periods (Good and Stone 1991a). The quota-setting procedure has long-term effects that are very similar to those of the general compensation plan structure discussed in Chapter 9.

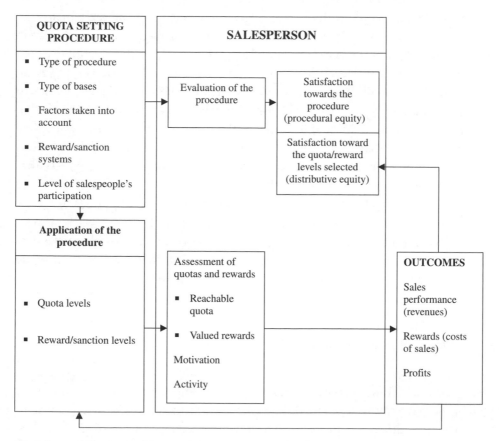

Fig. 8.2   Sales quota setting procedure and its consequences

A quota-setting procedure can be characterized as follows:

1. The type of procedure is essentially based on informal, qualitative, or judgment-based input, or on formal, quantitative, or model-based procedures and data (Darmon 1979; 1987b; Davis and Farley 1971; Farley and Weinberg 1975; Mantrala *et al.* 1994).

2. The bases selected for setting quotas, especially activities (e.g., sales calls) or performance (e.g., sales, profits, expenses). In addition, the bases can be overall measures (e.g., total sales volume) or they can be split according to some sales activities (e.g., sales volumes of various product lines).

3. The factors taken into account by the procedure for determining specific quotas and rewards (e.g., territory sales potential, present sales levels, salespeople's experience and skill levels, or workload).

4. The reward-sanction system linked to quota achievement or non-achievement.

5. The level of salespeople's involvement in the quota-setting procedure. The procedure can be exclusively top-down (i.e. from managers to salespeople), so it requires no involvement from salespeople whatsoever. Alternatively, the procedure can be bottom-up top-down (from salespeople to management, and back to salespeople). It then, requires complete cooperation from salespeople. The procedure can also involve an intermediate level of salesperson's involvement.

Implementation of the QRP procedure

A second aspect of quota setting relates to the application of the procedure itself to determine individual quotas. This involves a shorter time perspective, because the procedure is typically applied to a given quota-setting period. The application of the quota-setting procedure is characterized by the quota levels assigned to every salesperson for a given period of time, and by the amount of reward/sanction attached to the attainment/non-attainment of these quotas.

Centralization levels of QRPs

Although quota plans are by nature centralized management control devices, managers have some leeway for giving such plans a structure that can make them either strongly or moderately centralized management tools.

Highly-centralized QRPs

Fully centralized QRPs leave no (or very little) leeway to salespeople to decide their own effort levels and allocations. In some cases, however, QRPs can be designed to leave some initiative to salespeople in these areas, without reaching the status of highly-decentralized systems. Figure 8.3 provides examples of highly-centralized and moderately-centralized QRPs.

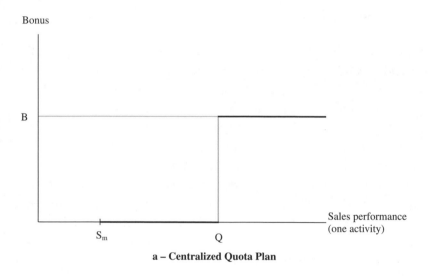

a – Centralized Quota Plan

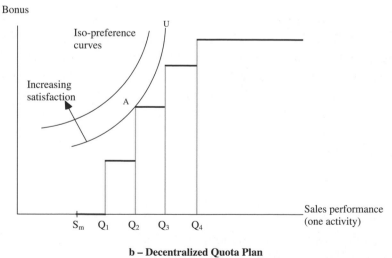

b – Decentralized Quota Plan

Fig. 8.3   Examples of centralized and decentralized quota/bonus plans

Under a fully-centralized QRP structure, (see Figure 8.3a), management sets the salespeople's objective for a given selling activity (a given product line sales quota Q) and its associated reward (a bonus B). The bonus is earned as soon as a salesperson achieves some percentage (typically, 100%) of the sales quota. From a managerial point of view, motivating quotas should be set in such a way as to induce salespeople to devote maximum time and effort to the various selling functions (Chowdhury 1993). Provided it has proper information, management can set quotas centrally and "force" a salesperson to devote maximum working time and effort by imposing the sales corresponding to maximum salesperson's working time. In agency theory terms (Basu *et al.* 1985; Dearden and Lilien 1990; Lal 1986; Lal and Srinivasan 1993; Lal and Staelin 1986; Rao 1990), this is a "forcing contract."

In this restricted case, a salesperson's decision space is essentially limited to only two possible courses of action, that is, strive to meet the quota (and earn the associated reward), or not (and in this case, deploy the most satisfying effort level which is also acceptable to management, S_m). As management attempts to set objectives centrally (e.g., for each product line, for each customer, etc.), QRPs tend to increase in details and complexity. Practically, different quotas and/or bonuses may be assigned to salespeople in the same sales force to account for salesperson and/or territory heterogeneity.

In addition, compared with moderately-centralized QRPs, fully-centralized quotas tend to be set at higher levels, so only a fraction of the sales force can be expected to meet them. Because highly-centralized QRPs assign the highest possible quotas, an important proportion of salespeople may be expected not to be able to meet them and earn the associated rewards. Sales managers should watch that this proportion does not exceed the limit at which salespeople perceive such quotas and rewards as being unattainable. This would result in an unmotivated group of people — the reverse of the intended effect.

Moderately-centralized QRPs

Moderately-centralized control systems depart from fully-centralized controls in several ways. Under a moderately-centralized control system, a sales manager attempts to offer a "set of options" under which salespeople can behave in their own best interests, and meet the firm's objectives at the same time (subject to a minimum satisfaction level). In this case, management gives the salespeople a wide range of effort level and allocation options. The major difficulty of moderately-centralized QRP design is to ensure that the salespeople will select the option which is the most profitable to management (Option A on Figure 8.3b).

Under a moderately-centralized QRP, salespeople are free to select their effort level and there is no guarantee that they will strive to achieve maximum sales. This requires management to have some information about their utility functions (Srinivasan 1981). Note that due to their very nature (specific objectives set by management) QRPs can never be fully decentralized control systems.

As an example, a moderately-centralized sales force QRP structure could provide increasing bonus amounts as salespeople exceed a basic quota by increasing percentages in a stepwise fashion (Figure 8.3b). For example, if a salesperson is given increasing bonuses after exceeding the quota by 5, 10, 15, 20, and 25 percent, their decision space is enlarged: not only may s/he decide to meet quota or not, but s/he may also decide to attempt to sell 5, 10, 15, 20, or 25 percent above that. Another example of a moderately-centralized QRP structure is a plan in which an overall quota is assigned to a salesperson across product lines. In this case, this salesperson is given complete freedom to allocate efforts the way s/he wishes, as long as total sales equal the quota, which can be achieved in an almost infinite number of ways.

Note that moderately-centralized QRPs may be convenient ways for management to account for salesperson heterogeneity. Each salesperson can select his/her most preferred solution along a quota-bonus function selected by management. Because moderately-centralized QRPs give some element of choice, they tend to be simpler and less detailed than fully-centralized QRPs. Because they require information on salesperson preferences and utilities, however, they may require more elaborate quota setting procedures than fully-centralized QRPs.

Under which circumstances is management likely to select a specific type of QRP structure, given its objectives and constraints? Figure 8.4 outlines the main managerial decision problem variables (i.e. objectives, constraints, and information requirements and processing) as well as their possible links to QRP structures and quota setting procedures.

QRP structures for different managerial objectives

Management may pursue several objectives through a QRP. They may be used to induce salespeople to elicit accurate sales forecasts (Gonick 1978;

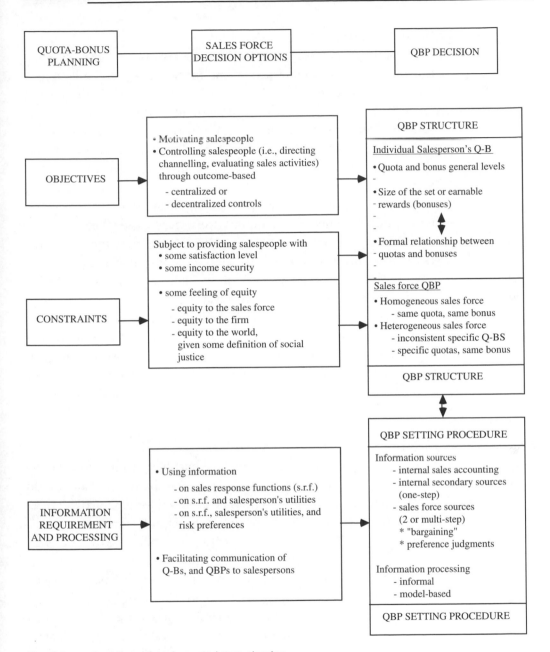

Fig. 8.4   Decision options for quota-bonus planning

Mantrala and Raman 1990). More frequently, they are used as devices
for motivating salespeople, channeling their efforts toward the most
profitable activities, and/or monitoring their short-term performance
(Jaworski 1988).

Control of effort levels: motivation

Setting motivating quotas is no easy task, because of the different perspectives and interests of salespeople and management. When designing QRPs, sales managers are naturally inclined to set quotas at the highest possible levels (i.e. to increase sales revenues and profits) and provide the lowest possible (but reasonable) bonus amounts (i.e. decrease selling costs). Consequently, quotas are generally set at a higher level than salespeople would have otherwise achieved (Futrell, Swan, and Todd 1976; Locke *et al.* 1981; Winer 1973; Wotruba 1989).

Sales managers' decisions, however, are constrained by their salespeople's response to the selected QRP. If quotas are unrealistically high (i.e. low expectancy estimates, in terms of Vroom's (1964) expectancy theory), or the bonuses too low (low reward valence), salespeople may find their objective unworthy of extra effort. As a result, a quota plan may lose its motivating factor, and may even have long-term adverse effects on profits through decay in sales force morale and/or sales personnel attrition. It is a controversial issue among practitioners and theorists as to whether the most motivating quotas are those that challenge salespeople the most or those that can be easily met. In any case, they should be set low enough to be judged attainable and worth the extra effort. Finding the right balance is fraught with difficulty.

Control of effort allocations: differentiated incentives

When the prime objective is to channel salespeople's efforts toward the most profitable selling activities (Ross 1991), a centralized QRP can best do the job by specifying which quota should be achieved for each activity (e.g., a specific quota for each product line and for each salesperson). A bonus may be earned when all the quotas are met (fully-centralized QRP), or when the total quota is met and the minimum percentages of product line quotas are also achieved (moderately-centralized QRP). Note that practically, management cannot control all possible effort allocations by sales staff because this would require setting too many quotas for each individual salesperson. Consequently, some implicit decentralization is unavoidable.

The most centralized quota plan structures are those that try to meet the dual objective of sales force motivation and salespeople's activity channeling. In this case, specifications to salespeople are so detailed and so strict that even slight performance departures from the assigned objectives result in the failure of some quota achievement, and consequently, the loss of the corresponding rewards. Under such circumstances, one could expect only a fraction of the sales force to be able to meet its objectives.

Performance control (evaluation)

When management's main purpose is to monitor and evaluate sales force performance through a QRP (Douthit 1976; Dubinsky and Barry 1982), quotas take on the role of performance standards that are expected from every salesperson, as achievement theory would suggest (McClelland *et al.* 1953). They are typically used because salespeople have been left to set their own activity levels and allocate their efforts, which is characteristic of moderately-centralized QRP structures. As a result, this objective is unlikely to be used concurrently with the motivation or effort-channeling objectives. Here, quotas are standards that everyone should achieve.

This is the reason why it may not be desirable for a firm to simultaneously pursue those objectives of evaluation and one of the two previously discussed objectives. Here, quotas should not be those challenging objectives that only a relatively small number of salespeople are likely to meet. They are minimum standards that every salesperson should be able to meet, and that should be met by any reasonable performer in the sales force. Because sales managers can use the sales quota control lever for diverse purposes, it is important for management to precisely define the objectives to be met, to explain them to salespeople, and to share them with the whole sales force.

QRP structures and behavioral constraints

Unless they accept the risks of incurring serious adverse effects in the long term, managers can meet their objectives only as long as salespeople do not experience feelings of bonus earnings insecurity, or inequity, but are generally satisfied (Wotruba 1989; Mantrala *et al.* 1994). These constraints to QRP design are somewhat related.

Satisfaction constraints

Management must try to keep individual salespeople as well as the whole sales force happy. As was seen in Chapter 4, unsatisfied salespeople are likely to be less motivated (Badovick *et al.* 1992; Brown and Peterson 1994) and possibly less efficient (Bagozzi 1980a; Hafer 1986; Sheridan and Slocum 1975). In the long term, dissatisfaction may mean that individuals will leave the company — which increases sales force turnover.

As noted above managers generally agree that salespeople should consider their quotas as achievable objectives (Chowdhury 1993). To set achievable quotas (from a salesperson's perspective), sales managers often involve salespeople in the quota setting process and try to anticipate their reactions (Wotruba and Thurlow 1976).

QRPs, however, are frequently a source of dissatisfaction for salespeople. One of the major reasons for this is the frequent lack of a clear understanding of the QRP structure and quota setting procedure, and the resulting pervasive suspicion that they might be treated unfairly. Unfortunately, QRP structures and quota setting procedures are often too complicated to be readily understood and/or memorized by salespeople, especially in the case of highly-centralized QRP structures which tend to be more complex (Churchill, Ford, and Walker 1993, pp. 268–270). In addition, because centralized QRPs provide less bonus-earnings security, less equity, provide salespeople with limited initiative, and yield quotas that can be easily challenged, they are likely to provide salespeople with less satisfaction than moderately-centralized QRP structures.

In addition, highly-centralized QRPs leave only limited initiative to salespeople, assign quotas that are generally more difficult to achieve and consequently, offer less opportunity to earn the rewards, and involve typically more complex setting procedures that are easy for salespeople to challenge. As a result, such QRPs are likely to generate higher levels of dissatisfaction.

Reward-earning security constraints

Salespeople may experience a feeling of insecurity when they are unsure about whether or not they will earn the QRP's rewards, in spite of an adequate effort level on their part. The risk of not meeting a quota (and consequently of not receiving the expected rewards), is part of the uncertainty that prevails in a given sales territory environment. Given a certain level of effort they display in their territories, the probability of not achieving (or passing) quotas depends on the extent to which environmental changes (that are beyond their control) can be anticipated, as well as on the quota plan structure.

Sales variability and reward-earnings risks

Whatever a QRP structure, a salesperson bears all or part of the risks associated with territory sales variability. Consequently, a risk-averse salesperson is likely to display an effort level and make effort allocation decisions *as if* sales territory sensitivities to his/her selling efforts were lower than the ones they actually anticipate. These "conservative" sales territory sensitivities are as low as the salesperson is risk-averse, and conversely. To accurately predict how a salesperson will respond to a given QRP, management should know which "conservative" sales territory sensitivity function they will select. This is illustrated in Figure 8.5.

One can show that sales variability results in increased dissatisfaction as the salesperson is risk-averse (Darmon 1979; Mantrala *et al.* 1994; Srinivasan 1981). This is the reason why, in this case, a salesperson is likely to react by increasing efforts, resulting in a lower level of satisfaction (Darmon 1997a).

Environmental uncertainty and QRP structures

Each QRP structure involves different risk levels for a salesperson. For example, research has shown, through a numerical example, that a QRP in which:

- quotas are thresholds above which salespeople start earning commission on additional sales (in addition to a fixed salary);
- the salary and commission rate are the same for all salespeople;

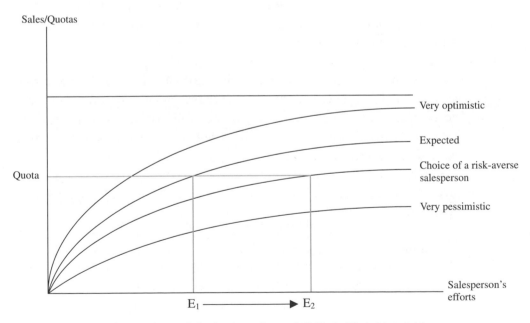

Fig. 8.5   Effect of uncertainty on behavior depending on individual attitude toward risk

- only quotas are salesperson-specific, and reflect sales force heterogeneity, i.e., sales variability in the different territories as well as salespeople's attitude toward risk,

is very close to the optimal curvilinear remuneration function suggested by the agency-theory-based plan discussed in Chapter 9 (Raju and Srinivasan 1994). This QRP structure, however, is not often found in practice (Joseph and Kalwani 1994).

A more prevalent QRP structure has found support in sales force research. Individual sales quotas, either for one single product line (Darmon 1979; 1987b) or for multiple product lines (Mantrala *et al.* 1994) have been proposed. Research based on agency theory shows that the best option is a multi-product QBP, in which a bonus for quota achievement is paid in addition to a fixed salary. Bonus amounts are linked to the quota levels assigned to salespeople. If, as is usual, a bonus constitutes a relatively small part of a salesperson's total compensation, the risk attached to earning the bonus is also relatively small.

Forcing contracts, however, have often been criticized on the grounds that they make salespeople bear all the risks. They are often difficult to implement because salespeople are in an all-or-nothing situation. In typical situations, where bonuses represent a relatively small part of remuneration, such centralized QRP "forcing contracts" are likely to provide higher profits to a firm (although they may be more difficult and costly to administer than a moderately-centralized QRP structure).

The reason for this is that under any QRP structure, a salesperson bears the risk that the actual sales territory sensitivity function is lower than anticipated. In such occurrences, a salesperson does not meet the quota, and consequently earns no bonus. If, on the contrary, the actual sensitivity function is higher than anticipated, the salespeople will earn a bonus even at lower effort levels than expected.

Under a stepwise QRP structure, the bonus amount increases with the size of the discrepancy between the actual and expected sales territory sensitivity functions. This is not the case with "forcing contracts." In the former QRP structure, when windfall sales occur, a firm pays the salesperson a premium directly linked to the size of the windfall sales. Under the fully centralized QRP structure, this premium has a set value, and is less costly to the firm. As a result, forcing contract QRPs are likely to be more cost efficient, despite their slightly higher administration cost.

As a result, as salespeople are risk-averse, they are more likely to prefer moderately-centralized QRPs, because they allow the risks to be shared with their firm. A firm which wants to provide (risk-averse) salespeople with some reward security, should adopt a relatively moderately-centralized QRP which would see a much larger proportion of its salespeople meeting their quotas.

Equity constraints

The motivating and directing effects of sales quota setting are important, but not sufficient. Salespeople may well perceive their quotas as achievable and motivating (as a result of the associated rewards), but also as inequitable. For example, salespeople may (rightly or wrongly) believe that easier quotas have been assigned to some of their colleagues. As discussed in Chapter 3, a feeling of inequity may result from the fact that salespeople, who are likely to compare their assignments with one another (Livingstone *et al.* 1995), may perceive that they do not receive their fair share of the common welfare relative to their contribution (Greenberg 1982; Lawler 1971). The notion of "equitable objective" refers to the effort level that every salesperson must deploy in order to meet it, taking into account all the specificities of the selling situations they face, including the characteristics of their respective territories and/or their different characteristics and abilities.

In Chapter 4, it was seen that according to equity theory (Adams 1965; Homans 1974), a state of equity exists among different parties when their respective ratios of outputs-to-inputs (or profits-to-investments), that is bonus-to-effort in a QRP context, are equal. As discussed, inequity can have several aspects. In the context of a quota-bonus plan, salespeople are likely to be more sensitive to functional equity (Scholl *et al.* 1987). Perceptions of inequity have a number of negative consequences for job satisfaction, morale, performance, as well as increasing dysfunctional turnover (Adams and Jacobsen 1964). In a QRP context, it has been shown also that inequity has long-term implications for sales force morale and attrition (Good and Stone 1991a), as well as for pay satisfaction (Joseph and Kalwani 1996).

Functional equity of QRPs

Salespeople can experience feelings of inequity *vis-à-vis* quota plans for two types of reason. One is related to the procedure that has been used to set up quotas. The other is related to how the application and outcome of this procedure affects them personally.

Procedural equity of QRPs   The quota setting procedure is evaluated by all the salespeople in the sales force. The salespeople judge whether it is fair or unfair, participative or autocratic, accurate or inaccurate. This is called procedural equity. This evaluation develops as individual salespeople gain experience with the procedure and as other salespeople develop their own judgments about it.

Because of the effects of this reward/sanction system on sales force satisfaction and morale, the importance of setting the "right" quotas should be underscored (Adams and Jacobsen 1964). In fact the only way to persuade salespeople that their quotas are equitable is to demonstrate that the procedure which has been followed for setting them is fair. Management should always try to find a method or procedure that is simple enough to be explained to, and understood by, the sales force. This may explain why some sales managers often use very simple (some would say simplistic) methods to set quotas. Such methods include, for example, quotas that are proportional to past territory sales or to sales potential. As discussed below, these rules do not yield equitable quotas. The following section outlines a simple allocation rule that ensures equitable quotas (i.e. quotas requiring equal effort levels from every salesperson).

Distributive equity of QRPs   Salespeople also evaluate the quota assigned to them for a given period. They may perceive this quota as fair or unfair, easy or difficult, sensible or not, worthy of being attained or not. This is different from the evaluation of the quota-setting procedure itself, although both evaluations cannot be considered as completely independent. Depending on how salespeople perceive the quota and the attached reward, they may be motivated to perform a certain level of activity that they expect to result in some performance and satisfaction levels (Brown and Peterson 1994), and, consequently, in sales revenues, costs, and profits (see Figure 8.2).

Sales forces are generally heterogeneous, and salespeople are likely to be assigned different quota-bonus levels. Salespeople can accurately assess QRP equity only as long as they know which quotas have been assigned and which rewards have been granted to other salespeople. If salespeople do not interact with one another, from a strictly economic point of view, and ethical considerations notwithstanding, management does not need to be concerned with QRP equity. In practice, however, this is seldom the case. And salespeople are likely to discuss and compare quotas among themselves.

Note that the practice of quota and pay secrecy is not only undesirable (Futrell and Jenkins 1978) but difficult, if not impossible, to implement. As a result, salespeople are likely to make up their own mind on how equitable a QRP is, and how their own quota-reward compares with those assigned to others. Consequently, for most firms, salespeople's QRP equity perceptions are unavoidable constraints.

Equity and social justice   Feelings of equity remain in the eyes of the beholder. Because no two subjects are likely to share the same perceptions, preferences, or have the same conception of equity, the same QRP may well be perceived as fair by some and unfair by others.

A second issue is related to the definition of "equity." What should be included in the definitions of a salesperson's outcome (or reward) and input (or investment) in the equity ratio. What salespeople consider to be their inputs leads to different definitions of fairness or equity (Edwards 1991). As everyone knows, social justice is a matter of appreciation and a philosophical issue. Some salespeople may feel that only the amount of effort (irrespective of competence or experience) constitute the real input, because they may not feel accountable for their natural aptitudes (or lack thereof). Like one author puts it: "no one deserves his place in the distribution of natural endowments, any more than one deserves one's initial starting place in society." (Rawls 1971, p. 74). Consequently, one should "regard the distribution of natural talents as a common asset and to share in the benefits of this distribution whatever it turns out to be."

The opposite idea has been advocated (see Nozick 1974). Such philosophers assert that an individual's basic assets and talents cannot be denied and should not be considered as part of the common welfare. According to this view, salespeople's competencies should be considered as part of their inputs, because they are valuable assets for which they should receive a fair compensation, even though they may not have a direct control over their own natural aptitudes. In fact, there is room for compromise between these two extreme positions. But the various ways of enforcing the self-ownership or collective sharing in talents may be more or less favorable to the talented (Fleurbaey and Maniquet 1994).

Because of salesperson's heterogeneous perceptions and conceptions of equity, there is certainly no universally accepted definition of equity. To devise a fair QRP, management needs to impose its own definition of equity, and may apply this definition through a centralized quota plan

Table 8.1. Views of a QBP's equity

Management's conception of a QBP as being	Salespeople's perceptions of the QBP as being	
	Equitable	Inequitable
Equitable	"True" equity	Semblance of inequity
Inequitable	Semblance of equity	"True" inequity

structure. It is up to management to explain this conception of equity to salespeople and to demonstrate that it is actually implemented in the QRP.

Equity perceptions and QRP structures

Depending on management's decisions to account for a QRP equity constraint or not, individuals may think that they are being treated fairly (or unfairly) by a firm. There are at least four types of equity situations, depending on salespeople's perceptions of QRP equity and on the equity constraint selected by management (see Table 8.1).

"True" inequity At one extreme, management may decide to ignore equity issues (and their possible consequences), and to provide salespeople with quota and reward levels that they deem as "satisfactory." In this case, salespeople are likely to receive personalized quotas and bonus amounts, typically based on their individual preferences. Needless to say, under those circumstances, the probability of obtaining an equitable QRP is practically nil at the individual level. These quota-bonus assignments, however, may well end up being inconsistent with one another. For example, for very similar territories, one work-averse salesperson could receive a small quota and a large bonus, and work-prone salesperson, a large quota and a small bonus. Alternatively, "true" inequity can also be achieved when all salespeople are assumed to be homogeneous and are assigned the same quota and bonus amounts, although they actually face different territory conditions, and have different perceptions, utilities, and/or risk preferences.

Semblance of inequity In some cases, management may decide to enforce equity in the QRP, according to its own vision of what equity should be. However, the salespeople who are using different criteria, do not perceive the QRP as equitable. For example, management may conceive equity as granting the same rewards to salespeople displaying identical effort levels, irrespective of their different competencies and abilities. This may be perceived as unfair, especially by the most experienced salespeople. In other instances, a moderately-centralized QRP structure could lead to personalized and consistent quota-bonus assignments that take into account territory specificities and salespeople's preferences and utilities (Darmon 1987b). According to the author's experience, in such cases, salespeople may well accept different quotas (on the grounds that they might reflect true territory differences). However, they often resent being given different bonus amounts when they achieve their quota.

Semblance of equity   In such cases, management may not provide equal sales quota-bonuses across the sales force, but the salespeople do not have the possibility to detect this because they lack some relevant information. Consequently, salespeople may behave as if the QRP were equitable. In the preceding case, for example, managers could easily assign personalized quotas based on territory as well as salespeople utility differences, and grant the same bonus to every salesperson. Because the quotas rely on salespeople's different preferences, it will not require the same work inputs from every individual, so, it cannot be equitable. If the salespeople do not know this, and attribute the quota difference to diverse territory conditions, they are unlikely to detect these inequities. This solution, of course, disregards any ethical concern!

"True" equity   Finally, sales managers may attempt to devise "truly" equitable QRPs in the sense of equity theory, and to make sure that this is perceived as such by individual salespeople. In order to do this, sales managers should *not* account for individual idiosyncratic preferences, but should only account for actual effort, competencies and abilities, and select one definition for equity and social justice. In other words, a QRP can provide "true" equity only under a highly-centralized control system. In this case, management needs to "demonstrate" that the QRP is equitable by explaining the quota setting procedure and its rationale to the sales force.

To sum up, when management wishes to implement a fair quota plan for the sales force, it should use a centralized approach, unless it is ready to provide only a "semblance of equity" by capitalizing on information that is just available to management.

Information requirement and costs of QRPs

Several factors may induce a firm to select a fully or moderately-centralized or decentralized QRP. More specifically, the extent and quality of its knowledge base, as well as the quality/cost ratios of its dashboard elements are determinant factors. There are some costs involved in a quota-reward procedure that should be considered by managers when adopting centralized control devices. Some of these are listed in Table 8.2.

Thus, for a firm to select highly-centralized control levers (e.g., sales quotas on each product line, or the imposition of pre-specified sales presentations), it needs to have some good knowledge of sales territory sensitivities to salespeople's selling efforts. In the former example, this knowledge is needed to estimate the quotas that correspond to maximum efforts that salespeople can provide. In the latter example, it is needed to design the most effective "universal" presentation. Information (even about sales territory sensitivities to salespeople's efforts) can always be acquired at some cost. Those costs depend on the extent to which salespeople's activities and/or performances are predictable and/or observable. The relative costs of obtaining such information probably explain why sales managers select an outcome- or a behavior-based control device.

Table 8.2. Variable and fixed costs associated with quota plan administration

Fixed costs (over a quota period)
—Costs of the managerial and administrative time spent devising the structure of the quota-reward plan
—Costs of setting up support for administering the plan (computer time, software development, clerical work, etc.)
—Fixed costs of collecting data for setting up the quota plan
—Costs of processing the data for determining quotas and rewards
—Costs of time for pre-testing the plan
—Costs of time to revise the plan
—Costs of the time for communicating and explaining the plan to the sales force
—Costs of evaluating the quota reward plan structure performance.

Variable costs (according to sales force size)
—Costs of time for providing the data that will be used for quota plan setting
—Costs of time for an explanation of and learning the quota plan
—Costs of time spent discussing quota issues with individual salespeople
—Costs of time for following up sales/quota and reward achievements, and to provide feedback to the sales force
—Costs of managerial and administrative time for implementing the quota plan and for controlling sales quota performance (clerical work, etc.)
—Opportunity costs of possible misperceptions of the quota-reward plan by some salespeople.

Table 8.3a hypothesizes how sales managers are likely to use various highly-centralized control devices depending on the characteristics of the situation they face, especially the availability and/or costs of territory sales sensitivity estimates. Some examples are provided in the last row of the table.

In addition, because highly-centralized controls provide salespeople with specific objective targets, management does not need information on their reactions to the selected control instrument (at least for that purpose). Consequently, a given control lever is likely to be used as a highly-centralized control device in a sales force control system, when management can secure (at a reasonable cost) extensive and accurate information about sales territory sensitivities to salespeople's effort, and when management has little or no knowledge of salespeople's reactions to control levers. As Table 8.3b shows, this is not the case when moderately-centralized controls are used.

In addition, because their purpose is to establish comparisons between expectations and realizations, one can expect those control elements to be more frequently quantitative (and typically less costly) when the sales objectives are short- rather than long-term, specific rather than directional. Consequently, control elements that enter a management's dashboard are likely to be essentially quantitative in nature when salespeople's objectives are specific and short-term. Conversely, they are more frequently qualitative in nature (and consequently more costly to collect and interpret) when salespeople's objectives are only defined directionally and over the long-term.

Research on QRPs

Search for optimal QRPs

Because QRPs have short- and long-term impacts on sales force motivation and morale, their design has always been a delicate task. In spite of these difficulties and of extensive work in control theory (see e.g., Eisenhardt 1985; Ouchi 1979; Ouchi and McGuire 1975; Williamson 1975; 1985; Stathakopoulos 1996), quota setting does not seem to have received the attention it deserves from sales management researchers. Presently, there is a lack of substantive knowledge for helping managers to select an adequate QRP structure and related quota setting procedures for specific types of managerial objective, constraint, and/or available relevant information.

Table 8.3a. Conditions that lead to the selection of a highly-centralized sales force control system

	Poor knowledge of salespeople's sensitivities			
	Easily observable and objectively measurable control entity		*Not easily observable and objectively measurable control entity*	
Situational characteristics	Predictability/Observability costs higher for behaviors	Predictability/Observability costs higher for outcomes	Predictability/Observability costs higher for behaviors	Predictability/Observability costs higher for outcomes
Characteristics of the control system	**Centralized** Behavior-based quantitative	**Centralized** Outcome-based quantitative	**Centralized** Behavior-based qualitative	**Centralized** Behavior-based qualitative
Example	Call quota for each market segment/customer	Sales quota for each product line/customer	Canned sales presentations to be followed strictly	Target satisfaction level for each client

Table 8.3b. Conditions that lead to the selection of a moderately-centralized sales force control system

	High knowledge of salespeople's sensitivities			
	Easily observable and objectively measurable control entity		*Not easily observable and objectively measurable control entity*	
Situational characteristics	Predictability/Observability costs higher for behaviors	Predictability/Observability costs higher for outcomes	Predictability/Observability costs higher for behaviors	Predictability/Observability costs higher for outcomes
Characteristics of the control system	**Moderately centralized** Behavior-based quantitative	**Moderately centralized** Outcome-based quantitative	**Moderately centralized** Behavior-based qualitative	**Moderately centralized** Outcome-based qualitative
Example	Overall call quota	Overall sales quota	Different selling strategies to be followed for different customers	Target satisfaction level (across customers)

The main theoretical research studies that have been carried in this area (Darmon 1979; 1987b; Mantrala *et al.* 1994) have also proposed operational procedures for determining the sales quota levels and the bonuses that should be linked to the achievement of those quotas. Because this problem implies some knowledge of the utilities (or preferences) of salespeople, these approaches are based on a conjoint analysis to determine the best salespeople's preferred plans (derived from simple preference judgments), subject to managerial constraints. Because they emphasize the motivating aspects of the plans, these approaches tend to adopt a short-term perspective.

For example, such a procedure proposes a quota-bonus plan structure in which the bonus constitutes a relatively small part of the salesperson's compensation (Darmon 1979; 1987b). Other compensation elements are a fixed salary which may account for territory and salesperson hetero-geneity, and/or commissions on sales. In this case, the quota-bonus assigned to each salesperson may be considered as a "forcing contract," according to which they earn a pre-specified bonus as soon as they meet quota. Quota and bonus amounts may be specific to each salesperson, and the various quota-bonus contracts can be made "consistent" (i.e. "equitable") across the sales force.

Search for equitable QRPs

There have only been a few research studies about the equity of sales quotas. One such study (Darmon 1995) has attempted to start bridging this gap by (1) investigating the conditions under which a firm's sales objectives can be allocated among various sales territories (and salespeople), to achieve a fair (i.e. equal effort) allocation, and (2) comparing this allocation procedure with other rules frequently used in practice. The main objectives were:

- to devise a simple, objective, and quantitative quota-setting procedure for allocating a firm's total sales objectives (e.g., one product line or several aggregated product lines) to achieve equal effort requirements in all territories;
- to take into account the most relevant sales territory and salespeople characteristics.

It was concluded that a firm wishing to allocate a sales objective to its sales territories to equalize salespeople's efforts across territories (taking into account different sales sensitivities to selling efforts) should assign a quota to each territory made up of the summation of two elements: (1) the territory's carryover sales from previous periods, and (2) a part of the firm's sales objectives less the carryover sales, proportional to the territory's weighted untapped potential. These weights reflect the relative competencies and skills of the different salespeople. Table 8.4 provides a simplified application of the method.

This principle of objective allocation, which is based on the weighted (or not weighted) untapped sales potential (1) is the only allocation procedure based on sales territory sensitivities to salespeople's efforts, and (2) is designed to provide salespeople with sales quotas that require equal effort levels, irrespective of the territory and salesperson characteristics. Frequently applied procedures of quotas allocations based on past sales, or territory sales potential, or salespeople's sales estimates cannot lead to equitable allocation of the collective effort. In contrast, the proposed rule is simple to implement, and requires few parameter estimates, provided that the firm can secure sufficiently good estimates of each territory market potential (a frequent occurrence in many selling situations).

QRPs: from theory to practice

Motivating and controlling salespeople's activities through quota plans are widespread industry practices (Douthit 1976; Dubinsky and Barry 1982). QRPs always apply to short periods of time, from a few weeks to a few months. They are based on salespeople's inputs or outputs. Sometimes, input quotas (e.g., call, demonstration, or expense quotas) are used, but more frequently, output (or performance) quotas (such as sales, profit, or new account quotas) are selected as outcome-based controls (Anderson 1985; Cravens *et al.* 1993; Oliver and Anderson 1994; 1995). A survey has found that sales relative to quota were the most widely used performance criterion and that bonuses were used by 72 percent of the responding companies (Joseph and Kalwani 1994).

Control of sales force activities with QSPs

Quota plans that involve sanctions (rather than rewards) when quotas are not met (QSP) are less frequent. However, they are sometimes used in practice. In these cases, quotas often involve quantitative measures of activity, such as a certain number of demonstrations or customer calls to be made over a given period of time. The sanctions can range from warnings to poor evaluation, and even dismissal.

Table 8.4. Equitable allocation of sales objectives among salespeople (in thousands of euros)

Territory	Sales potential	Sales in period t	Untapped sales potential	Competence index of salesperson	Weighted untapped potential	Percentage of weighted untapped potential	Expected sales even without effort	Allocation of actual objective	Total objective for period t + 1
(1)	(2)	(3)	(4)	(5)	(6)	(7)	(8)	(9)	(10)
A	1,000	200	800	1.1	880	15.7	50	278	328
B	2,000	300	1,700	0.8	1,360	24.3	80	430	510
C	1,500	400	1,100	1	1,100	19.7	100	349	449
D	1,000	500	500	0.9	450	8.1	100	143	243
E	2,000	500	1,500	1.2	1,800	32.2	100	570	670
Total	7,500	1,900	5,600		5,590	100	430	1,770	2,200

Total sales objective for t+1: 2,200 (to be allocated among five salespeople A, B, C, D and E)

Actual sales objective for t+1: Total sales objective − total (6): 2,200 − 430 = 1,770

(4) = (2) − (3)

(5) = Index of relative competence (average salesperson = 1.0)

(6) = (4) × (5)

(7) = 100 × (6)/Total (6)

(9) = (7) × Actual objective l/100

(10) = (9) + (8)

This type of sales management control lever is not concerned with the motivation of sales staff, just with sales force activity control (from a strictly quantitative point of view). Consequently, it is a truly centralized control tool. Like any centralized control, it implies that management has accurate information to establish the right numbers for each salesperson. For example, to determine the right number of sales calls a salesperson should make, management must estimate the sensitivities of customers and prospects to additional calls. Unfortunately, management seldom enjoys such a level of information and, frequently, uses impressions and beliefs rather than hard facts to establish these standards.

Conclusion

In order to set up efficient quota-reward plans, managers must make some key decisions about the objectives they want to achieve with such plans, on the constraints they want to take into account, especially in terms of satisfaction and the feelings they want to convey to salespeople in terms of reward-earnings security and equity. These decisions are likely to affect whether they use a fully or moderately-centralized QRP, and whether (and how) they will obtain the information they need to set the best possible QRP through proper involvement of the sales force in the quota setting procedure.

Although a quota setting procedure depends on the specifics of each sales force situation, a number of general conclusions do emerge. First, because salespeople are likely to have different preferences and perceptions, they are unlikely to make the same assessment of a QRP's equity. Consequently, management can only provide an equitable QRP to the whole sales force by "imposing" its own conception of equity, and by demonstrating to salespeople that the selected procedure provides fair quota-bonus amounts for every person in the sales force.

Second, because QRPs are more or less centralized sales force control systems, management always need some information from salespeople to set up an acceptable QRP. As this information level increases, management can devise a more centralized (controllable) system. The most centralized system involves a set of "forcing contracts" according to which a salesperson earns a bonus when quotas (set by management) for various sales activities are achieved or exceeded. It is suggested that this is the most cost effective QRP structure, when sales are affected by territory environmental uncertainty.

Third, management can secure valuable information for setting up even fully-centralized QRPs by involving the sales force in the quota setting procedure. Some of these procedures allow management to obtain enough information to set up a fully-centralized QRP. In some extreme cases, and short of any ethical considerations, management can even create an information asymmetry in its favor and capitalize on this information advantage for devising QRPs that provide salespeople with only a "semblance of equity."

Although a few operational procedures have already been proposed for setting up QRPs, more research work is still needed to provide management with operational ways to devise quota-bonus plans offering a wide variety of managerial options in different selling situations.

Tools for controlling decentralized processes: directional objective programs

A sales force motivation program at American Express

American Express' management considers that team work contributes substantially to the firm's success. The proximity of a sales team with customers, the continuous concern for quality, the constant search for improvements, as well as the importance of every salesperson's commitment are the bases that this firm uses to motivate the sales force. When they succeed in opening a new account, a salesperson gets a bonus on top of commission that is a percentage of the amounts that the new customer deposits during the first six years. In addition, every year, the highest performing salespeople are offered a luxury holiday. In order to fall into this category, the salespersons must have been singled out for some action in which they demonstrated exceptional team spirit.

American Express does not just recognize its top sales producers. The sales managers let their salespeople know that they appreciate good performance and show that the company appreciates even modest successes whenever they occur.

The objective of this American Express incentive program is to bring salespeople's motivation to its highest possible level, to foster a spirit of team work and high morale in the sales force. Contrasting with the type of centralized motivation programs that have been discussed in the preceding chapter, American Express has developed a highly decentralized motivation program that gives salespeople the leeway to select their own performance levels. They are provided with only directional objectives: they are instructed to increase the number of new accounts and consequently, new business volumes, as much as possible.

One year after implementing this motivation program, American Express has seen its number of new accounts jump by 27 percent (Marchetti 1998).

As the American Express case suggests, sales force motivation cannot just be declared. It must be communicated to salespeople through formal programs and policies that should inspire them to act to achieve management's priorities. For that purpose, sales managers often use decentralized control programs.

In this chapter, decentralized financial and non-financial incentive programs are discussed in turn (excluding quota plans that have been discussed in Chapter 8). This chapter also attempts to provide a prospective vision of the trends that may affect salespeople's compensation and incentive plans over the next few years.

Objectives of decentralized directional controls

Sales force motivation is often best generated by highly decentralized control programs. Not surprisingly, sales managers use such programs extensively. To motivate their sales forces, managers have at their disposal tools and techniques that tend to evolve over time. A few years ago, tools such as annual sales conventions, sales contests, and big motivational shows were intensively used. A recent survey of large firms has revealed that over fifty percent of them have set up motivational programs for their employees. Only 17.5 percent of them think that such motivation programs should be limited to sales force motivation and over 56 percent of them consider that motivation programs should be an important part of any firm's effective management. Only 9 percent of firms do not believe in motivation campaigns. Sales force motivation programs top the list of communication techniques (other than media campaigns) that firms use and consider to be very important.

Fully decentralized controls imply providing only directional objectives to salespeople. Individuals are given extensive leeway to select the means that will achieve their objectives. For example, management may pay salespeople a commission based on the gross margins of sales generated. This should induce income-maximizing salespeople (under quite restrictive conditions) to display activities that are in accordance with the firm's priorities (Farley 1964). In such cases, managers exert indirect control. Salespeople make their own effort allocation decisions, and enjoy an extended decision space. They are only given directional objectives, such as trying to achieve maximum sales (performance) or making maximum calls to prospects (activity). Management tries to set up programs that induce salespeople to act in their own best interests as well as those of the firm. In other words, decentralized control is liberal management whereby

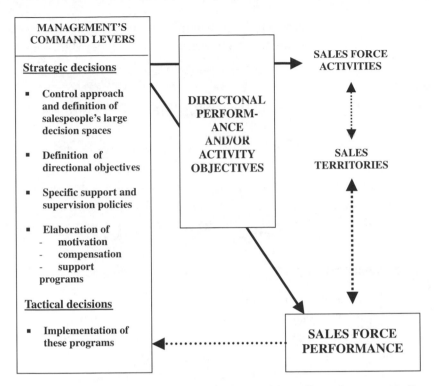

Fig. 9.1   Decentralized sales force control through directional activity and/or performance objectives

salespeople are independent entrepreneurs responsible for their own activities and performance (Anderson and Oliver 1987) (Figure 9.1).

There are essentially two types of control levers for increasing salespeople's motivation. Some of them are based on financial incentives (such as an incentive compensation plan or sales contests). Others appeal to personal and/or social achievements, or self-fulfillment in their jobs. Promotion opportunities as well as formal or informal recognition fall into the latter category. Every control lever may be appropriate depending on the situation. It should be clear however, that sales force motivation does not result from one single managerial tool. Trying to motivate salespeople through the compensation plan alone, and disregarding promotions, advancement opportunities, or informal performance recognition, may well be doomed to failure. However, providing excellent work conditions without a sufficient and motivating compensation package is unlikely to be a successful strategy. Even though these topics are addressed in turn in the following paragraphs, one should bear in mind that sales managers can motivate a sales force only through a consistent mix of all the motivational tools available.

Control of salespeople's activities with financial incentives

Among the financial incentive tools, one should differentiate between those that aim to control a salespeople's performance over relatively lengthy periods of time (such as a compensation plan that applies during periods ranging from several months to a few years), and those that control salespeople's activities over a relatively short period of time (such as sales contests).

Sales force compensation plans

Sales force compensation is a complex management tool that plays a key role in the management of a sales force, because of its effects on salespeople's motivation and morale, as well as its ability to serve as an indirect control device for salespeople's activities. A sales force compensation plan also has a strong influence on a firm's ability to recruit valuable salespeople at the required competence and ability levels, as well as on the sales force turnover rate (Coughlan 1993).

Sales force compensation is often given quite specific roles. Traditionally, sales managers have tried to meet varied and complex objectives using their sales force compensation plans. These go well past the mere remuneration of employees for their work, as is typically the case for most other employees. This explains why the sales force compensation plan structures that one can observe in practice range from the very simple (e.g., straight salary) to very complex structures. These structures often vary according to industry, firm, and type of selling function.

This is why it may be instructive to look at the reasons why sales force compensation plans frequently have special and specific structures, taking into account the substantial body of theoretical research that has been undertaken in this area over the last few decades, as well as the frequently observed departures of some current practices from theoretical findings.

Specifics of sales force compensation

Like any other employee, salespeople are assigned a specific mission by their firm. As discussed in Part I of this book, they are responsible for calling on customers and obtaining sales on behalf of their firm, for building lasting relationships with key accounts, and for increasing the client base by locating and calling on prospects. Rightly or wrongly, salespeople are often held responsible for the sales volume that their respective sales territories generate.

Because they are in charge of direct contacts with markets, salespeople are known as "boundary spanners." They are often far removed from direct supervision and may enjoy a large amount of freedom when exerting their duties. They know that their activities are often difficult for management to observe directly. Some salespeople may be tempted to behave opportunistically, and pursue their own interests rather than those of the firm. For example, salespeople are sometimes inclined to sell products that are easy for them to sell, rather than those that are more profitable to the firm. They may also avoid those tasks that do not translate immediately into financial or non-financial gain. Consequently, management's task is to induce salespeople to behave in the best interest of their firm, and to channel selling effort toward those activities that management has set as priorities. This is the task of controlling salespeople's effort and activity allocations (Anderson and Oliver 1987; Oliver and Anderson 1994; Darmon 1997a).

Selling functions are often difficult to fulfill. As already mentioned, salespeople typically play the role of buffer between a firm and its clients. For the clients, they *are* the supplier. As a result, they are often held responsible for all the problems that clients may face during their interactions with their supplier, even those which cannot be attributed to the salesperson (e.g., faulty production problems, delivery delays or errors). Inversely, for many functional personnel within their own firm, salespeople *are* the clients. Salespeople are often accused of having granted price concessions too easily. Production people may be resentful when they have agreed tight delivery schedules that are difficult to meet, even though these conditions were essential to get the customer order.

Salespeople are frequently subject to more or less rebuttals from prospects or face more or less deserved and expected customer losses to competition. From a psychological point of view, these failures are generally difficult to manage by a salesperson. Let us add also that salespeople hold a position that has never been highly valued by the general public. For all these reasons, more than any other type of employee, salespeople are more subject to loss of motivation, stress, and even burnout. Management must try to keep salespeople's motivation at its highest possible level (Walker, Churchill, and Ford 1977).

Because of the difficulties of their job, a substantial number of salespeople end up leaving and moving into a different career. However, the demand for successful salespeople is great and high sales performers are continuously solicited by other firms. These two factors acting together generate, as already pointed out, high sales force turnover rates. A firm must act to control sales force turnover by ensuring as high a morale level as possible in the sales force.

Although the sales force compensation plan is not the only control lever that can be used to reach those objectives, sales managers have extensively used it as a control device. Especially, they use it (often along with other control tools) to increase salespeople's motivation, to channel their efforts toward various selling activities, and, to a lesser extent, to indirectly control the morale of sales personnel and the sales force turnover rate.

Compensation as a means to control selling activities

These considerations lead to the specification of the desirable characteristics of a sales force compensation plan. First, the fundamental role of any compensation scheme is to remunerate salespeople for their work. If a firm wants to keep and attract competent new salespeople, this remuneration level must be fair, and should be set at a level that is competitive on the labor market.

Second, a compensation plan must motivate salespeople to devote the largest possible amount of time and effort to their tasks, and to perform these tasks at the highest level of quality possible. It is a powerful device to motivate and indirectly control salespeople's activities. For that purpose, it must clearly link the remuneration to the performance level achieved, and, if possible, only to that part of the performance for which salespeople are responsible. The case of a producer of business forms illustrates this point. This producer switched the sales force compensation plan from straight salary to strict commission to better motivate the sales force. Customers tended to remain loyal, as they would otherwise have experienced very high switching costs (changing business forms is often a very costly operation), so the salespeople had little selling to do to maintain their sales volumes. In this case, it would have been more appropriate to link incentive pay to any new business generated (Sinha and Zoltners 2001).

In addition, the compensation plan must be equitable to all the salespeople in a sales force, and be simple enough to be easily understood by salespeople (to keep its imitative effect). The compensation plan must also ensure some income security to the sales force, especially by protecting them from wide market fluctuations for which they cannot be held responsible. In addition, the compensation plan must be designed to induce salespeople to devote more time and effort to those activities that have been identified as priorities by management. For example, if maximum profits are a priority, salespeople should be induced to spend more time selling the most profitable products.

Control of effort levels: sales force motivation

A motivating compensation plan links salespeople's earnings and results. Ideally, only those results for which they have been instrumental should be taken into account. In most cases, remuneration is linked to sales (or a related measure, such as gross margins). This link is somewhat easy to specify, because selling activities yield sales volume, which is a quantifiable outcome. As a result, it is not surprising that a part of a salesperson's compensation (and sometimes their whole remuneration) is directly linked to performance. Commission on sales (or gross margins, or new business), tends to motivate salespeople to reach their highest performance level.

A large number of studies about salespeople's motivation have been carried out. Most of them rely on the circular relationships that have been outlined in Chapter 4, and which have received some empirical validation (Walker, Churchill, and Ford 1977):

Motivation $\rightarrow$ Performance $\rightarrow$ Rewards/Compensation $\rightarrow$
Satisfaction $\rightarrow$ Motivation

These relationships suggest that it is possible to control (at least to some extent) motivation through extrinsic rewards (including compensation) as well as intrinsic rewards. One recalls from Chapter 4 that in order to be motivated, salespeople must perceive three interrelated relationships: that a given effort in a certain activity is likely to result in higher performance, that this high performance will result in higher financial rewards, and that financial rewards are still valuable to them (Vroom 1964).

Consequently, many authors and managers have concluded that financial gains are a powerful motivational device. A few research studies, however, have proposed that this is not always the most important reward for employees (Lawler 1971) or salespeople (Churchill, Ford, and Walker 1976b). Salespeople's reactions may depend on the satisfaction with remuneration level they have already reached, or the behavior they display *vis-à-vis* financial incentives (Darmon 1974). Motivating effects could well decrease as compensation increases (Churchill and Pecotich 1982; Oliver 1974). In addition, the size of those motivating effects may depend on individual characteristics (Oliver 1974). Unexpectedly, the importance of these effects does not decrease as salesperson move on in their careers (Ford, Walker, and Churchill 1985).

The relationships outlined above underscore the necessary and sufficient conditions for a compensation plan to motivate salespeople. From a practical point of view, a salesperson must feel able and competent to accomplish the required tasks. Targets that are too high can quickly become ineffective. Salespeople must also understand their compensation plan. It should be simple enough to be easily understood and memorized (which is not always the case in practice). Finally, a compensation plan can only motivate if salespeople attach enough value to additional remuneration.

Control of effort allocations: channeling effects

Sales managers often use the compensation plan to channel salespeople's efforts toward those activities that are corporate priorities, for example, selling the most profitable product lines, making more calls to prospects, or selling to clients in certain industrial sectors that have been identified as priorities.

To meet such objectives, the compensation plan must specify different remuneration rates for the various relevant activities. Obviously, it is appropriate to grant higher remuneration rates for those activities (or performances) that a firm wishes to favor. For example, a firm may pay higher commission rates on sales of the most profitable products (Farley 1964).

As illustrated by the American Express case at the beginning of this chapter, a firm induces salespeople to spend more time prospecting by granting them a bonus for every new account. A communication object producer has changed its sales force compensation plan from fixed salary plus a 5 percent commission on sales to a plan in which the variable part is a function of the gross margins earned and the type of client. A full commission rate is applied to new account sales, but the commission falls to 50 percent of the full rate for new accounts that are identified by external sources and to 25 percent of the full rate for existing clients.

Control of sales force turnover
Control through financial incentives Controlling sales force turnover (especially dysfunctional turnover) is always a major concern for sales managers. Some firms, especially in the new technology sector, grant long-term bonuses to curb a high turnover rate. Salespeople can cash these bonuses in only after say five years, provided they have not left the firm. The bonus increases with tenure and can sometimes be as high as a full year's salary.

In some organizations like Microsoft, about half of the one hundred member sales force can subscribe to stock options that can bring substantial gains to their holders. Because such options can be exercised only after four years, the sales force turnover rate is as low as 3 percent per year.

Control through compensation equity The major *raison d'être* of a sales force compensation plan is to offer fair remuneration for the work achieved. Here, equity consists of providing salespeople with a competitive compensation package and to give a fair treatment to every member of the sales force. A compensation plan that is fair to every salesperson must account for every situation, the perceptions and preferences of every salesperson, as well as organizational and labor market factors.

It may not be surprising that, given the multiplicity of managerial objectives, compensation plan structures are often complex and require technical knowledge that sales managers often do not master. It may not be surprising either, that the sales force compensation problem has been among the first to have attracted researchers' attention in the marketing and OR/MS disciplines, yielding some of the most abundant literature in sales force management.

Theory of sales force compensation

Research into sales force compensation is relatively recent. The first significant contribution was about forty years ago. Most research originates from the United States, and has followed two major trends. The first is a theoretical and analytical approach, where attempts have been made to determine optimal compensation plan structures. A second trend relies more heavily on empirical work, so, these contributions are closer to the field and have been more concerned with concrete and immediate managerial applications. The typical questions that have been addressed are, for example, the assessment of salespeople's reactions to financial incentives and other compensation elements.

The problem of optimal compensation plans has often been placed within the framework of sales force control, especially decentralized control. In this case, the problem is to find conditions under which salespeople, acting in their own best interests, optimize the firm's objectives at the same time. This route has been followed in the first research trend mentioned above.

Optimal simultaneous conditions

This trend was initiated by a study that demonstrated that a firm using a commission plan to compensate its sales force, should pay equal commission rates on gross margins of each product line (Farley 1964). In this case, salespeople who maximize their financial gains would allocate their time and efforts to maximize their firm's profits at the same time. A strictly equivalent rule is to use (different) commission rates on the sales of each product line (and not on gross margins). These rates must be proportional to the various product margin rates. This rule has the distinct advantage of not revealing to the sales force what the gross margins of all product lines are. Furthermore, it may be more understandable for salespeople to have commissions set on sales instead of gross margins for which they may not feel completely responsible (especially if they have not be given the authority to negotiate prices with their clients).

As stated above, the compensation problem is exclusively concerned with the effort-channeling effect, but does not address the important issue of the motivation to work more and better. This latter objective cannot be examined as only commission plans are considered. Under such plans, it should be evident that remuneration-maximizing salespeople would work as much as possible to achieve more sales and consequently, get more commission.

The prescriptions of this pioneering study rest on a large a number of simplifying assumptions, many of which are questionable. As a result, several subsequent studies have tried to extend the analysis to more general situations, such as the following:

- the product marginal costs are variable (Davis and Farley 1971; Farley and Weinberg 1975);
- salespeople are given price initiative (Weinberg 1975);
- management wishes to devise a compensation plan that could be fair to salespeople (Darmon 1980; Srinivasan 1981);
- time-related factors (such as carryover effects) are taken into account (Tapiero and Farley 1975; Darmon 1978b);

- salespeople display behavioral patterns other than those which maximize short-term financial gain (Darmon 1981; Srinivasan 1981; Weinberg 1978);
- salespeople are uncertain about their territory sales sensitivities to their efforts and are risk-averse (Berger 1972; 1975);
- salespeople's time must be allocated among client and prospect calls (Darmon 1990a).

In most cases, these studies have shown that the constant rate on gross margins does not hold anymore, and that more complex compensation rules are required. The simple commission plan structure first hypothesized is not adequate to capture the complexity of most situations. This approach to optimal compensation has failed to address the sales force motivation problem because it assumes that salespeople always attempt to maximize income — this is not always the case.

Some exceptions aside, all the research studies previously mentioned have hypothesized a certain environment and have assumed that a straight commission plan was an adequate remuneration plan structure. In practice, one can observe that sales managers frequently use mixed compensation plan structures (e.g., fixed salary plus commission), especially for preventing (at least partially) salespeople from environmental uncertainties that may cause their remuneration to vary substantially and unexpectedly. These limitations have given rise to the second trend in sales force compensation research.

Optimal compensation plan structures

Agency theory (Eisenhardt 1985) provides an apt framework to analyze the sales force compensation plan structure problem. This theory addresses the problem of how principals (sales managers) can control the activities of agents (salespeople) to whom they delegate decision-making authority. Principals and agents are assumed to pursue different goals. They often do not share the same information level (information asymmetry) because salespeople usually have better information on their own territory sales response functions than management (Lal and Staelin 1986). Principals can control agents by observing either their activities (or purchasing information, if they cannot be observed directly), or their results. In the latter case, because of environmental uncertainties, risk-averse agents, who bear the risk that proper activities may not yield the expected results, should be given a premium.

The application of this theory to sales force control can be summarized as follows: How can a sales manager control salespeople's activities in an uncertain environment, using the most efficient compensation plan possible in such a way as to induce salespeople acting according to their own interests, to meet the firm's objectives at the same time? Sales managers cannot directly observe salespeople's efforts or activities, and properly infer the quality of these efforts from the observed performance because the sales territory sensitivities to salespeople's efforts cannot be predicted (Eisenhardt 1989; Bartol 1999).

In addition, sales managers and salespeople do not share the same interests. They do not always pursue the same objectives. They do not have the same attitudes toward risk: salespeople are assumed to be risk-averse, while managers are supposed to be risk-neutral. Finally, management and salespeople do not enjoy the same level and quality of information: salespeople have better information and knowledge about their sales territories than management.

The first study that applied those principles to sales force compensation suggests that, salespeople should be compensated with a combination plan — a plan that combines a fixed part (a salary) with a variable part (e.g., commission) (Basu *et al.* 1985). In addition, the relative proportions of these two elements in the total remuneration package are likely to vary depending on the level of market uncertainty, and the salesperson's attitude toward risk. When uncertainty, or marginal costs, or a salesperson's minimal utility increase, they then, reduce their efforts, the optimal salary part increases, the commission rates decrease, and the optimal profits decrease (Basu *et al.* 1985; Lal 1994). Because the original study only applied to one single selling activity (one product line), it is worth noting that the focus of new research has moved from the optimal effort allocation control problem to management's objective of reaching maximum sales force motivation.

Like previous contributions, this first study relies on a number of restrictive assumptions (individual salesperson analysis, one single product line situation, no dynamic effects accounted for, etc.). Several subsequent studies have attempted to remove one or several of the original assumptions. For example, researchers have analytically estimated the effects of various factors on the optimal contract, namely:

- the pricing authority delegation problem (Lal 1986);
- environmental uncertainties (Joseph and Kalwani 1995);
- salespeople's risk aversion (Lal and Srinivasan 1993);

- efforts quality (Rao 1990);
- salespeople's negative valence of efforts (Lal and Srinivasan 1993);
- the level of available information (Mantrala, Raman, and Desiraju 1997);
- the temporal dimension of salespeople's effort adjustment (Lal and Srinivasan 1993);
- production learning effects (Dearden and Lilien 1990);
- sales force heterogeneity (Lal and Staelin 1986; Raju and Srinivasan 1996);
- multiple independent (Berger and Jaffe 1991) and interdependent product lines (Zhang and Mahajan 1995);
- controls exerted on the sales force (Joseph and Thevaranjan 1998);
- multidimensional sales effort and salesperson efficiency (Erevelles, Dutta, and Galantine 2004);
- a combination of many of the preceding factors (Darmon and Rouziès 1999).

(For a detailed review of most of these studies, see Coughlan 1993; Coughlan and Sen 1989.)

Thus, from these studies, a sales manager can draw a number of general conclusions about the relevant factors to be considered when designing a compensation plan, and also the likely impact of such factors on the compensation plan control effects (Lal 1994). Although some of these studies rely on experimental simulations (Basu and Kalyanaram 1990; Raju and Srinivasan 1996; Darmon and Rouziès 1999), none propose truly operational procedures for solving the immediate and practical problems that many managers face when they actually design a compensation plan for their sales forces — namely what actual values should be given to salaries and/or commission rates.

Compensation effect on sales force turnover

Another research trend (Williamson 1979) that has strong implications for sales force compensation plan design was initiated a few years ago (Anderson 1985; John and Weitz 1989). According to this approach, it is sufficient to let the market mechanisms work, which, short of unusual circumstances, tends to regulate the economic relationships efficiently. As a result, sales force compensation should be based on salespeople's performance. However, when salespeople know that a firm cannot replace them easily without incurring the high training costs of new hires, they can display opportunistic behavior. Here, a firm may grant a high proportion of fixed salary in the compensation package and lose control over its sales force, as the market mechanisms are insufficient for controlling salespeople.

In this case, controlling (and remunerating) salespeople for their activities rather than their performance would be preferable. Inversely, when the sales process is uncertain, or when salespeople can be easily replaced, it would be preferable to increase the variable part because the firm can attract and retain those individuals who can best handle market uncertainties. In this case, a firm can deal with market uncertainty by increasing functional sales force turnover through the compensation plan.

This research trend is the only one to fill the gap between the nature of a compensation plan and sales force turnover. Like other research studies in this area, it has the merit of establishing a relationship between compensation and salespeople's behavior or performance. It fails, however, to provide help to practitioners when it comes to quantifying or estimating the parameter values of such relationships.

Equity conditions

Contrasting with the operational contributions that are briefly described in the following sections, few studies have addressed the equity problem in sales force compensation plans. One study (Darmon 2000) suggests that individuals tend to compare the perception they have of their ratio of their own investment (in time, efforts, resources, etc.) to their return on investment (financial and/or non-financial gains) with their perception of the ratios of "relevant others" (Adams 1965; Adams and Jacobsen 1964). When the ratios are equal, an individual does not experience any feelings of inequity. Inversely, when the ratios are perceived as being sufficiently unequal, an individual experiences a feeling of inequity. In this case, individuals behave in such a way as to restore equity (e.g., by working more, or alternatively, reducing effort). Thus a salesperson who feels overqualified for the job (and therefore not being compensated for his/her level) can decide to decrease efforts to restore equity.

Considering the various types of equity that have been discussed in Chapter 4 (external, interpersonal, and corporate − collective or individual equity), the study concludes that by selecting the proper compensation levels, a firm can provide salespeople with only certain types of equity at a time. Thus, a firm can ensure individual or collective corporate equity to salespeople or occupational equity. In any case, a firm can optimize profits using some form of equity constraint. It is only in very special circumstances, however, that a firm can provide salespeople with several types of equity simultaneously. In such cases, a firm will not be able to maximize profits. Consequently, providing equity implies some costs to a firm, so the decision concerning the type of equity to provide should follow from a deliberate personnel policy.

Another study (Darmon 2001), has shown that it may be in management's best interest to let salespeople enjoy their perception of a "semblance of equity" rather than providing them with "true equity," because they are unlikely to enjoy the same level of market information about every sales territory as management.

Operational methods

Several research studies have proposed decision support systems that lead to operational procedures for designing and implementing sales force compensation plans (Albers 1996). Some methods lead to the determination of optimal compensation plans (Farley and Weinberg 1975). Another method is relatively easy to implement (Darmon 1987a; 1997a). It allows managers to infer their salespersons' behavioral reactions to motivation and compensation programs. It relies on an estimation of the elasticity of salespeople's reactions to a change in their compensation plan (inferred from the resulting sales volume and compensation changes).

Another procedure is also relatively simple to implement. It predicts the effects (sales, profits, turnover rate) that a new sales force compensation plan might have in the long term, even before the plan is actually implemented (Darmon 1997b). Although it does not determine the optimal structure of a sales force compensation plan, this decision support system allows a simulation and comparison of the long-term effects of several possible compensation plan structures taking into account the probable effects of the plan on salespeople's motivation, turnover rates, as well as its attractiveness to potential new recruits.

Another method simulates and predicts the reactions of salespeople to even complex compensation plan structures (Darmon and Rouziès 1999). Supplemented by optimization techniques, this method allows sales management to determine the optimal compensation plan structure, taking into account the actual situation of a sales force. It specifies the various elements of the optimal compensation package, that is fixed salaries, commissions, quotas, bonuses for quota achievement, etc., and estimates the quantitative values for all these elements.

From compensation theory to practice

Theoretical and analytical developments concerning sales force compensation have become highly sophisticated. They typically propose compensation plan structures that are simple, which contrasts with the results of surveys carried out among firms about their compensation plan structures. These suggest that most firms use more elaborate compensation plan structures than the salary plus incentive formulae proposed by theory. They generally include (Heide 1999): (1) a fixed salary which ensures a minimum income level, while compensating salespeople for accomplishing certain tasks that do not immediately result in sales (such as customer servicing), (2) commission to motivate salespeople to cultivate their territories and generate more revenue and profits, and (3) bonuses rewarding those individuals who achieve performance targets beyond a set level.

It has been estimated that about 7 percent of firms compensate their salesforce with straight salaries only and about 10 percent with commission-only (Jackson, Schlacter, and Wolfe 1995). In other words, 17 percent of firms seem to depart from theoretical prescriptions that advocate using combination plans for sales force motivation. About 72 percent of firms offer a bonus as part of their sales force incentive plans. As discussed below, these figures may well reflect the deep changes in the selling function that have been described in Chapter 6, which could indicate future trends in sales force compensation.

Consequently, short of some general commonsense guidelines, sales managers are often left with little guidance when designing sales force compensation plans. In practice, when designing the sales compensation program, sales managers must strike a balance between two opposing objectives. On the one hand, they must account for an increasingly complex sales environment. On the other, they must keep the program simple, understandable, and pay for true performance. Simplicity and pay-for-performance are important characteristics of effective sales force compensation plans (Deloitte 2005). A recent survey by this well known consulting group suggests that over 65 percent of respondents are dissatisfied with the efficiency of their sales force compensation plan. Based on these results, Deloitte offers the following guidelines that are in line with up-to-date sales force compensation research findings:

- emphasize simplicity;
- understand and account for the behaviors that lead to superior sales performance;
- rigorously enforce the notion of pay-for-performance;
- employ the most effective compensation administration.

Sales contests

Sales contests are frequently used by sales managers to induce salespeople to deploy extra efforts on a given activity over a relatively short period of time. For example, management may wish to achieve quick market penetration for a new product, before competitors can retaliate. By using a special incentive program, salespeople may make the extra effort to meet that goal.

Frequently, sales contests are based on competition among salespeople, and only individuals that obtain the best results get a reward. Sometimes, all salespeople that have achieved a certain (short-term) objective are granted a reward.

It is clear that within the framework of lasting customer relationship strategies, sales contests should be used by management with extreme care. By definition, sales contests emphasize short-term performance. In order to win a contest, it is not unusual for salespeople to employ hard sell techniques and obviously, this is incompatible with building customer satisfaction and loyalty over time. In addition, because of time constraints inducing sales staff to make a special efforts in one area can only be done at the expense of other (often more profitable) activities. This is why management must carefully define what is expected from the sales force in the short and long term before deciding to implement sales contests (Murphy and Dacin 1998).

Control using non-financial incentives

In addition to motivation programs that are based on financial incentives, sales managers can take a wider view of sales force motivation. The strong motivating effects of salesperson empowerment that results from an increase in their decisional space (Perry, Pearce, and Sims 1999), as well as building trust in salesperson-sales manager relationships (Flaherty and Pappas 2000; Sallee and Flaherty 2003), have already been underlined. Sales force motivation can also be enhanced by favoring clan controls, or involving salespeople in their own objective setting, in order to build a consensus. They can also achieve similar objectives by planned management of their careers and/or by providing adequate organizational support.

Sales force clan controls

The strategy of controls through clans may be considered as an example of highly decentralized control (Ouchi 1979). According to this strategy, managers have only limited information and are subject to bounded rationality (i.e. they are unable to process large amounts of information simultaneously). Consequently, organizations can at best try to exert control over their employees through socialization within clans. Clans should build loyalty towards the organization, and enhance acceptance of the firm's objectives and goals. Firms can build up employees' loyalty through the development of a warm and human atmosphere in the workplace, the provision of excellent working conditions and adequate remuneration for their employees.

Obviously, clans are influential factors in individuals' behavior. However, the major difficulty that management faces when attempting to implement such control methods is that it is almost impossible to identify which actions and decisions to make to properly control sales force behavior. Although recognizing the logic of control through clans, one may question its practical usefulness when it comes to actual implementation.

Involving salespeople in objective setting

In some cases, sales managers prefer to establish sales objectives through general consensus with the various members of a sales force, and avoiding directly linking objective realization to salespeople's compensation. In the most extreme cases, salespeople are exclusively compensated with a straight salary, and the only way for management to reward higher performers is to unilaterally increase their salary.

In this case, the most frequently used method for objective setting is management by objectives (MBO). It consists of discussing and negotiating with every salesperson precise and quantified objectives to be met over a certain period of time, of making provisions for the means that are necessary to meet those objectives, and finally, comparing the actual performance with the objectives at the end of the planning period. A major difficulty with this approach lies, as one could easily surmise, in the negotiated aspects of objective setting. Good negotiators can obtain objectives that can be more easily attained than less efficient negotiators. This might possibly result in a lack of efficiency and equity in the sales force.

Career and promotion management

Career life cycle

Organizational psychologists have long recognized that employees go through career cycles (Dalton, Thompson, and Price 1977; Ference, Stoner, and Warren 1977). Each career stage is characterized by specific needs, attitudes, perceptions, and behaviors (Rabinowitz and Hall 1981; Stumpf and Rabiniwitz 1981; Flaherty and Pappas 2002). The same phenomenon applies to salespeople (Jolson 1974; Cron 1984), as evidenced by empirical research (Cron and Slocum 1984, 1986; Slocum and Cron 1985). A salesperson's career is likely to move through four basic stages: preparation, development, maturity, and decline. In the exploration (or preparation) phase, new salespeople must learn everything, including their role in an organization. These individuals may not be sure how to pursue a career in selling – this largely depends on how successful they are during their early selling experience. In the establishment (or development) phase, they have decided to establish themselves as salespeople. They want to improve, and are eager to learn and assert themselves. At the maintenance (or maturity) phase, productivity levels off. They try to maintain their status and previous performance levels. Finally, at the disengagement (or decline) phase that occurs during the last few years of their professional lives, they start to psychologically prepare for retirement.

Because objectives and interests tend to vary depending on their phase in the career cycle, and given the very definition of those phases, one can expect salespeople to assign different priorities to various aspects of their function, at every stage. In the exploration phase, when they do not know if they will pursue a selling career, they may give more weight to the constraining aspects of the job, such as travel, and might be less concerned by the type of clients on which they must call or their supervision level.

Research suggests that salespeople tend to give higher priority to extrinsic rewards (except promotions) at the establishment phase of their career (Rabinowitz and Hall 1981; Schein 1971). In other instances, financial reward has been given the highest weight at the establishment phase, probably because it is used as a yardstick to measure performance and to assess how successful they are in their selling function. Finally, extrinsic rewards (especially compensation, promotion opportunities, and formal recognition by supervisors) are less important at the salesperson's disengagement phase. In this phase, salespeople are more likely to value security or visible indicators of the prestige of their job.

Importance of promotion

Promotion has a special importance at different phases of the career cycle. It has been shown that the importance given to promotion was inversely related to a salesperson's age, itself related to the stage they have reached in their career (Ingram and Bellenger 1983; Churchill, Ford, and Walker 1979). In fact, promotions reach their highest importance level at the establishment phase (Cron, Dubinsky, and Michaels 1988; Hall 1976; Hall and Mansfield 1975). The role of promotion policies on sales force turnover has already been underlined. Like any other employee in a firm, salespeople wish to see their career evolve, either within or outside the firm for which they work. As a result, many firms have a deliberate policy of promoting their best salespeople to managerial levels.

The morale and motivation of the whole sales force depends to a large extent on the quality of middle sales management. They motivate, train, support, and coach field staff. The problem sales managers often face is that frequently the characteristics and qualities that made them a successful salesperson are not necessarily the same as those that are required to manage a sales force. Hence, before deciding to promote a salesperson management has to consider if they might be losing a high caliber salesperson and creating a mediocre manager.

For a firm to manage salespeople's careers, it must be able to fire poor performers who have little prospect of improvement in the near future. Consequently, sales managers must set a minimum performance criterion below which it would not be reasonable to keep a salesperson in the field. In practice, a firm should set these minimum standards at a high level. The opportunity costs that can be generated by a salesperson whose performance is only marginal can be substantial. These marginal salespeople hold a position that could be better filled by another. The opportunity costs are as high as the minimum acceptable performance level for a salesperson is low. This is why it is essential to have a very demanding selection and recruitment process, because it can limit the number of marginal sales producers in a sales force.

Control of motivation through organizational support

Although a firm can develop specific sales force motivation programs, one should keep in mind that any management decision and action, even the most trivial ones, are likely to have a positive or negative effect on sales force motivation and morale. As will be seen in Chapter 10, sales managers who provide strong organizational support to sales staff to make their tasks easier, increase sales force motivation. Providing adequate training, fostering a climate of confidence, and encouraging initiative all help to develop a high level of motivation in a sales force. Conversely, a poor organizational climate, and too-tight supervision, can decrease the effects of a motivation program that could have been adequate otherwise. These are some of the reasons why sales force motivation should not be considered as a result of specific motivation programs, but rather as a management style and philosophy for the sales force.

It is important for salespeople to share the same vision of management's role in supporting them to fulfill their mission. Unfortunately, it seems that a gap frequently exists between the respective visions of management and salespeople. A recent survey suggests that salespeople expect management to essentially develop their knowledge, provide information about the firm's strategy, recognize achievements, and be available when needed. A substantial proportion of those surveyed reported that management was not available – a fact that was acknowledged by a very small fraction of sales managers surveyed.

Control of motivation though CRM support

Salespeople may achieve a high motivation level when their firm directly and indirectly supports and helps them manage their own management of customer relationships and sales territories. For example, managers can provide the tools to help them allocate their time among various accounts. The CRM approach helps salespeople to segment customers according to their potential for the firm. An analysis of the customer portfolio in each territory leads to the identification of the most profitable segments for the firm (and consequently for sales staffs) and can help to make their tasks more effective. Because time is one of the most precious resource, a salesperson has, it is vital for a firm to identify those customers and prospects that should receive priority treatment. With such help, salespeople can make choices on a rational basis. A certain number of tools are currently available and are marketed by specialized institutions.

Control of motivation in critical situations

It should be clear by now that motivating the sales force is a constant problem and concern of sales management. This task, however, takes a special dimension when a crisis arises and when a firm faces difficult times. In such cases, management has a number of special tools at its disposal that can be adapted to the needs of the situation. When the rumor that Coca-Cola was about to purchase Orangina, the large fruit juice manufacturer, hit the sales force of the Pernod-Ricard group, there was a risk that uncertainty would adversely affect salespeople's motivation. The 250 salespeople that were in charge either of the immediate consumption sector or supermarkets had been surprised to learn this news from the media. To maintain the sales force morale, sales management reacted by implementing a personal communication program. Management organized meetings with salespeople in every region, to explain the actual situation and reassure the sales force. In addition, all the new sales initiatives were maintained as scheduled and announced during a national sales meeting.

Another example is provided by the Class A model of Mercedes-Benz. It was all over the media that the car had failed certain safety tests. The company recognized its errors and made all the necessary technical adjustments. This was enough to keep the sales force and the distribution network motivated. These actions were supported by transparent communications, an advertising campaign, a contest for the best Class A salesperson, and weekly letters. A quick managerial response and transparent communication programs seem to have been instrumental in keeping the sales force morale and motivation at a high level.

Information and costs

Chapter 9 discussed the main factors inducing management to select a more or less centralized or decentralized control system. These were the extent and quality of its knowledge base, as well as the quality/cost ratios of its dashboard elements. In order to devise effective fully decentralized control systems, in which salespeople are given the freedom to select the most appropriate courses of action, managers must be able to predict the behavior of its sales force and consequently, how they are likely to make choices from the options open to them — how they should react to management's control levers. This is why they must have accurate information on salespeople's preferences and utilities.

As a result, a given control element is likely to be used as a decentralized control lever, when management cannot secure at a reasonable cost sufficient information about sales territory sensitivities to salespeople's effort, but can acquire good knowledge of salespeople's reactions to control levers. For example, if salespeople are instructed to increase overall

Table 9.1. Conditions that lead to the selection of a highly decentralized sales force control system

Situational characteristics	High knowledge of salespeople's sensitivities			
	Easily observable and objectively measurable control entity		*Not easily observable and objectively measurable control entity*	
	Predictability/Observability costs higher for behaviors	Predictability/Observability costs higher for outcomes	Predictability/Observability costs higher for behaviors	Predictability/Observability costs higher for outcomes
Characteristics of the control system	**Decentralized** behavior-based quantitative	**Decentralized** outcome-based qualitative	**Decentralized** behavior-based qualitative	**Decentralized** outcome-based qualitative
Example	Evaluation based on number of calls	Commissions based on sales volume (unique rate)	Evaluation based on quality of sales presentations	Evaluation based on overall customer satisfaction

customer satisfaction as much as possible (a directional decentralized objective) and that they will be rewarded for it, management only needs to know if this reward is sufficiently appealing to induce the right behavior.

Table 9.1 shows the main characteristics of a fully decentralized sales force control system, depending on various situational characteristics and constraints, and provides some examples in the last row.

In the above-mentioned Deloitte survey (2005), 34 percent of the respondents reported that the cost of their compensation plans was either too high or too low. A balance between the two is not easy to strike. Spending too little can mean that a firm cannot attract or retain strong sales performers. However, spending too much means that the firm uses its resources ineffectively. In addition, 77 percent of respondents reported some difficulty in administering the plan, and 97 percent declared that they were making changes to their sales compensation program.

Control of activities with hybrid programs

To implement a dynamic management process, sales managers need more than one single control procedure. Ideally, they try to control not only the quantity but also the quality of their salespersons' efforts (Sujan 1986; Challagalla and Shervani 1996). This is why they are likely to select, out of their command center, several control mechanisms with various characteristics. For example, it is quite conceivable for a manager to assign sales quotas to its sales force (a centralized quantitative outcome-based control), to impose simultaneously the use of strictly pre-specified and organized presentations (a centralized qualitative behavior-based control), and give them some price initiative (a decentralized qualitative behavior-based control).

In practice, the dynamic management processes require sometimes highly centralized and sometimes decentralized controls. These types of hybrid control systems have often been observed in practice (Oliver and Anderson 1994). According to Transaction Cost Analysis (TCA) (Williamson 1975; 1981), this choice is generally made using imperfect information because of environmental uncertainties and managers' bounded rationality. Managers select the control mechanisms that minimize the transaction costs (i.e. the cost of performing, monitoring, and controlling salespeoples' activities).

In the same way, transaction-specific assets induce salespeople to engage in opportunistic behaviors. They may get away with it because they have acquired specialized and valued knowledge and experience, so it would be too expensive for a firm to replace them (John and Weitz 1989). In fact, in the presence of transaction-specific assets, a firm loses all or part of its authority over its salespeople. This makes it difficult for management to use a centralized control system based strictly on authority. In addition, this situation often involves a decline in salespeople's sensitivities to various control levers. The firm's problem is to design a decentralized control system that can best accommodate its objectives and salespeople's preferences.

The evolution of incentive programs

In order to understand and predict how incentive control levers are likely to evolve over the next few decades, one should first consider the current and future evolutions of the selling functions, and the causes of such evolutions. As discussed in Chapter 6, there are currently strong evolutionary trends in the selling environment. Such trends will no doubt also affect the direction which incentive programs are likely to take.

Compensation plans

First, because personal selling is becoming much more professional, more competent and better educated salespeople will require higher remuneration levels. One should expect the cost of personal selling to increase dramatically in the next few years.

The structure of the sales force compensation plan should also evolve. Building long-term relationships with customers requires large investments in time and effort on the part of salespeople. Consequently, compensation plans that are exclusively (or to a large extent) based on short-term performance measures (such as current sales volumes) should disappear. A recent survey of 584 companies on their sales force compensation practices has found that there is no relationship between a company's sales incentive plan structure and its gain or loss in market share. It was also found that the differentiating factor was the fit between the incentive structure and the company's marketing objectives. Successful companies did not pay for sales volume if their goal was to increase profits, or did not pay for short-term results if they intended to build long-term relationships with their clients (Marks and Emerson 2002). Given the prevalent philosophy of long-term customer orientation taken by many firms, one should expect short-term incentive plans to be de-emphasized. For example, when consumers must rely on a salesperson to evaluate alternatives, this salesperson may be tempted to oversell the value of the firm's product features. This leads to reduced consumer satisfaction and lower profits for the firm (Kalra, Shi, and Srinivasan 2003).

Fixed salaries should constitute the largest part of the remuneration package, even though some variable part will still remain. In fact, one can observe that a variable element in the remuneration package has become general practice. The proportion of salespeople that have some variable part in their compensation plan is currently estimated at around 90 percent.

If this trend lasts, a variable element (even a modest one) of remuneration will continue to be part of the sales force compensation. It will, however, be based on different types of performance measures. First, quantitative criteria (such as sales) will lose importance to more qualitative criteria that will reflect the quality of the relationships that have been established with customers, the services rendered to clients, and customer satisfaction. One should logically see the bonus practice to be extended to a larger number of sales forces in the next few years and to account for a large part (if not all) of the incentive compensation. In addition, even when quantitative criteria are used to determine the variable part of compensation, they will become more sophisticated than sales volumes or gross margins. They may be based on such strategic criteria as market share (Darmon 2004b).

Another trend follows from the expanding practice of team selling, especially for servicing the firm's key accounts. Part or all of the variable part of compensation could be attributed to the team. Note that equitable ways to share the common bonus among all the team members remains to be found. These are a few major trends that are likely to shape the structure of the sales force compensation plans over the years to come.

Other incentives

Due to the evolution of the selling functions, and consequently of salespeople's profiles, many motivational devices that sales managers have used extensively in the past are likely to change drastically or become obsolete. Most sales managers presently think that sales force motivation is best achieved through personal development, empowerment, career path management, relevant continuing education and training, in addition to a fair and equitable compensation plan and good job conditions.

One can safely predict that such devices as sales contests in which salespeople compete with one another are likely to disappear. In contrast, given the ever-increasing costs of personal selling, one can expect most firms to provide salespeople with the most up-to-date and sophisticated means to make them more efficient in the field. Call centers, telemarketing, and computerization, and all sorts of demonstration aids are available to make the selling function more efficient.

Conclusion

The control levers that sales managers use to motivate salespeople and ensure a high level of morale in their sales force are financial and/or non-financial in nature. Traditionally, sales managers have had a tendency to heavily rely on the sales force compensation plan for that purpose. No doubt, financial incentives are always strong motivators. Nevertheless, sales force management is becoming increasingly aware that other types of incentive programs should also be used to ensure a high level of sales force motivation. More specifically, non-financial incentive programs such as well established promotion policies, career management, or personal development programs are becoming increasingly important at a time when the personal selling function is being recognized as a true profession.

One can also consider that salespeople's knowledge development programs have also a strong impact on sales force motivation. These programs are the subject matter of the following chapter.

10 Controlling effort quality improvement programs

Does better training result in an increase in sales?

Raleigh, an important independent distributor of bicycles, had just hired a new sales manager. Shortly after taking the job, this sales manager realized that in order to increase the firm's customer basis, it was essential to redefine the sales force mission. Salespeople had to become the best consultants for their clients. A prerequisite to do this was to provide salespeople with knowledge, not just about products, but also to give them some basic understanding of fields such as accounting and inventory management so they could provide their independent clients with useful advice when needed. The objective was to develop high value-added partnerships with customers.

The sales manager quickly realized that all the field salespeople needed additional education and training. The objectives of the necessary training program have been defined as "developing a basis for mutual understanding and dialogues between customers and salespeople in order to implement a more consultative approach to selling." An external trainer was hired to provide the training. The sales manager looked at several training agencies so he could select the organization that was best equipped for providing the required service, and which could eventually provide the best follow up program.

All the regional sales managers worked closely with the trainers in order to define twelve areas in which sales staff needed to make some progress (for example, the best ways to uncover and address customers' needs and problems, or to handle customers' objections). Shortly after the training seminars, salespeople had to follow rehearsal, feedback, and corrective sessions.

The results were first noticed by the salespeople themselves. They felt they had become much more self-confident — even the senior salespeople. Shortly after the end of the training programs, the firm had doubled the number of its accounts and increased its sales volume by 35 percent in an industry characterized by an average sales increase of less than 3 percent (Rasmusson 1999).

This example provides a clear illustration that the dynamic management process is exerted not only through the control of salespeople's effort levels, but also through the quality of those efforts. This quality aspect of sales force control is the subject matter of this chapter. In order to increase the quality of salespeople's efforts, several conditions must be met. First, the competence and efficiency of the sales personnel must be raised. Second, salespeople need the motivation to improve their skills and to be trained to achieve higher professional goals. The motivational aspects that have already been covered in other chapters will not be addressed in this chapter, which is concerned with salespeople's competence improvement dimension.

Several control levers can be handled by sales management in order to raise the overall sales force competence level (Figure 10.1). They consist essentially of the initial training program provided by a firm, the periodic

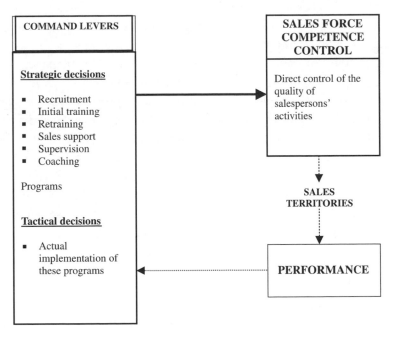

Fig. 10.1   Selling effort quality and deployment controls

retraining programs for well established salespeople, and coaching by sales supervisors and managers. One should not overlook the role of the sales force recruiting programs. Although these programs do not provide a short-term control of a sales force competence level, it exerts a considerable influence on a sales force quality, especially in the long-run.

Control of competencies through initial training programs

When a firm has a decentralized approach to the management of its sales force, it generally sets up an extensive and complete initial training program. Because salespeople are given an extended decision space, are empowered, and given leeway for managing their territories as independent managers, they must be well trained in order to be efficient once in the field. Conversely, a firm that selects a highly centralized management strategy typically stresses continuing education, and retraining, as well as close supervision of the sales force. In this case, the initial training period may be shorter. As a result, it is useful to make a distinction between the initial training that sales management provides to new recruits before they are assigned to a territory, and retraining programs that fulfill quite different situational needs and objectives.

To provide this training, managers may either call upon professional trainers whose unique mission is to educate and train newly hired salespeople, or assign this responsibility to field managers or senior salespeople. In practice, over one-third of the firms involve senior and experienced salespeople in their initial training programs. This practice is often challenged on the grounds that "old timers" may have developed bad habits over time that they might transmit to new staff. Another argument may be even more convincing: it may be unwise to believe that successful senior salespeople have the ability to teach young recruits what it has taken them many years to learn. In addition, high performing salespeople are not always good trainers. As a result, sales managers should use senior sales staff for training purposes only with extreme care.

Initial training programs

Initial training as a managerial control lever

At a time when economic conditions are booming, when there is a need to build loyal relationships with customers and keep sales force turnover under control, it is essential to provide salespeople with extensive training before giving them full field responsibilities (Cron *et al.* 2005). When they take charge of their sales territories, poorly prepared staff do not feel integrated, may lack self-confidence, distrust their supervisors, and may try to quit their job at the first opportunity. Consequently, initial training decisions are vital, not only for the direct control of the competence levels and work quality, but also for their potential impact on sales force turnover.

Initial training programs, however, constitute a costly and risky investment, the return from which is difficult for a firm to estimate (Evered 1988; Honeycutt *et al.* 2001). It involves the direct training costs, but also heavy opportunity costs, because a salesperson in a training program is not (or in any case not completely) operational in the field. Consequently, cost-wise, this constitutes a burden to a firm and a potential loss of revenue. In addition, because training is always an investment that pays off at some point in the future, sales managers whose sales forces are plagued with high turnover rates, may be inclined to shorten training programs, thus avoiding the risk of no return on their investment.

Some firms, like Xerox, have always been known to be very effective sales schools because of the quality of their training programs. It prompted the company to sell its sales force training programs to its distributors and external firms through their Erudia training branch. When a firm invests heavily in building its salespeoples' competencies, it should also invest in a strong loyalty-building program to keep its better trained people.

Finally, like any other educational program, training programs are very difficult to evaluate in terms of return on investment (Attia, Honeycutt, and Leach 2005). Most people think that education ends up being beneficial. It is less obvious however, which type of training is most efficient, with what rate of return, and how long it will take to feel its effects. As a result, except possibly when it comes to teaching salespeople very factual knowledge, or immediately useable techniques, developing sales-people's skills and aptitudes remains no more than a credo for many sales managers.

Like salespeople's objective programs, training programs involve two aspects. One concerns the relatively stable structure and processes that management follows for sales force training. A firm must determine its training strategy, select between an internal or outsourced training program, and specify the objectives that such programs should achieve. These training program structures and processes are pretty stable over time and are generally implemented for several cohorts of new recruits.

A second aspect relates to the actual implementation of the general processes to specific training programs. This implies, for example, the choice of the specific trainers who are in charge of given training sessions, the time schedule followed by trainees during a given program, as well as the activities involved during each session. It is quite conceivable that a well structured training program can be poorly implemented. This is unlikely to meet managers' expectations and objectives. If, for example, the training leaders are not sufficiently competent, or the program is not adequately planned, or the program is shortened in order to send the trainees in to the field too quickly, the *implementation* of the program is at fault, not its conception or structure.

Objectives of an initial training program

Before being formally assigned a sales territory, every new sales recruit, even experienced salespeople, must follow an initial training period (Dubinsky and Staples 1982; Wilson, Strutton, and Farris 2002). The natural starting point for making training decisions is to specify which objectives this training program should achieve over a given period of time. The objective is always to fill the gap between the effectiveness of salespeople at the time they are recruited and the competence level that is necessary to manage a sales territory and to be effective at managing customer relationships.

Methods for defining training objectives

Most training and development programs are designed for providing salespeople with the KSAs (knowledge, skills and abilities) they need to hold their customer relationship management responsibilities (Dubinsky 1996). Newly recruited salespeople should not only have an adequate knowledge of their firm and identify themselves with it, but they also need to acquire the necessary information and knowledge about the products they have to sell, as well as those of the competition. They must obtain a certain amount of information about the customers that will be part of their territories, have a thorough understanding of the policies and administrative procedures of their firm, and they must be fully aware of the limits of their responsibilities (for example, in terms of the price concessions that they may be authorized to make to their clients). More recently, customer-centered selling and relationship building approaches to training programs tend to focus on salespeople's skills (Johnston and Marshall 2005).

To precisely define the objectives of their training programs, sales managers can take a complete inventory of salespeople's necessary knowledge and competencies (Table 4.1), and compare it with the current knowledge of the new recruits (Erffmeyer, Russ, and Hair 1991).

Unfortunately, it seems that in practice, a systematic and formal need analysis is seldom made before building initial training programs. However, filling the gap between current and desired knowledge bases should logically be the best way to define training program objectives. Such an analysis may well show that all the new recruits do not share exactly the same training needs. In this case, devising a unique standardized training program for all the new hires would not be efficient. While some salespeople would attend sessions in which they would learn very little, others could still have knowledge gaps by the end of the sessions. It is in a firm's best interest to customize initial training programs, or at least to make them modular. Every salesperson can then follow selected modules according to his/her needs. It is only when such gap analyses have been performed that sales management can specify the content, duration, and organization of their initial training programs.

Training for new market responsibilities

Sometimes, a firm has to create a new sales force from scratch, especially in the case of new market penetration or where new products are introduced by the firm. Here, the firm must also create a new training program. This situation was faced by a leading manufacturer of suspended ceilings when the firm entered the individual home market. Selling to this market requires special knowledge and competencies that the current sales force, which was accustomed to selling directly to the industrial market, did not have. To solve the problem, management created a completely new sales force made up of young college graduates, and give them a new training program which had been specifically designed, which was based on a blend of theory and field practice.

Program contents

The content of a training program must unfold naturally when a systematic list of all the gaps between actual and desired skills, knowledge, and competence levels is drawn. In practice, it seems that most programs emphasize knowledge acquisition and selling techniques. According to several studies, substantial differences do exist between what sales managers think salespeople in their sales force should know and the actual content of training programs (Kerr and Burzynski 1988). In spite of the more recent trend towards skill development mentioned above, developing essential qualities and attitudes that constitute a prerequisite to selling competence, such as self-confidence or persistence, are seldom part of initial training programs. The IBM consultative sales training program focuses on building ties with clients, working as consultants, and solving problems jointly (Cron *et al.* 2005). Salespeople should be trained in five related skills of failure analysis and recovery effort (Gonzalez, Hoffman, and Ingram 2005). Given the role of performance attributions in personal selling that have been described in Chapter 4 (see Dixon, Forbes, Schertzer 2005), salespeople should be taught to identify failures, make proper attributions, select and implement a proper recovery strategy, and assess the effectiveness of these strategies.

Program duration

In practice, the duration of training programs varies considerably, from a few days to several months. Obviously, the length of time depends on how much the new hire has to learn between the beginning and the end of the program, as well as the learning speed of the new recruits. If the gap between salespeoples' competence levels at the beginning of the program and the time they are ready to be assigned to a territory is wide, the longer and the more important the training program should be. In the same way, when a training program has for objectives a change of attitudes and behaviors or know-how development (by opposition to factual knowledge), it takes longer to train and teach salespeople, and consequently, the duration of the training programs also tends to be longer.

Because of the high direct and opportunity costs of sales force initial training mentioned earlier, sales managers sometimes try to cut the length of initial training as much as possible. Others deliberately recruit experienced salespeople so they can avoid expensive training programs. In the latter case, however, they should account for additional costs (and revenues) that such experienced staff may generate.

An international pharmaceutical product company carried out an investigation to find out what was the most desirable initial education level of its salespeople at the time of recruitment, taking into account all the cost structures and revenues that each candidate profile was likely to generate for the firm in the long term. The analysis took five candidate profiles into account, each one with varying competence levels:

- a salesperson entering the job market for the first time, such as new college graduates without any practical experience or older people entering the job market for the first time (no experience);
- a salesperson who has been employed in other companies in non-selling jobs (modest experience);
- a salesperson who is currently employed by the company, but in a non-selling position (average experience);
- a salesperson with previous sales experience, but not in the pharmaceutical industry (substantial experience);
- a salesperson coming from a competing sales force in a similar type of industry (extensive experience).

The results (Figure 10.2) suggest that in the case of this firm (one should guard against generalizing results that are based on a single company's experience), salespeople that displayed average initial competence, not only generated the lowest costs (remuneration costs plus other selling costs), but also produced the highest profits for the firm (Darmon 1993b).

Program methods

The choice of training methods must logically follow from the program's objectives and content. Classroom sessions, on-the-job training with a trained supervisor, mentoring, or any combination of those methods are most frequently used in practice.

Classroom training

Classroom training is the most frequently used method. It is often supplemented by one or several other training methods. Training sessions may take place either at the firm's head office or at the trainers' office when training has been outsourced. The method is best suited for transmitting factual information to sales trainees or for role playing, sales demonstrations or simulation of sales negotiations. It allows teamwork with a group leader to foster thinking and learning.

More recently, electronic devices and equipment have been added to the training kits of many companies. These include interactive computers with videodisks that make it possible to simulate sales calls to different types of customers and prospects (Urbanski 1988). Even more recently, expert systems have entered the trainers' tool kit (Rubash, Sullivan, and

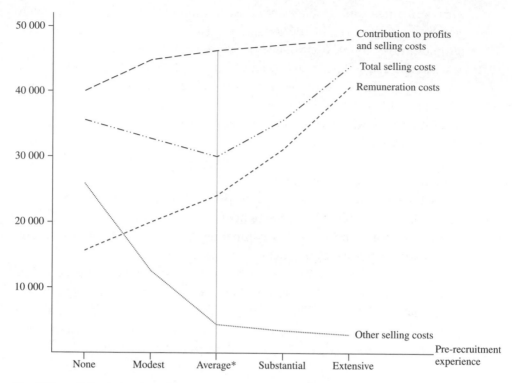

Fig. 10.2   Estimated costs and revenues at different initial competence levels

Herzog 1987). These programs require salespeople to provide information about themselves and about the customer. The system then suggests a selling strategy that fits the needs of the situation and demonstrates the best way to approach a customer.

Classroom training is relatively inexpensive, because it can handle several sales trainees at a time (ideally, six to ten). It can be used for initial training as well as for retraining sessions.

On-the-job training

Whatever their quality, classroom training sessions are not sufficient. As underlined in Part 1 of this book, competencies cannot be developed unless trainers get some practical know-how and on-the-job experience. A sales trainee can only acquire such experience by actually calling on customers along with a trainer, a supervisor, or an experienced salesperson (keeping in mind the above-mentioned restrictions). In addition, on-the-job training is best suited to teach salespeople how to develop the declarative and procedural knowledge that is specific to their own territories and industry. Some authors have even suggested that the procedural knowledge developed by experienced salespeople should be formally recorded, and that this material should be used to train inexperienced staff (Leigh and McGraw 1989).

As already discussed, research has shown that salespeople have identifiable cognitive structures. These can be used to train new staff (Bandura 1977). Complex tasks, such as personal selling can be best learned through observation, imitation, and role playing. Such methods are even more effective when they precede and immediately follow some cognitive type of learning (Leigh 1987).

Volkswagen has recently used an original method to train the salespeople of its some 560 distributors in France. The mission was to improve the customer reception function that, according to surveys, was often deficient. A program called "Client 2000" was launched a few years ago to solve this problem. It is based on a delegation of training. Every participating distributor is helped by a Volkswagen salesperson who plays the role of a mentor. Each distributor selects a delegate among its own sales force. This delegate goes through a training program (lasting about an hour-and-a-half every month) and is in charge of training all the salespeople in his/her own agency. The program resulted in a ten percentage point increase in the customer satisfaction level index (ranging from 0 to 100).

Mentoring

Recognizing that the personal selling activities and duties cannot be learned exclusively in textbooks, some firms like L'Oreal (following the North American lead) are increasingly turning to tutoring or mentoring. Mentoring is the process by which an experienced salesperson takes the responsibility to transmit certain knowledge and know-how to young new recruits. In principle, there is no hierarchical link between a mentor and the trainee. Tutoring has the effect of actualizing new salespeople's potential, to enhance their performance, to teach the trainees the firm's organizational culture, and consequently, to build commitment and loyalty to the organization. Although it has definite advantages, this training method has also its limits (Bolman Pullins and Fine 2002). It forces mentors and trainees to work in dyads at least for a certain period of time. It assumes complete cooperation of the mentor (which may not be always automatically acquired). Finally, it requires the mentors to play their role effectively.

Quality control

Periodically, sales management must evaluate the quality of its training programs. This should take place at at least three levels. Sales trainees should be assessed before and after the training program to make sure that the program has met its objectives. In the same way, trainers should also be evaluated on their results and their ability to enforce the changes for which they are responsible. Finally, a third type of periodical evaluation should question the relevance and quality of the overall training processes that the firm has set up and used in the past (Leach and Liu 2003).

Control of competencies through retraining programs

Many aspects of initial training also apply to retraining programs. In this section, only those aspects that are specific to the latter type of program are discussed.

Retraining program objectives

Besides initial training, salespeople need to be periodically retrained during their careers. There are several reasons for this. First, most of a salesperson's knowledge is likely to become obsolete within a few years of completing the initial training program. Like any other type of knowledge, it also decays over time. At a time when technological advances happen very quickly, individuals who do not keep up-to-date may find themselves unable to communicate effectively with their customers. To maintain sales force effectiveness at peak level, it is essential to periodically up-date individual knowledge and skill.

Sales managers and supervisors should be able to recognize those salespeople who may be affected by professional obsolescence. Typically, they tend to call on the same clients, with whom they feel most at ease. They avoid calling on young new buyers who have acquired more up-to-date technical knowledge. They are often reluctant to sell new products that they do not know well or know how to sell, and they frequently suffer from motivation problems (Goodman 1971). Finally, one should not forget that senior salespeople are often considered as role models for new recruits.

They refer (consciously or not) to such models. If they can find their role models within the firm itself, the probability is high that they will remain loyal to it.

Undertaking training during their careers often has the salespeople being retrained a new lease of life. Unfortunately, firms are sometimes reluctant to send their salespeople to refresher training programs for a simple reason: sales managers must withdraw salespeople from their territories to send them for retraining. Consequently, they incur sales losses. Frequently, sales managers are not convinced (often wrongly) that the hypothetical benefits that might result from a retraining program will override the actual losses of removing a salesperson (even temporarily) from his/her territory. As the example at the beginning of this chapter suggests, this underestimates the benefits of retraining programs.

Most firms that have adopted a policy of periodic retraining for their sales forces have harvested positive results. Dolphin Telecom, a subsidiary of the Canadian Group Mobile Telesystems International Inc., has not recorded one single voluntary leave in over a year. Kuka Automatism, another hi-tech firm, submits its highly technical sales force to periodic retraining programs twice a year. Salespeople are updated on sales negotiation and closing techniques, with highly positive impacts on sales volumes.

Contents and methods

Sometimes firms combine retraining programs and sales meetings. During these meetings, some event that is likely to catch the salespeoples' imagination is organized. This develops team spirit and their commitment to their job and firm. One major industrial firm includes boat races for its salespeople.

"Event" training

Some "event" training programs are held during sales meetings. Sometimes, events are organized during a sales meeting that is devoted to the launch of a new product, or to provoke a major change in sales force attitude or behavior. Those events are intended to trigger a consciousness reaction. Generally, they imply short and specific training actions addressed to large groups of salespeople, sometimes even to the whole sales force. Such an action has been recently undertaken by Merck Laboratories. The four competing sales forces that had resulted from their recent acquisitions (Prolabo, Cofralab, and Poly Labo) had been called to a meeting which was to last for two days. This event concluded an eighteen-month training program. Management thought that this action was instrumental in bringing an organizational culture change in the company.

Concerning this type of action, one caveat is in order. Training, like any form of education, is a serious matter that should be treated as such by sales management. Some firms still apply (or have applied) so-called motivation methods that are more reminiscent of the circus than of serious educational programs, possibly a residual of door-to-door salesmanship, when salespeople had to be motivated by any means. In some cases, football players or coaches have been hired as trainers for the sales forces. Questionable practices are also offered by certain specialized agencies (Chitwood 1988; Falvey 1989; Alessandra and Wexler 1988). If sales managers want their salespeople to be professionals who can develop relationships with clients, and build strong customer loyalty, they should treat them seriously, with well designed and professional meetings. It is quite possible to conduct good taste events training that shows respect to the sales force. At a time when personal selling aspires to become a well recognized profession that requires higher educational levels from salespeople, it is time for sales managers to adapt their control levers accordingly.

Coaching

Instead of one-shot training programs, firms prefer sometimes to resort to continuous highly-personalized training programs that are fully tailored to the needs of each individual. These firms recognize that salespeople often have a need to constantly update or sometimes change their working methods, attitudes, and/or priorities. More and more frequently, field sales managers are given responsibility for this type of continuous training (Rich 1998). Helena Rubinstein, one of the L'Oreal Group's brands, has recently designed a multimedia training program that is being used by all the firm's trainers in 35 countries. This gives salespeople some important scientific knowledge about the cosmetology properties of the brand.

Self-training and self-learning

Increasingly, salespeople participate actively in their own training through self-regulation training (Leach, Liu, and Johnston 2005), and sometimes, with the help of new information technological devices, such as CD-Rom, the internet, or intranets. Such a practice is followed, for example, at

Pernod-Ricard with a CD-Rom entitled "At the conquest of Pernodland." The program involves eight stages, including a self-administered test that measures progresses. One should make a distinction between self-learning, which is based on the help of such technological devices, and self-regulation training that is part of an integrated training process. While the former does not seem to give satisfactory results, the latter is more adequate because of the integration of the NTI into a logical and consistent training program. One should point out that such applications to sales force training are still in their infancy and have not yet proven to be effective on a large scale.

Retraining quality control

Nabisco has recently undertaken a study to evaluate the benefits of its regular training program. It compared the sales results of those salespeople who had followed the training program and those who had not (all other things being equal). It produced some interesting findings. The average sales increase in the first group had been multiplied by a factor of 122 and profits had increased by a factor of 20. These spectacular results, however, constitute a relatively modest investment for Nabisco. The training program was only two days long and salespeople were taught how to plan and make professional sales presentations. The training method was interactive, including role playing, discussions, video presentations, tests, and group exercises. The cost was about $1,000 per salesperson. This should be compared with an estimated $123,000 dollars of additional profits per salesperson that could be attributed to the training program alone (Klein 1997).

Control of competencies through supervision policies

To ensure high efficiency, direct supervisors and field sales managers must provide salespeople with adequate help and support. For that purpose, supervisors must take a series of tactical decisions that should steer salespeople in the desired direction in their everyday tasks. As already discussed, supervision can be limited to a strict control of selling activities and to an assessment of performance. Alternatively, supervision could (and should) have the more positive role of increasing salespeople's competencies through continuous sales training. Nowadays, this latter vision tends to prevail. This conception of supervision is discussed further in the following section.

Main levers of sales leadership

Sales managers exert their leadership essentially through the continuous coaching of salespeople, as well as during the meetings they organize and plan for all or part of the sales force.

Control of competencies through coaching

Coaching salespeople consists of ensuring their continuous professional development. Salespeople can be coached in groups or individually (although in most cases, individual coaching is preferable). Typically, this is accomplished by a supervisor going along with a salesperson when they call on customers. During these calls, a supervisor can observe those behaviors which can be improved — they can thus teach more appropriate selling techniques and more adequate behaviors. A good sales coach applies two basic learning principles: those of recency and repetition. Learning is always much faster when one can immediately apply what has just been learned. Because coaching occurs in the field, just before and after a customer call has taken place, a salesperson has the opportunity to apply what has just been learned. In addition, coaching is more effective when supervisors address the questions of understanding behaviors and of finding the means to change them, rather than stressing the outcomes (Challagalla, Shervani, and Huber 2000).

In order to play this role model, sales managers must be respected and trusted by the salespeople they are coaching. This is an essential condition that must be accounted for when management offers a salesperson promotion, or when a new sales supervisor is hired. An army's Commander-in-Chief needs the respect of the soldiers if he is to command them effectively.

Research has shown the existence of a relationship between the feedback that a manager gives to a salesperson about his/her performance, and the satisfaction level of a salesperson towards her or her management. Surprisingly, negative feedback does not affect satisfaction levels. In contrast, negative feedback on behaviors results in a slight increase in satisfaction (Jaworski and Kholi 1991). Ther research suggests that salespeople are more inclined to receive suggestions from supervisors for improving their own competencies.

Another study of 25,000 employees (including 2,000 salespeople) has found that 69 percent of job satisfaction could be traced back to the leadership qualities of management (Rich 1997; Campanelli 1994). Such conclusions can only reinforce the leadership role of management for constantly improving the salespeople's competencies, and consequently, their performance and outcomes.

Control of competencies and motivation through sales meetings

Periodical sales meetings are opportunities for sales managers to exercise their leadership. These meetings generally pursue several objectives, such as training, motivation, strategic planning, and rewarding the best performers. However, they all share the objective of building a strong selling team with common objectives and to give salespeople the feeling that they are not isolated employees, but that they are part of a team and a larger organization.

Centralized versus decentralized supervision

Although supervision tends to be a typical centralized management tool, it can also be used in a decentralized management context. In ther case, supervision plays the role of a resource that a salesperson can access in case of need (e.g., for dealing with a very delicate situation with a client).

Sales managers may decide to supervise salespeople more or less closely, depending on their control philosophy and management style. They have to choose between a centralized and a decentralized approach. Some managers think that salespeople should enjoy a large autonomy in their actions and want to encourage individual initiative. In this case, they provide only a light supervision, which is less expensive to a firm. Others prefer a very tight supervision to best control salespeople's activities (and consequently reduce their decision space). The advantage is that they can implement corrective actions as soon as they are needed. Due to the supervisory time involved, this approach is more costly than the preceding one.

Irrespective of the approach selected, adequate supervision can result in high sales force motivation, by helping every salesperson to reach the highest possible performance level. For that purpose, sales supervisors can help salespeople to make good (if not optimal) allocations of their time and to reduce unproductive time as much as possible. A number of decision aids have been proposed to that effect (e.g., Lodish 1971). In addition, salespeople often expect management to provide them with help, advice, and support, especially when they face difficult and unusual situations in the field. In any case, it is essential for management to provide constructive and positive supervision to foster a good organizational climate in a sales force. Research suggests that close supervision has a positive effect on job satisfaction, and that a clear and precise perception of their role and function results in higher performance (Teas 1981; 1983).

Research has also shown that experience, self-esteem, and perceptions of their own performance had some impact on supervision behaviors (Kholi 1989). A recent research study suggests that salespeople's supervisory participation is an effective control lever for reducing dysfunctional behaviors because of the resulting increase in trust in their supervisors (Choi, Dixon, and Jung 2004). This suggests also that supervision should be tailored to the needs of the individual. Close supervision may prove to be more adequate when salespeople are inexperienced or when they have not yet fully grasped the extent of their role and function. Inversely, experienced salespeople may require much lighter supervision.

Control of competencies through other programs

Several managerial actions may have an indirect effect on the quality of salespeople's actions. For example, all the decisions that lead to the recruitment and selection of salespeople, or to their assignment to specific sales territories, as well as all the support actions, can enhance (or decrease) sales force effectiveness.

Selection and recruitment programs

It is especially important for a firm to recruit highly competent salespeople or individuals who will quickly reach the highest competence levels. The main reason lies in the heavy costs that will be generated from the recruitment of poor sales performers (who will soon need to be replaced). In addition to the direct recruitment and training costs they involve, poor recruits also provoke a series of opportunity costs, such as the sales they have not been able to make, or the possible damage caused to customer relationships.

Recruitment: a vicious cycle?

The sales force recruitment process may lead to a vicious cycle. A firm may suffer from a high turnover rate and may need to develop recruitment activities to keep the sales force at the desired level. When such a firm has not developed highly valid recruitment procedures, or when it is unable to keep up with this required sustained recruiting effort, it may well recruit salespeople that do not possess the desired qualities and potential performance levels. These new hires are unlikely to stay long with the firm, either because they will have to be fired, or because low performers often experience stress and burnout, and prefer to leave the company voluntarily. As a result, the sales force turnover rate keeps increasing, which requires even more recruiting activities. The firm is locked in a vicious cycle (Figure 10.3). To avoid this, a firm must develop and apply extremely rigorous recruitment procedures (Ganesan, Weitz, and John 1993).

An adequate recruitment procedure implies a series of difficult decisions. The choices that a firm makes are likely to have a considerable impact on the quality and competence levels of the selected salespeople, and consequently, on the efficiency of the whole sales force. The sales manager (in connection with human resources) should carefully design a recruiting strategy which defines adequate and valid selection procedures.

This strategy must specify the objectives of each recruiting campaign, especially the number of salespeople to be hired over a certain period of time. As already discussed, the size of the sales force constitutes a strategic management decision which has direct consequences for recruitment. But it is not the only factor. One should also account for the current sales force turnover rate. Because these aspects have already been discussed in preceding chapters, they will not be considered here explicitly. They should, however, be part of the recruiting decision process. In addition, the recruitment procedures also imply that management defines an "ideal" salesperson's profile, identifies the best possible sources of candidates for the job, and specifies all the steps that will be followed to effectively recruit the desired number of new trainees (Figure 10.4).

"Ideal" recruit profile

First, sales managers should precisely specify the aptitudes, competencies, knowledge, as well as the personal characteristics and preferences that a candidate should ideally possess to be able to effectively carry the mission, as defined in their job description. There are no general innate characteristics that can accurately predict the future sales aptitudes of an individual, so

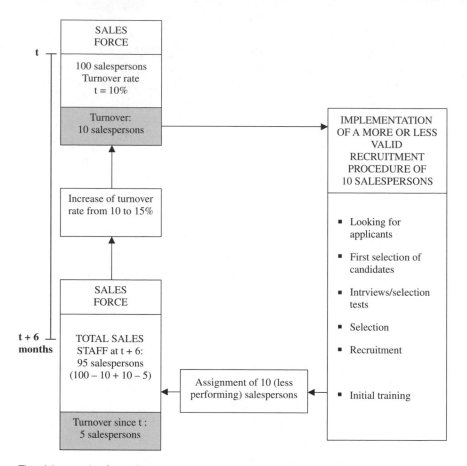

Fig. 10.3   The vicious cycle of recruitment

each firm should set up its own best profile, that is, the profile that best suits its current needs. A detailed job description is a natural starting point.

All companies have explicit or implicit criteria for evaluating, selecting, and hiring. This suggests that they believe it is possible to predict performance from easily-observable characteristics. Typically, these criteria are based on background or personal characteristics. A survey of forty-four top sales executives from large manufacturing companies has assessed the importance those executives granted to ten attributes often believed to be tied to successful salesmanship (Moss 1978; Rollins 1990). It turned out that enthusiasm was ranked as the most important characteristic, followed by good organizational skills, ambition, persuasiveness, general sales experience, superior verbal skills, and sales experience acquired in the same industry. The three characteristics believed to be the least important were,

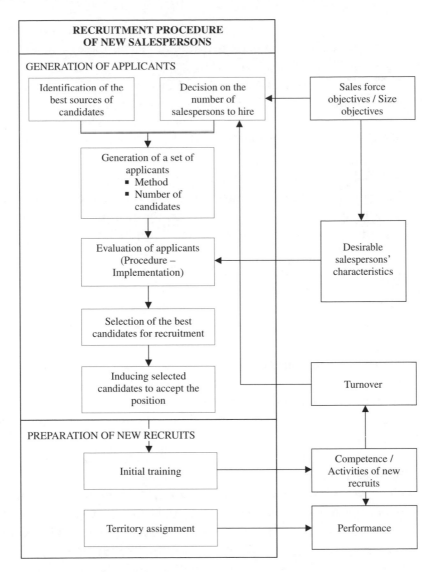

Fig. 10.4   Setting up the recruiting process

good recommendations, ability to follow instructions, and sociability. It is interesting to note that this is at odds with the commonly held belief that a sociable and outgoing personality is a prerequisite to success in selling.

To draw up a list of characteristics of the ideal profile for a given sales force, sales managers should also consider the extent to which they want to (or can) provide the new recruits with the additional training they need to become efficient and competent salespeople. Firms follow a wide variety of strategies for recruitment. Xerox, for example, essentially recruits young inexperienced sales trainees. Canon, its Japanese competitor, recruits salespeople who already have at least some sales experience.

The list of recruiting criteria should then be refined to include only those characteristics that can be observed or measured at the time of recruitment and that are known to be good predictors of a salesperson's quality and efficiency for accomplishing the tasks that management has specified. Drawing a list of recruiting criteria is a delicate task. Any mistake is costly as it translates into less efficient recruits. Including characteristics that are irrelevant causes good candidates to be eliminated, even though they could have been better sales producers than the selected candidates. Omitting important characteristics may lead to similar results.

How to find the best candidate sources

Once the desired profile has been defined, the next question is where are such individuals most likely to be found? (Darmon 1993b). Depending on the profile, some sources of salespeople are better than others. In this context, a source of candidates is defined as "where are the potential sales candidates with various experience levels, who could possibly be hired as salespeople in the organization," rather than "which are the means (or methods) to be used to generate applications for sales jobs." As a result, a firm can find its salespeople from different sources, such as those indicated in Figure 10.2.

Once the most promising sources of candidates with the desired profiles have been identified, then, and only then, should one select the most adequate means to try to communicate with them, to inform them of the firm's job opportunities, and induce them to apply. In practice, visits to university campuses, direct solicitation, advertisements in newspapers and specialized periodicals and magazines, unsolicited applications, referrals from other salespeople within the firm, are most frequently used. At Xerox, one-third of the salespeople recruited had answered a job advertisement in the daily press, but most of them have been recommended by the firm's employees or had sent in spontaneous applications.

Not addressing the best sources, or not using the right communication channels would result in inefficiencies, in the sense that these inefficiencies may prevent the best candidates from being recruited, with the resulting loss of efficiency and competence for the whole sales force.

A question that is frequently neglected in practice, but which may have a strong impact on the quality of the new recruits, is to find out how to generate a sufficient number of candidates, and determine the right amount to spend for that purpose (Darmon 1978a). Logically, it should be profitable to start the recruiting process with as large a pool of candidates as possible. If, for example, ten salespeople need to be recruited, one can show that the average quality of the ten best candidates (assuming that one can properly identify them), is much better if they are selected from a pool of one thousand applicants than if they have been selected from a pool of, say, twenty applicants. From this point of view, it is always profitable to increase the starting pool of potential candidates to avoid recruiting those who are only marginally acceptable salespeople (Hyman and Sager 1999). However, the costs of evaluating every candidate using an elaborate selection procedure may be substantial and may increase drastically with the number of candidates to evaluate. There is a point at which trying to further improve the quality of the recruits is not worth the cost. A research study based on this logic has shown that many firms spend well below the optimal level on recruitment (Darmon 1978a).

Candidate selection procedure

The candidate selection procedure must utilize the best means to observe or detect the presence (or absence) of desirable characteristics and traits at the time of recruitment. Many firms use a multi-step approach to candidate evaluation and selection. After each step, a number of candidates are eliminated until only those that will be recruited remain. Canon, for example, generates about 12,000 applications for its sales force every year. Eight hundred are asked for an interview at the head office, and finally about fifty of them (less than 0.5 percent) are hired (plus ten others in non-selling positions).

Devising a proper evaluation and selection procedure implies the correct specification of the various steps of the procedure: What should be observed at each step? Who, internally or externally, should be implied in the various evaluation tasks? Who should decide on the number of candidates to be eliminated at the end of each step, and how? All these procedures and recruiting methods must be carefully examined by sales management and by human resources. They should be based on scientific criteria for evaluating relevant characteristics and personality traits that are sound predictors of a salesperson's future performance. Unfortunately, these principles are not always applied in practice. Some firms use unorthodox evaluation processes such as graphology (an analysis of candidate's handwriting), which has been elevated to the rank of a valid personality detector. Others use, esoteric methods like numerology, chirographic evaluation, and even the candidate's blood type! Needless to say that there is a lack of scientific evidence for relating a candidate's selling aptitudes to the outcome of those pseudo recruiting techniques (Schmidt and Hunter 1998). Eliminating a candidate after looking at his/her hand writing for a few seconds is roughly equivalent to throwing a substantial number of application forms in the bin. These methods go against the elementary logic of efficient recruiting practices.

Evaluation methods

Three evaluation techniques, are most frequently used in practice. These are: application blank evaluation, personal interviews, and psychological testing. Many companies use a combination of several or all of them, at different steps of the recruiting process. At Xerox, although all the candidates go through a battery of personality tests, face-to-face interview remains the method that carries the most weight. Every candidate who is asked for an interview must spend three one-hour meetings successively with the recruitment office, the future sales manager, and the regional sales manager who validates the final choice. Many large firms also use assessment centers which evaluate selected candidates through interviews, tests, exercises, presentations over a more, or less, extended period of time.

Résumé analysis   Résumés (or the data requested on the firm's application form), provide a quick assessment of an applicant's background and experience. In addition to demographic characteristics, they allow a quick appraisal of a candidate's education, professional experience, and general profile. This analysis frequently allows managers to infer some of the candidate's qualities (or shortcomings), especially when they have had a very active (or inactive) life in the past. To an extent, it can provide some clues as to whether individuals will integrate well into the sales force, their potential for performing well, and if they may quit the sales force too quickly (Gable, Hollon, and Danyello 1992). Finally, résumé analysis leads to the elimination of a number of candidates that do not have the required education level or experience. Research has shown that biodata are relatively effective at predicting objective sales performance (Farrell and Hakastian 2001).

Face-to-face interviews   This is the most frequently used selection technique. In fact it would be difficult to imagine that a salesperson could be recruited without first being interviewed by the relevant sales manager. Through personal interview, sales managers can assess the personality profile of a candidate, but it is also the only way a recruiter can evaluate a candidate's physical appearance, behavior, and communication abilities and observe all the non-verbal information that a candidate is likely to give about him/herself. Some firms use evaluation centers that put candidates in simulated situation conditions, close enough to those that a salesperson is likely to experience (Cohen 1980). These centers can be helpful to evaluate the candidate's behaviors as close to the real world as possible.

In spite of their great notoriety, face-to-face interviews have been the target of a number of criticisms that have not yet found theoretical answers. Who, in the firm, should be the interviewer(s)? Should these interviews be carried out individually or in groups (on both sides)? How long should each interview last? Should the interview be highly structured or informal? Should it be carried out in a relaxed atmosphere or under stress? How should divergent opinions from different interviewers be reconciled to arrive at a hire/fire decision? Anyone who has carried out evaluation and selection interviews knows that different judges who have observed exactly the same situation often reach different, and sometimes opposite, conclusions. Some research has suggested that personal interviews are probably the least valid and the least reliable tool for predicting the future performance level of a salesperson (Hunter and Hunter 1984; Johnston and Cooper 1981). More recent evidence suggests that interviews can be a reasonably good predictor of future sales performance, provided they are highly structured (Salgado 1999). Of course, this does not mean that salespeople should not be interviewed before recruitment. It means, however, that the weight given to interviews should be discounted at the selection time. This proposition is easier to state than to apply. Interviewers have the tendency to be extremely confident about their judgments and few are generally ready to admit that even occasionally, they could be wrong.

Psychometric tests   Psychological tests allow an assessment of the intellectual aptitudes and personality traits that could be difficult to measure otherwise. Firms frequently use tests that measure the IQ (intelligence quotient) or aptitudes that are assumed to be important. Others use personality tests to make sure that candidates have traits that they consider essential to good salesmanship (such as empathy) (Maxwell *et al.* 2005). Still others use tests that assess the vocation that an individual has for a selling career, and for the types of situation that this individual will have to face eventually. The major problem with such tests is that they can be easily faked by providing the obvious answers.

Another problem concerns the validity of such tests (i.e. the extent to which they actually measure what they are supposed to measure) as well as their reliability (i.e. their ability to provide the same scores when repeated in identical situations). Thus, cognitive ability test scores have been found to be the best predictors of future sales performance, followed by integrity tests. They out-perform personality tests, and biographical data (Schmidt and Hunter 1998; Robertson and Smith 2001).

Recruitment decisions

A candidate's evaluation by different measuring instruments and different managers does not end the recruiting process. The procedures must make explicit or implicit provisions for the type of tradeoffs that are necessary to arrive at a final decision for each candidate, especially when such evaluations are inconsistent. These compromises should be acceptable to a firm, because some lack of a given desirable characteristic may have to be compensated by another. Finally, sales managers should determine which arguments are the best for "selling" the job and the company to prospective candidates. Candidates' perceptions of the selling job and training programs they will undertake are crucial (Barksdale *et al.* 2003). One should not forget that, especially when the job market is tight, salespeople select their job at least as much as they are selected by a firm (Wotruba, Simpson, and Reed-Draznick 1989; Wiles and Spiro 2004).

All the decisions in a recruiting process are likely to have a strong impact on the quality and competence levels of those recruited and consequently, the overall quality of a sales force. Although recruiting new salespeople is not *per se* a process control lever, it constitutes a major constraint to which sales managers should pay constant attention. It must be used to keep the sales force at the desired size, and to ensure the desired competence level over the more or less distant future.

Support programs

Sales support programs can considerably increase sales force efficiency and improve the quality of salespeople's activities and performance. These programs tend to help with the administrative work that must be performed, as well as with the relationships that salespeople enjoy with their customers.

"Classic" support devices

Motivation and morale can be considerably enhanced when salespeople feel supported by their hierarchy and their firm. As a result, management should make available any useful means for helping salespeople in the field. These means are varied and obviously depend on the type of selling situation and clientele. They encompass such concrete devices as detailed sales catalogues and literature, easy access to such information as price lists or inventory levels, samples to be given away to customers and prospect, and to electronic aids (Table 10.1). They also include even more subtle devices, such as providing salespeople with an ethical organizational climate. Research has shown that such an ethical climate is positively linked to individual commitment to quality and organizational commitment (Weeks *et al.* 2004).

Sales support tools also include demonstration material. This is material that helps salespeople to answer typical customers' objections and reminds them of the best selling arguments and problem-solving strategies. Salespeople can see that their task is made easier when they can hand in descriptive and technical brochures specifically written for the various functional representatives of their clients.

Expense accounts can also help. Obviously, the rules concerning the use of such accounts should be made very clear and be well understood to avoid any potential problems with this dimension of their role.

Support through NTI

A firm can achieve high motivation and satisfaction levels in its sales force by providing the communication and information processing means that can help salespeople to become more efficient and make their tasks easier. All salespeople are now equipped with mobiles and laptops essential for those who work in the field, far away from the firm and clients. As discussed in Chapter 6, this practice tends to generalize.

Firms now equip their sales force with all kinds of electronic devices to permit their salespeople to work from home. Many firms like Viessman, a leading heater manufacturer, for example, have organized their sales forces in such a way as to make it possible for salespeople to send relevant information directly to their headquarters using laptops. The objective is to

Table 10.1. Main sales force support tools

Informational support
- Information about prospects identified by the head office (call centers, telemarketing, etc.)
- Information available about clients
- Information available about sales territories
- Information available about products/services
- Information about inventory levels

Informational aids
- Laptops
- Customer management software
- Time and sales tour management software
- Mobile phone

Organizational support
- Secretarial help
- Support from technical personnel, whenever needed
- Support from administrative personnel
- Support from sales supervisors, whenever needed

Communication aids support
- Equipment for demonstration
- Selling arguments
- Literature on products and services for customer usage
- Price lists
- Samples to be given away to customers/prospects
- Supplies necessary for building sales proposals (measuring instruments, tables, etc)
- Order forms and other administrative forms

Travel support
- Cars

Financial support
- Credit cards, expense accounts for inviting clients
- Refunds of travel expenses

reduce travel time and allow salespeople to spend more time on more productive tasks.

In the same way, all the sales staff at Villeroy & Boch, a major distributor of kitchens, bathrooms, and tiles, work from home. This has allowed the firm to close down most of its agencies. The company covers the cost of installing two telephone lines at each salesperson's home, one for telephone calls, and one for a fax, special computer outlets, a mobile, and a laptop with an e-mail address. These laptops are connected to a central server which gives access to internal data bases that can be used to report market intelligence.

As mentioned in Chapter 6, although this tends to become a part of a salesperson's tool kit, electronic equipment and computer devices are not always easily accepted by salespeople who have not used this type of equipment before. Many salespeople will not readily use laptops. Consequently, management must introduce this technology gradually, involving the sales force in the process, and providing adequate training to demonstrate the benefits of using such equipment.

Conclusion

The last four chapters have discussed most of the control levers that are available to management. These control levers include programs and policies that can be used to more or less control salespeople's activities, depending on the level of centralized or decentralized controls that management wishes to implement.

Although some interactions among all those tools do exist, it should be clear that some of them are more appropriate for achieving certain specific sales force objectives, others for increasing levels of effort and activities, others for improving the quality of those activities and efforts (through enhancement of sales force competence). All these programs can be used within the framework of a centralized or decentralized approach to control by selecting the right mix of centralized and decentralized control levers.

Besides control levers, a sales manager's command center also includes a dashboard. It is up to sales management to select those elements that it wishes to have in its dashboard, and consequently, to organize the information flow that will provide the necessary control elements over the activities and/or performances of salespeople. This is the subject matter of the next chapter.

Using dashboards and organizing information flows

Performance indicators to watch

Recently, the sales manager of a leading paint product manufacturer that distributed its product through wholesalers to retail outlets, major retailers (such as do-it-yourself chain stores and supermarkets), and directly to building contractors, was given the mission to make a major inroad in the market segment of professional builders and substantially increase the firm's market share in this segment.

The sales manager developed a program for the sales force that included contests and bonuses for salespeople who could reach the highest sales volumes in this market segment over a one-year period. After one year, management proudly claimed that the firm's market share objective had been reached and even surpassed. Given the success of this incentive program, the sales manager decided to keep it running for another year. Quite unexpectedly, the sales to building contractors showed a sharp decrease the following year.

The sales manager decided to investigate and analyze the situation to find out why this sharp sales decline had happened. Salespeople, clients who had ordered that year, as well as those that had not ordered, were questioned. It quickly became obvious that the market share increase gained the previous year had been the result of hard-sell tactics from a sales force that had been motivated to reach the highest sales volume possible. To that effect, salespeople had overstated the quality of the products and promised delivery times that could not possibly be met by the production department. Consequently, many clients had not had deliveries on time, and many of them had been forced to turn to other suppliers to meeting their deadlines. As a result, these contractors were still carrying excess inventories of the firm's products. All this had resulted in customer dissatisfaction, and many of them had decided to switch to other suppliers.

As a result, the firm decided to drop its incentive program, and undertook a new policy of customer orientation which involved a direct advertising campaign to inform customers of the new policy. They also retrained the sales force using a new and more ethical and effective selling approach.

Evaluation and control of a sales force generally go together. A good evaluation (and consequently control) system is an essential part of an effective process. When implemented, a dynamic management process must quickly point out unexpected facts, particularly large gaps between actual and planned performances. This is a prerequisite to taking corrective action.

In the above case, the sharp sales decrease could have been avoided, if in the first year, instead of just watching market share gains (the firm's objective) and being satisfied with the results, the sales manager had also watched other indicators of sales performance, such as customer satisfaction.

Any evaluation and control system involves some comparison of actual results and explicit or implicit objectives or pre-established norms. A dynamic management process implies constant reactions and adjustments over time to close gaps. At first glance, one could say that it is always clear which indicators of performance sales managers should be constantly watching. In practice, this is seldom the case. Obviously, any action should eventually result in sales, either in the short or the long term. However, there are many relevant performance indicators other than sales volumes that must be watched. For example, profits, market share variations, customer satisfaction, may be highly relevant indicators, too, and sales managers should watch them systematically. The outcomes of selling activities should always be measured with the same yardstick as final or intermediate objectives.

It would be erroneous, however, to only use such measures. As demonstrated throughout this book, any sales force management action is likely to have some impact at various levels and in different parts of the sales force system. Logically, then one should constantly monitor all facets of the sales force to detect such desirable and/or undesirable effects as soon as possible.

Designing a dashboard for effectively managing a sales force is a very delicate task. A dashboard is stable over time, as is the dashboard in the cockpit of an aircraft. It is designed for an extended usage over time. Altering or significantly changing the dashboard design cannot be achieved without involving sometimes quite substantial costs and delays.

A dashboard structure is the most stable element in a dynamic management process. As a result, it should be carefully designed to provide the information that a sales manager needs. In addition, the information flows required for feeding the dashboard should have been properly organized.

One difficulty of this task lies in the fact that general and sales managers are themselves frequently affected by high turnover rates. The information and control devices that are used are often specific to a given sales manager. The simplest solution in this case might seem to set up the most complete dashboard as possible. The costs for setting up and operating such a detailed system, however, can very quickly become substantial, especially if some parts of the system are not used optimally by management. In fact, a sales force management dashboard should be the best possible compromise between the cost of "complete" information and the actual informational needs of sales managers.

In the following sections, the different types of market feedbacks that management can use are described. Then, the criteria that sales managers can use to select their specific set of feedback elements in their dashboards are discussed.

Different types of feedback

Sales management can and should collect information about their sales force performances, as well as the sales outcomes of various entities, such as sales regions or other geographical splits of the market, and/or about salespeople's activities. In the latter case, one should make a clear distinction between the quantitative amount of activities deployed and the quality of these activities (Weitz, Sujan, and Sujan 1986).

Sales performance

Sales managers always get some feedback about the performance of their sales force. The most basic feedback from the market is the sales volumes that have been achieved during a certain period of time. This is indicated by the simple addition of customer orders during a given time period. Performance measures, however, can also apply to the resulting profits, market share, or percentage of satisfied customers. At a more disaggregated level, individual feedback always constitutes a challenge for sales management, because it is usually difficult to obtain a complete picture of a salesperson's performance. Sales results alone can sometimes provide a distorted picture of performance. For example, there are frequent cases where impressive sales results could be attributed, not to the current salesperson, but to the salesperson formerly in charge of the same territory, who may have efficiently cultivated this territory in the past. Inversely, the preceding salesperson may have caused some damage, resulting in lower than anticipated actual sales performance. Hence, there is a need for accessing reliable and complete information about sales results. Such information may come from different sources, in particular, the firm (through its analyses of customer orders), internal sources (supervisors or salespeople themselves), or external sources (syndicated services or customers).

Customer order analysis

As discussed in the case of generally centralized controls, salespeople are frequently assigned explicit sales objectives or sales quotas. These objectives are convenient benchmarks against which managers can evaluate performance. Salespeople generally earn a bonus or other types of reward when they meet or surpass their sales quotas. Sales managers can effectively follow progresses toward the firm's (or region's or sales territory's) objectives by closely monitoring sales achievements over time and comparing the sales results with what they normally expect to be achieved at any time to see an objective met at the end of the planning period.

An analysis of customers' orders can provide extremely rich information, and involves relatively low costs. Table 11.1 provides a list of such analyses. This list is not exhaustive by any means, but it shows the large amount of relevant information they can yield. Sales managers must select the information that they find most useful. Note, however, that information overload is to be avoided. One possibility for avoiding this pitfall is to exert "management by exception" in which only those observations that depart sharply from expectations are singled out for thorough analysis.

Supervisors

Field sales managers and direct supervisors are usually in the best position to observe salespeoples' performances and outcomes. They frequently use either formal grading systems or more participative procedures. Grading

Table 11.1. Sales force control based on sales performance analysis

Performance measures	Relative usage frequency (5-level scales)
Sales volume (revenues)	
Sales volume (in euros)	3.77
Sales volume to previous year's sales	3.60
Sales to new accounts (in euros)	3.23
Sales volume versus quota	3.21
Sales volume versus market potentials	3.16
Sales volume (in units)	3.14
Percentage of market share achieved	2.84
Sales volume by product type	2.62
Payments overdue	2.62
Sales volume by customer type	2.52
Customer flows	
Number of lost accounts	3.36
Number of new accounts	3.18
Number of customer complaints	3.15
Accounts buying full line	2.65
Profits	
Net profits (in euros)	3.23
Net profit margins	3.21
Gross profit margins	3.06
Gross profit margin as a percentage of sales	3.02
Return on sales cost	2.87
All these analyses can be done for the whole sales force level but they can also be done for sales region, district, or salesperson.	

Source: Adapted from Michael Morris *et al.* (1991).

systems are often used to evaluate performance, and are implemented in many large companies like 3M or Microsoft. Here, salespeople are evaluated on a term basis by their direct supervisors using a five-point scale. At Microsoft, the bonus that a salesperson earns is directly linked to their term grade. Salespeople are assigned six-month objectives per product or product line, such as for example, selling Windows NT to a given number of clients or to sign up a number of licensing contracts with key accounts. Note that the time and type of performance measurement is important: research has shown that they could lead to different evaluations (Chonko *et al.* 2000).

Sometimes, managers and salespeople discuss and agree on objectives to be reached, on the feedback, and on the rewards to be earned.

According to this system, managers play the role of partners and salespeople are in charge of their own careers and development. Research suggests that firms who follow such an approach tend to reach higher productivity levels and achieve better financial results than the industry average (Rheem 1995). This approach is fully consistent with the total quality management philosophy, which attempts to conciliate both a customer orientation and an organizational culture oriented toward team work and on the continuous improvement of procedures and behaviors, including those of salespeople.

Salespeople

Salespeople are also likely to provide interesting feedback on their own performance, and especially on their own performance expectations. For example, they can give their own explanations about lost orders and accounts. As already mentioned, salespeople can be instrumental in developing realistic sales forecasts and can play a useful role in the quota setting process.

Customers

At a time when most firms are fully devoted to building customer loyalty, customer satisfaction has become a directional or specific objective. Although customer satisfaction is no guarantee of loyalty, it is an essential prerequisite. Not surprisingly, progress toward such objectives deserves to be constantly monitored and frequently and accurately measured. Customer satisfaction surveys are extremely important inputs into sales force evaluations. They are currently used by more than 25 percent of North American firms, including such large corporations as Xerox and General Electric (Knouse and Strutton 1996; Cohen 1997; Mentzer, Bienstock, and Khan 1995).

Most firms that achieve a certain sales volume have generally developed or use some measure of customer satisfaction. This is an extremely important performance indicator and should be included in any sales force management dashboard. Many firms collect customer satisfaction data themselves, either through telephone, mail, or internet surveys. However, firms should be wary of using the sales force to collect this information. Because they are involved in the customer satisfaction enhancement process, salespeople should not be put in a role conflict situation. To evaluate the performance of sedentary salespeople, many firms use the fake customer method. Originated from the United States several years ago, this technique consists of using anonymous evaluators who pretend to be clients to assess the quality of the services provided.

Customer satisfaction surveys are carried out more or less frequently. They are also more or less detailed. They measure either global customer satisfaction or customers' satisfaction with various aspects of the relationship and service quality. In the same way, customer satisfaction may be measured either at the overall satisfaction level of a firm's clientele only or, alternatively, in each territory, and even at the customer level in the case of key accounts.

The systematic analysis of customer claims also constitutes an important source of information on customer satisfaction, or more likely, on customer dissatisfaction. Because all these measurements can be taken at a more or less frequent pace and level of detail, their costs can also vary considerably from one firm to another.

Other external sources

Sales managers can also obtain feedback about their firm and their salespeople from external sources. Pharmaceutical companies purchase the services of other firms like the GERS to estimate the sales volumes that have been registered by drugstores in every region, as well as their market shares and those of competitors. Nielsen provides similar services for consumer markets. Firms may also secure information from external firms to estimate market potential or competitors' sales to estimate their market share.

Salespeople's activities

The performance of various selling activities may be monitored using feedback on salespeoples' activity levels and quality, their usage of the firm's resources, as well as their general behaviors. The advantage of this is that management can assess whether these behaviors are desirable, either in the short or a long term. Traditionally, a large number of dimensions of salespeople's behavior have been monitored by sales managers (Table 11.2).

Resource usage

When managers have not met objectives, they tend to blame insufficient or inadequate activity levels from their employees (occasionally from themselves), and/or to external factors. They often overlook that another frequent cause of failure to meet objectives, can be attributed to the fact that all the required resources that have been allocated to the mission have not

Table 11.2. Sales force control based on quantitative measures of sales force activities

Activity measures	Percentage of firms using this criterion
Customer calls	
Number of customer calls	48
Number of calls per day (or period)	42
Use of promotional materials	37
Number of planned calls	24
Number of calls per account	23
Number of formal sales presentations	22
Number of quotes	21
Number of calls per number of customers – by product class (call frequency ratio)	18
Number of service calls	17
Number of formal proposals	15
Advertising displays set up	13
Number of demonstrations conducted	12
Number of unplanned calls	7
Planned to unplanned call ratio	3
Time management	
Number of worked days (per period)	33
Time spent selling compared to other activities	27
Average time spent per call	8
Administrative activities	
Number of required reports handed in	38
Training meetings conducted	26
Number of dealer meetings held	17
Amounts recovered on overdue accounts	10
Number of letters/telephone calls to prospects	9

Measures	Relative usage frequency (5-level scales)
Number of reports turned in	2.63
Selling expenses for selling activities	
Selling expenses versus sales budget	2.93
Selling expenses as a percentage of sales	2.65

Source: Adapted from Thomas N. Ingram *et al.* (2001), *Sales Management: Analysis and Decision Making*, 4th edn. Fort Worth, Harcourt, 283; Michael Morris *et al.* (1991).

been spent according to the marketing and/or sales plans. Consequently, while keeping an eye on the various performance outcomes, a manager must also make sure that all the resources that had been anticipated are actually used efficiently, at the right time. As a result, an essential part of a sales manager's dashboard should be timely information about the current sales force size, anticipated and actual recruitments and departures for all the reasons that have been discussed previously. A dashboard should also provide information about the expenses charged by each salesperson, not necessarily with the objective of curtailing them, but to make sure that the resources that have been used can generate the target performance level. In the same way, sales managers should have enough direct control (and consequently information) over the effective use of selling material and support aids by salespeople.

Information concerning resource usage by the sales personnel generally originates from internal sources. Consequently, it is less costly and requires relatively less time to collect than most other feedback information. This information should be part of any sales management's dashboard.

Salespeoples' activities

When they are not provided by salespeople themselves, information about selling activities must be collected from various sources, especially from field supervisors or from customers (Powell Mantel *et al.* 2002). It may be useful here to make a distinction between feedback using quantitative and qualitative criteria.

From salespeople

Customer call reports written by salespeople and/or e-mailed to management constitute a good information basis about salespeople's quantitative activities. They can be used to assess the extent to which salespeople follow some pre-established norms concerning the number of calls that they should make over a set period of time. Salespeople can provide good indicators of the level of their selling activities, they probably are a much less reliable and valid information source concerning the quality of those activities. It would be wise to question the validity of these kinds of reports. A first prerequisite is for salespeople to have a genuine interest in transmitting information to managers. A second prerequisite is their interest in transmitting *accurate* information.

For example, a large electronic equipment firm had undertaken a study about the actual time the sales force spent in direct contact with customers, and the relationships between contact time and sales. Sales managers had requested salespeople to send anonymous detailed reports with the necessary information about the preceding week's activities to headquarters.

When the data was reviewed, the analyst was surprised to find a series of identical reports. When he investigated the problem, it became clear that in every sales region, the sales staff had designated one of them to make up the daily reports for everybody. It transpired that, management had not taken the time to explain the aim and relevance of this study to the sales staff. As a result, they developed the feeling that some member of the administrative staff had decided to control them and ask them to establish one more "useless and time consuming report."

In addition, salespeople may be afraid to report the truth and receive a poor evaluation from their supervisors. Thus, some salespeople may well report an artificially inflated number of calls to prospects, if they fear negative feedback from management. For all these reasons, salespeople can only be a questionable source of information when reporting the quantity and especially the quality of their efforts and work. Any such information should be supplemented with other sources, whenever possible.

Supervisors

Sales supervisors are a superior source of information about the quantity and quality of salespeople's activities (see Table 11.3). As management is centralized and as sales forces are under close supervision, managers have plenty of relevant information.

One should not believe, however, that field sales supervisors are completely unbiased. Like any other human beings, they are subject to perceptual biases or emotional reactions toward their subordinates. Consequently any such information should be supplemented by other more objective and reliable data, whenever feasible.

Customers

Customers often constitute another source of information that enable supervisors to appraise their salespeople. Obviously, clients are also subject to perceptual biases and have emotional reactions. However, several clients independently assess the same salesperson's activities, which should result in an averaging out of this effect. When a firm intends to collect information about salespeople's activities, it might be helpful to look for customers' appreciation, even if such appraisals are spaced over time. Customer appraisals can be collected either through direct solicitation or mail or e-mail surveys.

Managers sometimes resort to ingenious ways to get feedback. The sales manager of a cleaning product manufacturer wished to assess the activities

Table 11.3. Qualitative control of aptitudes and competencies

Competence measure	Percentage of firms using this criterion
Knowledge	
Product knowledge	85
Knowledge of competition	71
Pricing knowledge	55
Knowledge of company policies	48
Aptitudes and skills	
Communication skills	88
Selling skills	79
Team player	67
Time management	63
Planning ability	58
Customer goodwill generation	41
General dispositions	
Attitude	82
Initiative and aggressiveness	76
Appearance and manner	75
Enthusiasm	66
Judgment	62
Cooperation	62
Motivation	61
Ethics/moral behavior	59
Report preparation and submission	54
Creativity	54
Punctuality	49
Resourcefulness	49
Self-improvement efforts	40
Care of company property	39
Degree of respect from trade and competition	38
Source of new product ideas	35
Use of marketing/technical backup means	33
Good citizenship	22

Source: Adapted from Thomas N. Ingram *et al.* (2001).

and behaviors of newly trained salespeople. To do this, he used to send them prospecting an area in which he had customers who were personal acquaintances. After the salesperson returned from this assignment, the sales manager called on these customers to check that they had actually been called by the new hire, and asked them to provide a detailed report on the qualities of the (unknowingly tested) salesperson. Sometimes, the client was called in advance and instructed by the sales manager to give the salesperson a hard time, in order to assess their attitudes and behavior under stressful situations. Without resorting to such questionable methods from an ethical point of view, questioning customers remains the best way to collect valid information on salespeople's activities.

One of the best ways to collect customer feedback is to ask them to rate a salesperson on a series of scales that capture the various quantitative and qualitative aspects of the relationship that the salesperson has built with them. However, the major drawback of using customers for that purpose is the fact that the method cannot be used too often, for fear of irritating clients.

Multiple sources: 360 degree evaluation

To obtain a more accurate assessment of their salespeople's performance and activities, some firms like Bell Atlantic or Chrysler use a circular or 360 degree evaluation method. With this method, a sales manager can assess a salesperson's performances, taking into account their work environment. It consists of getting a self-evaluation from every salesperson. Then, comments are also obtained from all the individuals with whom they have regular working relationships. Finally, an evaluation form is also completed externally, for example by customers, who are asked to rate the various dimensions of the salesperson's work. These various evaluative reports may indicate differences of perception as well as areas where improvements are needed. When this process is done well, salespeople can correct any revealed weaknesses in a constructive and non-threatening way (Snader 1997). This type of method, which does not seem to have gained general acceptance in Europe can help to develop salespeople's abilities and competencies.

Salespeople's behaviors: BARS procedures

All these quantitative measures that are limited to salespeople's performance only provide a partial view of actual performance. The analysis of salespeople's sales outcomes does not account for the specific events that can occur in every salesperson's environment and can affect their performance. When customers or supervisors evaluate salespeople using a set of rating scales, the resulting evaluations do not say much about the behaviors that should be adopted in order to improve selling performance.

Generally, experts criticize control measures of the current evaluation systems on the grounds that they fail to account exclusively for those outcomes that are specifically and exclusively attributable to salespeople, rather than on often ill-defined personality traits. When these evaluations involve rating scales, the scales are sensitive to halo effects. Halo effects result from the tendency of an evaluator to let the score given to one dimension that is judged as important to affect all other scores, including those that should be completely unrelated. Rating scales always reflect the severity or indulgence of some evaluators. They have a tendency to evaluate toward the mean and to have interpersonal biases. In addition, they cannot adequately cover the functional domain of the salesperson to be evaluated.

This is why some firms prefer to use behavioral anchored rating scales (BARS) for measuring their salespeople's behavioral performances (Cocanougher and Ivancevich 1978). Using this technique, sales managers can identify behaviors that are associated with some outcomes. An adequate BARS program identifies the contributions of a given salesperson to different outcomes because they are anchored on controllable behaviors. Table 11.4 lists the different steps that one should follow in order to implement such a procedure.

The BARS procedure involves building a parsimonious series of scales (see Figure 11.1) which allows an evaluation of performance based on a number of relevant dimensions of their function. This provides individuals and their supervisors with very precise indications as to which aspect of performance needs to be improved. The main advantage of this method is that it can be applied to specific selling positions. Consequently, it is relevant to evaluate the sales force for which the specific dimensions have been identified. However, because of quick identification, salespeople can almost immediately adjust their faulty behavior.

Morale and satisfaction

Throughout the preceding chapters, in order to secure a harmonious process, the importance of securing high morale and satisfaction among salespeople has been underlined. Indicators of sales force dissatisfaction can be linked in the short- or long-term to motivation problems, intentions to quit, and to dysfunctional sales force turnover. Naturally, salespeople are the best possible information sources about their own satisfaction/dissatisfaction. As already seen, job satisfaction is a multidimensional concept that

Table 11.4. Five steps in developing sales oriented BARS

Step 1: Critical incidents generated

Persons with knowledge of the job to be investigated (sales personnel, managers, or clients) are asked to describe specific critical incidents of effective and ineffective sales performance behavior. These incidents are analyzed and classified into a small number of categories.

Step 2: Refinement and creation of dimensions

Those developing the performance appraisal form (e.g., a group of sales personnel and/or managers) review the reduced set of critical incidents and refine them further into a smaller set of performance dimensions (generally between five and twelve dimensions).

Step 3: Retranslation

The set of critical incidents is presented to another group of sales personnel who have knowledge of the job. They are also provided with the performance dimensions found after step 2. They are instructed to relate the incidents to appropriate dimensions. Typically, an incident is kept if approximately 60% or more of the group assigns it to the same dimension as did the other group in Step 2.

Step 4: Weighting the incidents

The second group is asked to rate on a 7- or 10-point scale the behavior described in the critical incident as to how effectively or ineffectively it represents performance on the dimension. The standard deviation of the ratings for each incident represents the amount of agreement among raters regarding the effectiveness level of performance specified by the incident. Typically, incidents that have standard deviations of 1.5 or less on a 7-point scale and 1.75 or less on a 10-point scale are retained for the final BARS.

Step 5: The final "BARS"

A set of incidents, usually six to eight per dimension, that meet both the retranslation and standard deviation (Steps 3 and 4) criteria are used as behavioral anchors for the performance dimension. The final BARS consists of vertical scales, one for each dimension to be evaluated, anchored by the retained dimension (see example for one dimension in Figure 11.1).

Source: Adapted from Cocanougher and Ivancevich (1978).

includes such aspects as work itself, work colleagues, supervision, compensation, promotion opportunities, and customers.

In order to measure job satisfaction on those various dimensions, sales managers can use INDSALES, a scale that has been especially developed to that effect, validated, and revised for special application to selling situations (Churchill, Ford, and Walker 1974; Futrell 1979; Nonis and Erdem 1997). Salespeople are invited to react to a certain number of items for each of the seven job dimensions. The summation of all the item scores for one dimension provides a basis for analyzing a salesperson's satisfaction with

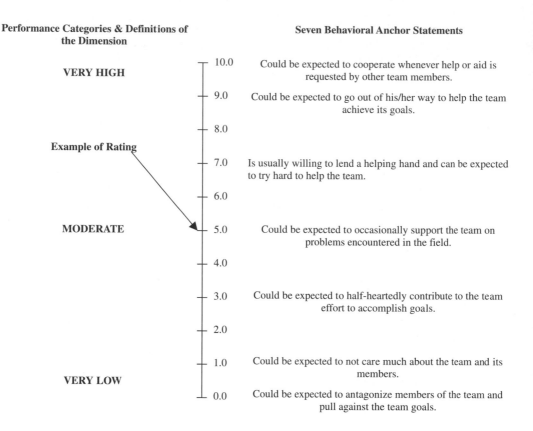

Source : Cocanougher and Ivancevich (1978).

Fig. 11.1   Example of BARS scales for one performance dimension

various aspects of the job. The summation of the seven scores provides a global assessment of job satisfaction.

INDSALES is more than just a simple device for measuring job satisfaction: it can also be used to diagnose job dissatisfaction. Sales managers can analyze not only every dimension of job satisfaction, but also the items that are responsible for the overall low score on a given job dimension. Managers can also analyze salespeople's satisfaction according to their performance level. As one can expect, research generally shows different satisfaction levels for high and low performers. Consequently, it is important to carry separate analyses for both groups in order to avoid changing practices that do not satisfy less productive salespeople, but that are well accepted by high sales performers.

Market environments

In the same way as the commandant of an aircraft would not be able to do without meteorological reports, a sales manager could not efficiently manage a sales force without carefully monitoring the evolution of the market and sales territory environments. For that purpose, they should try to receive information through internal departments (especially marketing and market research) and/or through the sales force network itself.

Syndicated sources

Every firm has developed a more or less sophisticated and organized market intelligence system. As discussed previously, many firms purchase the services of firms who specialize in collecting market information on a syndicated basis, such as Nielsen, to provide estimates of their own market shares as well as those of their competitors. To have access to relevant market information, A.S., a firm that implements electronic financial management solutions for their clients, systematically peruse the financial and electronic papers and watch all the mergers and acquisitions that take place in those industries. Sales managers should be able to set up and use such market intelligence systems to receive up-to-date and relevant information on a continual basis.

Sales force network

Salespeople remain one of the best sources of intelligence about market environments. As already underlined, they are often the first people to learn about facts that are extremely important to their firm's sales and marketing managers. Translating individual knowledge into meaningful intelligence for the community, collecting, and storing the experience and information that has originated from all a firm's employees for the benefits of organizational community are the major functions of what has been labeled *knowledge management*. Knowledge management may also constitute a partial answer to the sales force turnover problem. Many firms have lost business because the person in charge of the account left the company, taking with them essential knowledge and know-how. A study by Arthur Andersen Management has revealed that 80 percent of the managers surveyed reported that knowledge management is an important project for their firm, even though many of them recognize the difficulties in implementing such a program. If salespeople are recognized as good users of market information, they are also often accused of being poor providers of knowledge. One plausible reason for that lack of communication is that they generally do not benefit directly from the performance of such tasks. Consequently, it is up to management to facilitate this market intelligence reporting function that has been described earlier. To effectively organize market intelligence reporting salespeople should have been taught how to process, verify the accuracy, and present the collected information in a timely fashion and in such a way as to be useful to management.

Unfortunately, as this function often lacks any formal structure, it often happens that relevant market information is lost or does not reach the right person at the right time and in the right format to be useful for decision making. When this function is not formally organized, it may happen that a salesperson has no clue that a certain piece of information could have been vital to management, or that management has not already been aware of this information for some time. Even when they know that the information is extremely important, the salesperson may not know who to report it to if no formal procedure has been set up.

Finally, it should be emphasised that market intelligence reporting is not a natural part of the selling function. It is typically assigned to salespeople because they are the first to be exposed to the relevant market intelligence. As a result, salespeople have no direct or obvious incentive to accomplish the function to the best of their abilities. Sales managers often design motivation programs that emphasize other types of activity (e.g., sales and commission). In such occurrences, salespeople may resent that they have to carry out a task for which they do not receive any compensation, but which also prevents them from spending more time on their basic selling tasks.

In order to organize the sales force market intelligence function, sales managers should explicitly include this responsibility in the salesperson function description. They must train salespeople to accomplish this mission and give it as much importance as sales training or knowledge of administrative duties and procedures. Among other facts, salespeople should be instructed about the type of intelligence the firm wishes to collect, and which methods can be used (and those that should not be used) to obtain this information. Salespeople must also be taught how to check the accuracy of information before transmitting it to management. In addition, salespeople should know to whom every type of market intelligence should be addressed in their organization. For that purpose, the task of salespeople should be facilitated as much as possible. The objectives are to avoid inefficiencies in intelligence transmission, but without adversely affecting their core selling mission. Finally, salespeople should be given some feedback every time they transmit a piece of intelligence to management. When some relevant piece of intelligence is timely transmitted to the right manager, this should be clearly acknowledged. If this does not happen,

Table 11.5. Partial inventory of elements that could be part of a DSMP dashboard

	Percentage of firms using this element
Observation/measures of performance	
1. Observation/measures of sales	
Sales volume in €	79
Sales volume to previous year's sales	76
Sales volume versus quota (in €)	65
Percentage of increase in sales volume	55
Sales volume by product or product line	48
Sales volume by customer	44
Sales volume to new accounts	42
Sales volume in units	35
Sales volume versus market sales potential	27
Sales volume by customer type	22
Sales volume versus quota (in units)	9
Sales volume per order	7
Sales volume per call	6
Sales volume by outlet type	4
Percentage of sales made by telephone or mail	1
2. Observation/measures of market shares	
Current market share achieved	59
Market share per quota	18
3. Customer accounts	
Number of new accounts	69
Number of lost accounts	33
Number of accounts buying the full line	22
Receivable accounts (in €)	17
Number of accounts overdue	15
Lost account ratio	6
Observation/measures of selling activities (see Table 11.2)	
Observation/measures of salespeople' behavioral characteristics (see Table 11.3)	

Source: Adapted from Thomas N. Ingram, *et al.* (2001).

salespeople may quickly conclude that this market intelligence reporting function is useless.

To sum up, an extremely large number of indicators can be part of a sales manager's dashboard. Table 11.5 provides a list that is not exhaustive by any means. Obviously, it is out of question for sales managers to use them all. They must, however, carefully select those that they need and wish to use, depending on their preferences, management style, and the costs involved. This is discussed in the following section.

Management's control of salespeoples' dashboards

One should recall from Chapter 4 that salespeople try to establish and nurture relationships with clients in their sales territories. Consequently, they, too, need a dashboard to effectively exert their managerial functions. Part I showed how salespeople feed their dashboard using feedback from their customers, supervisors, management, and their market environment. The information that salespeople need for their managerial activities is collected as they work in the field, for example, salespeople need to have access to detailed information about the purchasing decision process of every customer. They should be constantly updated on all relevant information about buyers and their firms. As stated above, management has the responsibility to provide salespeople with adequate electronic and technical support that can help them efficiently store, process, and retrieve this information.

Management must make up part of the salespeople's dashboard by providing them with relevant information at the right time, according to their needs. Most salespeople need quick feedback on their sales, as well as essential statistics on their position relative to the previous year, or their progress toward the objectives they have been assigned during a planning period. They also need some feedback on how they compare with their colleagues in similar territories.

Wolkswagen Finance provides its salespeople with a decision tool accessible on Intranet. This has cost the firm about €500,000. Every morning, salespeople receive on their mobile a management fed dashboard with a number of updated indicators, for example, sales volume, products sold, and credit rates. This information is especially useful to salespeople when they are preparing their calls and identifying any problems to be discussed during their customer and prospect calls. Before this was implemented, salespeople had to build their own system, which took a large amount of time away from more productive customer contact time.

Management dashboard design

In order to select elements as parts of their dashboards, sales managers explicitly or implicitly use certain criteria. This section provides an overview of such criteria, as well as a discussion of dashboard design principles in a few specific instances.

Dashboard selection: element and design criteria

A control dashboard should provide any information that management needs to implement specific types of process. Another key dashboard design factor is the cost/benefit of including certain elements in the dashboard.

Management's specific need for information

As shown in the preceding chapters, there are some basic informational needs that management must satisfy, irrespective of the selected process. Current information about their firm, sales force, or market situations must be collected and regularly updated. Note that information needs are not the same for all the sales force members, so dashboards must be tailored to the needs of everyone. To establish strong communication links between headquarters and regional managers and to process information in real time, S. C. Johnson, the leading manufacturer of maintenance products such as Brise, K2R, Pliz, Raid, or Sol Plus has developed an Intranet network. The sales force is divided into regions. Seven regional sales managers report to a general sales manager at head office and supervise seven regional merchandisers and 37 field staff. Depending on the needs of their function, every sales force has access to all or part of the information that is relevant to his/her function. This information is kept current for every user. This example illustrates that, a good dashboard that is tailored to the needs of managers and salespeople requires special information flows to be set up and organized.

In addition, management experiences quantitative and qualitative informational needs that depend on the type of process it intends to follow, especially the centralization versus decentralization level of the controls it wishes to exert.

Information needs for any type of process

Whether sales managers set specific objectives within the framework of centralized controls, or provide only directional objectives within the framework of a decentralized control approach, they must be able to follow how the sales force is progressing toward those objectives. They must secure relevant information at different intervals during a planning period to exert such controls. Obviously, the dashboard should provide the type of information that allows such comparisons. If market share objectives have been assigned, the dashboard must regularly provide data on market share. If customer satisfaction objectives are used, the dashboard should monitor customer satisfaction. And so on.

In addition, dashboard indicators must go well beyond ensuring that current objectives are being met. It is important to remember that even when managers observe that the sales force is on course to achieve its objectives, this does not necessarily means that everything is going well. Sales managers must constantly ensure that salespeople and the whole sales force remains in satisfactory shape. This point is well illustrated by the case outlined at the beginning of this chapter.

Information needs for centralized-decentralized processes

When sales managers select a centralized or decentralized management control approach, the quality of their knowledge bases as well as the completeness of their dashboards should be adapted to their approach to management. Conversely, one can say that the quality (and cost) of the information that is available to them through their dashboards can induce sales managers to adopt a centralized or decentralized management approach.

Table 11.6 shows the main characteristics of a fully centralized and a fully decentralized control sales force management, with the corresponding informational needs for sales managers. One should be aware, however, that such extreme situations are seldom encountered in practice. More frequently, a sales force is managed and controlled by a more or less centralized and/or decentralized approach, depending on the circumstances, the situation, the availability and/or costs of the required information.

Table 11.6. Main characteristics of a sales force according to its DSMP style

Sales force characteristic	Centralized management	Decentralized management
At the whole sales force level		
Sales force size	No significant difference	No significant difference
Type of sales force organization	Internal sales force	Possibility to externalize the sales force
Type of sales force supervision	Close supervision	Light or no supervision
Span of control	Small	Large
Sales territory design	No significant difference	No significant difference
Sales force functional turnover rate	Smaller as a result of closer supervision	Larger as a result of the lack of close supervision
Sales force dysfunctional turnover rate	Depends on salespeople's reactions to close supervision	Depends on salespeople's reactions to light (or no) supervision
Supervision costs	Very high	Relatively low
At the salesperson level		
Definition of salespeople's decisional space	Narrow decision space	Wide decisional space
Definition of a salesperson's function	Very precise and detailed job description	None or sketchy job description
Specification of a salesperson's objectives	Specific, precise, and detailed objectives (example: sales quotas for each product and client)	Directional objectives only (example: increase sales volume)
Salesperson's motivation level	Depends on salesperson's personal characteristics	Depends on salesperson's personal characteristics
Salesperson's satisfaction level	Depends on salesperson's personal characteristics	Depends on salesperson's personal characteristics
Salesperson's competence level	Generally higher, provided supervisors are competent	Generally lower as a result of a lack of direct supervision
Management programs		
Salesperson motivation program	Motivation essentially provided by supervisors and assigned objectives (quota-rewards) and long term rewards (promotions, etc.)	Motivation essentially provided by the compensation plan and long-term rewards (promotions, etc.)
Salesperson initial training program	Light training programs, essentially field training provided by supervisors	More elaborate training programs because of the leeway eventually left to salespeople

Table 11.6 (*cont.*)

Sales force characteristic	Centralized management	Decentralized management
Salesperson retraining programs	Light training programs, essentially field training provided by supervisors	More elaborate retraining programs because of lack of field supervision
Salesperson compensation plan	Essentially or exclusively fixed salary	Essentially or exclusively incentive pay
Programs for salesperson's activity support	No significant difference	No significant difference
Salesperson recruitment programs	Recruitment of young inexperienced (or with little sales experience) salespeople with substantial supervision needs	Recruitment of more experienced salespeople that can do with little or no supervision
Costs of management programs	Relatively lower costs	Higher costs of training, compensation, and recruitment programs

Information needed on the dashboard

At the sales force level

On the sales force progress toward the firm's short-term objectives	Essential	Essential
On the sales force progress toward the firm's long-term objectives	Essential	Essential
On customer satisfaction	Essential	Essential
On the environment (market intelligence)	As extensive as possible	As extensive as possible
On functional sales force turnover	Essential	Essential
On dysfunctional sales force turnover	Essential	Essential
On market sensitivities to selling efforts for every product line	Essential for assessing the proper sales force size and organization	Essential for assessing the proper sales force size and organization

At the salesperson and territory levels

On salesperson's progress toward short-term objectives	Essential	Essential
On salesperson's progress toward long-term objectives	Essential	Essential

Table 11.6 (*cont.*)

Sales force characteristic	Centralized management	Decentralized management
On customer satisfaction in the territory	Essential	Essential
On the territory environment	As extensive as possible	As extensive as possible
On salesperson's satisfaction	Desirable	Essential
On salesperson's motivation	Desirable	Essential
On salesperson's competence level	Essential	Not Essential
On territory sensitivities to salesperson's activities	Not Essential	Essential
On salesperson's reactivity (preferences) to the various management programs	Not Essential	Essential
Cost of the dashboard	Depends on the relative costs of collecting information about territory sensitivities to salesperson's activities compared to those on information about salesperson's motivation, satisfaction and preferences	Depends on the relative costs of collecting information about territory sensitivities to salesperson's activities compared to those on information about salesperson's motivation, satisfaction and preferences
Cost of the DSMP	Depends on the relative costs of management programs and those of the dashboard for both types of DSMP	Depends on the relative costs of management programs and those of the dashboard for both types of DSMP

Observable behaviors and information costs

Management should consider if it is easy to collect the information that could be part of a dashboard. If it is not readily available or observable, information is likely to be costly, because special procedures must be set up. The decision to include some information in the dashboard requires a careful examination of cost-benefit ratios.

Sometimes, collecting information can be immediate and inexpensive, such as information about the number of customer or prospect calls.

In other cases, it may be difficult, and certainly more expensive, to monitor the quality of sales presentations and demonstrations that salespeople make during sales calls, because this may require close supervision from managers. As a result, the control elements that are part of management's dashboard are more likely to be based on salespeople's behaviors when these behaviors are more easily observable and predictable (and consequently less costly to observe) than the behaviors' outcomes. Conversely, control elements are more likely to be based on results when performance is more easily predicted and observable (and consequently less costly to collect) than salespeople's behavior.

Information flows for specific control levers

This section provides a few examples of the dashboard elements and information flows that are typically associated with some sales force control levers. In the following paragraphs full salary compensation, sales commissions, and quota-reward plans (QRPs) are considered in turn.

Fixed salary

A fixed salary often indicates centralized management control — management decides the compensation level of each salesperson. Because of a lack of built-in incentives management must either impose specific objectives to control selling activities and performance, or provide close supervision to ensure that salespeople effectively deploy those activities that are sought by management. Because managers have to make decisions about what salespeople need to do in order reach their desired objectives, they need as much information as possible. This can only be inferred from adequate knowledge of how the market is likely to respond to various activities and efforts. Sales managers may obtain this type of information through experience, market research, or eventually from the salespeople themselves.

Straight commission

Firms that use a straight commission plan follow, at least in this area, a fully decentralized approach to salespeople's control. In this case, salespeople are often given full responsibility for deciding on their own activities, so it is up to them to secure and manage the information they need to make the best possible decisions concerning their effort levels and allocations. In this case, the responsibility of collecting information about territory sensitivities to their own efforts and activities is transferred to salespeople. When, for example, management wishes to influence selling activities in a particular direction, it must determine the appropriate commission levels to be paid (e.g., for multi-product line selling). To do this, management only needs to know how salespeople react to financial earnings (i.e. whether they respond to financial rewards and whether they attempt to maximize their revenues). In the case of such decentralized controls, sales managers have fewer information needs, and consequently, are likely to design less elaborate dashboards.

QRP

In Chapter 8, it was shown that QRPs are efficient only if management has sufficient information and adequate procedures for setting quotas and bonuses within the selected QRP structure. To do this, management needs information on territory sales sensitivities to salespeople's efforts, on salespeople's utilities and risk preferences. To set optimal quotas using a fully-centralized approach, management needs precise knowledge of territory sales sensitivities for each type of activity to be controlled (Davis and Farley 1971).

A frequent reason for providing salespeople with some freedom through a decentralized control system lies in the information asymmetry that exists between management and salespeople. Salespeople control their own effort levels and allocations. Management cannot directly observe their input when they are working in the field. Salespeople have better information about their own territory responses than management. As a result, management cannot infer and accurately evaluate an individual's activity just by observing sales. In addition, salespeople should be able to make better decisions (for both parties), provided they are offered the "right contract," and given the freedom to select the best alternative among an adequate set of possible courses of action. This is why the use of effective decentralized control levers typically requires much less information about sales territory sensitivities to selling efforts.

When building a moderately-centralized QRP, however, management's major difficulty is to have enough information on the selling situations and on salespeople's behavior patterns in order to offer the right set of options, and be able to predict which option a salesperson should choose in any given situation (Lal and Staelin 1986). This cannot be easily predicted unless managers know the preferences and utility functions of their sales force and have some information about its attitude toward risk.

How can managers obtain this essential information? They are unlikely to have the relevant data available for every salesperson's territory sensitivities, utilities for rewards, disutility for high quotas, and attitudes toward risk. Because most of this information is readily available to salespeople, but not to management, a typical information asymmetry exists between the two parties. QRP-setting procedures are likely to differ depending on the ways management attempts (or not) to fill this information gap.

Exclusive usage of readily available information

At one extreme end of the spectrum, management does not collect specific information, and determines individual quota and reward levels using the best information available. This generally includes past sales data and managerial judgments (Churchill *et al.* 1993; Strahle and Spiro 1986). For example, quotas are often set using last year's performance. In this case, sales are augmented or reduced according to the increase or decrease in new total sales objective, and judgmentally adjusted for any environmental changes that can be anticipated in the territories. Although salespeople are sometimes asked to provide some input, this is a typical one-way, top-down process.

This is unlikely to produce optimal QRPs or even satisfactory quota-rewards for salespeople. With such a limited database, it is generally impossible to "enforce" an efficient and equitable QRP, which frequently leads to some tough bargaining between salespeople and their supervisors. Salespeople may challenge their quota assignments on the grounds that they have better information than management on the prevalant conditions in their own territories.

Territory sensitivity to efforts

In the middle of the spectrum, management may collect information on sales territory sensitivities from secondary sources and/or from salespeople themselves. In the former case, sales managers may use such data as territory sales potential, market penetration, or territory competition levels. The firm sets up a one-way (or top-down) procedure, quite suited to centralized controls. Because in this case management relies on "objective" market data, it may be easier to "impose" its conception of equity onto the sales force.

Alternatively, a firm may obtain some information on sales territory sensitivities using a two-way participative process (Wotruba and Thurlow 1976). Thus, salespeople may be asked to provide sales forecasts for the whole territory, or for the individual customers that should reflect their knowledge of their territories. Research suggests that generally, salespeople tend to give sales forecasts that are neither overestimated (as a result of a presumably optimistic nature) nor underestimated (even if they know that their forecasts will serve as a basis for setting their own quotas). In contrast, managers who do not ask salespeople to submit estimates for their quota levels, anticipate larger errors and more frequent overestimates (should they ask for them) than experienced managers who actually request such estimates (Wotruba and Thurlow 1976).

This type of procedure is a typical two-way quota-setting process. Salespeople are required to provide some information, possibly in the form of proposed sales quotas or estimates (a bottom-up process). When these estimates are aggregated, they provide a basis to set the firm's overall sales objectives. Then, the (typically) revised objective is allocated among the sales force, very much like the one-way (top-down) process, except that this time, there is usually a rule which links the sales allocation process to the salespeople's original estimates. In this case, however, the sales quota-setting procedure includes some way to embody salespeople's information on their anticipated sales (and consequently on their sales territory sensitivities to their intended efforts). Because such data collection procedures provide only information on sales territory sensitivities, they probably are used to set centrally-controlled QRPs.

Additional use of preference information

Whenever preference (or utility) information is needed, salespeople's involvement in the quota setting procedure is mandatory because only they are likely to know about their own preferences and attitudes toward risk. Obviously, it is not easy to question salespeople about their preferences directly, so only indirect methods can be used. By definition, this always involves a two-way procedure.

Such an approach has been proposed and applied (Darmon 1979; 1987b; Mantrala *et al.* 1994). It estimates salespeople's utilities for rewards and quotas through conjoint analysis. Preference judgments for combinations of quotas and financial bonuses (for example) are collected from salespeople, *within the context of their specific territories.* When salespeople are asked to provide information on their preferences for quota and bonus amounts, and when they are asked to provide these preference judgments in the context of their own efforts in their own territories, their disutility for quotas (efforts) revealed by these preferences account for:

- expected sales territory sensitivities to this salesperson's efforts;
- perceived environmental uncertainty;
- attitudes toward risk;
- disutility for efforts (quotas);
- utilities for earning larger reward amounts.

When properly carried out, such analyses provide management with as much relevant information as salespeople have. When this approach is followed, it is not necessary for management to *explicitly* take into account environmental uncertainty, attitude toward risk, or sales territory sensitivities: all these elements are already embodied in salespeople's preference judgments.

In such cases, it is clear that it is in management's best interest to use this information to provide each salesperson with the "optimal" centrally set quota-reward "forcing contracts." Because this optimal QRP is based on every salesperson's preferences, it is unlikely to be equitable. Note, however, that in this case, from an equity assessment point of view, management has *better* information. While management has information on every salesperson's utilities, individual salespeople only know their own utilities and sales territory sensitivities. As discussed in Chapter 8, salespeople are unable to assess a QRP's equity properly, because they cannot figure out up to what point the different sales quotas assigned to their colleagues reflect different territory conditions or different preferences for efforts and rewards. If management capitalizes on this advantage, it provides salespeople with only some "semblance of equity." Note that when such an approach is applied, the data processing may be substantial and may require a model-based procedure (see Albers 1996).

Conclusion

This chapter highlights the information needed for various types of control system. This should provide a clear indication to management as to which type of information it actually needs to devise an effective control system. Managers should organize the information flows that feed their dashboards.

These should be designed according to the control approach that managers wish to exercise and to the control levers they intend to use. The ability to obtain this information, the procedures through which such information may be obtained, as well as the costs involved, should be key elements in the decision to select a specific control system. Management will often enforce sales force quota plans, even when sufficiently valid and reliable information on sales territory sensitivities is unavailable. This is often the reason why these plans fail — salespeople, who may have better information than management about their territory sensitivities, can challenge the quotas they have been set.

Conclusion

The vision of a Dynamic Sales Force Management Process that has been developed throughout this book is a general vision. It recognizes that any sales force management/control system is typically made up of several elements or sub-systems. The two major sub-systems that constitute a manager's command center are a set of control levers (or programs) and a dashboard. Control levers are constantly activated and adjusted as sales managers, the leaders in charge of the process, watch on their dashboard whether they are on track toward meeting their short- and long-term objectives. All the control center elements should be designed so as to help management achieve its multiple selling objectives, and in such a way as to directly or indirectly adjust salespeople's decision spaces, and consequently, their levels of autonomy and initiative.

Every control element may be characterized along one fundamental dimension, that is, its ability to provide a centralized versus decentralized control. The selection by management of a position on the centralized-decentralized continuum generally depends on the firm's specific sales force selling and control objectives, and on the relative availability and costs of obtaining and using the relevant information.

The proposed vision of a dynamic sales force management process has a number of implications for the practice of sales management and for sales research.

Some managerial perspectives

First, this book has proposed a vision of sales management that is still under-used in practice. This is, however, an integrative vision. It permits management to predict the effects of any contemplated action on the different aspects of a sales force, and consequently, to foresee the consequences of these actions and their positive or negative contribution to the firm's short- and long-term objectives. This vision is especially suited to the management of complex human systems like sales force management. It accounts for a firm's specific objectives, as well as all the human, behavioral, informational, and financial constraints that sales managers always face when accomplishing their missions.

This approach shows how specific management objectives, information constraints, and situation conditions should lead management to select specific centralized or decentralized control devices (that may include outcome- or behavior-based, qualitative (subjective) or quantitative (objective) elements). Knowing such basic control element characteristics leads to very specific control mechanisms. For example, Tables 8.3 and 9.1 provide a few examples of control devices frequently used in practice, which display different levels of the three main control characteristics.

In order to control a sales force, managers will probably need more than one procedure. Ideally, managers attempt to control not only the quantity but also the quality of their salespeople's efforts (Sujan 1986; Challagalla and Shervani 1996). This is why they will probably select several control mechanisms with different characteristics. For example, it is quite conceivable for a firm to use sales quotas for its sales force (a centralized quantitative outcome-based control) and to impose simultaneously the use of well-structured sales presentations to customers (a centralized qualitative behavior-based control).

Finally, the present framework highlights the informational requirements of the various types of control system and provides clear indications to management as to which type of information is actually needed. This helps management to devise an effective control system made up of specific sales force control devices characterized along the main centralized-decentralized control dimension (see Table 11.6). The ability to obtain this information, the procedures through which such information is obtained, as well as the costs involved, should be key elements in the decision to select a specific control system. For example, it often happens that management enforces sales force quota plans, even when there is not enough valid and reliable information on the territory sensitivities to salespeople's efforts. This is a frequent cause of failure for such plans, because the individual salesperson, who may enjoy better information than management about territory sensitivities to their own efforts, can challenge the quotas they have been assigned. In general, it is clear that management must rely more heavily on the size and quality of the control system dashboard under a centralized than under a decentralized approach.

Generally speaking, a firm should select a more or less centralized process depending on the most favorable cost/quality ratio it can secure to set up and feed an adequate dashboard.

Some research perspectives

Until recently, management and control have been areas of personal selling that have not received much attention, except in textbooks and professional literature. Over the last decade, however, a certain number of research studies have been reported in academic journals for marketing and sales management. All of them have essentially characterized sales force control along a behavior-based versus outcome-based dimension (Anderson 1985; Cravens *et al.* 1993; Oliver and Anderson 1994; 1995; Stathakopoulos 1996; Challagalla and Shervani 1997). The general conclusion of these studies is that most sales managers use hybrid control systems that combine behavior- and outcome-based controls. Predictions about anticipated consequences of both types of control approach, although sometimes supported by empirical data, show generally relatively weak relationships (Oliver and Anderson 1995).

In addition, if these research studies suggest that firms use behavior- or outcome-based sales force control systems, they cannot explain why in practice, sales managers use a whole gamut of devices from both types of control approach. For example, outcome-based controls can be exercised through (among others) sales quotas, commissions on gross margins, or customer satisfaction scores. In the same way, behavior-based control can include customer and prospect call norms and the requirement for salespeople to limit themselves to deliver highly-structured sales presentations. The process discussed throughout this book, accounts for the key time dimension of management, and consequently provides better explanations of what induces sales managers to use certain control instruments rather than others. The centralized versus decentralized aspect of controls remains a central concept in such explanations.

The present framework has a number of implications for research into sales force control. First it suggests that previous studies may have not always focused on the correct unit of analysis. Instead of considering sales force control as a whole, it might have been more fruitful to recognize that a firm is likely to use a mix of control devices because multiple objectives may be pursued at the same time. Consequently, these analyses could be supplemented by studies carried out at the level of each single control device rather than the control system as a whole. In light of this analysis, it may not be surprising that the recurring conclusions of these studies are that elements of different types of control systems are likely to be observed in the same sales force, although in various proportions. It would be useful to conduct similar studies using both types of unit of analysis, and compare the results.

In addition, the vision of a dynamic management process outlined in this book suggests that management's choice of a sales force control system cannot be meaningfully studied without consideration of the specific control objectives, and without a sufficiently detailed view of the control mechanisms that take place when specific control devices are used. Even within one single process, control elements play different roles, such as those of control levers or dashboard feedbacks. As a result, specific processes need to consider the various elements of the command center that are used, and in which sequence, given management's objectives and situational constraints.

Several questions remain to be answered and point at possible future research avenues. For example, are all control devices compatible among themselves? Is it always advisable for a firm to use simultaneously centralized and decentralized control devices? Some managers may argue that both types of control reflect opposite managerial styles and would prefer to select those control devices that could fit with the prevalent firm's culture. Other managers, however, may assert that both types of control should be used simultaneously, in order to fit the various needs of the firm and of salespeople. Obviously more research is needed to answer these questions precisely.

Another unanswered question is the extent to which a selected process and its various devices are compatible with some types of salesperson profiles, as well as with the kind of selling situation (especially the type of salesperson mission). Although managers can still exercise judgment to decide which set of controls are likely to be the most appropriate for their own sales forces, there is still a lack of substantive research-based knowledge in this area.

Finally, some research propositions can be easily derived from the various conceptual frameworks that have been outlined in this book (see, e.g., Table 11.6). Many of these propositions may deserve to be tested empirically, which suggests other possible areas for future research into the Dynamic Sales Force Management Process.

References

Adams, John S. (1965), "Inequity in Social Exchange," in L. Berkowitz, (ed.) *Advances in Experimental Social Psychology*, Academic Press, New York, 267–299.

Adams, John S. and R. Jacobsen (1964), "Effects of Wage Inequities on Work Quality," *Journal of Abnormal and Social Psychology*, **69**, 19–25.

Agarwal, Sanjeey (1999), "Impact of Job Formalization and Administrative Controls on Attitudes of Industrial Salespeople," *Industrial Marketing Management*, **28**, 4 (July), 359–368.

Ahearne, Michael, Narasimhan Srinivasan and L. Weinstein (2004), "Effect of Technology on Sales Performance: Progressing from Technology Acceptance to Technology Usage and Consequence," *Journal of Personal Selling and Sales Management*, **24**, 4 (Fall), 297–310.

Albers, Sönke (1981), "Incorporation of Turnovers and Long-run Planning Periods in Compensation Schemes for Controlling a Sales Force," *Zeitschrift für betriebswirtschaftliche Forschung*, **33**, 1, 47–94 (in German).

(1996), "Optimization Models for Salesforce Compensation," *European Journal of Operational Research*, **89**, 1–17.

Alderfer, Clayton P. (1969), "An Empirical Test of a New Theory of Human Needs," *Organizational Behavior and Human Performance*, **4**, 142–175.

(1972), *Existence, Relatedness, and Growth*, New York: Free Press.

Alessandra, A. and P. Wexler (1988), "The Professionalization of Selling," *Sales and Marketing Training*, **33** (March), 140–145.

Alwin, D. F. (1987), "Distributive Justice and Satisfaction with Material Well-Being," *American Sociological Review*, **52** (February), 83–95.

Anderson, Erin (1985), "The Salesperson as Outside Agent or Employee: A Transaction Cost Analysis," *Marketing Science*, **4** (Summer), 234–254.

Anderson, Erin and R. L. Oliver (1987), "Perspectives on Behavior-Based Versus Outcome-Based Salesforce Control Systems," *Journal of Marketing*, **51** (October), 76–88.

Anderson, Erin and R. Trinkle (2005), *Outsourcing the Sales Function: The Real Costs of Field Sales*, Mason, Ohio, Thomson.

Anderson, Rolph E. (1995), *Essentials of Personal Selling*, Englewood Cliffs, NJ: Prentice-Hall, 50.

(1996), "Personal Selling and Sales Management in the New Millennium," *Journal of Personal Selling and Sales Management*, **16** (Fall), 17–32.

Arnett, Dennis B., B. A. Macy and J. B. Wilcox (2005), "The Role of Core Selling Teams in Supplier-Buyer Relationships," *Journal of Personal Selling and Sales Management*, **25**, 1 (Winter), 27–42.

Arnott, N. (1995), "It's a woman's world," *Sales and Marketing Management*, (March), 54–59.

Attia, Ashraf M., E. D. Honeycutt Jr. and M. P. Leach (2005), "A Three-Stage Model for Assessing and Improving Sales Force Training and Development," *Journal of Personal Selling & Sales Management*, **25**, 3 (Summer), 253–268.

Aulakh, Preet S. and E. F. Gencturk (2000), "International Principal-Agent Relationships—Control, Governance, and Performance," *Industrial Marketing Management*, **29**, 6 (November), 521–538.

Austin, W. and E. Hatfield (1975), "Equity with the World: The Transrelational Effects of Equity and Inequity," *Sociometry*, **38**, 474–496.

Avila, Ramon A. and E. F. Fern (1986), "The Selling Situation as a Moderator of the Personality-Sales Performance Relationship: An Empirical Investigation," *The Journal of Personal Selling and Sales Management*, **6** (November), 53–63.

Avila, Ramon A., E. F. Fern and O. K. Mann (1988), "Unraveling Criteria for Assessing the Performance of Salespeople: A Causal Analysis," *The Journal of Personal Selling and Sales Management*, **8** (May), 45–54.

Badovick, Gordon J., F. J. Hadaway and P. F. Kaminski (1992), "Attributions and Emotions: The Effects on Salesperson Motivation after Successful vs Unsuccessful Quota Performance," *Journal of Personal Selling and Sales Management*, **12**, 3 (Summer), 1–11.

Bagozzi, Richard C. (1978), "Salesforce Performance and Satisfaction as a Function of Individual Difference, Interpersonal, and Situational Factors," *Journal of Marketing Research*, (November), 517–531.

(1980a), "Performance and Satisfaction in an Industrial Sales Force: An Examination of their Antecedents and Simultaneity," *Journal of Marketing*, **44** (Spring), 65–77.

(1980b), "The Nature and Causes of Self-Esteem, Performance, and Satisfaction in the Salesforce: A Structural Equation Approach," *Journal of Business*, 315–331.

Baldauf, Arthur, D. W. Cravens and N. F. Piercy (2001a), "Examining Business Strategy, Sales Management, and Salesperson Antecedents of Sales Organization Effectiveness," *Journal of Personal Selling and Sales Management*, **21**, 2 (Spring), 109–123.

(2001b), "Examining the Consequences and Sales Management Control Strategies in European Field Sales Organizations," *International Marketing Review*, **18**, 5, 474–508.

(2005), "Sales Management Control Research—Synthesis and Agenda for Future Research," *Journal of Personal Selling and Sales Management*, **25**, 1 (Winter), 7–26.

Bandura, A. (1977), *Social Learning Theory*, Englewood Cliffs, N.J.: Prentice-Hall.

Barksdale, Hiram C. Jr., D. N. Bellanger, J. S. Boles and T. G. Brashear (2003), "The Impact of Realistic Job Previews and Perceptions of Training on Sales Force Performance and Continuance Commitment: A Longitudinal Test," *Journal of Personal Selling and Sales Management*, **23**, 2 (Spring), 125–138.

Bartkus, K. R., M. F. Peterson and D. N. Bellenger (1989), "Type A Behavior Experience and Salesperson Performance," *The Journal of Personal Selling and Sales Management*, **9** (Summer), 11–18.

Bartol, Kathryn M. (1979), "Professionalism as a Predictor of Organizational Commitment, Role Stress, and Turnover: A Multidimensional Approach," *Academy of Management Journal*, **22** (December), 815–821.

—— (1999), "Reframing Salesforce Compensation Systems: An Agency Theory-Based Performance Management Perspective," *Journal of Personal Selling and Sales Management*, **19**, 3 (Summer), 1–16.

Bass, Ken, T. Barnett and G. Brown (1998), "The Moral Philosophy of Sales Managers and its Influence on Ethical Decision Making," *Journal of Personal Selling and Sales Management*, **18**, 2 (Spring), 1–18.

Basu, Amya K. and G. Kalyanaram (1990) "On the Relative Performance of Linear Versus Nonlinear Compensation Plans," *International Journal of Research in Marketing*, **7**, 171–178.

Basu, Amya K., R. Lal, V. Srinivasan and R. Staelin (1985), "Salesforce Compensation Plans: An Agency Theoretic Perspective," *Marketing Science*, **4**, 267–291.

Bateman, Thomas S. and S. Strasser (1984), "A Longitudinal Analysis of the Antecedents of Organizational Commitment," *Academy of Management Journal*, **27** (March), 95–112.

Bello, Daniel C. and W. I. Gilliland (1997), "The Effect of Output Control, Process Controls, and Flexibility on Export Channel Performance," *Journal of Marketing*, **61** (January), 22–38.

Beltramini, Richard F. and K. R. Evans (1988), "Salesperson Motivation to Perform and Job Satisfaction: A Sales Contest Participant Perspective," *Journal of Personal Selling and Sales Management*, **8** (Fall), 35–42.

Bennett, Rebekah, C. E. J. Hartel and J. R. McColl-Kennedy (2005), "Experience as a Moderator of Involvement and Satisfaction on Brand Loyalty in a Business-to-Business Setting," *Industrial Marketing Management*, **34**, 1 (January), 97–107.

Berger, Paul D. (1972), "On Setting Optimal Sales Commissions," *Operational Research Quarterly*, **23**, 213–215.

—— (1975), "Optimal Compensation Plans: The Effect of Uncertainty and Attitude Toward Risk on the Salesman Effort Allocation Decision," in E. M. Mazze, (ed.) *Combined Proceedings*, Series 37, American Marketing Association, Chicago.

Berger, Paul D. and L. J. Jaffe (1991), "The Impact of Risk Attitude on the Optimal Compensation Plan in a Multi-product Situation," *Journal of the Operational Research Society*, **42**, 4, 323–330.

Berkowitz, Leonard, C. Fraser, F. P. Treasurer and S. Cochran (1987), "Pay Equity, Job Gratifications, and Comparisons in Pay Satisfaction," *Journal of Applied Psychology*, **72** (November), 544–551.

Beswick, Charles A. and D. W. Cravens (1977), "A Multi-Stage Decision Model for Sales Force Management," *Journal of Marketing Research*, **4** (May), 135–144.

Beverland, Michael (2001), "Contextual Influences and the Adoption and Practice of Relationship Selling in a Business-to-Business Setting: An Exploratory Study," *Journal of Personal Selling and Sales Management*, **21**, 3 (Summer), 207–216.

Bhaskar, Rahul (2004), "A Customer Relationship Management System to Target Customers at Cisco," *Journal of Electronic Commerce in Organizations*, **2**, 4, 63–73.

Blausfuss, Judy, J. Murray and G. Schollars (1992), "Methods for Evaluating Turnover Costs," *Nursing Management*, **23** (May), 52–57.

Bluedorn, Allen C. (1982a), "A Unified Model of Turnover from Organizations," *Human Relations*, **35** (February), 135–153.

(1982b), "The Theories of Turnover: Causes, Effects, and Meanings," in B. Bacharach Samuel, (ed.) *Research in the Sociology of Organizations*, Greenwich, Conn.: JAI Press, **1**, 75–128.

Boles, James S., J. A. Wood and J. Johnson (2003), "Interrelationships of Role Conflict, Role Ambiguity, and Work-Family Conflict with Different Facets of Job Satisfaction and the Moderating Effect of Gender," *Journal of Personal Selling and Sales Management*, **23**, 2 (Spring), 99–114.

Bolman Pullins, Ellen and L. M. Fine (2002), "How the Performance of Mentoring Activities Affects the Mentor's Job Outcomes," *Journal of Personal Selling and Sales Management*, **22**, 4 (Fall), 259–272.

Bonner, Joseph M. and R. J. Calantone (2005), "Buyer Attentiveness in Buyer-Supplier Relationships," *Industrial Marketing Management*, **34**, 1 (January), 53–61.

Boulding, William, R. Staelin, M. Ehret and W. J. Johnston (2005), "A Customer Relationship Management Roadmap: What Is Known, Potential Pitfalls, and Where to Go," *Journal of Marketing*, **69**, 4 (October), 155–166.

Brashear, Thomas G., C. M. Brooks and J. S. Boles (2004), "Distributive and Procedural Justice in a Sales Force Context: Scale Development and Validation," *Journal of Business Research*, **57**, 86–93.

Brewer, Geoffrey (1997), "Hewlett-Packard," *Sales and Marketing Management*, (October), 58.

Brown, Roger (1986), *Social Psychology*. 2nd edn, New York: The Free Press.

Brown, Steven P., K. R. Evans, M. K. Mantrala and G. Challagalla (2005), "Adapting Motivation, Control, and Compensation Research to a New Environment," *Journal of Personal Selling & Sales Management*, **25**, 2 (Spring), 155–167.

Brown, Steven P. and R. A. Paterson (1993), "Antecedents and Consequences of Salesperson Job Satisfaction: Meta-Analysis and Assessment of Causal Effects," *Journal of Marketing Research*, **30** (February), 63–77.

(1994), "The Effect of Effort on Sales Performance and Job Satisfaction," *Journal of Marketing*, **58** (April), 70–80.

Busch, P. S. and R. F. Bush (1978), "Women Contrasted to Men in the Industrial Sales Force: Job Satisfaction, Values, Role Clarity, Performance, and Propensity to Leave," *Journal of Marketing Research*, **15**, 3, 438–448.

Buzzell, Richard D. and P. W. Farris (1976), Industrial Marketing Costs. Working Paper, Cambridge, MA: Marketing Science Institute.

Campanelli, Melissa (1994), "What Price Salesforce Satisfaction," *Sales and Marketing Management*, (July), 37.

Carlisle, John A. and R. C. Parker (1989), *Beyond Negotiation: Redeeming Customer-Supplier Relationships*, New York: John Wiley.

Cawsey, T. F. and W. C. Wedley (1979), "Labor Turnover Costs: Measurement and Control," *Personnel Journal*, **58**, 2, 90–95.

Cellich, Claude and S. Jain (2003), *Global Business Negotiation: A Practical Guide*, New York: Southwestern-Thomson.

Challagalla, Goutam and T. Shervani (1996), "Dimensions and Types of Supervisory Controls: Effects on Salesperson Performance and Satisfaction," *Journal of Marketing*, **60** (January), 89–105.

——— (1997), "A Measurement Model of the Dimensions of Types of Output and Behavior Control: An Empirical Test in a Sales Force Context," *Journal of Business Research*, **39** (January), 159–172.

Challagalla, Goutam, T. Shervani and G. Huber (2000), "Supervisory Orientations and Salesperson Work Outcomes: The Moderating Effect of Salesperson Location," *Journal of Personal Selling and Sales Management*, **20**, 3 (Summer), 161–172.

Chen, Ja-Shen and R. K. H. Ching (2004), "An Empirical Study of the Relationship of IT Intensity and Organizational Absorptive Capability on CRM Performance," *Journal of Global Information Management*, **12**, 1, 1–17.

Cherry, John and J. Fraedrich (2000), "An Empirical Investigation of Locus of Control and the Structure of Moral Reasoning: Examining the Ethical Decision-Making Processes of Sales Managers," *Journal of Personal Selling and Sales Management*, **20**, 3 (Summer), 173–188.

Chitwood, R. (1988), "Let's Get Back to Basic Training," *Sales and Marketing Management*, (September), 10.

Choffray, Jean-Marie and G. Lilien (1978), "Assessing Response to Industrial Marketing Strategy," *Journal of Marketing*, **42**, 2 (April), 20–32.

Choi, Nak Hwan, A. L. Dixon and J. M. Jung (2004), "Dysfunctional Behavior among Sales Representatives: The Effect of Supervisory Trust, Participation, and Information Controls," *Journal of Personal Selling and Sales Management*, **24**, 3 (Summer), 181–198.

Chonko, Lawrence B., E. Jones, J. A. Roberts and A. J. Dubinsky (2002), "The Role of Environmental Turbulence, Readiness for Change, and Salesperson Learning in the Success of Sales Force Change," *Journal of Personal Selling and Sales Management*, **22**, 4 (Fall), 227–246.

Chonko, Lawrence B., T. W. Loe, J. A. Roberts and J. F. Tanner (2000), "Sales Performance: Timing of Measurement and Type of Measurement make a Difference," *Journal of Personal Selling and Sales Management*, **20**, 1 (Winter), 23–36.

Chonko, Lawrence B., J. F. Tanner, Jr. and W. A. Weeks (1993), "Sales Training: Status and Needs," *Journal of Personal Selling and Sales Management*, **13** (Fall), 81–86.

Chonko, Lawrence B., T. R. Wotruba and T. W. Loe (2002), "Direct Selling Ethics at the Top: An Industry Audit and Status Report," *Journal of Personal Selling and Sales Management*, **22**, 2 (Spring), 87–96.

Chowdhury, Jtinuk (1993), "The Motivational Impact of Sales Quotas on Effort," *Journal of Marketing Research*, **30**, 1, 28–41.

Churchill, Gilbert A. Jr., R. H. Collins and W. A. Strang (1975), "Should Retail Salespersons be Similar to their Customers?" *Journal of Retailing*, **51** (Fall), 29–42.

Churchill, Gilbert A. Jr., N. M. Ford, S. Hartley and O. C. Walker, Jr. (1985), "Determinants of Sales Performance: A Meta-Analysis," *Journal of Marketing Research*, **22**, 103–118.

Churchill, Gilbert A. Jr., N. M. Ford and O. C. Walker, Jr. (1974), "Measuring the Job Satisfaction of Industrial Salesmen," *Journal of Marketing Research*, **11**, 254–260.

(1976a), "Organizational Climate and Job Satisfaction in the Sales Force," *Journal of Marketing Research*, (November), 323–332.

(1976b), "Motivating the Industrial Sales Force: The Attractiveness of Alternative Rewards," Report # 76–115, Cambridge, Mass.: Marketing Science Institute.

(1979), "Personal Characteristics of Salespeople and the Attractiveness of Alternative Rewards," *Journal of Business Research*, 7 (June), 25–50.

(1993), *Sales Force Management: Planning, Implementation, and Control*, 4th edn, Homewood, Ill.: Irwin

Churchill, Gilbert A. Jr., N. M. Ford, S. Hartley, O. C. Walker, Jr. and A. Pecotich (1982), "A Structural Equation Investigation of the Pay-Satisfaction-Valence Relationship Among Salespeople," *Journal of Marketing*, 46 (Fall), 114–124.

Clancy, Kevin J. and R. S. Shulman (1994), *Marketing Myths that Are Killing Business*, New York: McGraw-Hill.

Cocanougher, A. B. and J. Ivancevich (1978), "'BARS' Performance Rating for Salesforce Personnel," *Journal of Marketing*, (July), 87.

Cohen, Andy (1997), "General Electric," *Sales and Marketing Management*, 149 (October), 57.

Cohen, S. (1980), "The Bottom Line on Assessment Center Technology," *The Personnel Administrator*, (February), 50–55.

Coleman, L. G. (1989), "Sales Force Turnover Has Managers Wondering Why," *Marketing News*, 4 (December), 6–7.

Colletti, J. A. and L. J. Mahoney (1991), "Should You Pay Your Sales Force for Customer Satisfaction?" *Perspectives in Total Compensation*, 2, Scottsdale, Ariz.: American Compensation Association.

Costa, Paul T. and R. E. McCrae (1988), "From Catalog to Classification: Murray's Needs and the Five-Factor Model," *Journal of Personality and Social Psychology*, 55, 2, 258–265.

Coughlan, Anne T. (1993), "Salesforce Compensation: A Review of MS/OR Advances," in J. Eliashberg and G. L. Lilien, (eds.) *Handbooks in Operations Research and Management Science*, 5, Amsterdam, North-Holland, 1993, 611–651.

Coughlan, Anne T. and S. K. Sen (1989), "Salesforce Compensation: Theory and Managerial Implications," *Marketing Science*, 8, 4, 324–342.

Crane, Michael J. (2000), "Clean Databases Score National Accounts," *Marketing News*, 9 (October), 20.

Cravens, David W., T. Ingram, R. LaForge and C. Young (1993), "Behavior-Based and Outcome-Based Salesforce Control Systems," *Journal of Marketing*, 57 (October), 47–59.

Cravens, David W., F. G. Lassk, G. S. Low, G. W. Marshall and W. C. Moncrief (2004), "Formal and Informal Management Control Combinations in Sales Organizations—The Impact on Salesperson Consequences," *Journal of Business Research*, 57, 3 (March), 241–248.

Creery, Presley T. (1986), "The High Cost of Turnover," *American Bankers Association, ABA Banking Journal*, 78 (September), 113–114.

Cron, William L. (1984), "Industrial Salesperson Development: A Career Stage Perspective," *Journal of Marketing*, 48, 41–52.

Cron, William L. and T. E. DeCarlo (2006), *Dalrymple's Sales Management: Concepts and Cases*, 9th edn, New York: John Wiley.

Cron, William L., A. J. Dubinsky and R. E. Michaels (1988), "The Influence of Career Stages on Components of Salesperson Motivation," *Journal of Marketing*, **52** (January), 78–92.

Cron, William L., G. W. Marshall, J. Singh, R. L. Spiro and H. Sujan (2005), "Salesperson Selection, Training, and Development Trends, Implications, and Research Opportunities," *Journal of Personal Selling & Sales Management*, **25**, 2 (Spring), 123–136.

Cron, William L. and W. J. Slocum Jr. (1984), "Career Stages Effects in Industrial Sales Forces," in R. W. Belk, *et al.*, (eds.) *AMA Educators' Proceedings*, Chicago, Ill.: American Marketing Association, 148–152.

(1986), "The Influence of Career Stages on Salespeople's Job Attitudes, Work Perceptions and Performance," *Journal of Marketing Research*, **23** (May), 119–129.

Cronin, J. J. (1994), "Analysis of the Buyer-Seller Dyad: The Social Relation Model," *Journal of Personal Selling and Sales Management*, **14**, 3 (Summer), 69–78.

Crosby, L., K. Evans and D. Cowles (1986), "Relationship Quality in Services Selling: An Interpersonal Influence Perspective," *Journal of Marketing*, **54** (July), 68–81.

Dailey, Robert C. and D. J. Kirk (1992), "Distributive and Procedural Justice as Antecedents of Job Satisfaction and Intent to Turnover," *Human Relations*, **45**, 305–317.

Dalrymple, Douglas. J. and W. L. Cron (1998), *Sales Management: Concepts and Cases*, 6th edn, New York: John Wiley, 540–541.

Dalton, D. R., W. D. Todor and D. M. Krachhardt (1982), "Turnover Overstated: The Functional Taxonomy," *Academy of Management Review*, **7**, 2, 117–123.

Dalton, G. W., P. H. Thompson and R. L. Price (1977), "The Four Stages of Professional Careers – A New Look at Performance by Professionals," *Organizational Dynamics*, **6** (Summer), 19–42.

Dana, James (1999), "Hit the Bricks: Internet Shifts in B-to-B Sales World Means 'Get up and Go' or Risk Losing Jobs," *Marketing News*, 13 (September), 1–15.

Darmon, René Y. (1974), "Salesmen's Reactions to Financial Incentives: An Empirical Study," *Journal of Marketing Research*, **11** (October), 418–426.

(1978a), "Sales Force Management: Optimizing the Recruiting Process," *The Sloan Management Review*, **20** (Fall), 47–59.

(1978b), "Optimal Salesmen's Compensation Plans: A Multi-Period Approach," *Journal of the Operational Research Society*, **29** (November), 1061–1069.

(1979), "Setting Sales Quotas with Conjoint Analysis," *Journal of Marketing Research*, **16**, 1, 133–140.

(1980), "Fair vs. Optimal Salesmen's Compensation Plans," *Journal of the Operational Research Society*, **31**, 43–50.

(1981), "Optimal Compensation Plans for Salesmen Who Trade-off Leisure Time Against Income," *Journal of the Operational Research Society*, **32**, 381–390.

(1987a), "The Impact of Incentive Compensation on the Salesperson's Work Habits: An Economic Model," *Journal of Personal Selling and Sales Management*, (May), 21–33.

(1987b), "QUOPLAN: A System for Optimizing Sales Quota-Bonus Plans," *Journal of the Operational Research Society*, **38**, 12, 1121–1132.

(1990a), "Setting Commission Rates for the Control of the Salesperson's Client-Prospect Effort Allocation," *Journal of the Operational Research Society*, **41** (1990), 151–163.

(1990b), "Identifying Sources of Turnover Costs: A Segmental Approach," *Journal of Marketing*, **54** (April), 46–56.

(1993a), Effective Human Resource Management of the Sales Force, New York: Quorum Books.

(1993b), "Where Do the Best Sales Force Profit Producers Come From?" *The Journal of Personal Selling and Sales Management*, **13** (Summer), 17–30.

(1995), "Linking Sales Quotas to Territory Untapped Market Potential," in Dan C. Weilbacher and Timothy A. Longfellow, (eds.) *Professional Sales and Sales Management Practices Leading Toward the 21st Century*. Proceedings of the National Conference in Sales Management, Atlanta, GA: 112–120.

(1997a), "Selecting Appropriate Sales Quota Plan Structures and Quota Setting Procedures," *Journal of Personal Selling and Sales Management*, **17**, (Winter 1997), 1–16.

(1997b), "Predicting the Long-run Profit Impact of a Contemplated Sales Force Compensation Plan," *Journal of the Operational Research Society*, **48**, 1215–1225.

(1998a), "The Effects of Some Situational Variables on Sales Force Governance System Characteristics," *Journal of Personal Selling and Sales Management*, **18**, 1 (Winter), 17–30.

(1998b), "A Conceptual Scheme and Procedure for Classifying Sales Positions," *Journal of Personal Selling and Sales Management*, **18** (Summer), 31–46.

(1998c), "La vente: quelques grandes tendances actuelles," *Revue Française du Marketing*, **164**, 121–128.

(2000), "Optimal Conditions for Sales Force Equitable Compensation," *Operations Research Spektrum*, **22**, 1 (January), 35–57.

(2001), "Optimal Salesforce Quota Plans Under Salesperson Job Equity Constraints," *Canadian Journal of Administrative Sciences*, **18**, 2, 87–100.

(2004a), "Controlling Sales Force Turnover Costs Through Optimal Recruiting and Training Policies," *European Journal of Operational Research*, **154**, 1 (April), 291–303.

(2004b), "Market Share and Sales Variations as Bases for Sales Force Incentive Compensation," Document de Recherche, Cergy, Centre de Recherche de l'ESSEC.

(2005), "Joint Assessment of Optimal Sales Force Sizes and Sales Call Guidelines: A Management-Oriented Tool," *Canadian Journal of Administrative Sciences*, (September).

Darmon, René Y., B. Rigaux-Bricmont and P. Balloffet (2003), "Designing Sales Force Satisfying Selling Positions: A Conjoint Measurement Approach," *Industrial Marketing Management*, **32**, 6 (August 2003), 501–515.

Darmon, René Y. and D. Rouziès (1999), "Optimal Sales Force Compensation Plans: An Operational Procedure," *Journal of the Operational Research Society*, **53** (2002), 447–456.

Davis, Otto A. and J. U. Farley (1971), "Allocating Sales Force Effort with Commissions and Quotas," *Management Science*, **18**, 55–63.

Day, George (2001), "Capabilities for Forging Customer Relationships," Marketing Science Institute Report 00–118, Cambridge, MA.

Dearden, J. A. and G. L. Lilien (1990), "On Optimal Salesforce Compensation in the Presence of Production Learning Effects," *International Journal of Research in Marketing*, **7** (2/3), 179–188.

Deci, E. and R. Ryan (1985), *Intrinsic Motivation and Self-Determination in Human Behavior*, New York: Plenum Press.

Deloitte (2005), *2005 Strategic Sales Compensation Survey*, www.deloitte.com/dtt/cda/doc/content/us_humancapital_salescompsurvey05.pdf.

DelVecchio, Susan K. (1998), "The Quality of Salesperson-Manager Relationship: The Effect of Latitude, Loyalty, and Competence," *Journal of Personal Selling and Sales Management*, **18**, 1 (Winter), 31−48.

DelVecchio, Susan K., J. E. Zemanek, R. P. McIntyre and R. P. Claxton (2002), "Buyers' Perceptions of Salesperson Tactical Approaches," *Journal of Personal Selling and Sales Management*, **23**, 1 (Winter), 39−50.

Dixon, Andrea L., L. P. Forbes and S. M. B. Schertzer (2005), "Early Success: How Attributions for Sales Success Shape Inexperienced Salespersons' Behavioral Intentions," *Journal of Personal Selling and Sales Management*, **25**, 1 (Winter), 67−77.

Dixon, Andrea L., J. B. Gassenheimer and T. F. Barr (2003), "Identifying the Lone Wolf: A Team Perspective," *Journal of Personal Selling and Sales Management*, **23**, 3 (Summer), 205−220.

Donath, Bob (1999), "Get Marketing, Sales on the Same Wavelength," *Marketing News*, 13 (September), 16.

Douthit, James C. (1976), "The Use of Sales Quotas by Industrial Firms," *Journal of the Academy of Marketing Science*, **4** (Spring), 467−472.

Doyle, Stephen X., C. Pignatelli and K. Florman (1985), "The Hawthorne Legacy and the Motivation of Salespeople," *Journal of Personal Selling and Sales Management*, **5** (November), 1−6.

Doyle, Stephen X. and G. T. Roth (1992), "The Use of Insight Coaching to Improve Relationship Selling," *Journal of Personal Selling and Sales Management*, **12** (Winter), 59−64.

Dreher, G. F. (1982), "The Role of Performance in the Turnover Process," *Academy of Management Journal*, **25**, 2, 137−147.

Dubinsky, Alan J. (1996), "Some Assumptions About the Effectiveness of Sales Training," *Journal of Personal Selling and Sales Management*, **16**, 3 (Summer), 67−76.

 (1998), "A Research Odyssey in Sales Management," *Academy of Marketing Science Review*, available at www.amsreview.org/articles/dubinsky10−1998.pdf.

Dubinsky, Alan J. and T. E. Barry (1982), "A Survey of Sales Management Practices," *Industrial Marketing Management*, **11**, 2, 133−141.

Dubinsky, Alan J., T. W. Dougherty and R. S. Wunder (1990), "Influence of Role Stress on Turnover of Sales Personnel and Sales Managers," *International Journal of Research in Marketing*, **7**, 4, 121−133.

Dubinsky, Alan J. and S. W. Hartley (1986), "A Path-Analytic Study of a Model of Salesperson Performance," *Journal of the Academy of Marketing Science*, **14** (Spring), 36−46.

Dubinsky, Alan J., R. D. Howell, T. N. Ingram and D. N. Bellenger (1986), "Salesforce Socialization," *Journal of Marketing*, **50** (October), 192−207.

Dubinsky, Alan J. and M. Levy (1989), "Influence of Organizational Fairness on Work Outcomes of Retail Salespeople," *Journal of Retailing*, **65** (April), 221−239.

Dubinsky, Alan J. and W. A. Staples (1981–1982), "Sales Training: Salespeople Preparedness and Managerial Implications," *Journal of Personal Selling and Sales Management*, **2**, (Fall–Winter), 24–31.

Dubinsky, Alan J. and F. J. Yammarino (1984), "Differential Impact of Role Conflict and Ambiguity on Selected Correlates: A Two-Sample Test," *Psychological Reports*, **55** (December), 699–707.

Dubinsky, Alan J., F. J. Yammarino, M. A. Jolson and W. D. Spangler (1995), "Transformational Leadership: An Initial Investigation in Sales Management," *Journal of Personal Selling and Sales Management*, **15** (Spring), 17.

Duncan, Tom and C. Caywood (1996), "The Concept, Process, and Evolution of Integrated Marketing Communication," in Esther Thorson and Jerry Moore, (eds.) *Integrated Communication: Synergy of Persuasive Voices*, Mahwah, NJ: Lawrence Erlbaum Associates.

Dwyer, Sean, O. Richard and C. David Shepherd (1998), "An Exploratory Study of Gender and Age Matching in the Salesperson-Prospective Customer Dyad: Testing Similarity-Performance Predictions," *Journal of Personal Selling and Sales Management*, **18**, 4 (Fall), 55–70.

Edwards, Jeff R. (1991), "Person-Job Fit: A Conceptual Integration, Literature Review, and Methodological Critique," *International Review of Industrial and Organizational Psychology*, **6**, 283–357.

Eisenhardt, Kathleen M. (1985), "Control: Organizational and Economic Approaches," *Management Science*, **31** (February), 134–149.

(1989), "Agency Theory: An Assessment and Review," *Academy of Management Review*, **14**, 1, 57–74.

Erevelles, Sunil, Indranil Dutta and Carolyn Galantine (2004), "Sales Compensation Plans Incorporating Multidimensional Sales Effort and Salesperson Efficiency," *Journal of Personal Selling and Sales Management*, **24**, 2 (Spring), 101–112.

Erffmeyer, Robert C. and D. A. Johnson (2001), "An Exploratory Study of Sales Force Automation Practices Expectations and Realities," *Journal of Personal Selling and Sales Management*, **21**, 2 (Spring), 167–176.

Erffmeyer, Robert C., R. K. Russ and J. F. Hair (1991), "Needs Assessment and Evaluation in Sales Training Programs," *Journal of Personal Selling and Sales Management*, **11** (Winter), 17–30.

Evans, F. (1963), "Selling as a Dyadic Relationship–A New Approach," *American Behavioral Scientist*, (May), 76–79.

Evans, Kenneth R., L. Margheim and J. L. Schlacter (1982), "A Review of Expectancy Theory Research in Selling," *Journal of Personal Selling and Sales Management*, **2** (November), 33–40.

Evans, M. (1970), "The Effects of Supervisory Behavior on the Path-Goal Relationships," *Organizational Behavior and Human Performance*, (May), 277–298.

Evered, J. F. (1988), "Measuring Sales Training Effectiveness," *Sales and Marketing Training*, (February), 9–18.

Falvey, J. (1999), "Compare Football to Selling? Nonsense," *Sales and Marketing Management*, (January), 15–17.

Farber, B. and J. Wycoff (1991), "Customer Service: Evolution or Revolution," *Sales and Marketing Management*, (May), 44–51.

Farley, John U. (1964), "An Optimal Plan for Salesmen's Compensation," *Journal of Marketing Research*, **1**, 39–44.

Farley, John U. and C. B. Weinberg (1975), "Determining Optimal Sales Commissions for Multiproduct Sales Forces: An Algorithm in Inferential Optimization," *Operational Research Quarterly*, **25**, 2, 413–418.

Farrell, Mark A. and B. Schroder (1996), "Influence Strategies in Organizational Buying Decisions," *Industrial Marketing Management*, **25**, 293–303.

Farrell, Seonaid and A. R. Hakstian (2001), "Improving Sales Force Performance: A Meta-Analytic Investigation of the Effectiveness and Utility of Personnel Selection Procedures and Training Interventions," *Psychology and Marketing*, **18**, 3, 281–316.

Ference, T. P., J. A. F. Stoner and E. K. Warren (1977), "Managing the Career Plateau," *Academy of Management Review*, **2** (October), 602–612.

Festinger, Leon (1967), *A Theory of Cognitive Dissonance*, New York: Harper and Row.

Flaherty, Karen E. and J. M. Pappas (2000), "The Role of Trust in Salesperson-Sales Manager Relationships," *Journal of Personal Selling and Sales Management*, **20**, 4 (Fall), 271–278.

(2002), "The Influence of Career Stage on Job Attitudes: Toward a Contingency Perspective," *Journal of Personal Selling and Sales Management*, **22**, 3 (Summer), 135–144.

Flamholtz, E. (1974), *Human Resource Accounting*, Encino, CA: Dickenson.

Fleurbaey, Marc and F. Maniquet (1994), "Fair Allocation with Unequal Production Skills: The Solidarity Approach to Compensation," Working Paper 9419, Paris: Université de Cergy-Pontoise.

Fogg, C. D. and J. W. Rokus (1973), "A Quantitative Method for Structuring a Profitable Sales Force," *Journal of Marketing*, **37** (2), 8–17.

Folkes, Valerie (1984), "Consumer Reactions to Product Failure: An Attributional Approach," *Journal of Consumer Research*, **10** (March), 398–409.

Folkes, Valerie, S. Koletsky and J. Graham (1987), "A Field Study of Causal Inferences and Consumer Reaction: The View from the Airport," *Journal of Consumer Research*, **13** (March), 534–539.

Ford, Neil M., O. C. Walker Jr. and G. A. Churchill Jr. (1975), "Expectation-Specific Measures of the Intersender Conflict and Role Ambiguity Experienced by Industrial Salesmen," *Journal of Business Research*, **3** (April), 95–112.

(1985), "Differences in the Attractiveness of Alternative Rewards among Industrial Salespeople: Additional Evidence," *Journal of Business Research*, (April), 123–138.

Fournier, S., S. Dolsha and D. G. Mick (1998), "Preventing the Mature Death of Relationship Marketing," *Harvard Business Review*, **76**, 1 (January/February), 42–51.

Franckwick, Gary L., S. S. Porter and L. A. Crosby (2001), "Dynamics of Relationship Selling: A Longitudinal Examination of Changes in Salesperson-Customer Relationship Status," *Journal of Personal Selling and Sales Management*, **21**, 2 (Spring), 135–146.

Franco, John (1984), "Managing Sales Success," *Business Marketing*, **69** (December), 48–57.

Furey, Tim R. (1999), "Sales Rep Not Dead, Just Redefined," *Marketing News*, 6 (December), 16.

Futrell, Charles M. (1979), "Measurement of Salespeople's Job Satisfaction: Convergent and Discriminant Validity of Corresponding INDSALES and Job Descriptive Index Scales," *Journal of Marketing Research*, (November), 594.

(2005), *ABCs of Relationship Selling*, 9th edn, Homewood, Ill., Irwin McGraw Hill.

(2006), *Fundamentals of Selling: Customers for Life through Service*, 9th edn, New York: Irwin-McGraw-Hill Publishers.

Futrell, Charles M. and Omer C. Jenkins (1978), "Pay Secrecy versus Disclosure for Salesmen: A Longitudinal Study," *Journal of Marketing Research*, **15** (May), 214–219.

Futrell, Charles M. and A. Parasuraman (1984), "The Relationship of Satisfaction and Performance to Salesforce Turnover," *Journal of Marketing*, **48** (Fall), 33–40.

Futrell, Charles M., J. E. Swan and J. T. Todd (1976), "Job Performance Related to Management Control Systems for Pharmaceutical Salesmen," *Journal of Marketing Research*, **13** (February), 25–33.

Gable, M., C. Hollon and F. Danyello (1992), "Increasing the Utility of the Application Blank: Relationship between Job Application Information and Subsequent Performance and Turnover of Salespeople," *Journal of Personal Selling and Sales Management*, **12** (Summer), 39–56.

Ganesan, S., B. A. Weitz and G. John (1993), "Hiring and Promotion Policies in Sales Force Management," *The Journal of Personal Selling and Sales Management*, **13** (Spring), 15–26.

Geykens, Inge and J-B. E. M. Steenkamp (1997), "An Examination of Comparison Standards Used in the Evaluation of Channel Members' Outcomes," in *Proceedings*, 24th EMAC Conference. University of Warwick, **4**, 1698–1706.

Giannini, Gaetan (2005), "Outsourcing the Sales Function," *Ezine Articles*, www://ezinearticles.com

Giunipero, Larry C., D. Denslow and R. Eltantawy (2005), "Purchasing/Supply Chain Management Flexibility: Moving to an Entrepreneurial Skill Set," *Industrial Marketing Management*, **34**, 6 (August), 602–613.

Gonick, Jacob (1978), "Tie the Salesmen's Bonuses to Their Forecasts," *Harvard Business Review*, **56** (May–June), 116–123.

Gonzalez, Gabriel R., K. Douglas Hoffman and T. N. Ingram (2005), "Improving Relationship Selling through Failure Analysis and Recovery Efforts: A Framework and Call for Action," *Journal of Personal Selling and Sales Management*, **25**, 1 (Winter), 57–65.

Good, David J. and R. W. Stone (1991a), "How Sales Quotas Are Developed," *Industrial Marketing Management*, **20**, 1, 51–55.

(1991b), "Attitudes and Applications of Quotas by Sales Executives and Sales Managers," *Journal of Personal Selling and Sales Management*, **11** (Summer), 57–60.

Goodman, Charles S. (1971), *Management of the Personal Selling Function*, New York: Holt, Rinehart, and Winston, 340.

Goodwin, Cathy and I. Ross (1992), "Consumer Responses to Service Failures: Influence of Procedural and Interactional Fairness Perceptions," *Journal of Business Research*, **25**, 149–163.

Green, Donna H. (1987), "The Effects of Risk Preference on Salesperson Time Allocation: A Critical Review and Integrative Model," in AMA *Educators' Proceedings*,

Susan P. Douglas and Michael R. Solomon, (eds.), Chicago: American Marketing Association, 112.

Greenberg, Jerald (1982), "Approaching Equity and Avoiding Inequity in Groups and Organizations," in *Equity and Justice in Social Behavior*, Jerald Greenberg and Ronald L. Cohen, (eds.), New York: Academic Press, 389–435.

Guest, D. B. and H. J. Meric (1989), "The Fortune 500 Companies Selection Criteria for Promotion to First Level Sales Management: An Empirical Study," *Journal of Personal Selling and Sales Management*, **9**, 4, 47–58.

Gustafson, Anders, M. D. Johnson and I. Ross (2005), "The Effects of Customer Satisfaction, Relationship Commitment Dimensions, and Triggers on Customer Retention," *Journal of Marketing*, **69**, 4 (October), 210–218.

Gutman, Jonathan (1982), "A Means-End Chain Model Based on Consumer Categorization Process," *Journal of Marketing*, **46** (Spring), 60–72.

Hackman, J. R. and G. R. Oldham (1980), *Work Redesign*, Readings, Mass.: Addison-Wesley.

Hafer, J. (1986), "An Empirical Investigation of the Salesperson's Career Stage Perspective," *Journal of Personal Selling and Sales Management*, **6** (November), 1–7.

Hall, D. T. (1976), *Careers in Organizations*, Pacific Palisades, CA: Goodyear Publishing Company.

Hall, D. T. and R. Mansfield (1975), "Relationships of Age and Seniority with Career Variables of Engineers and Scientists," *Journal of Applied Psychology*, **60** (April), 201–210.

Harris, C. E. and R. L. Spiro (1981), "Training Implications of Salesperson Influence Strategy," *Journal of Personal Selling and Sales Management*, **11**, 1 (Spring/Summer), 10–17.

Hastings, Bill, J. Kiely and T. Watkins (1988), "Sales Force Motivation Using Travel Incentives: Some Empirical Evidence," *Journal of Personal Selling and Sales Management*, **8** (August), 43–51.

Hawes, Jon M., K. Mast and J. Swan (1989), "Trust Earning Perceptions of Sellers and Buyers," *Journal of Personal Selling and Sales Management*, **19**, 2 (Spring), 1–8.

Hawes, Jon M., A. K. Rich and S. M. Widmier (2004), "Assessing the Development of the Sales Profession," *Journal of Personal Selling and Sales Management*, **24**, 1 (Winter), 27–37.

Heide, C. P. (1999), *Dartnell's 30th Sales Force Compensation Survey*, Chicago, IL: Dartnell Corporation.

Heider, Fritz (1958), *The Psychology of Interpersonal Relations*, New York: Wiley.

Henthorne, Tony L., M. S. LaTour and R. Natarajan (1993), "How Organizational Buyers Reduce Risk," *Industrial Marketing Management*, **22**, 41–48.

Herzberg, Frederick B., B. Mausner and B. Snyderman (1986), *The Motivation to Work*, 2nd edn, New York: Wiley.

Hess, S. W. and S. A. Samuels (1971), "Experiences with a Sales Districting Model: Criteria and Implementation," *Management Science*, **18**, Part II, 1971, 41–54.

Hom, P. W. and C. L. Hulin (1981), "A Competitive Test of the Prediction of Reenlistment by Several Models," *Journal of Applied Psychology*, **66**, 3, 23–29.

Hom, P. W., R. Katerberg and C. L. Hulin (1979), "Comparative Examination of Three Approaches to the Prediction of Turnover," *Journal of Applied Psychology*, **64**, 3, 280–290.

Homans, George (1974), *Social Behavior: Its Elementary Forms*, (Rev. edn), Harcourt, Brace, and Jovanovich, New York.

Homburg, Christian, J.P. Workman and O. Jensen (2000), "Fundamental Changes in Marketing Organizations: The Movement toward a Customer-Focused Organizational Structure," *Journal of the Academy of Marketing Science*, **28**, 4, 459–478.

Honeycutt, Earl D. Jr., K. Karande, A. Attia and S.D. Maurer (2001), "An Utility Based Framework for Evaluating the Financial Impact of Sales Force Training Programs," *Journal of Personal Selling and Sales Management*, **21**, 3 (Summer), 229–238.

Hong-Kit Yim, Frederick, R.E. Anderson and S. Swaminathan (2004), "Customer Relationship Management: Its Dimensions and Effect on Customer Outcomes," *Journal of Personal Selling and Sales Management*, **24**, 4 (Fall), 263–278.

Horsky, D. and P. Nelson (1996). "Evaluation of Salesforce Size and Productivity Through Efficient Frontier Benchmarking," *Management Science*, **15** (4), 301–320.

House, R., A. Filley and S. Kerr (1971), "Relation of Leader Consideration and Initiating Structure to R and D Subordinates' Satisfaction," *Administrative Science Quarterly*, 19–30.

Huffman, Cyntia and L.B. Cain (2001), "Adjustments in Performance Measures: Distributive and Procedural Justice Effects on Outcome Satisfaction," *Psychology and Marketing*, **18**, 593–615.

Hull, C.L. (1952), *A Behavior System*, New Haven, Conn.: Yale.

Hunt, H. Keith (1977), "CS/D: Overview and Future Research Directions," in H.K. Hunt, (ed.) *Conceptualization and Measurement of Consumer Satisfaction and Complaining Behavior*, Cambridge, Mass.: Marketing Science Institute.

Hunter, Gary L. (2004), "Information Overload: Guidance for Identifying When Information Becomes Detrimental to Sales Force Performance," *Journal of Personal Selling and Sales Management*, **24**, 2 (Spring), 91–100.

Hunter, John E. and R.F. Hunter (1984), "Validity and Utility of Alternative Predictors of Job Performance," *Psychological Bulletin*, **96** (July), 73–96.

Huppertz, John W., S.J. Arenson and R.H. Evans (1978), "An Application of Equity Theory to Buyer-Seller Exchange Situations," *Journal of Marketing Research*, **15** (May), 250–260.

Hyman, Michael R. and J.K. Sager (1999), "Marginally Performing Salespeople: A Definition," *Journal of Personal Selling and Sales Management*, **19**, 4 (Fall), 67–74.

Iacobucci, D. and A. Ostrom (1996), "Commercial and interpersonal relationships; Using the structure of interpersonal relationships to understand individual-to-individual, individual-to-firm, and firm-to-firm relationships in commerce," *International Journal of Research in Marketing*, **13** (February), 53–72.

Ingram, Thomas N. and D.N. Bellenger (1983), "Personal and Organizational Variables: Their Relative Effect on Reward Valences of Industrial Salespeople," *Journal of Marketing Research*, **20** (May), 198–205.

Ingram, Thomas N., R.W. LaForge, R.A. Avila, C.H. Schwepker Jr. and M.R. Williams (2001), *Sales Management: Analysis and Decision Making*, 4th edn, Fort Worth, Harcourt.

—— (2006), *Professional Selling: A Trust-Based Approach*, 2nd edn, Mason, OH: Thomson South-Western.

Ingram, Thomas N., R. W. LaForge and Thomas W. Leigh (2002), "Selling in the New Millennium: A Joint Agenda," *Industrial Marketing Management*, **31**, 6, 559–567.

Ingram, Thomas N., R. W. LaForge, W. B. Locander, S. B. MacKenzie and P. M. Podsakoff (2005), "New Directions in Sales Leadership Research," *Journal of Personal Selling and Sales Management*, **25**, 2 (Spring), 137–154.

Ingram, Thomas N. and K. S. Lee (1990), "Sales Force Commitment and Turnover," *Industrial Marketing Management*, **19** (May), 149–154.

Jackson, Donald W. Jr., J. E. Keith and J. L. Schlacter (1983), "Evaluation of Selling Performance: A Study of Current Practices," *Journal of Personal Selling and Sales Management*, **13**, 3 (November), 42–51.

Jackson, Donald W. Jr., J. L. Schlacter and W. G. Wolfe (1995), "Examining the Bases Utilized for Evaluating Salespeoples' Performance," *Journal of Personal Selling and Sales Management*, **15**, 4 (Fall), 59.

Jap, Sandy D. (2001), "The Strategic Role of the Salesforce in Developing Customer Satisfaction Across the Relationship Lifecycle," *Journal of Personal Selling and Sales Management*, **21**, 2 (Spring), 95–108.

Jaworski, Bernard J. (1988), "Toward a Theory of Marketing Control: Environmental Context, Control Types, and Consequences," *Journal of Marketing*, **52** (July), 23–39.

Jaworski, Bernard J. and A. Kohli (1991), "Supervisory Feedback: Alternative Types and Their Impact on Salespeople's Performance and Satisfaction," *Journal of Marketing Research*, **28** (May), 190.

Jaworski, Bernard J. and D. J. MacInnis (1989), "Marketing Jobs and Management Controls: Toward a Framework," *Journal of Marketing Research*, **24** (November), 406–419.

Jaworski, Bernard J., V. Stathakopoulos and H. Shanker Krishnan (1993) "Control Combinations in Marketing: Conceptual Framework and Empirical Evidence," *Journal of Marketing*, **57** (January), 57–69.

Jayachandran, Satish, S. Sharma, P. Kaufman and P. Raman (2005), "The Role of Relational Information Processes and Technology Use in Customer Relationship Management," *Journal of Marketing*, **69**, 4 (October), 177–192.

Jennings, R. G. and R. E. Plank (1995), "When the Purchasing Agent is a Committee: Implications for Industrial Marketing," *Industrial Marketing Management*, **24** (November), 411–419.

Joetan, Edwin and B. H. Kleiner (2004), "Incentive Practices in the US Automobile Industry," *Management Research News.*, **27**, 7, 49–56.

John, George and B. Weitz (1989), "Salesforce Compensation: An Empirical Investigation of Factors Related to Use of Salary Versus Incentive Compensation," *Journal of Marketing Research*, **26** (February), 1–14.

Johnson, A. M. (1991), "The Incentive Program's Contribution to Quality," *Sales and Marketing Management*, (April), 91–93.

Johnson, Julie T., H. C. Barksdale Jr. and J. S. Boles (2001), "The Strategic Role of the Salesperson in Reducing Customer Defection in Business Relationships," *Journal of Personal Selling and Sales Management*, **21**, 2 (Spring), 123–134.

Johnston, Mark W. and C. M. Futrell (1989), "Functional Salesforce Turnover: An Empirical Investigation into the Positive Effects of Turnover," *Journal of Business Research*, **18**, 2, 141–157.

Johnston, Mark W., C. M. Futrell, A. Parasuraman and J. Sager (1988), "Performance and Job Satisfaction Effects on Salesperson Turnover: A Replication and Extension," *Journal of Business Research*, **16**, 3, 67–83.

Johnston, Mark W. and G. W. Marshall (2005), *Relationship Selling and Sales Management*, New York: McGraw-Hill/Irwin.

(2006), *Churchill/Ford/Walkers's Sales Force Management*, 8th edn, New York: McGraw-Hill/Irwin.

Johnston, Mark W., G. W. Marshall, C. M. Futrell and W. C. Black (1990), "A Longitudinal Assessment of the Impact of Selected Organizational Influences on Salespeople's Organizational Commitment During Early Employment," *Journal of Marketing Research*, **27** (August), 333–344.

Johnston, Mark W., R. R. Varadarajan, C. M. Futrell and J. Sager (1987), "The Relationship between Organizational Commitment, Job Satisfaction and Turnover among Salespeople," *Journal of Personal Selling and Sales Management*, **7**, 3, 29–38.

Johnston, Wesley J. and M. C. Cooper (1981), "Industrial Sales Force Selection: Current Knowledge and Needed Research," *Journal of Personal Selling and Sales Management*, **2** (Spring-Summer), 49–57.

Jolson, M. A. (1974), "The Salesman's Career Cycle," *Journal of Marketing*, **38** (July), 39–46.

(1975), "The Underestimated Potential of the Canned Sales Presentation," *Journal of Marketing*, **39** (January), 75–78.

(1977), *Sales Management: A Tactical Approach*, New York: Petrocelli/Charter.

Jolson, M. A., A. J. Dubinsky and R. E. Anderson (1987), "Correlates and Determinants of Sales Force Tenure: An Exploratory Study," *The Journal of Personal Selling and Sales Management*, **7** (November), 9–27.

Jones, Edward E., D. E. Kanouse, H. H. Kelley, R. E. Nisbett, S. Valins and B. Weiner (1972), *Attribution: Perceiving the Causes of Behavior*, Morristown, NJ: General Learning Press.

Jones, Eli, S. P. Brown, A. A. Zoltners and B. A. Weitz (2005), "The Changing Environment of Selling and Sales Management," *Journal of Personal Selling & Sales Management*, **25**, 2 (Spring), 105–111.

Jones, Eli, A. L. Dixon, L. B. Chonko and J. P. Cannon (2005), "Key Accounts and Team Selling: A Review, Framework, and Research Agenda," *Journal of Personal Selling & Sales Management*, **25**, 2 (Spring), 181–198.

Jones, Eli, J. N. Moore, A. J. S. Stanaland and R. A. J. Wyatt (1998), "Salesperson Race and Gender and the Access and Legitimacy Paradigm: Does Difference Make a Difference?" *Journal of Personal Selling and Sales Management*, **18**, 4 (Fall), 71–88.

Jones, Eli, S. Sundaraman and W. Chin (2002), "Factors Leading to Sales Force Automation Use: A Longitudinal Analysis," *Journal of Personal Selling and Sales Management*, **22**, 3 (Summer), 145–156.

Joseph, Kissan and M. U. Kalwani (1994), "Bonus Payment Practices and their Impact on the Efficiency of Sales Organizations," Working Papers, Lawrence, Kansas: University of Kansas.

(1995), "The Impact of Environmental Uncertainty on the Design of Salesforce Compensation Plans," *Marketing Letters*, **6**, 3, 183–197.

(1996), "The Role of Incentive Pay in the Design of Salesforce Compensation Plans: An Empirical Study," Working Paper, Lawrence, Kansas: University of Kansas.

Joseph, Kissan and A. Thevaranjan (1998), "Monitoring and Incentives in Sales Organizations: An Agency-Theoretic Perspective," *Marketing Science*, **17**, 2, 107–123.

Joshi, Ashwin W. and S. Randall (2001), "The Indirect Effects of Organizational Controls on Salesperson Performance and Customer Orientation," *Journal of Business Research*, **54**, 1 (October), 1–9.

Kalra, Ajay, M. Shi and K. Srinivasan (2003), "Salesforce Compensation Scheme and Consumer Inferences," *Management Science*, **49**, 5 (May), 655–673.

Kassarjian, Harold H. and M. J. Sheffet (1981), "Personality and Consumer Behavior: An Update," in *Perspectives in Consumer Behavior*, Harold H. Kassarjian and Thomas S. Robertson, (eds.), Glenview, Ill.: Scott, Foresman, 160–180.

Keenan, William Jr. (1993), "Time Is Everything," *Sales and Marketing Management*, **145**, 9 (August), 60.

Keiser, Thomas C. (1988), "Negotiating With a Customer You Can't Afford to Lose," *Harvard Business Review*, **66** (November–December), 30–34.

Keller, R. T. (1975), "Role Conflict and Ambiguity: Correlates with Job Satisfaction and Values," *Personnel Psychology*, (Spring), 57–64.

—— (1984), "The Role of Performance and Absenteeism in the Prediction of Turnover," *Academy of Management Journal*, **27**, 2, 176–183.

Kelley, B. (1991), "Selling in a man's world," *Sales and Marketing Management*, (January), 28–35.

Kelley, Harold H. (1972), "Attribution in Social Interaction," in E. E. Jones, D. E. Kanous, H. H. Kelley, R. E. Nisbett, S. Valin and B. Weiner, (eds.) *Attribution: Perceiving the Causes of Behavior*, Morristown, NJ: General Learning Press, 1–26.

Kennedy, Karen N. and D. R. Deeter-Schmelz (2001), "Descriptive and Predictive Analyses of Industrial Buyers' Use of Online Information for Purchasing," *Journal of Personal Selling and Sales Management*, **21**, 4 (Fall), 279–290.

Kerber, K. W. and J. P. Campbell (1987), "Correlates of Objective Performance among Computer Salespeople: Tenure, Work Activities and Turnover," *The Journal of Personal Selling and Sales Management*, **7**, 3, 39–50.

Kerr, M. and B. Burzynski (1988), "Missing the Target: Sales Training in America," *Training and Development Journal*, (July), 68–70.

Kiesche, Elizabeth S. (1997), "Nalco Attacks Sales Force Turnover," *Chemical Week*, New York (May 5), **152**, 17, 12.

Kimmons, G. and J. Greenhaus (1976), "Relationship between Locus of Control and Reactions of Employees to Work Characteristics," *Psychological Reports*, (December), 815–820.

Kitchen, Philip J. and Patrick de Pelsmaker (2004), *Integrated Marketing Communication: A Primer*, London: Routledge.

Klein, Howard J. and J. S. Kim (1998), "A Field Study of the Influence of Situational Constraints, Leader-Member Exchange, and Goal Commitment on Performance," *Academy of Management Journal*, **41** (February), 88.

Klein, Robert (1997), "Nabisco Sales Soar after Sales Training," *Marketing News*, 7 (January), 23.

Klein, Stuart M. (1973), "Pay Factors as Predictors to Satisfaction: A Comparison of Reinforcement, Equity, and Expectancy," *Academy of Management Journal*, **16** (December), 598–610.

Knouse, Stephen B. and D. Strutton (1996), "Modeling a Total Quality Salesforce through Managing Empowerment, Evaluation, and Reward and Recognition Processes," *Journal of Marketing Theory & Practice*, **4** (Summer), 24.

Knowles, Patricia A., S. J. Grove and K. Keck (1994), "Signal Detection Theory and Sales Effectiveness," *Journal of Personal Selling and Sales Management*, **14** (Spring), 1–14.

Ko, Dong-Gil and A. R. Dennis (2004), "Sales Force Automation and Sales Performance: Do Experience and Expertise Matter?" *Journal of Personal Selling and Sales Management*, **24**, 4 (Fall), 311–322.

Kohli, Ajay K. (1989), "Effects of Supervisory Behavior: The Role of Individual Differences Among Salespeople," *Journal of Marketing*, **53** (October), 40–50.

Krafft, Manfred (1999), "An Empirical Investigation of the Antecedents of Sales Force Control Systems," *Journal of Marketing*, **63**, 3, 120–134.

Krishnan, Balaji C., R. G. Netemeyer and J. S. Boles (2002), "Self-efficacy, Competitiveness, and Effort as Antecedents of Salesperson Performance," *Journal of Personal Selling and Sales Management*, **22**, 4 (Fall), 285–296.

LaForge, Raymond W., D. W. Cravens and C. E. Young (1986). "Using Contingency Analysis to Select Selling Allocation Methods," *Journal of Personal Selling and Sales Management*, **6**, 19–28.

Lagace, Rosemary R. (1991), "An Exploratory Study of Trust Between Sales Managers and Salespersons," *Journal of Personal Selling and Sales Management*, **11**, 2 (Spring), 49.

Lal, Rajiv (1986), "Delegating Pricing Responsibility to the Salesforce," *Marketing Science*, **5**, 2, 159–168.

— (1994), "Plans de rémunération de la force de vente: les conséquences managériales des derniers développements théoriques," *Recherche et Applications en Marketing*, **9**, 51–72.

Lal, Rajiv and V. Srinivasan (1993), "Compensation Plans for Single- and Multi-product Salesforces: An Application of the Holmstrom-Milgrom Model," *Management Science*, **39**, 7, 777–793.

Lal, Rajiv and R. Staelin (1986), "Salesforce Compensation Plans in Environments with Asymmetric Information," *Marketing Science*, **5** (Summer), 179–198.

Lamont, Laurence M. and W. G. Lundstrom (1974), "Defining Industrial Sales Behavior: A Factor Analytic Study," in R. C. Curhan, (ed.) *1974 Combined Proceedings: New Marketing for Social and Economic Progress and Marketing's Contributions to the Firm and Society*, Chicago, Ill.: American Marketing Association, 493–498.

Landry, Timothy. D., T. J. Arnold and A. Arndt (2005), "A Compendium of Sales-Related Literature in Customer Relationship Management: Processes and Technologies with Managerial Implications," *Journal of Personal Selling & Sales Management*, **25**, 3 (Summer), 231–251.

Langerack, Fred and P. C. Verhoef (2003), "Strategically Embedding CRM," *Business Strategy Review*, **14**, 4, 73–80.

Lavidge, R. J. and G. A. Steiner (1961), "A Model of Predictive Measurement of Advertising Effectiveness," *Journal of Marketing*, (October), 61–65.

Lawler, Edward E. III (1970), "Job Attitudes and Employee Motivation: Theory, Research, and Practice," *Personnel Psychology*, **23**, 223–237.

(1971), *Pay and Organizational Effectiveness: A Psychological Review*, New York: McGraw-Hill.

(1973), *Motivation in Work Organizations*, Monterey, Calif.: Brooks/Cole.

(1976), "Control Systems in Organizations", in M. Dunnette, (ed.) *Handbook of Industrial and Organizational Psychology*, Chicago: Rand McNally.

Leach, Mark P. and A. H. Liu (2003), "Investigating Interrelationships Among Sales Training Evaluation Methods," *Journal of Personal Selling and Sales Management*, **23**, 4 (Fall), 327–340.

Leach, Mark P., A. H. Liu and W. J. Johnston (2005), "The Role of the Self-Regulation Training in Developing the Motivation Management Capabilities of Salespeople," *Journal of Personal Selling & Sales Management*, **25**, 3 (Summer), 269–281.

Learning International (1989), *What Does Sales Force Turnover Cost You?* Stamford, Conn.: Learning International.

LeBon, Joël and D. Merunka (2004), "Understanding, Explaining, and Managing Salespeople's Effort Toward Competitive Intelligence," Working Paper, Institute for the Study of Business Markets, Pennsylvania State University, Smeal College of Business.

Leigh, Thomas W. (1987), "Cognitive Selling Scripts and Sales Training," *Journal of Personal Selling and Sales Management*, **7** (August), 39–48.

Leigh, Thomas W. and P. McGraw (1989), "Mapping the Procedural Knowledge of Industrial Sales Personnel: A Script-Theoretic Investigation," *Journal of Marketing*, **53** (October), 16–34.

Leigh, Thomas W. and A. J. Rethans (1984), "A Script-Theoretic Analysis of Industrial Purchasing Behavior," *Journal of Marketing*, **48** (Fall), 22–32.

Leigh, Thomas W. and J. O. Summers (2002), "An Initial Evaluation of Industrial Buyers' Impressions of Salespersons' Nonverbal Cues," *Journal of Personal Selling and Sales Management*, **22**, 1 (Winter), 41–54.

Leong Siew Meng, P. S. Bush and D. R. John (1989), "Knowledge Bases and Salesperson Effectiveness: A Script Theoretic Analysis," *Journal of Marketing Research*, **26** (May), 164–178.

Lewin, Kurt (1935), *A Dynamic Theory of Personality*, New York: McGraw-Hill.

Lichtenthal, David J. and T. Tellefsen (2001), "Toward a Theory of Business Buyer-Seller Similarity," *Journal of Personal Selling and Sales Management*, **21**, 1 (Winter), 1–14.

Lilien, Gary L. (1979), "Advisor 2: Modeling the Marketing Mix for Industrial Products," *Management Science*, **25** (2), 191–204.

Lilien, Gary L., P. Kotler and K. S. Moorthy (1992). *Marketing Models*, Upper Saddle River, NJ: Prentice-Hall.

Lilien, Gary L. and D. Weinstein (1984), "An International Comparison of the Determinants of Industrial Marketing Expenditures," *Journal of Marketing*, **48**, 48–53.

Lilly, Bryan, T. W. Porter and A. William Meo (2003), "How Good Are Managers at Evaluating Sales Problems?" *Journal of Personal Selling and Sales Management*, **23**, 1 (Winter), 51–60.

Lind, Allen E. and T. R. Tyler (1988), *The Social Psychology of Procedural Justice*, New York: Plenum Press.

Linda, Gerald (1979), "New Research Works on Consumer Satisfaction/Dissatisfaction Model," *Marketing News*, 21 (September), 8.

Liu, Annie H. and M. P. Leach (2001), "Developing Loyal Customers with a Value-Adding Sales Force: Examining Customer Satisfaction and the Perceived Credibility of Consultative Salespeople," *Journal of Personal Selling and Sales Management*, **21**, 2 (Spring), 147–156.

Livingstone, Linda P., J. A. Roberts and L. B. Chonko (1995), "Perceptions of Internal and External Equity as Predictors of Outside Salespeople's Job Satisfaction," *Journal of Personal Selling and Sales Management*, **15** (Spring), 33–46.

Locke, Edwin A. (1969), "What Is Job Satisfaction?" *Organizational Behavior and Human Performance*, **4**, 309–336.

 (1976), "The Nature and Causes of Job Satisfaction," in Marvin. D. Dunnette, (ed.) *Handbook of Industrial and Organizational Psychology*, Rand McNally, Chicago, 1297–1350.

Locke, Edwin A. and G. P. Latham (1990), *A Theory of Goal Setting and Task Performance*, Englewood Cliffs, NJ: Prentice-Hall.

Locke, Edwin A., K. N. Shaw, L. M. Soari and G. P. Latham (1981), "Goal Setting and Task Performance: 1969–1980," *Psychological Bulletin*, **90**, 1, 125–152.

Lodish, Leonard M. (1971), "CALLPLAN: An Interactive Sales Call Planning System," *Management Science*, **18**, Part II (December), 25–40.

 (1975), "Sales Territory Alignment to Maximize Profits," *Journal of Marketing Research*, **12**(1), 30–36.

 (1976), "Assigning Salesmen to Accounts to Maximize Profits," *Journal of Marketing Research*, **13**(4), 440–444.

Lodish, Leonard M., E. Curtis, M. Ness and M. K. Simpson (1988), "Sales Force Sizing and Development Using a Decision Calculus Model at Syntex Laboratories," *Interfaces*, **18**, 1 (January/February), 5–20.

Louderback, Jim (1997), "HP Divisions Are Getting Leaner and Meaner," *PC Week*, 21 (July), 165.

Lucas, G. A., A. Parasraman, R. A. Davis and B. M. Enis (1987), "An Empirical Study of Salespeople Turnover," *Journal of Marketing*, **11**, 3, 34–59.

Lucas, H. C., C. B. Weinberg and K. Clowes (1975), "Sales Response as a Function of Territory Potential and Sales Representative Workload," *Journal of Marketing Research*, **12**, 298–305.

Macintosh, Gerrard, K. A. Anglin, D. M. Szymanski and J. W. Gentry (1992), "Relationship Development in Selling: A Cognitive Analysis," *Journal of Personal Selling and Sales Management*, **12** (Fall), 23–34.

Magrath, A. J. (1997), "From the Practitioner's Desk: A Comment on 'Personal Selling and Sales Management in the New Millennium'", *Journal of Personal Selling and Sales Management*, **17** (Winter), 45–47.

Mangione, T. W. (1973), "Turnover: Some Psychological and Demographic Correlates", in R. P. Quinn and T. W. Mangione, (eds.) *1969–1970 Survey of Working Conditions*, Ann Arbor: University of Michigan, Research Centre.

Mantrala, Murali K. and K. Raman (1990), "Analysis of Sales Force Incentive Plans for Accurate Sales Forecasting and Performance," *International Journal of Research in Marketing*, **7** (December), 189–202.

Mantrala, Murali K., K. Raman and R. Desiraju (1997), "Sales Quota Plans: Mechanisms for Adaptive Learning," *Marketing Letters*, **8**, 4, 393–405.

Mantrala, Murali K., P. Sinha and A. A. Zoltners (1994), "Structuring a Multiproduct Sales Quota-bonus Plan for a Heterogeneous Sales Force: A Practical Model-based Approach," *Marketing Science*, **13**, 2 (Spring), 121–144.

Marchetti, Michelle (1998), "Master Motivators," *Sales & Marketing Management*, **150** (April), 38–44.

Marks, Mike and M. Emerson (2002), *What's Your Plan? Smart Sales Force Compensation in Wholesale Distribution*, Washington, DC: National Distribution of Wholesalers.

Martin, T. N., J. L. Price and C. W. Mueller (1981), "Research Note on Job Performance and Turnover," *Journal of Applied Psychology*, **66**, 1, 116–119.

Maslow, Abraham H. (1943), "A Theory of Human Motivation," *Psychological Review*, **50** (July), 370–396.

(1970), *Motivation and Personality*, 2nd edn, New York: Harper and Row.

Mathieu, John E. and D. M. Zajac (1990), "A Review and Meta-Analysis of the Antecedents, Correlates, and Consequences of Organizational Commitment," *Psychological Bulletin*, **108** (2), 171–194.

Mattson, M. R. (1988), "How to Determinate the Composition and Influence of a Buying Center," *Industrial Marketing Management*, **17**(3), 205–214.

Maxwell, Sarah, G. Reed, J. Saker and V. Story (2005), "The Two Faces of Playfulness: A New Tool to Select Potentially Successful Sales Reps," *Journal of Personal Selling & Sales Management*, **25**, 3 (Summer), 215–229.

McClelland, David C. (1962), "Business Drive and National Achievement," *Harvard Business Review*, **40** (July–August), 99–112.

McClelland, David C., J. W. Atkinson, R. A. Clark and E. L. Lowell (1953), *The Achievement Motive*, New York: Appleton, Century-Crofts.

McFarland, Richard G. (2003), "Crisis of Conscience: The Use of Coercive Sales Tactics and Resultant Felt Stress in the Salesperson," *Journal of Personal Selling and Sales Management*, **23**, 4 (Fall), 311–326.

McMurry, Robert N. (1961), "The Mystique of Super-Salesmanship," *Harvard Business Review*, **39** (March–April), 113–122.

McNeilly, Kevin M. and F. A. Russ (1992), "The Moderating Effect of Sales Force Performance on Relationships Involving Antecedents of Turnover," *Journal of Personal Selling and Sales Management*, **12**, 9–24.

(2000), "Does Relational Demography Matter in a Personal Selling Context?" *Journal of Personal Selling and Sales Management*, **20**, 4 (Fall), 279–288.

Mengüç, Bülent (1996), "The Influence of the Market Orientation of the Firm on Sales Force Behavior and Attitudes: Further Empirical Results," *International Journal of Research in Marketing*, **13** (July), 277–291.

Mengüç, Bülent and A. T. Barker (2003), "The Performance Effects of Outcome-Based Incentive Pay Plans on Sales Organizations: A Contextual Analysis," *Journal of Personal Selling and Sales Management*, **23**, 4 (Fall), 341–358.

Mentzer, John, C. Bienstock and K. Khan (1995), "Benchmarking Satisfaction," *Marketing Management*, **4** (Summer), 41.

Miller, H. E., R. Katerberg and C. L. Hulin (1979), "Evaluation of the Mobley, Horner, and Hollingsworth Model of Employee Turnover," *Journal of Applied Psychology*, **64**, 5, 509–517.

Mirvis, P. H. and E. E. Lawler (1977), "Measuring the Financial Impact of Employee Attitudes," *Journal of Applied Psychology*, **62**, 1, 1–8.

Misra, S., E. J. Pinker and R. A. Shumsky (2004), "Salesforce Design with Experience-Based Learning," *IIE Transactions*, **36**, 941–956.

Mitchell, T. R. (1973), "Motivation and Participation: An Integration," *Academy of Management Journal*, 670–679.

 (1974), "Expectancy Models of Job Satisfaction, Occupational Preference, and Effort: A Theoretical, Methodological, and Empirical Appraisal," *Psychological Bulletin*, **81**, 1053–1077.

Mithas, Sunil, M. S. Krishnan and C. Fornell (2005), "Why Do Customer Relationship Management Applications Affect Customer Satisfaction?" *Journal of Marketing*, **69**, 4 (October), 201–209.

Mizerski, Richard W., L. L. Golden and J. B. Kerman (1979), "The Attribution Process in Consumer Decision Making," *Journal of Consumer Research*, **6** (September), 123–140.

Mobley, W. H. (1977), "Intermediate Linkages in the Relationship between Job Satisfaction and Employee Turnover," *Journal of Applied Psychology*, **62**, 2, 237–240.

 (1982), *Employee Turnover: Causes, Consequences and Control*, Reading, Mass.: Addison-Wesley.

Moncrief, W. C. (1986), "Selling Activity and Sales Position Taxonomies for Industrial Salesforces," *Journal of Marketing Research*, **23** (August), 261–270.

Montgomery, David B., A. J. Silk and C. E. Zaragoza (1971), "A Multiple-Product Sales Force Allocation Model," *Management Science*, **18**, 4 (December), II, 3–24.

Moon, Mark A. and G. M. Armstrong (1994), "Selling Teams: A Conceptual Framework and Research Agenda," *Journal of Personal Selling and Sales Management*, **14** (Winter), 17–30.

Morris, Michael, D. Davis, J. Allen, R. Avila and J. Chapman (1991), "Assessing the Relationships among Performance Measures, Managerial Practies, and Satisfaction when translating the Sales force: A Replication and Extension," *Journal of Personal Selling and Sales Management*, **11**(Summer).

Moss, Stan (1978), "What Sales Executives Look for in New Salespeople," *Sales & Marketing Management*, (March), 47.

Motowidlo, S. J. (1983), "Predicting Sales Turnover from Pay Satisfaction and Expectation," *Journal of Applied Psychology*, **68**, 4, 484–489.

Mowday, Richard T., R. M. Steers and L. W. Porter (1979), "The Measurement of Organizational Commitment," *Journal of Vocational Behavior*, **14** (April), 224–247.

Muchinsky, P. M. and P. C. Morrow (1980), "A Multi-disciplinary Model of Voluntary Employee Turnover," *Journal of Vocational Behavior*, **17**, 4, 263–290.

Muchinsky, P. M. and M. L. Tuttle (1979), "Employee Turnover: An Empirical and Methodological Assessment," *Journal of Vocational Behavior*, **14**, 1, 43–77.

Murphy, Kevin (2004), "The Psychology of Buying," *Industrial Distribution*, **93**, 11 (November), 66.

Murphy, William H. and P. A. Dacin (1998), "Sales Contests: A Research Agenda," *Journal of Personal Selling and Sales Management*, **18**, 1 (Winter), 1–16.

Netemeyer, Richard G., J. S. Boles, D. O. McKee and R. McMurrian (1997), "An Investigation into the Antecedents of Organizational Citizenship Behaviors in a Personal Selling Context," *Journal of Marketing*, **61**, 85–99.

Newman, J. (1974), "Predicting Absenteeism and Turnover: A Field Comparison of Fishbein's Model and Traditional Job Attitude Measures," *Journal of Applied Psychology*, **59**, 5, 610–615.

Newton, Derek A. (1973), *Sales Force Performance and Turnover*, Cambridge, MA: Marketing Science Institute.

Nonis, Sarath A. and S. Altan Erdem (1997), "A Refinement of INDSALES to Measure Job Satisfaction of Sales Personnel in General Marketing Settings," *Journal of Marketing Management*, **7** (Spring/Summer), 34.

Nonis, Sarath A. and J. K. Sager (2003), "Coping Strategy Profiles Used by Salespeople: Their Relationships with Personal Characteristics and Work Outcomes," *Journal of Personal Selling and Sales Management*, **23**, 2 (Spring), 139–150.

Nozick, R. (1974), *Anarchy, State, and Utopia*, New York: Basic Books.

O'Connor, Joseph and J. Seymour (1993), *Introducing Neuro-Linguistic Programming: Psychological Skills for Understanding and Influencing People*, 2nd edn, New York: Thorsons.

Oldham, Greg R., C. T. Kulik, M. L. Ambrose, L. P. Stepina and J. F. Brand (1986), "Relations between Job Facet Comparisons and Employee Reactions," *Organizational Behavior and Human Decision Processes*, **38** (February), 28–47.

Oliver, Richard L. (1974), "Expectancy Theory Predictions of Salesmen's Performance," *Journal of Marketing Research*, **11**, 243–253.

  (1980), "A Cognitive Model of the Antecedents and Consequences of Satisfaction Decisions," *Journal of Marketing Research*, **17** (November), 460–469.

Oliver, Richard L. and E. Anderson (1994), "An Empirical Test of the Consequences of Behavior- and Outcome-Based Sales Control Systems," *Journal of Marketing*, **58** (October), 53–67.

  (1995), "Behavior- and Outcome-Based Sales Control Systems: Evidence and Consequences of Pure-Form and Hybrid Governance," *Journal of Personal Selling and Sales Management*, **15** (Fall), 1–16.

Oliver, Richard L. and W. S. DeSarbo (1988), "Response Determinants in Satisfaction Judgments," *Journal of Consumer Research*, **14**, 495–507.

Oliver, Richard L. and J. Swan (1989), "Consumer Perceptions of Interpersonal Equity and Satisfaction in Transactions: A Field Survey Approach," *Journal of Marketing*, **52**, 21–35.

Ouchi, William G. (1979), "A Conceptual Framework for the Design of Organizational Control Mechanisms," *Management Science*, **25** (September), 833–847.

Ouchi, William G. and M. Maguire (1975), "Organizational Control: Two Functions," *Administrative Science Quarterly*, **20** (December), 559–569.

Ozanne, Urban B. and G. A. Churchill (1971), "Five Dimensions of the Industrial Adoption Process," *Journal of Marketing Research*, **8**, 3 (August), 322–329.

Parasuraman, A. and C.M. Futrell (1983), "Demographics, Job Satisfaction and Propensity to Leave of Industrial Salesmen," *Journal of Business Research*, **11**, 1, 33—48.

Park, Jeong-Eun and B.B. Holloway (2003), "Adaptive Selling Behavior Revisited: An Empirical Examination of Learning Orientation, Sales Performance, and Job Satisfaction," *Journal of Personal Selling and Sales Management*, **23**, 3 (Summer), 239—252.

Parsons, Leonard J. and P. Vanden Abeele (1981), "Analysis of Sales Call Effectiveness," *Journal of Marketing Research*, **18** (1), 107—113.

Pass, Michael W., K.R. Evans and J.L. Schlacter (2004), "Sales Force Involvement in CRM Information Systems: Participation, Support, and Focus," *Journal of Personal Selling and Sales Management*, **24**, 3 (Summer), 229—234.

Pavalko, R.M. (1970), "Recruitment of Teaching: Patterns of Selection and Retention," *Sociology of Education*, **43**, 3, 340—353.

Payne, Adrian and P. Frow (2005), "A Strategic Framework for Customer Relationship Management," *Journal of Marketing*, **69**, 4 (October), 167—176.

Perdue, B.C. and J.O. Summers (1991), "Purchasing Agents: Use of Negotiation Strategies," *Journal of Marketing Research*, **28** (May), 175—189.

Perry, Monica L., C.L. Pearce and H.P. Sims Jr. (1999), "Empowered Selling Teams: How Shared Leadership Can Contribute to Selling Team Outcomes," *Journal of Personal Selling and Sales Management*, **19**, 3 (Summer), 35—52.

Piercy, Nigel F., D.W. Cravens and N. Lane (2001), "Sales Manager Behavior Control Strategy and Its Consequences: The Impact of Gender Differences," *Journal of Personal Selling and Sales Management*, **21**, 1 (Winter), 39—49.

Pilling, Bruce K., N. Donthu and S. Henson (1999), "Accounting for the Impact of Territory Characteristics on Sales Performance: Relative Efficiency as a Measure of Salesperson Performance," *Journal of Personal Selling and Sales Management*, **19**, 2 (Spring), 35—46.

Plank, Richard E. and D.A. Reid (1996), "Difference Between Success, Failure in Selling," *Marketing News*, 4 (November), 6—14.

Porter, Lyman W. and E.E. Lawler, III (1968), *Managerial Attitudes and Performance*, Homewood, Ill.: Dorsey Press.

Porter, Lyman W. and R.M. Steers (1973), "Organizational, Work and Personal Factors in Employee Turnover and Absenteeism," *Psychological Bulletin*, **80**, 2, 151—176.

Porter, Stephen S. and L.W. Inks (2000), "Cognitive Complexity and Salesperson Adaptability: An Exploratory Investigation," *Journal of Personal Selling and Sales Management*, **20**, 1 (Winter), 15—22.

Powell Mantel, Susan (2005), "Choice or Perception: How Affect Influences Ethical Choices Among Salespeople," *Journal of Personal Selling and Sales Management*, **25**, 1 (Winter), 43—55.

Powell Mantel, Susan, E. Bolman Pullins, D.A. Reid and R.E. Buehrer (2002), "A Realistic Sales Experience: Providing Feedback by Integrating Buying, Selling, and Management Experiences," *Journal of Personal Selling and Sales Management*, **22**, 1 (Winter), 33—40.

Price, J.L. (1977), *The Study of Turnover*, Ames, IA: The Iowa State University Press.

Pritchard, Robert D. (1969), "Equity Theory: A Review and Critique," *Organizational Behavior and Human Performance*, **4** (May), 176—211.

Rabinowitz, S. and D. T. Hall (1981), "Changing Correlates of Job Involvement in Three Career Stages," *Journal of Vocational Behavior*, **18** (April), 138–144.

Rackham, Neil (1996), *The SPIN Selling Fieldbook*, New York: McGraw-Hill.

Raju, Jagmohan S. and V. Srinivasan (1996), "Quota-based Compensation Plans for Multi-territory Heterogeneous Salesforces," *Management Science*, **42**, 10, 1454–1462.

Ramaswami, Sridhar N. (2002), "Influence of Control Systems on Opportunistic Behaviors of Salespeople: A Test of Gender Differences," *Journal of Personal Selling and Sales Management*, **22**, 3 (Summer), 173–188.

Ramaswami, Sridhar N. and Jagdip Singh (2003), "Antecedents and Consequences of Merit Pay Fairness for Industrial Salespeople," *Journal of Marketing*, **67**, 46–66.

Rangaswamy, A., P. Sinha and A. A. Zoltners (1990), "An Integrated Model-Based Approach for Sales Force Structuring," *Marketing Science*, **9**(4), 279–298.

Rao, Ram C. (1990), "Compensating Heterogeneous Salesforces: Some Explicit Solutions," *Marketing Science*, **9** (Fall), 319–341.

Rasmusson, Erika (1999), "Getting School in Outsourcing," *Sales and Marketing Management*, **151** (January), 48–53.

Rawls, J. (1971), *A Theory of Justice*, Cambridge: Harvard University Press.

Reichers, Arnon E. (1985), "A Review and Reconceptualization of Organizational Commitment," *Academy of Management Review*, **10** (July), 465–476.

Rheem, Helen (1995), "Performance Management: A Progress Report," *Harvard Business Review*, (March–April), 11.

Rice, R. W., D. B. McFarlin and D. E. Bennett (1989), "Standards of Comparison and Job Satisfaction," *Journal of Applied Psychology*, **74**, 591–598.

Rich, Gregory A. (1997), "The Sales Manager as a Role Model: Effects on Trust, Job Satisfaction, and Performance of Salespeople," *Journal of the Academy of Marketing Science*, **25** (Fall), 319.

(1998), "The Constructs of Sales Coaching: Supervisory Feedback, Role Modeling, and Trust," *Journal of Personal Selling and Sales Management*, **18**, 1 (Winter), 53–64.

Richardson, Robert (1999), "Measuring the Impact of Turnover on Sales," *Journal of Personal Selling and Sales Management*, **19**, 4 (Fall), 53–66.

Rigby, Darrell K. and D. Ledingham (2004), "CRM Done Right," *Harvard Business Review*, **82**, 11 (November), 118–121.

Roberts, J. A., K. R. Coulson and L. B. Chonko (1999), "Salesperson Perceptions of Equity and Justice and Their Impact on Organizational Commitment and Turnover," *Journal of Marketing Theory and Practice*, **7**, 1–6.

Robertson, Ivan T. and M. Smith (2001), "Personnel Selection," *Journal of Occupational and Organizational Psychology*, **74**, 4, 441–472.

Robinson, Patrick. J., C. W. Farris and Y. Wind (1967), *Industrial Buying and Creative Marketing*, Boston: Allyn and Bacon.

Rodriguez Cano, Cynthia, J. S. Boles and C. J. Bean (2005), "Communication Media Preferences in Business-to-Business Transactions: An Examination of the Purchase Process," *Journal of Personal Selling & Sales Management*, **25**, 3 (Summer), 283–294.

Roethlisberger, F. J. and W. J. Dickson (1946), *Management and the Worker*, Cambridge, Mass.: Harvard University Press.

Rollins, Thomas (1990), "How to Tell Competent Salespeople from the Other Kind," *Sales & Marketing Management*, (September), 116–117.

Ronen, Simsha (1986), "Equity Perception in Multiple Comparisons: A Field Study," *Human Relations*, **39** (April), 333–346.

Ross, William T. (1991), "Performance Against Quota and the Call Selection Decision," *Journal of Marketing Research*, **28** (August), 296–306.

Rotter, J. B. (1966), "Generalized Expectancies for Internal versus External Control of Reinforcement," *Psychological Monographs*, **809**, 1–28.

Rouziès, Dominique, E. Anderson, A. K. Kohli, R. E. Michaels, *et al.* (2005) "Sales and Marketing Integration: A Proposed Framework," *Journal of Personal Selling & Sales Management*, **25**, 2 (Spring), 113–122.

Rouziès, Dominique and A. Macquin (2002), "An Exploratory Investigation of the Impact of Culture on Sales Force Management Control Systems in Europe," *Journal of Personal Selling and Sales Management*, **23**, 1 (Winter), 61–72.

Rubash, A. R., R. R. Sullivan and P. H. Herzog (1987), "The use of an Expert to Train Salespeople," *Journal of Personal Selling and Sales Management*, (August), 49–56.

Ryans, Adrian B. and C. B. Weinberg (1987), "Territory Sales Response Models: Stability Over Time," *Journal of Marketing Research*, **24**(2), 229–233.

Sager, Jeffrey K., R. R. Varadarajan and C. M. Futrell (1988), "Understanding Salesperson Turnover: A Partial Evaluation of Mobley's Turnover Process Model," *Journal of Personal Selling and Sales Management*, **8**, 1, 21–35.

Sager, Jeffrey K., J. Yi and C. M. Futrell (1998), "A Model Depicting Salespeople's Perceptions," *Journal of Personal Selling and Sales Management*, **18**, 3 (Summer), 1–22.

Sales and Marketing Management (1987), Survey of selling costs, **136**, 16 (February).

— (1994), "Does This Compute?" (September), **115**.

Salgado, Jesus (1999), "Personnel Selection Methods," in *International Review of Industrial and Organizational Psychology*, Vol. **14**, Cary Cooper and Ivan Robertson, (eds.), New York: John Wiley and Sons, 74–101.

Sallee, Amy and K. Flaherty (2003), "Enhancing Salesperson Trust: An Examination of Managerial Values, Empowerment, and the Moderating Influence of SBU Strategy," *Journal of Personal Selling and Sales Management*, **23**, 4 (Fall), 299–310.

Sauers, Daniel A., J. B. Hunt and K. Bass (1990), "Behavioral Self-Management as a Supplement to External Sales Force Control," *Journal of Personal Selling and Sales Management*, **10** (Summer), 81.

Schank, R. and R. Abelson (1977), *Scripts, Plans and Knowledge*, Hillsdale, NJ: Erlbaum.

Schein, E. H. (1971), "The Individual, the Organization, and the Career: A Conceptual Scheme," *Journal of Applied Behavioral Science*, **7** (July–August), 401–426.

Schmidt, Frank and J. Hunter (1998), "The Validity and Utility of Selection Methods in Personnel Psychology: Practical and Theoretical Implications of 85 Years of Research Findings," *Psychological Bulletin*, **124**, 2, 262–274.

Scholl, Richard W., E. Cooper and J. F. McKenna (1987), "Referent Selection in Determining Equity Perceptions: Differential Effects on Behavioral and Attitudinal Outcomes," *Personnel Psychology*, **40** (Spring), 113–124.

Schultz, Roberta J. and K. R. Evans (2002), "Strategic Collaborative Communication by Key Account Representatives," *Journal of Personal Selling and Sales Management*, **22**, 1 (Winter), 23–32.

Schwepker, Charles H. Jr. (1999), "The Relationship Between Ethical Conflict, Organizational Commitment, and Turnover Intentions in the Salesforce," *Journal of Personal Selling and Sales Management*, **19**, 1 (Winter), 42–49.

——— (2003), "Customer-Oriented Selling: A Review, Extension, and Direction for Future Research," *Journal of Personal Selling and Sales Management*, **23**, 2 (Spring), 151–172.

Schwepker, Charles H. Jr. and D. J. Good (2004), "Marketing Control and Sales Force Customer Orientation," *Journal of Personal Selling and Sales Management*, **24**, 3 (Summer), 167–179.

Semlow, Walter J. (1959). "How Many Salesmen do You Need?" *Harvard Business Review*, **37**, 126–132.

Sengupta, Sanjit, R. E. Krapfel and M. A. Pusateri (2000), "An Empirical Investigation of Key Account Salesperson Effectiveness," *Journal of Personal Selling and Sales Management*, **20**, 4 (Fall), 253–262.

Sharma, Arun, M. Levy and A. Kumar (2001), "Knowledge Structure and Retail Sales Performance: An Empirical Examination," *Journal of Retailing*, **76**, 1, 53–69.

Sharma Arun and R. Pillai (1996), "Customers' Decision-Making Styles and their Preference for Sales Strategies: Conceptual Examination and an Empirical Study," *Journal of Personal Selling and Sales Management*, **16**, 1 (Winter), 21–33.

Shepherd, C. David and J. C. Heartfield (1991), "Discrimination Issues in the Selection of Salespeople: A Review and Managerial Suggestions," *Journal of Personal Selling and Sales Management*, **11** (Fall), 65–75.

Shepherd, C. David and J. O. Rentz (1990), "A Method for Investigating the Cognitive Processes and Knowledge Structures of Expert Salespeople," *Journal of Personal Selling and Sales Management*, **10** (Fall), 55–70.

Sheridan, J. E. and J. W. Slocum Jr. (1975), "The Direction of the Causal Relationship Between Job Satisfaction and Work Performance," *Organizational Behavior and Human Performance*, **14** (April), 159–172.

Sheth, Jagdish. N. (1973), "A Model of Industrial Buyer Behavior," *Journal of Marketing*, **37** (October), 50–56.

——— (1995), "Selling Without the Sales Force," Presentation at the National Conference in Sales Management, Atlanta, Georgia.

Shoemaker, Mary E. (1999), "Leadership Practices in Sales Managers Associated with the Self-Efficacy, Role Clarity, and Job Satisfaction of Individual Industrial Salespeople," *Journal of Personal Selling and Sales Management*, **19**, 4 (Fall), 1–20.

Silvester, Joanne, F. Patterson and E. Fergusson (2003), "Comparing Two Attributional Models of Job Performance in Retail Sales: A Field Study," *Journal of Occupational and Organizational Psychology*, **76**, 115–132.

Sims, H., A. Szilagyi and D. McKemey (1976), "Antecedents of Work Related Expectancies," *Academy of Management Journal*, (December), 547–559.

Singh, Jagdip, J. Goolsby and G. K. Rhoads (1994), "Behavioral and Psychological Consequences of Boundary Spanning Burnout for Customer Service Representatives," *Journal of Marketing Research*, **31** (November), 558–569.

Sinha, Prabhakant and A. A. Zoltners (2001), "Sales-Force Decision Models: Insights from 25 Years of Implementation," *Interfaces*, **31**, 3 (May–June), S8–S44.

Sivadas, Eugene, S. Bardi Kleiser, J. Kellaris and R. Dahlstrom (2002), "Moral Philosophy, Ethical Evaluations, and Sales Manager Hiring Intentions," *Journal of Personal Selling and Sales Management*, **23**, 1 (Winter), 7–22.

Slocum, J. Jr. and W. L. Cron (1985), "Job Attitudes and Performance During Three Career Stages," *Journal of Vocational Behavior*, **26** (April), 126–145.

Smith, Kirk, E. Jones and E. Blair (2000), "Managing Salesperson Motivation in a Territory Realignment," *Journal of Personal Selling and Sales Management*, **20**, 4 (Fall), 215–226.

Snader, Jack (1997), "How Sales Reps Make 360-degree Turnaround," *Marketing News*, **17** (February), 11.

Spencer, D. G. and R. M. Steers (1981), "Performance as a Moderator of the Job-Satisfaction-Turnover Relationship," *Journal of Applied Psychology*, **66**, 4, 511–514.

Spiller, Brenda and J. Thomas, (eds.) (2003), *Perfecting the Art of Telesales Spiced with the Magic of Neuro-Linguistic Programming*, New York: Gardners Books.

Srinivasan, V. (1981), "An investigation of the Equal Commission Rate Policy for a Multiproduct Sales Force," *Management Science*, **27** (July), 731–756.

Stafford, T. F. (1996), "Conscious and Unconscious Processing of Priming Cues in Selling Encounters," *Journal of Personal Selling and Sales Management*, **16** (Spring), 37–44.

Stanton, William J., R. A. Buskirk and R. L. Spiro (1995), *Management of a Sales Force*, 9th edn, Chicago: Irwin.

Stathakopoulos, Vlasis (1996), "Sales Force Control: A Synthesis of Three Theories," *Journal of Personal Selling and Sales Management*, **16**, 2 (Spring), 1–12.

Steers, R. M. and R. T. Mowday (1981), "Employee Turnover and Post-decision Accommodation Processes," in L. L. Cummings and M. B. Staw, (eds.) *Research in Organizational Behavior*, Greenwich, Conn.: JAI Press, **3**, 235–281.

Stefanou, Constantinos, C. Sarmanioris and A. Stafyla (2003), "CRM and Customer-Centric Knowledge Management: An Empirical Research," *Business Process Management Journal*, **9**, 5, 617–634.

Steinbrinck, John P. (1970), "How to Pay Your Sales Force," *Harvard Business Review*, (July–August), 111–122.

Stevens, Charles C. and G. Macintosh (2003), "Personality and Attractiveness of Activities Within Sales Jobs," *Journal of Personal Selling and Sales Management*, **23**, 1 (Winter), 23–38.

Strahle, William and R. L. Spiro (1986), "Linking Market Share Strategies to Salesforce Objectives, Activities, and Compensation Policies," *Journal of Personal Selling and Sales Management*, **6** (August), 11–18.

Strong, E. K. (1925), *The Psychology of Selling*, New York: McGraw-Hill.

Strutton, David, L. E. Pelton and J. R. Lumpkin (1993), "The Relationship between Psychological Climate and Salesperson-Sales Manager Trust in Sales Organizations," *Journal of Personal Selling and Sales Management*, **13** (Fall), 1.

Stumpf, S. A. and P. K. Dawley (1981), "Predicting Voluntary and Involuntary Turnover Using Absenteeism and Performance Indices," *Academy of Management Journal*, **24**, 2, 148–163.

Stumpf, S. A. and S. Rabinowitz (1981), "Career Stages as a Moderator of Performance Relationships with Facets of Job Satisfaction and Role Perceptions," *Journal of Vocational Behavior*, **18** (April), 202–218.

Sujan, Harish (1986), "Smarter versus Harder: An Exploratory Attributional Analysis of Salespeople's Motivation," *Journal of Marketing Research*, **23** (February), 41–49.

Sujan, Harish, M. Sujan and J. R. Bettman (1988), "Knowledge Structure Differences Between More Effective and Less Effective Salespeople," *Journal of Marketing Research*, **25** (February), 81–86.

Sujan, Harish, B. A. Weitz and N. Kumar (1994), "Learning Orientation, Working Smart, and Effective Selling," *Journal of Marketing*, **58** (July), 39–52.

Summers, Timothy P. and W. H. Hendrix (1991), "Modeling the Role of Pay Equity Perceptions: A Field Study," *Journal of Occupational Psychology*, **64**, 145–158.

Swan, J. and R. L. Oliver (1991), "An Applied Analysis of Buyer Equity Perceptions and Satisfaction with Automobile Salespeople," *Journal of Personal Selling and Sales Management*, **11**, 15–26.

Swan, J., F. Trawick and D. Rink (1988), "Measuring Dimensions of Purchaser Trust of Industrial Salespeople," *Journal of Personal Selling and Sales Management*, **18**, 3 (May), 1–9.

Swift, Ronald S. (2000), *Accelerating Customer Relationships: Using CRM and Relationship Technologies*, Upper Saddle River, NJ: Prentice-Hall PTR.

Szymanski, D. M. (1988), "Determinants of Selling Effectiveness: The Importance of Declarative Knowledge to the Personal Selling Concept," *Journal of Marketing*, **52** (January), 64–77.

Szymanski, D. M. and G. A. Churchill (1990), "Client Evaluation Cues: A Comparison of Successful and Unsuccessful Salespeople," *Journal of Marketing Research*, **17** (May), 163–170.

Talley, Walter J. Jr. (1961), "How to Design Sales Territories," *Journal of Marketing*, **25**(1), 7–31.

Tanner, John F. Jr. (1996), "Buyer Perceptions of the Purchase Process and its Effect on Customer Satisfaction," *Industrial Marketing Management*, **25**, 125–133.

Tanner, John F. Jr., M. Ahearne, T. W. Leigh, C. H. Mason and W. C. Moncrief (2005), "CRM in Sales-Intensive Organizations: A Review and Future Directions," *Journal of Personal Selling & Sales Management*, **25**, 2 (Spring), 169–180.

Tanner, John F. Jr. and S. B. Castleberry (1993), "The Participation Model: Factors Related to Buying Decision Participation," *Journal of Business to Business Marketing*, **1**, 3, 35–61.

Tapiero, C. S. and J. U. Farley (1975), "Optimal Control of Sales Force Effort in Time," *Management Science*, **21**, 9 (May), 976–985.

Taylor, Terry (1993), "The True Cost of Turnover and How to Prevent It," *Journal of Property Management*, (December), 20–22.

Teas, R. Kenneth (1981), "An Empirical Test of Models of Salespersons' Job Expectancy and Instrumentality Perceptions," *Journal of Marketing Research*, **18** (May), 209–226.

(1983), "Supervisory Behavior, Role Stress, and Job Satisfaction of Industrial Salespeople," *Journal of Marketing Research*, **20** (February), 84–89.

Teas, R. Kenneth and J. C. McElroy (1986), "Causal Attributions and Expectancy Estimates: A Framework for Understanding the Dynamics of Salesforce Motivation," *Journal of Marketing*, (January), 75–86.

Tse, David K. and P. C. Wilton (1988), "Models of Consumer Satisfaction Formation: An Extension," *Journal of Marketing Research*, **25**, 204–212.

Tuggle, F. D. (1978), "An Analysis of Employee Turnover," *Behavorial Science*, **23**, 2, 32–37.

Tyagi, Pradeep K. (1982), "Perceived Organizational Climate and the Process of Salesperson Motivation," *Journal of Marketing Research*, (May), 240–254.

——— (1985a), "Relative Importance of Key Job Dimensions and Leadership Behaviors in Motivating Salesperson Work Performance," *Journal of Marketing*, **49** (Summer), 76–86.

——— (1985b), "Work Motivation through the Design of Salesperson Jobs," *Journal of Personal Selling and Sales Management*, **5** (May), 41–51.

Urbanski, A. (1988), "Electronic Training May Be in Your Future," *Sales and Marketing Management*, (March), 46–48.

Valentine, Sean and T. Barnett (2003), "Ethics Code Awareness, Perceived Ethical Values, and Organizational Commitment," *Journal of Personal Selling and Sales Management*, **23**, 4 (Fall), 359–368.

Vandenbosch, Mark B. and C. B. Weinberg (1993) "Salesforce Operations," in J. Eliashberg and G. L. Lilien, (eds.) *Handbook on OR and MS*, Vol. **5**, Amsterdam: North-Holland, 653–694.

Vandermerwe, Sandra (2004), "Achieving Deep Customer Focus," *MIT Sloan Management Review*, **45**, 3, 26–34.

Van Weele, Arjan J. (2004), *Purchasing and Supply Chain Management: Analysis, Strategy, Planning, and Practice*, New York: International Thomson Business.

Vroom, Victor H. (1964), *Work and Motivation*, New York: John Wiley and Sons.

Walker, Orville C., G. A. Churchill and N. M. Ford (1977), "Motivation and Performance in Industrial Selling: Present Knowledge and Needed Research," *Journal of Marketing Research*, **14** (May), 156–168.

Waters, L. K., D. Roach and C. W. Waters (1976), "Estimates of Future Tenure, Satisfaction and Biographical Variables as Predictors of Termination," *Personnel Psychology*, **29**, 2, 57–60.

Webster, Frederick. E. and Y. Wind (1972), "A General Model of Organizational Buying Behavior," *Journal of Marketing*, **36**, 2, 12–19.

Wedell, A. and D. Dempeck (1987), "Sales Force Automation - Here and Now," *Journal of Personal Selling and Sales Management*, **7** (August), 11–16.

Weeks, William A. and Lynn R. Kahle (1990), "Salespeople's Time Use and Performance," *Journal of Personal Selling and Sales Management*, **10** (February), 29–37.

Weeks, William A., T. W. Loe, L. B. Chonko and K. Wakefield (2004), "The Effect of Perceived Ethical Climate on the Search for Sales Force Excellence," *Journal of Personal Selling and Sales Management*, **24**, 3 (Summer), 199–214.

Weeks, William A., James Roberts, Lawrence B. Chonko and Eli Jones (2004), "Organizational Readiness for Change, Individual Fear of Change, and Sales Manager Performance: An Empirical Investigation," *Journal of Personal Selling and Sales Management*, **24**, 1 (Winter), 7–17.

Weeks, D. A. and J. M. Stark (1972), *Salesmen's Turnover in Early Employment*, New York: The Conference Board.

Weinberg, Charles B. (1975), "An Optimal Compensation Plan for Salesman's Control over Price," *Management Science*, **21**, 937–943.

(1978), "Jointly Optimal Sales Commissions for Non-income Maximizing Sales Forces," *Management Science*, **24**, 12 (August), 1253–1258.

Weinberg, Charles B. and H. C. Lucas (1977), "Letter to the Editor," *Journal of Marketing*, **41**(2), 147.

Weiner, B. (1972), *Theories of Motivation: From Mechanism to Cognition*, Chicago: Markham.

Weiner, B., H. Heckhausen, W. Meyer and R. E. Cook (1972), "Causal Ascriptions and Achievement Behavior: A Conceptual Analysis of Effort and Reanalysis of Locus of Control," *Journal of Personality and Social Psychology*, **21**, 239–248.

Weitz, Barton A. (1978), "The Relationship between Salesperson Performance and Understanding of Customer Decision Making," *Journal of Marketing*, **15** (November), 501–516.

(1979), "A Critical Review of Personal Selling Research: The Need for Contingency Approaches," in G. Albaum and G. A. Churchill, (eds.) *Critical Issues in Sales Management: State-of-the-Art and Future Research Needs*, Eugene: University of Oregon.

Weitz, Barton A., H. Sujan and M. Sujan (1986), "Knowledge, Motivation, and Adaptive Behavior: A Framework for Improving Selling Effectiveness," *Journal of Marketing*, **50** (October), 174–191.

Wells, D. L. and P. M. Munchinsky (1985), "Performance Antecedents of Voluntary Managerial Turnover," *Journal of Applied Psychology*, **70**, 3, 329–336.

Whittler, T. E. (1994), "Eliciting Consumer Choice Heuristics: Sales Representatives' Persuasion Strategy," *Journal of Personal Selling and Sales Management*, **14** (Fall), 41–54.

Widmier, Scott M., D. W. Jackson Jr. and D. Brown McCabe (2002), "Infusing Technology into Personal Selling," *Journal of Personal Selling and Sales Management*, **22**, 3 (Summer), 189–198.

Wiles, Michael A. and R. L. Spiro (2004), "Attracting Graduates to Sales Positions and the Role of Recruiter Knowledge: A Reexamination," *Journal of Personal Selling and Sales Management*, **24**, 1 (Winter), 39–48.

Wilkins, Alan L. and W. G. Ouchi (1983), "Efficient Cultures: Exploring the Relationship Between Culture and Organizational Performance," *Administrative Science Quarterly*, **28** (September), 468–481.

Williams, Kaylene C., R. L. Spiro and L. M. Fine (1990), "The Customer-Salesperson Dyad: An Interaction/Communication Model and Review," *Journal of Personal Selling and Sales Management*, **10** (Summer), 29–43.

Williamson, N. C. (1983), "A Method for Determining the Causes of Salesperson Turnover," *The Journal of Personal Selling and Sales Management*, **3**, 1, 26–35.

Williamson, Oliver E. (1975), *Markets and Hierarchies: analysis and Antitrust Implications*, New York: The Free Press.

(1979), "Transaction-Cost Economics: The Governance of Contractual Relations", *Journal of Law and Economics*, **22** (October), 233–261.

(1981), "The Economics of Organization: Origins, Evolution, Attributes," *American Journal of Sociology*, **87**, 3, 548–577.

(1985), *The Economic Institutions of Capitalism*. New York: The Free Press.

Wilson, E. J. (1994), "The Relative Importance of Supplier Selection Criteria: A Review and Update," *International Journal of Purchasing and Materials Management*, **30** (Summer), 35–41.

Wilson, Phillip H., D. Strutton and M. Theodore Farris II (2002), "Investigating the Perceptual Aspects of Sales Training," *Journal of Personal Selling and Sales Management*, **22**, 2 (Spring), 77–86.

Winer, Leon (1973), "The Effect of Product Sales Quotas on Sales Force Productivity," *Journal of Marketing Research*, **10** (May), 180–183.

Wotruba, Thomas R. (1989), "The Effect of Goal Setting on the Performance of Independent Sales Agents in Direct Selling," *Journal of Personal Selling and Sales Management*, **9** (Spring), 22–29.

(1990), "Full-time vs. Part-time Salespeople: A Comparison on Job Satisfaction, Performance and Turnover in Direct Selling," *International Journal of Research in Marketing*, **7**, 4, 97–119.

(1991), "The Evolution of Personal Selling," *Journal of Personal Selling and Sales Management*, **11**, 3 (Summer), 1–12.

Wotruba, Thomas R., E. K. Simpson and J. L. Reed-Draznick (1989), "The Recruiting Interview as Perceived by College Student Applicants for Sales Positions," *Journal of Personal Selling and Sales Management*, **9** (Fall), 13–24.

Wotruba, Thomas R. and M. L. Thurlow (1976), "Sales Force Participation in Quota Setting and Sales Forecasting," *Journal of Marketing*, **40** (April), 11–16.

Wotruba, Thomas R. and P. K. Tyagi (1991), "Met Expectations and Turnover in Direct Selling," *Journal of Marketing*, **55**, 3, 24–35.

Zablah, Alex R., D. N. Bellenger and W. J. Johnson (2004), "Customer Relationship Management Implementation Gaps," *Journal of Personal Selling and Sales Management*, **24**, 4 (Fall), 279–295.

Zemanek, James E. Jr. (1997), "Manufacturer Influence versus Manufacturer Salesperson Influence over the Industrial Distributor," *Industrial Marketing Management*, **26**, 59–66.

Zhang, C. and V. Mahajan (1995), "Development of Optimal Salesforce Compensation Plans for Independent, Complementary and Substitutable Products," *International Journal of Research in Marketing*, **12**, 355–362.

Zoltners, Andris A. and S. E. Lorimer (2000), "Sales Territory Alignment: An Overlooked Productivity Tool," *Journal of Personal Selling and Sales Management*, **20**, 3 (Summer), 139–145.

Zoltners, Andris A. and P. Sinha (1980), "Integer Programming Models for Sales Resource Allocation," *Management Science*, **26**, 242–260.

(1983), "Sales Territory Alignment: A Review and Model," *Management Science*, **29** (11), 1237–1256.

Zoltners, Andris A., P. Sinha and G. A. Zoltners (2001), *The Complete Guide to Accelerating Sales Force Performance*, New York, NY: American Management Association.

Index